Politics and Poetry
in the Fifteenth Century

BLANDFORD HISTORY SERIES

(General Editor R. W. Harris)

PROBLEMS OF HISTORY

HISTORY OF ENGLAND

HISTORY OF EUROPE

HISTORY AND LITERATURE

1399-1485

Politics and Poetry
in the Fifteenth Century

V. J. SCATTERGOOD

Lecturer, English Department
University of Bristol

Blandford Press · London

First Published 1971
First paperback edition 1971
© 1971 Blandford Press Ltd
167 High Holborn
London WC1V 6PH

ISBN 07137 3608 9 *Casebound*
07137 3628 3 *Paperback*

Printed and bound in Great Britain by
C. Tinling & Co. Ltd., London and Prescot

Contents

ACKNOWLEDGEMENTS

Acknowledgement is due to the following for their kind permission to reproduce photographs:

British Museum, Nos. 1, 2, 4, 5, 14
The Librarian, The John Rylands Library, Manchester, No. 3
Library of the Inner Temple, No. 16
National Portrait Gallery, Nos. 6–9
Master and Fellows of Corpus Christi College, Cambridge, No. 15
National Monuments Record, Nos. 10, 11, 13

List of Illustrations

Author's Note

Abbreviated references to the more frequently used primary sources are normally made in the text itself, and for fuller bibliographical details the reader should refer to the list of Abbreviations and the Bibliography. Reference to less frequently used primary sources and to secondary material is made in the Notes following each chapter.

I should like to express my gratitude to the Librarian and Staff of the University Library, Bristol, for supplying me with books; to the Trustees of the British Museum for allowing me to consult manuscripts in their possession; to the National Library of Wales for supplying me with microfilm copies of manuscripts; and particularly to my colleague Dr A. B. Cottle for his advice and encouragement.

1 : Introduction

THE importance of late Middle English poetry on political and social subjects is generally recognised. Except for a number of prophecies, which are still largely unstudied, almost all the known extant political verses are available in print, the largest collections being those of Thomas Wright[1] and R. H. Robbins.[2] In the more recent standard histories of literature these verses are usually accorded a brief mention. Thus, in 1939, W. L. Renwick and H. Orton remark that 'casual verses on contemporary affairs—the cry of the oppressed commons, and the song of exultation over fallen enemies—may be expected at any time', and they proceed to devote a paragraph to fifteenth-century verses, noting as particularly significant the 'treatises on government'. They conclude that '. . . men were thinking about the technique and ethics of government, and trying to influence others, creating the rudiments of a public opinion'.[3] Writing in 1945, Sir E. K. Chambers has a little over a page on those fifteenth-century lyrics 'which can best be described as political'.[4] In 1960 David Daiches mentions 'satirical, topical and political verse of little literary merit but of considerable historical interest' as one of the 'three main categories of fifteenth-century English literature', but he has nothing further to say about them.[5]

Though these poems are regarded as of some importance, they have been little studied. The best general accounts of political verse appear in the introductions to the collections of Wright and Robbins, though these are necessarily fairly short. Various individual aspects of these verses have been treated from time to time: in 1911, for example, Rupert Taylor wrote a *genre* study of the prophecy;[6] both R. H. Hilton and Maurice Keen, from differing points of view, have studied the social aspects of the Robin Hood ballads;[7] G. A. Holmes has written on the political implications of *The Libelle of Englyshe Polycye*;[8] and a few specialist scholarly articles have been produced on other verses. But these verses have most often been considered simply as historical source material. In 1913, C. L. Kingsford wrote: 'The student of historical sources can never afford to disregard contemporary poetry altogether. Least of all can he do so in an age such as the fifteenth century, when ballads are the most natural form of popular historical narrative, and verse is not only the commonest vehicle for political satire, but for political controversy as well. Though the fifteenth century was singularly barren of good poetry other than lyrics, the volume of contemporary verse was considerable, and it would be possible to construct from it a tolerably consecutive commentary on the History of the Age.'[9] This is followed by a discussion of some of the verse. Very recently J. J. Bagley has assumed a similar position: 'No wise historian neglects the literature of the age he sets out to study. At the least it will tell him what matters interested the people of that time, what virtues they admired, and what evils they denounced; at the best it will describe for him their towns, countryside, means of travel, houses, furniture, dress, food and drink, education and entertainment, and illustrate and discuss the problems that most vexed their minds.'[10] This statement is made in the immediate context of fourteenth-century poems, but he also uses fifteenth-century authors, such as Hoccleve, in this way. In Bagley's view poems which express opinions and attitudes of a partisan sort can be useful to the historian, but it is notable that he sets more value on texts which describe the life of the times in detail and give factual information.

Of course, a historian may use any materials which come to hand, including contemporary verses, in any way he feels is legitimate. Verses are indeed useful as evidence for social history, for insights into the life of the times, and they can occasionally enable historical facts to be verified or established. The fact that verses were sometimes incorporated into chronicles goes to show that, in the fifteenth century, poems were regarded as furnishing reasonably accurate accounts of some events. R. H. Robbins has pointed to various examples of close similarity between the accounts of events preserved in prose chronicles and the accounts which appear in verses. He shows that the ballad on *The Siege of Calais* (1436) is, in one respect, more detailed than the prose chronicle accounts of the same events: it gives the names of the defenders of the various gates of Calais—'details not found elsewhere'. But Robbins' own limiting criticism is relevant here: 'Admitting the importance of literature for historical research, one must place equal or greater reliance on documents—charters, parish records, wills, inventories and so forth. . . .'[11] It is also relevant to remark that to look for accuracy of detail in these poems is almost certainly to look for something with which the poet was not primarily concerned. Nor is a poet's analysis of contemporary events and society usually meant to be definitive. His response to a situation is usually immediate, primarily personal or sectional, and above all, to some degree biased. When a writer chooses to comment on contemporary political events or social conditions he is almost always concerned to express his own feelings, his attitudes and opinions, his hopes and fears. Frequently he intends his poem to influence others to feel the same way.

Accordingly, the present study is principally concerned with ideas, attitudes and opinions about fifteenth-century politics and society as they are expressed in contemporary verses. Of course, other sets of documents also reveal attitudes to these problems: some fifteenth-century chronicles (for example the Yorkist *English Chronicle*) are almost as partisan as the verses; the letters of the Pastons, the Celys, the Stonors and the Plumpton family give important insights into the activities and attitudes of the landed and commercial middle classes; and contemporary sermons give a fairly comprehensive picture of society from a clerical point of view. But these sets of documents have been extensively studied already, and are only used incidentally in the pages which follow.[12]

NOTES

[1] *Political Poems and Songs*, Rolls Series 14, 1861, 2 vols.

[2] *Historical Poems of the Fourteenth and Fifteenth Centuries*, New York 1959.

[3] *The Beginnings of English Literature to Skelton*, 1939, p. 105.

[4] *English Literature at the Close of the Middle Ages*, Oxford 1945, p. 117.

[5] *A Critical History of English Literature*, 1961, I, 132.

[6] *The Political Prophecy in England*, New York 1911.

[7] Respectively 'The Origin of Robin Hood', *Past and Present* 14, 1958, 30–44 and *The Outlaws of Medieval Legend*, London 1961.

[8] *EHR* 76, 1961, pp. 193–216.

[9] *English Historical Literature in the Fifteenth Century*, 1913, p. 228.

[10] *Historical Interpretation*, 1965, p. 131. See also pp. 227–31 for a treatment of fifteenth-century verses.

[11] *Op. cit.*, pp. xx–xxiii.

[12] See Kingsford and Bagley, *op. cit.*, on the subject as a whole. On *The Paston Letters* see H. S. Bennett, *The Pastons and their England*, Cambridge 1922, and on the sermons G. R. Owst, *Literature and Pulpit in Medieval England*, Cambridge 1933.

2 : Political Verse in Medieval England

ALTHOUGH it comprises neither the largest nor the most important body of medieval English literature, the surviving poetry dealing with political subjects is considerable. Political poems of varying lengths are extant in Latin, Anglo-Norman and English—the Latin and Anglo-Norman poems being most numerous in the two centuries after the conquest. The first extant Middle English political poem dates from 1265 and only a few political verses antedate 1300. At around this time there is much evidence of a resurgence in the use of the English language.[1] Gradually but surely its use increased throughout the fourteenth century, though it was long before it achieved any formal recognition. However, in 1362 English was made the official language of the law and in the same year the Chancellor first opened Parliament with a speech in English. In 1349 two schoolmasters, John Cornwall and Richard Pencrich, first began to use English as a teaching medium, and by about 1385 John Trevisa could complain that '. . . children of grammar scole conneþ na more Frensche þan con hir lift heele'. After the 1380s English begins to be used increasingly in wills. A few personal letters were also written in English towards the end of the fourteenth century, and in 1400 George Dunbar, Earl of March, in a letter to Henry IV, explained why:

> noble Prince, mervaile yhe nocht that I write my letters in English, fore that ys mare clere to myne understanding than Latyne or Fraunche.

In 1422, the Brewers' Guild of London determined to keep their records in English because many of their members could not understand Latin or French. After the reign of Henry V, who himself encouraged the use of the vernacular, English was in fairly general use. Almost all fifteenth-century political verses are in English, and only a few in French or Latin.

It should occasion no surprise that verse was used in the treatment of political themes. Verse was considered a suitable medium for most subjects—astrology, topography, alchemy, hunting and so forth—topics which would in later periods have been treated in prose. There is no adequate general account of the conditions under which political verses were composed and disseminated in medieval England. They bear some relation to the conditions governing the composition of other types of verse, but there are important differences. In broad terms political verse has practical intentions and practical consequences. It aims to have an effect on government, the fabric of society and public life. It seeks to establish certain ideas, parties or individuals at the expense of others. And it is this single and important fact that gave rise to many of the unique circumstances of its composition and dissemination. Political verse was subject to pressures and demands from which other types of verse were free. In this chapter an attempt is made to give a general account (but with particular reference to the fifteenth century) of some of the people who are known to have composed political verse, and of the conditions in which it was written and disseminated. An attempt is also made to assess its contemporary importance and to estimate how much of the verse has been lost.

I

Little is known of the writers of Middle English political verse. Ten Brink was of the opinion that they were to be found 'among two classes: the gleemen and the clergy, in the broadest sense'. Developing this, he distinguishes between the characteristic productions of the two groups of writers: '. . . the English gleeman was very little initiated into the mysteries of parties; his audience was a very mixed one, and only in rare cases had he a powerful patron, as did the Norman minstrel, in the higher circles of society. Hence his poetry was in the service of national interests, as they

were understood by the people. His proper mission was to celebrate victorious battles, to praise the heroes of the nation and to
pursue its enemies with scorn.' On the other hand, he considers
that 'satire was, as a whole, the province of the clergy, the learned.
Neither rank nor power shielded men from their attacks; all classes
of society had to be pilloried by them. The abuses in church and
state, especially the latter, bad measures of government, social
evils, moral rottenness in clergy and laity, all served as material for
satire.'[2] Courthope, following this, says that 'Many, perhaps most',
of these political poems, 'seem to have been composed by the
clergy',[3] and Owst expounds the same opinion even more vigor-
ously.[4] This analysis is accurate enough as applied to verses of the
thirteenth and earlier fourteenth centuries. But in the fifteenth
century a rather different picture emerges. Clerics are still responsible for many verses. And minstrels were still employed in the
royal household, in the households of lords, in monasteries, and by
various city corporations.[5] The author of the poems in MS Digby
102 mentions 'mynstrallis' as capable of giving advice to lords
(IV, 82), so perhaps they were responsible for the composition (or
at least the dissemination) of verses of some political relevance.
But by this time minstrels were primarily musicians, and few, if
any, political verses can be attributed to them.

A certain amount of evidence can be derived from the careers of
the few authors who are known to have composed fifteenth-century
political verse. John Gower (c. 1327–1408) had ecclesiastical and
legal connections, but he probably lived on the rents of his considerable lands. In his native county of Kent he held land at
Throwley, Stalesfield and Aldington, and had a country house at
Otford. He drew rents from Wigborough in Essex and in 1382
acquired the manors of Feltwell in Norfolk and Moulton and
Kentwell in Suffolk. He was doubtless quite rich and spent some
time at court. He knew Chaucer, and both Richard II and Henry
IV were his patrons.[6] Unlike Chaucer he seems to have been little
involved in the political life of the time, but he was a keen observer
and critic of contemporary events.

Thomas Hoccleve (c. 1369–1426) had none of the leisure for
writing that Gower's considerable wealth must have given him.

Like his self-confessed master, Chaucer, Hoccleve was a government employee, though he was markedly less successful than
Chaucer. He is first recorded at the Office of the Privy Seal in
Westminster in 1387–8, and he worked there for practically the
whole of his life. For this he earned £4 annually, and after 12
November 1399 he also received an annuity of £10 from the
Crown. As these amounts were paid irregularly (and rarely in full),
and since Hoccleve had rather extravagant tastes, he was constantly
short of money. Perhaps he wrote verses to help supplement his
income. Many of his productions are 'begging poems' to the Chancellor for payment of his arrears. He also sought, with some
success, the patronage of the great and influential. He married in
1410 or 1411 and lived in Chester's Inn in the Strand, by this time
greatly impoverished, he tells us. He remained always poor. His
work at the Privy Seal Office was arduous, and this, together with
his irregular life, affected his health; in about 1416 or 1417, he
appears, from his own description of it, to have suffered a nervous
breakdown. In 1424 he was granted a corrody in Southwick Priory,
Hampshire, where he probably lived until his death in about 1426.[7]
It is hardly surprising that Hoccleve—living as he did in the capital
city and working in a government department—should have shown
an interest in contemporary political affairs. Many of his poems
deal explicitly with political topics, and in poems on other subjects
there is sometimes incidental political comment.

Hoccleve's contemporary, John Lydgate (c. 1370–1449), was in
orders from the time he became a novice at the Benedictine Abbey
of Bury St Edmunds at the age of fifteen. He must frequently have
been absent from his monastery. He was in France in 1421, and
spent some time in London. Until 1441 he received frequent gifts
and court pensions. The greater part of Lydgate's massive output
of verse was religious. But several poems are explicitly or implicitly
political. He was a nationalist and a Lancastrian supporter, and
wrote much in favour of Henry VI.[8] As will be seen below, much of
his political verse was commissioned and has to be read with this
in mind. But his interest in political questions seems to have been
real enough, and some of his most characteristic comments derive
from poems on non-political subjects.

The only other notable writer of political verse in the fifteenth century known by name is George Ashby (*c.* 1390–1475). His early life is obscure, but later it is known that he owned land in Middlesex. Like Chaucer and Hoccleve he was a government employee, a clerk of the Signet to Henry VI and later to Margaret of Anjou '. . . full fourty yere/As well beyond the see as on thys syde' (*Poems* I, 64–5). Evidently a Lancastrian, his *Prisoner's Reflections* was written while he was in the Fleet, confined no doubt by the conquerors of Henry VI. Subsequently, he seems to have directed the education of Henry's son Edward before the Prince's murder in 1471.[9] Thus Ashby was involved in contemporary politics, and obviously in a position to know about national issues. His works, however, consist mainly of advice to Prince Edward, and his interest inclined rather to theories about the proper conduct of a ruler than to explicit comment on particular events.

Of other writers of political verse in the fifteenth century very little is known. Dating probably from 1429, *A Recollection of Henry V* appears among the fifty-six poems in MS Douce 302 written by John Audelay, a chantry priest who received a corrody at Haughmond Abbey, near Shrewsbury, late in his life. From 1492 comes a *Remembrance of Henry VI* by James Ryman, a Franciscan, the author of more than one hundred and sixty religious songs and carols. The colophon to *Friar Daw's Reply to Jack Upland* gives the author's name as 'Iohannem Walssingham' but nobody of this name who is likely to have written the poem has so far been identified. Sometimes an author has been suggested by modern scholars: for example, Sir George Warner considered that *The Libelle of Englyshe Polycye* (1436) may have been written by Adam Moleyns (1396–1450), but the evidence for this is tenuous. For the rest, if an image of the author is necessary it must be derived from the verses themselves. Thus J. Kail postulates an author for the important sequence in MS Digby 102: 'In some passages the writer addresses the faithful like a clergyman; in others he speaks like the master of a monastery to his fellow monks. From this circumstance, as well as from his acquaintance with, and his frequent reference to the Bible, we may infer that the author was a priest, most probably an abbot or a prior. As such he occupied a seat in Parliament, and voted with the Commons. This makes us understand his rather detailed knowledge of the proceedings in Parliament, and his lively interest in the cause of the Commons.'[10]

The vast majority of political verse is anonymous, and it would be misleading to base too much on the careers of a few known authors. What is known about Gower, Hoccleve and Ashby, however, makes it possible to offer a partial corrective to the opinions of Ten Brink, Courthope and Owst. The verses which survive represent the opinions of a wider range of medieval society than these scholars admit. Of all types of medieval verse, that dealing with political subjects is the least exclusive.

II

The importance of political verse and the use made of it are bound up with the position of the poet in medieval England. Some poets had no desire other than their own amusement: George Ashby wrote some verses while in prison in 1463, he tells us, 'Thus occupying me' (*Poems* I, 339). If a poet had an audience in mind the chances are that it would consist of a small group of friends in his own locality: it is clear from BM MS Harley 1735 (his note-book) that John Crophill of Wix in Essex wrote verses to amuse his own circle;[11] and Osbern Bokenham's versified saints' legends seem to have been read only among the East Anglian gentry.[12] Crophill was apparently a doctor, and Bokenham was in orders, so neither depended on money received for writing verses. If a poet needed to obtain a reward for his verses he usually elected to write for a patron whose wishes he could seek to satisfy in return for financial support. Before the advent of printing there was no other way in which an author might benefit financially from his verse. Thus, in a sense, every type of medieval verse was a commodity which could be purchased. Many miniatures depict the poet on his knee obsequiously presenting the commissioned book to a patron. And since political verse, more than any other, had a real value in the formation and manipulation of opinion it was frequently utilized by the rich and powerful. Patronage of this sort of verse is found early. Richard I's Chancellor, William Longchamp, was accused of having employed minstrels and poets to sing adulatory verses about himself through the streets. In 1174 Henry II employed Jordan Fantosme to write an account of a battle against the Scots. Edward II in 1314 commissioned Roger Baston to celebrate the expected relief of Stirling Castle.[13] The potential influence of political verse is exploited in the same way throughout the fifteenth century, and it is doubtless in this that its main importance was thought to lie.

Even in verse only marginally political the effects of patronage are apparent. The case of Gower is interesting. He was fairly conventional in his political attitudes, and these included support for his King. But within these broad terms there seems to have been some shifting of position. This is most noticeable in his dedications to successive versions of the *Confessio Amantis* which is not primarily a political poem. The Prologue to the earlier versions contains a lengthy and circumstantial account of how the poem was commissioned by Richard II, and a respectful dedication to him:

> Richard by name the secounde
> In whom hath evere yit be founde
> Justice medled with pite.
> Largesce forth with Charite.
>
> (VIII, 2987–90)

Doubtless, like many of his contemporaries, Gower came to be dissatisfied with Richard's handling of national affairs and might have wanted to modify such fulsome praise. But, in 1393, Gower is recorded as having received gifts from Henry Bolingbroke, Duke of Lancaster, and it is at around this time that the dedications to Richard II begin to be suppressed and replaced by references to 'myn oghne lord which of Lancastre/is Henri named'. After Henry IV's accession (of which Gower gave a favourable account in his *Chronica Tripartita* and his *Address to Henry IV*) he received further rewards. Chaucer, who had never been a political writer and who had been much more dependent on Richard II and much more committed to him, also felt it necessary in 1399 to switch his support to Henry IV, and, by means of a witty 'begging poem', pleads for a continuation of royal favour.

The effects of patronage are much more obvious in the cases of other writers. Lydgate was the favourite poet of the Lancastrian court of Henry VI and wrote most of the 'official' political verse, almost all of which must have been commissioned. The Prologue to one such poem gives an elaborate account of the circumstances of its composition. In 1423 John, Duke of Bedford, 'þe Regent of þe reme of Fraunce', had commissioned verses in French from Laurence Calot to establish Henry VI's just claim to the French throne. According to Lydgate, four years later the Earl of Warwick thought it would be useful to have these verses in English also and ordered Lydgate to translate them:

> And I, as he that durst not withsey,
> Humbly his biddyng did obey,
> Ful desirous him to do plesaunce,
> With fere suppressed for my ignoraunce,
> And in my hert quakyng for drede;
> And as I kend began to taken hede
> Vnto the Frenssh compiled by Laurence,
> In substaunce filowyng the substaunce
> Of his writyng and compilacioun.
> *(Minor Poems* II, 28, 55–63)

Lydgate was in most things the voice of the establishment and of political orthodoxy. He was a patriot and a Lancastrian, and, despite the conventional obsequious pose, he was doing nothing against his conscience. Nevertheless, the suggestion for this particular set of political verses came from the Earl of Warwick. and it is almost certain that Lydgate would not have written them without this prompting. Like Lydgate, Hoccleve wrote for patrons whenever he could. In one place he records with pride how he was commissioned to write verses for the Duke of York:

> ones at London, desired he,
> Of me þat am his seruant/& shal ay,
> To haue of my balades swich plentee
> As ther weren remeynynge vn-to me.
> *(MP* IX, 11–14)

His political verses are almost all dedicated to Henry V and were perhaps commissioned by him or on his behalf. George Ashby's political verses were written specifically for the benefit of the young Prince Edward, and it is likely, though not certain, that they were commissioned. During the course of the civil wars the power of verse as an instrument of propaganda was considerably exploited. Many pieces, both pro-Yorkist and pro-Lancastrian, must have been written by commissioned partisans, as Brotanek suggests is the case with the pro-Yorkist pieces in MS Trinity College Dublin 432.[14]

If political verse was important enough to be commissioned, it was also important enough to be suppressed. In writing some types of political verse the poet exposed himself to punishment. In 1124 Henry I condemned Lucas de la Barre to be deprived of his sight because he had written songs and had sung them so as to make the King a laughing-stock to his enemies, and only the poet's suicide prevented the punishment. In 1314 at Bannockburn, the Scots captured Roger Baston, who, as his ransom, had to compose verses in praise of their victory instead of that of the English. This almost humorous punishment was exceptional. More in keeping with the general trend was the Bishop of Bangor's threat to excommunicate the writers of lampoons against John of Gaunt in 1377. Sanctions against political propagandists continued throughout the fifteenth century. In 1456 John Holton was hung, drawn and quartered because he wrote 'bills' against the King. In 1484, for his couplet deriding Richard III, Ratcliff, Catesby and Lovell, Wyllyam Collyngbourne was

> put to the most cruel deth at the Tower Hylle, where for hym were made a newe payer of galowes. Vpon the whiche, after he hadde hangyd a shorte season, he was cutte down, beynge alyve, & his bowellys rypped out of his bely, and cast into the fyre there by hym, and lyved tyll the bowcher put his hande into the bulke of his body; insomuch that he sayd in the same instant, 'O Lorde Ihesu, yet more trowble,' & so dyed to the great compassion of moche people.[15]

The writing of political verse was dangerous for those in any way critical of the régime.

A further measure of its importance and potential influence may be derived from the legislation enacted against certain types of political verse.[16] In 1402 an act was passed which forbade the composition and dissemination of political prophecies. In 1406 an act against the Lollards mentions among its complaints their publication of false prophecies predicting the overthrow of the King, the Lords Temporal and the Lords Spiritual. The use of prophecies had reached such proportions in the fifteenth and sixteenth centuries that Henry VIII, Edward VI and Elizabeth I all found it necessary to pass laws against their composition. In the fifteenth century the posting up of 'bills' on the doors of churches, walls and gates had also become so common and potentially dangerous that a proclamation was issued forbidding it.[17] Yet it is hard to know whether political verse had any actual effect. According to one source, the prophecies of certain Welsh minstrels led to an insurrection in Wales, but there is no conclusive evidence.[18] It is clear enough, though, from the widespread commissioning of politically favourable poetry, and also from the frequent punishment of that which was considered subversive, that verse was thought to be a highly effective mode of propaganda.

III

Because this type of verse was essentially public and depended largely for its effectiveness on being brought before the notice of a large number of people, the methods of 'publication' or dissemination employed by its authors are of some interest and importance. The normal method of disseminating verse—through the multiplication of scribal copies—is, of course, much in evidence. Lydgate's *Kings of England*, a fairly simple versified account of the dynasty from William I to Henry VI, touching on such questions as the rightful claim of Henry VI to the English and French thrones, is preserved in no less than forty-six manuscripts and was clearly a favourite among patriotic Lancastrians. But political verse was also publicised by other methods.

Some political poems were oral and may have been sung before a noble audience in a castle assembly, or before burgesses and peasants in a market square, or by soldiers around the military camps. The earliest in date is a fragment preserved by Matthew Paris which was reputedly sung by the followers of Geoffrey de Mandeville about their plunderings in East Anglia:

> I ne mai a-live
> For Benoit ne for Ive.

The same chronicler also has a couplet which was sung by the Flemish mercenaries of the Earl of Leicester in 1173 predicting victory for themselves.[19] Both Peter of Langtoft and Robert Mannyng of Brunne record songs relating to the Scottish wars of Edward I.[20] Both the *Brut* and Fabyan's chronicle give the text of a song sung '... in daunces, in carolis of ye maydens and mynstrellys of Scotlande ...' deriding the English after the defeat at Bannockburn. According to other chroniclers, the Scottish soldiers, on the night before the Battle of Dupplin in 1332, sang songs optimistically predicting the overthrow and degradation of the English army on the morrow. There is a considerable reduction in the amount of oral verse in the fifteenth century. The *Brut* preserves verses purporting to have been sung by the English soldiery in derision of the Flemings after the failure of the Siege of Calais in 1436. From its opening lines, it appears that at least one of the Robin Hood ballads was delivered orally:

> Lythe and listin, gentilmen,
> That be of fre bore blode ...
> (*GRH*, 1–2)

But there are few others. In the fifteenth century political subjects were treated more frequently in sophisticated courtly songs, often of considerable musical elaboration. But the purpose of these sets them apart from the more popular songs. The writers of popular songs used the oral medium to make known ideas to an audience which was largely illiterate; the writers of court songs used it for aesthetic reasons.

The undoubted increase in literacy in the fifteenth century must have been an important factor in the decline of oral literature. The ever-broadening scope of educational facilities and the wider use of the vernacular brought the ability to read and write to classes other than the aristocracy and the clergy. In the towns, some apprentices were given educational opportunities in addition to the training connected with their particular trades. For example, a record survives of a complaint against one Robert Chirche, a merchant, who, in 1442, had bound himself to send one of his apprentices to school for one and a half years so that he could learn grammar, and for a further half year to learn to write. The boy's friends complained that Chirche had failed to fulfil his obligations, much to the boy's disadvantage. Tradesmen were also becoming increasingly literate: in 1422 most of the members of the Brewers' Guild of London could read English; among the witnesses to the will of Sir John Fastolf in 1466, were two merchants, two farmers, a tailor and a seaman who are described as literate; among the *Stonor Papers* for the years 1474–8 are several letters clearly written by tradesmen and apprentices. Bequests in wills of this century show that the middle classes were increasingly owning books: in 1403, for example, a London draper Thomas Walyngton left two volumes on religious subjects; in 1411 a mason of Southwark bequeathed books to St Olave's Church; Robert Skrayngham, a merchant, left a copy of Higden's *Polychronicon* to another merchant. Interesting in this context is a letter dated 1484, from Margery Paston to her husband, complaining that one of their servants is proving unsatisfactory because he '. . . will not take upon him to breve dayly as ye commandyt'. The word 'breve' means 'to note down' and almost always implies writing accounts, so it appears from this that literacy was expected in anyone with even a small amount of responsibility.

But exact contemporary estimates of overall literacy are lacking. The earliest general statement comes from Sir Thomas More, who in 1533 estimated that forty per cent of the population 'could never reade englische yet'. Literacy had doubtless increased considerably in the years since 1485 and it may be that J. W. Adamson's estimate of about forty per cent literacy in the fifteenth century is fairly accurate.[21] There were almost certainly considerable variations from place to place: the rich south-east was culturally more advanced than the rest of England, and townspeople would be more likely to read and write than countrymen. But overall there can be little doubt that literacy increased, and this seems to have influenced the methods by which political verse was publicised. In the fifteenth century political verse tended to be read rather than listened to.

In fact, apart from the usual method of scribal proliferation, some of the less usual methods of publicising verses assume a considerable literacy among the general public. Those verses posted up on the walls or gates of churches and towns depended for their effectiveness on the public's ability to read them. And this method was widely used. As early as 1327, during one of their periodic raids in Yorkshire, 'þe scotes made a bille þat was fastnede oppon þe cherche dores of Seint Peres toward Stangate' with some verses against the English on it. But the real vogue of this method of publicity comes in the fifteenth century. In 1418 certain scholars of Cambridge were accused of having 'affixed on the mayor's gate a certain schedule, to his great scandal, and so that the mayor and burgesses dared not to preserve the peace', and there followed some thirty lines of verse. In February 1424, when feelings ran high against the Flemings, 'bills' began to circulate, 'And somme were sette upon the Byshoppes gate of Wynchester and on other Byshops gates.' In 1448 John Piggot records that 'bills' in verse against William de la Pole, Duke of Suffolk, William Ayscough, Bishop of Salisbury, and Lord Say and Sele were posted up on the gates of St Paul's in London. Dating from 1460 comes a 'balat' of eighty-six lines in English and Latin which was set up on the gates of Canterbury to welcome the invasion of the Earls of Warwick and Salisbury. From 1484 comes Fabyan's account of the well-known couplet set up on the doors of St Paul's for which its author, Wyllyam Collyngbourne, was executed. In 1494, Laurence Saunders was imprisoned in Coventry, and '. . . within viij dayes after Lammasse ther was a bill sett vppon þe north Chirch durre in seynt Mighels Chirch be some evell disposed person vnknowen. . . .' This method of propaganda was apparently favoured by his supporters, for when he was imprisoned again in 1496 ij seducious billes wer founde i-sette vppon þe Mynster durre in þe feste of seynt Anne, & anoþer was cast &c. Whereof the tenour here-after ensuen.

There follow two poems in support of Saunders, perhaps by the 'evell disposed person vnknowen' responsible for the earlier 'bill'.[22] There are other instances of this method of publicising political verse. It had an extensive and enduring vogue.

Other methods of disseminating political verse, not so extensively used, also depended on the ability of the public to read. Capgrave relates that the Emperor Sigismund, travelling out of England after his visit in 1416, 'mad his servauntis for to throwe billes be the wey' containing poems in praise of the English.[23] More curious, and certainly more gruesome, are the circumstances in which *The Five Dogs of London* (1456) was publicised:

Item the XIX day of September in the nyght tyme wer sett upon the Standard in ffletestrete afore the duk of york being þer þan lodged in the Bisshop of Salisbury place certain dogges hedes with Scriptures in their mouthes balade wise which dogges wer slayn vengeably the same nyght.   (*HP*, p. 355)

This is a piece of Lancastrian propaganda designed to discredit Richard, Duke of York, in the eyes of his supporters in London. The 'bills' reflect on the Duke's integrity, since each dog in turn complains how he was sacrificed to the Duke's ambitions. Perhaps also displayed publicly was *The Epitaph for the Duke of Gloucester* (1447). R. H. Robbins has suggested that the refrain 'Have mercy on him buryed in this sepulture' indicates that the poem was written on a scroll exhibited on or near the tomb at the time of his burial (*HP*, p. xxxix).

Propagandist literature needs to make an immediate impact. Those who publicised verses by means of the methods outlined above knew it was essential to communicate their ideas as forcefully and as widely as possible. The audiences they were able to reach were, by modern standards, limited and local, but within a fifteenth-century context this was about the best a political poet could hope for.

IV

Despite the increasing tendency for poems to be written down, it is an unfortunate but well documented fact that much Middle English political verse has been lost. To some extent all types of verse were affected, but those on political subjects suffered more than most. As R. M. Wilson has shown, what survives is only part of a much more extensive literature.

It has been shown that political verses were important enough to be commissioned and important enough to be suppressed. But this importance was essentially temporary. As the political situation which gave rise to the verses changed, the verses became irrelevant. Consequently, it must often have been felt that there was very little point in preserving them. That the collection of these verses was frequently casual and haphazard is clear from the actual physical position and condition of some of the texts in the manuscripts in which they occur. Many political verses, for example, are to be found added to flyleaves or otherwise blank leaves of manuscripts: the well-known quatrain on the Peasants' Revolt of 1381 beginning 'Man be ware and be no fool . . .' is found on an originally blank leaf towards the end of Cambridge University Library MS Dd. xiv 2; *The Layman's Complaint* and *The Friar's Answer* are written without a break between them in a fifteenth-century hand on the flyleaf of the fourteenth-century MS St John's College Cambridge 195; the verses of the so-called *Advice to the Several Estates* II beginning 'ye that ar comons obey yovr kynge and lords . . .' are found written in an early sixteenth-century hand in MS Sloane 4031 on a flyleaf which was not part of the original manuscript. There are many other examples of this. Again, the relative unimportance of the preservation of political verses may be inferred from the unprofessional manner in which some of them are copied. For example, the texts of the two St John's College Cambridge MS 195 poems mentioned above contain many scribal errors and appear to have been copied at an odd moment by someone to whom they were of little significance. Many verses like them must have been lost because of the indifference of those who collected medieval poems.

Many medieval political verses must also have been lost simply because they were essentially oral and never achieved a written currency. Not surprisingly, the majority of these date from the earlier part of the Middle English period. In addition to the minstrel verses commissioned by William Longchamp and the lampoons against John of Gaunt already mentioned, R. M. Wilson gives many examples of allusions to songs now lost.[24] The earliest which are thought to have been in English date from the twelfth century and concerned an incident in the life of St Wulfstan. Other songs were apparently composed against Robert Fitzwalter and Sigar de Quincy for their surrender of the castle of Vaudreuil to Philip of France. In 1323, 'songs of Simon de Montfort and other songs' were sung before Edward II, but these cannot now be identified. Also lost are the verses made about Peter de la Mare in 1376, and those sung by certain Oxford scholars against Richard II in 1378. Perhaps fewer fifteenth-century songs have been lost. One that certainly has dated from 1453–4 and celebrated John Norman, Lord Mayor of London for that year. A contemporary chronicle gives an account of the incident to which the song related:

> and this yere, vpon the morne after Symound and Jude, John Norman befor-named, beyng chosyn Mair for that present yere, was rowed by water to Westmynster wt the Aldermen; and alle the chief of the Comoners of the Cite went also thedir by barges; which of tymes owte of mynd was vsed before season by the Mairs to ride allwey by land to take their charge. Wherefore the watermen of Themmys made a song of this John Norman, wherof the begynnyng was 'Rowe thy bote Norman'; which newe custome was welle allowed, & hathe contynued from his daies to this season.

Fabyan's account of the same incident adds a little more of the song, probably giving the whole of the first two lines: 'Rowe the bote, Norman, rowe to thy lemman', and Skelton perhaps gives the refrain in his reference in *The Bowge of Courte:* 'Heave and ho rumbelow, row the bote, Norman, row.'[25] From the evidence of rhyme in the fragments which survive it looks as though the song was originally in short lines. It refers to a comparatively unimportant local incident. But the three separate references to the song argue a certain popularity over a long period of time. Whether anyone copied it down in full is not known, but it is doubtful.

There is evidence also that many battle poems have been lost. Mention has already been made of the songs by Roger Baston in enforced praise of the Scots, but songs on the deeds of Edward Mortimer and Henry Percy have evidently disappeared also. In the late fifteenth-century accounts of Tattershall College appear the titles of two songs, now lost, one of which, *The Cry of Caleys* was apparently in English and probably political.[26] There is evidence that the compilers of the *Brut* chronicle used popular verses as source material for some incidents but these verses have disappeared. It was not uncommon for verses to be rewritten as prose for incorporation in chronicles. How often this happened is difficult to assess. An interesting example from BM MS Cotton Cleopatra C iv demonstrates the process. For his account of the Battle of Agincourt the chronicler begins by paraphrasing a current ballad. But, in his prose, either through the difficulty of rendering the heavily alliterated vocabulary, or the fairly difficult syntax, the ends of stanzas begin to appear, with the correct rhyme sequence and refrain:

> Cryste helpe me, so now in þis case,
> Bot þo þat been cause of this trespase.
> When þou sittest in Iugment,
> Þer holde me excused tofore þi face,
> As þou art god omnipotent.
>
> (*HP*, 27, x—aa)

This is a passage from Henry V's exhortation to his soldiers, and the end of it, like the beginning, is partly rendered into prose. But when the chronicler turns, in his rendering of the next stanza, to the battle itself his purpose falters and the end of the stanza appears practically unchanged:

> Þer men myght see a semble sade
> Þat turnyd many on to tene & tray,
> for many a lorde þer ryght low lay,

> þat commen was of blod full gent.
> By evensong tyme, soþely to say,
> Þer helpe vs god omnipotent.
>
> (*Ibid.*, gg—jj)

Finally the writer discards all pretence and the remaining sixty-four lines of the poem are written as verse. But had it not been for the chronicler's lack of application, or alternatively the domination of his mind by the verses he knew, the surviving part of what has been called 'the best and most spirited of the Agincourt poems' would have been lost like the beginning. Similarly, although some fifteenth-century verses against the Flemings are extant, some have probably been lost. On the failure of the siege of Calais of 1436 the *Brut* chronicler remarks: 'amonges Englisshmen were made many rymes of þe fflemmynges', and he follows this with the text of some verses. He knows of other poems, however, which he does not include: 'Such & many oþir rimes were made amonges englisshmen, aftir the fflemmynges were thus shamfully fled frome Caleis . . .', and which may well be lost.[27]

Some verses published as 'bills' have also disappeared. Single sheet manuscripts are rarely preserved. Unless, like some of the examples given above, they were connected with events important enough to be included in contemporary chronicles, or unless they were the subject of legal proceedings and the like, almost their only chance of survival would be if they appealed to someone sufficiently for him to copy them into a larger collection. This cannot have happened often, and it is demonstrable that some such verses have disappeared. In 1424, according to his own testimony, William Paston was the subject of many threatening 'bills' written by a certain Walter Azlak and posted up on various church doors in the city of Norwich:

> swich and so many manaces of deth and dismembryng maden and puttyn by certeyns Englische billes rymed in partye, and up on the yates of the Priorie of the Trinite chirche of Norwiche, and on the yates of the chyrche of the Freres Menures of Norwiche, and the yates of the same Cite called Nedeham yates and Westewyk yates, and in othre places

wyth inne the seyd Cite by the seyd Walter and Richard sette, making mension and beryng this undeyrstondyng that the seyd William, and hese clerkes, and servauntes should be slayn and mordered in lyke forme as the seyd John Grys in the seyd forme was slayne and mordered . . .   (*Paston Letters*, No. 6)

Evidently many copies of these 'bills' were distributed but none have survived. Again, in 1463, it is recorded that certain priests preached against the friars, who, in retaliation, set up 'bills' on the door of every church which they considered corrupt.[28] But none of these 'bills' have survived either.

Perhaps the most serious losses, however, are from the earlier years of the reign of Henry IV. In the second fragment of *Mum and the Sothsegger*, which was composed sometime after 1402, the author writes:

> Now forto conseille þe kyng vnknytte I a bagge
> Where many a pruye poyse is preyntid withynne
> Yn bokes vnbredid in balade-wise made
> Of vice and of vertue fulle to þe margyn . . .
>
> (*M*, 1343–6)

This is not an easy passage to interpret ('vnbredid' probably means 'opened' or 'unrolled', and 'balade-wise' may be 'in the manner of popular songs or poems') but the general intention is clear. The author, in his role of self-styled 'truthteller' or adviser to the King, intends to bring to his notice the extent and nature of contemporary grievances, as, he says, they appear in popular songs and verses. He lists 'a volume' about how the clergy forsake their real duties and seek financial gain in the service of lords, 'a rolle' on how endowments are misused, 'a payre of pamphiletz' on how pluralists and bishops neglect the people and spend 'þaire lyves in lustes and in sportes', a 'copie' of complaints made by the common people against the lords, a 'scrowe' against those jurors who will not bring just verdicts for poor men against the rich, another 'writte' about the waste of excessive litigation, a 'raggeman rolle' against interference in lawsuits and a book against the unfair advantages the rich enjoy over the poor in litigation, a whole collection ('a librarie') of books against those lords who diminish the King's revenue, an account of those who hoard wealth in their lifetimes so that they can make large endowments at their deaths, a piece on those who fail to carry out the intentions of generous bequests to the poor, a book of prophecies 'on þe mervailes þat Merlyn dide devyse', and, finally, before the unique manuscript breaks off, a 'cedule' (schedule) on the corruption of the knights and the clergy. Since the author is arguing a case it is possible that he has invented these books and their contents. But in most cases he is unusually specific. One book has 'viftene leves', another is 'y-writte al newe', a third is 'frayed a lite', and the last on the list is

> soutelly indited
> With tuly silke intachid right at rollis end
> (*M*, 1734–5)

so that it appears that he has specific books in mind. It would, in addition, be reasonable to suppose that the prophecies of Merlin he alludes to are versions of the 'six kings to follow John', which were sometimes attributed to Merlin, and were circulated at around this time by the supporters of Glyndwr, Mortimer and the Percies. It could well be that this entire list is of actual political pieces, now either lost or unidentified, all of which pointed out the short-comings of Henry IV's rule.

It is clear from the examples given above that much has been lost, but the verses discussed here have at least left some trace. Much must have disappeared completely and left no trace of its existence. About these verses it is impossible to speculate. But, from the information remaining, it is obvious that some types of political verse were more susceptible to loss than others. For example, 'official' verses composed for special occasions by poets such as Hoccleve and Lydgate, and commissioned by influential patrons, would have a better chance of survival than other types of verse such as those recited orally or 'bills'. Also, because they largely controlled the means by which literature was transmitted and preserved, it is fair to assume that more verse has survived which reflects the preoccupations and ideas of the noble and the clerical classes than that which represents the opinions of the less articulate artisans and peasants. However, a sufficiently large body of verse has survived, representing the opinions of a wide enough range of society, to make a study of it both possible and significant.

NOTES

[1] For the reestablishment of English see particularly A. C. Baugh, *A History of the English Language*, 2nd edition, 1959, especially pp. 171–84.

[2] *History of English Literature*, translated by H. M. Kennedy, 1887, I, 314, 316.

[3] *History of English Poetry*, 1895–1910, I, 187.

[4] *Literature and Pulpit in Medieval England*, Cambridge 1933, particularly pp. 210–36.

[5] On minstrels see especially E. K. Chambers, *The Medieval Stage*, Oxford 1903, I, 42–69.

[6] On Gower's life see vol. IV of the edition of his works by G. C. Macaulay, Oxford 1899–1902; and also J. H. Fisher, *John Gower: Moral Philosopher and Friend of Chaucer*, 1965, especially chapter 2.

[7] For details of Hoccleve's life see F. J. Furnivall ed. *Hoccleve's Works*, EETS ES 61, 1892, pp. vii–xxx, and the collection of documents on pp. li–lxx.

[8] For Lydgate's life see W. F. Schirmer, *John Lydgate*, translated by Ann E. Keep, 1961.

[9] See Mary Bateson ed. *George Ashby's Poems*, EETS ES 76, 1899, pp. v–vi.

[10] *Twenty Six Political and Other Poems*, EETS OS 124, 1904, p. ix.

[11] See R. H. Robbins *RES* 20, 1969, pp. 182–9 for details on this man, and my note *RES* 21, 1970, pp. 337–8.

[12] For Bokenham's literary activity see Samuel Moore, 'Patrons of Letters in Norfolk and Suffolk c. 1450', *PMLA* 27, 1912, pp. 188–207 and *ibid*. 28, 1913, pp. 79–105.

[13] For the songs on William of Longchamp see Roger of Hoveden, *Chronica* ed. W. Stubbs, Rolls Series 51, III, 143; for Fantosme and Baston see R. H. Robbins, *Historical Poems of the Fourteenth and Fifteenth Centuries*, 1959, p. xl.

[14] *Mittelenglische Dichtungen*, Halle 1940, especially pp. 6, 192–3, 198.

[15] For the stories in the above paragraph see Ordericus Vitalis, *Historiae Ecclesiasticae* ed. A. Le Prevost, Paris 1838–55, IV, 460; *Chronicon Angliae* ed. E. M. Thompson, Rolls Series 64, 1874, p. 129; *Registrum Abbatiae Johannis Whetamstede* ed. H. T. Riley, Rolls Series 28, 1872, I, 247–8; and Robert Fabyan, *The New Chronicles of England and France*, ed. H. Ellis, 1811, p. 672.

[16] For details of the legislation against political prophecies see Rupert Taylor, *The Political Prophecy* in England, New York 1911, pp. 104–7.

[17] T. Rymer, *Foedera*, 1727, XI, 268.

[18] See Taylor, *op. cit.*, p. 104.

[19] *Historia Anglorum* ed. Sir F. Madden, Rolls Series 44, 1866, I, 271, 381.

[20] For these songs see especially R. M. Wilson, *The Lost Literature of Medieval England*, 1952, pp. 207–12 where most of them are printed. For references to the other songs mentioned in this paragraph see *ibid.*, pp. 212–14.

[21] For much of the information used in this paragraph, and detailed references, see J. W. Adamson, 'The Extent of Literacy in England in the 15th and 16th centuries', *The Library* 10, 1929–30, pp. 163–93. For the ownership of books among the middle classes see E. A. Savage, *Old English Libraries*, 1911, pp. 274–85; and Sylvia Thrupp, *The Merchant Class of Medieval London*, Michigan 1962, pp. 161–3, 248–9.

[22] For the incidents alluded to in this paragraph see: *The Brut*, ed. W. F. D. Brie, EETS OS 131, 136, 1906–8, p. 249; G. G. Coulton, *Social Life in Britain*, Cambridge 1918, p. 66; C. L. Kingsford, *English Historical Literature in the Fifteenth Century*, Oxford 1913, p. 370; *English Chronicle* ed. J. S. Davies, 1858, p. 91; Fabyan's *New Chronicles of England and France* ed. H. Ellis, 1811, p. 672; *The Coventry Leet Book* ed. M. D. Harris, EETS OS 134, 135, 1907–8, pp. 566, 577–8 and generally R. M. Wilson, *op. cit.*, pp. 197–201.

[23] *Chronicle of England* ed. F. C. Hingeston, Rolls Series 1, 1858, p. 314.

[24] *Lost Literature of Medieval England, op. cit.*, pp. 193–202 for references to verses mentioned below, and to other verses.

[25] C. L. Kingsford, *Chronicles of London*, Oxford 1905, p. 164; Fabyan, *op. cit.*, p. 628.

[26] For references to these songs see R. M. Wilson, *op. cit.*, pp. 203–4.

[27] *Op. cit.*, pp. 582, 600.

[28] *Collections of a London Citizen* ed. J. Gairdner, Camden Society 1876, p. 228.

3 : Nationalism and Foreign Affairs

A TYPICAL early fifteenth-century map would have shown England on the north-westernmost edge of the known world. But the country which Henry IV came to rule was by no means isolated from European politics. England had commercial connections with most European countries. Various royal marriages provided other contacts. But the diplomatic and military involvement in a protracted war with France was the principal concern of English foreign policy in this century, and it is this which provoked most reaction from contemporary poets. Their contributions vary a great deal, but most testify to a growing English national awareness and most urge strong militaristic policies. As one might expect, the more sensational events provide the subject matter for most verses and English successes tend to provoke more comment than failures.

It is necessary first of all, however, to say something briefly of the historical situation. Most foreign contacts were relatively superficial in that they depended on commerce and involved at most a few merchants. England in the fifteenth century was becoming increasingly a trading nation and English merchants reached most of the civilized nations of Europe and sometimes beyond. The trade with the Low Countries had been established for several hundred years, and there were contacts further north round the shores of the Baltic with Norway, Denmark, Sweden and Prussia though the main trade in this area was in the hands of the merchants of the Hanse. During the fifteenth century some merchants found their way 'by nedle and by stone' to Iceland. There were also commercial contacts with the major cities of northern Italy, and the Genoese in their 'grete karrekkis' and the Venetians and Florentines in their 'grete galees' were frequent visitors to England. There was some trade with Spain and Portugal and the war with France did not cut off English contacts with Brittany and Gascony, though it disrupted them. For the most part contacts with these countries were confined to commerce with a minimum of diplomatic and political involvement. Of course there were disputes from time to time. The sea routes were never entirely safe. Trading ships were sometimes pirated and this could lead to diplomatic activity and reprisals. The Venetians, particularly, resented the growth of English trade in the Mediterranean. There were also wrangles, particularly with the Italians and the merchants of the Hanse, about technical conditions of trading. There were frequent complaints by the English that alien merchants here 'have more liberte/Then wee oure selfe' and that 'evere we have the worse in this contre'.[1] The Iceland trade caused difficulties too, for the Norwegians claimed a monopoly of it and trading was forbidden to the English by Henry V in 1415 and by Parliament in 1429. The ban was not always observed and there was some fighting between the English and the Norwegians. Nor did Henry V endear himself to foreigners by his habit of commandeering their trading ships to transport his armies to France. But for the most part commercial dealings were mutually advantageous and did not lead to trouble.

English involvement with Wales, Ireland and Scotland was of a rather different nature. Wales had, of course, its own language and customs, but since Edward I's successful campaigns of 1277–84 had been under English rule. It was a country of large lordships controlled either by the Marcher nobility or the King and dominated by the big castles designed by Master James of St George for Edward I. The Welsh nationalism which had flared briefly under Llywelyn ap Gruffydd at the end of the thirteenth century did not reappear until Glyndwr's revolt at the beginning of the fifteenth. This was never a very serious threat to the English Crown, though it proved difficult for Henry IV to eradicate resistance completely and there were still those later in the fifteenth century who looked upon the Welsh with a suspicious mistrust:

Beware of Walys, Criste Ihesu mutt us kepe,
That it make not oure childes childe to wepe,
Ne us also.

(Libelle, 784–6)

Ireland was also nominally under English rule. It had its own justiciary, parliament and council but all these were controlled by the Anglo-Irish. The Gaelic chieftains, who had formerly been provincial kings, had become vassals of the English king or of the Anglo-Irish nobles after the conquest of the twelfth century. But, in real terms, the English and Anglo-Irish controlled only Dublin and its neighbourhood together with one or two ports from which was conducted the fairly flourishing Irish trade. For the rest, the chiefs ruled in their own localities. There was constant friction between them and the Anglo-Irish both on constitutional and territorial questions and a whole series of governors failed to put matters right. The English kings lacked a coherent policy in Ireland. Only Richard II devoted much time and energy to the problem. His expedition of 1394 had some success in rationalising the situation: the chiefs swore a general oath of fealty and agreed to give up the lands they had 'usurped' in return for confirmation of their possession of lands held by hereditary right. But Richard II had no time to consolidate these gains. In 1394 he had to return to England to deal with the Lollards and his later expedition was called off because of Bolingbroke's invasion. Thereafter the rivalries continued much as before, and even the Anglo-Irish quarrelled amongst themselves. Few people were concerned. A notable exception is the author of *The Libelle of Englyshe Polycye* (1436), who seemed to have been well informed on Ireland through contact with 'a lorde and of ful grete astate' (763), who is identified by a marginal note in one manuscript as James Butler, fourth Earl of Ormond. This author recognises the potential richness of Ireland's resources and the possibilities for trade out of its 'havenes grete and godely bayes', but he also warns against allowing the native Irish too much power and draws attention to their constant encroachments which have, he says, seriously diminished Anglo-Irish territory:

> So wylde Yrishe have wonne on us unable
> It to defenden and of none powere,
> That oure grounde there is a lytell cornere
> To all Yrelonde in treue comparisone
>
> (725–8)

and he urges that money and resources should be shifted from the French war so that the English

> Myght wynne Yrelonde to a fynall conquest
> In one soole yere, to sette us all in reste.
>
> (770–1)

Though this poem seems to have been reasonably popular, and though the author apparently had influential friends, nobody appears to have paid much attention to his suggestions. The problems of Ireland played little part in English politics of the fifteenth century.

Nor, on the whole, did those of Scotland, though Scotland was a sovereign state, and for much of the time hostile to England. Edward I, after his intervention in the 'great cause' between John Balliol and Robert Bruce in 1290, had attempted to subjugate Scotland in the same way as he had Wales. In fact, after his defeat of the Scots at Dunbar in 1296 and Balliol's abdication, Edward I did briefly rule the whole of the British Isles. But first under Sir William Wallace, and then under Robert Bruce, grandson of the claimant to the throne in 1290, the Scots resisted English domination, and, at the Treaty of Northampton in 1328, Bruce was recognized as independent King of Scotland. Edward III's victory at Halidon Hll in 1333, which resulted in the exile of David II, and the capture of the Scottish King in 1346 after Neville's Cross gave the English an advantage once again, but thereafter all their attention was taken by events in France. Not that this meant that there was peace with Scotland, but the warfare was thereafter confined more or less to border raids. A Scottish army in 1388 defeated the English forces of the Percies at Otterburn, but, at Homildon Hill in 1402, the result was reversed. And such raids and counter-raids continued. The question of Scottish subjugation was not, however, seriously contemplated again by English kings, although in the version of his *Metrical Chronicle* which he presented to Edward IV, John Hardyng sought to persuade the King that he ought to claim the Scottish throne:

> Most cause was why I drew this ilke treatise,
> To make your father haue had perfecte knowlage,
> And you also of Scotlande in all wise,
> That percell was of your eldest heritage,
> And of all landes moste nere your auauntage,
> To haue it whole, no more to bee dismembred,
> Which might bee gote, as it is afore remembred.

Hardyng had been, at various times since the reign of Henry V, collecting material on Scotland, and was obsessed with the question of English overlordship. He even plots out a method of campaign by means of which 'within a moneth this land maye bee destroyed' and as a result of which:

> our enemies shall bee sore annoied
> And wasted bee, and eke for euer shent,

but there is no evidence that Edward IV was persuaded.[2] What the English feared most from the Scots, in fact, was their alliance with the French. This never amounted to a serious threat, principally because of the baronial rivalries in Scotland itself. Many verses had been provoked by the Scottish wars of the thirteenth and early fourteenth centuries, but fifteenth-century writers are interested in Scotland only in its connections with France and Burgundy. Typical is the position assumed by the author of the Latin verses against James I and Philip of Burgundy:

> Dux Burgundicus et rex Scoticus insidiantur,
> Sed rex Anglicus et grex publicus his dominantur.
> Anglia regna premit, Burgundia dedecus emit,
> Francia fracta tremit, Scotia victa gemit.
> Undique concursus stat et Anglia fortis et ursus;
> Anglia dum rugit, circula terra fugit.[3]
>
> > (*PPS*, II, p. 151)

The war with France dominated English foreign affairs to the exclusion of almost all else. England and France were at war from 1337 to 1453, and though large-scale military operations were sporadic, there existed at the best of times a climate of hostility. The causes of the war were complex and the issues which divided the nations varied throughout its course. Initially the trouble occurred because of the English possessions in France, particularly the rich territory of Gascony. The treaty of Paris of 1259 gave the King of France suzerainty over Gascony and Ponthieu which the King of England held from him in fief, a simple enough arrangement but one which was subsequently to cause difficulties, since English kings were reluctant to pay the formal homage. In addition there was constant friction about the exact authority held by the French and English in Gascony. Nor were its boundaries at all well defined and this resulted in territorial disputes also. As the situation worsened over the years, both the English and the French sought allies. Philip VI of France had the support, amongst others, of Spain and Bohemia, and had an alliance with Scotland against the English. Edward III, for his part, exploited the hostility in the Low Countries towards the French by means of a series of alliances, and at one time had the support of the Emperor Lewis IV.

The dynastic issue, with which the war came to be concerned in the fifteenth century, was not initially of very much importance. In 1328 Charles IV, last of the sons of Philip IV of Capet, died without male issue and the throne of France passed to Philip VI, son of Charles of Valois, Philip IV's brother. His accession to the throne did not go undisputed, but Edward III's claim was not pressed at this time. And the English King did have some sort of a claim, for his father Edward II had married Isabella, the daughter of Philip IV, whose grandson Edward III thus was. Edward III, however, had implicitly recognised Philip VI as the legitimate French King in 1329, when he paid his formal homage in Gascony. Yet when Philip VI declared Gascony confiscate in 1337, Edward III replied by stating his own claim to the French throne. It is difficult to decide how serious the claim was. It would seem he used it only as a bargaining point, for at the Treaty of Brétigny in 1360 he was prepared to drop his claim in return for substantial concessions by the French. Under the terms of the treaty Edward III was allowed full sovereignty of Gascony, Poitou and various towns and counties in northern France, most important of which was Calais. The French also agreed to pay three million gold crowns for the ransom of the French King, John II, who had been captured at Poitiers.

This was the high point of English success in the fourteenth century, following as it did the great naval success at Sluys in 1340, the notable military victories at Crécy in 1346 and Poitiers in 1356, and the capture of Calais in 1347. After 1361 English fortunes in France declined: the Gascon nobility revolted against the arrogant and tactless rule of Edward, the Black Prince, and Charles V began to reconquer many of the territories granted to Edward III at Brétigny. English counter-measures failed to have a great deal of effect: the expedition of 1370 into northern France under Sir Robert Knollys had no success, the march from Calais to Bordeaux in 1373 under John of Gaunt brought no long-term advantage, and an English fleet carrying reinforcements to Gascony was defeated off La Rochelle in 1372. By 1375, when a truce was settled at Bruges, England held only Calais, a few ports in Brittany and a severely diminished Gascony. Neither country at this time had the resources necessary for a protracted military effort and thereafter activity was only sporadic. There was piracy in the Channel, the French burnt Rye and Gravesend in 1377 and the English retaliated with an attack on St Malo in 1378, but for the most part the war petered out. In 1396 Richard II married Isabella, the young daughter of Charles VI, and sealed a long-term peace which was still operative when Henry IV came to the throne. But there had been no formal settlement and the problems which divided the nations were there to pursue when resources might permit.

This growing involvement in foreign affairs and the increased contacts with other nations gave the English a sense of their own identity and gave rise to sentiments which were distinctly national-istic. Such sentiments were not new. They appear not infrequently in earlier English writing, for example in the chronicles of Laʒamon and Robert of Gloucester, in the political verses connected with the Scottish wars of the late thirteenth century, in the patriotic songs of Laurence Minot, and even in romances. It is noticeable, however, in the fifteenth century that expressions of nationalistic feeling are more frequent. There is everywhere a concern with 'oure Englande', 'oure Englysshe men', 'our Englysshe marchauntes'. The triumphs and disasters of the nation come to be experienced collectively: after a military victory 'Englonde may calle & cry/Deo gracias', (*HP*, 32, 4–5), and when things go wrong 'England may say and syng Allas! Allas!' (*HP*, 58, 5). Nor were the English alone in this. A measure of the extent to which national consciousness was developing throughout Europe may be derived from some of the exchanges between the delegates at the Council of Constance. In one dispute the French cited as proof of the greatness of their country that it had more provinces, more episcopal churches, more universities, bigger towns and cities, and more clergy and people than England, to which the English retorted that their land had more counties and more parish churches, and even claimed, at one point, that England was bigger.[4] Claims of superiority were often absurd. Towards the end of the century, Sir John Fortescue, a man not noted for his irony, sees as an indication that Englishmen are braver than Frenchmen the fact that 'there bith . . . mo Men hanged in Englond, in a Yere, for Robberye, and Manslaughter, than there be hangid in Fraunce, for such maner of crime in seven Yers'.[5] The French, he implies, are not brave enough to be robbers or murderers. Some years earlier a poet had asserted the superiority of Englishmen to Flemings 'more of reputacioun ben englisshmen þen ye' and had sought to prove it on philological grounds by playing on the word 'fflemed' meaning 'banished' or 'put to fright':

> ffor flemmynges com of flemmed men, ye shal wel vndirstand,
> ffor fflemed men & banshid men enhabit first youre land.
>
> (*HP*, 29, 59–60)

Along with this contempt for foreigners usually went a deep distrust and suspicion. Particularly when things were going badly, the English were quick to suspect foreign treachery: the Flemish are readily characterised as 'fals' and 'ful of gyle', and one writer accuses Venetian and Florentine merchants of spying for England's enemies so that 'By wretynge ar discured oure counsayles'. On the other hand information given to the English by foreign informers is unreliable and 'false coloured alwey'. A particular fear, and one that appears to lie behind several contemporary poems, was that the country might be encircled by an alliance of hostile powers 'and so to have enmyes environ aboute'.[6]

Almost any topic could provoke a patriotic outburst. In the opinion of one writer late in the fifteenth century, the contemporary decadence of England, which he sees all around him and which has destroyed all the former 'chyvalry, manhode and ryche marchaundyse' of the country, has been caused by nothing more than the vain extravagance of contemporary clothes, which, he says, do not follow English fashions, but imitate continental ones.[7] In his *Debate between the Horse the Goose and the Sheep* (1437–40) John Lydgate's national pride is touched by the thought of the excellence of English wool:

> Alle naciouns afferme vp to þe fulle
> In al the world ther is no bettir wolle.
> (*Minor Poems*, II, 23, 356–7)

In the same poem he demonstrates the value of goose feathers which were used on arrows to which the English owed many of their military successes:

> Bi bowe & arwis sith the werr began
> Have Ynglysshmen, as it is red in story,
> On here enmyes had many gret victory.
> (215–17)

That 'the werr' refers to the war with France is made clear by a later reference to Poitiers. This debate is not chiefly a political work, nor for that matter is Lydgate's *Fall of Princes* (1431–8) but both poems contain nationalistic observations. *The Fall of Princes* is based on Laurent de Premierfait's French translation of Boccaccio's *De Casibus Virorum Illustrium* and as usual Lydgate feels free to modify his source. The account of King John II of France, who was captured at Poitiers in 1356, involves a particularly drastic alteration. Boccaccio had referred to 'anglis, inertissimis adque pavidis et nullius valoris hominibus' ('Englishmen, the laziest, most fearful and worthless of men') and Laurent renders this accurately

enough: 'des anglois, hommes faillis et vains et de nulle valeur.'
Lydgate is incensed at this slur on his country, ignores his source
completely, and instead reviles Boccaccio for his original sentiments:

> For to hyndre the famous cheualrie
> Of Inglisshmen, ful narwe he gan hym thynke,
> Lefft spere and sheelde, fauht with penne and inke.
>
> Thouh seide Bochas floured in poetrie,
> His parcial writyng gaf no mortal wounde;
> Kauhte a quarel in his melencolie,
> Which to his shame did afterward rebounde,
> In conclusion, lik as it was founde,
> Ageyn King John a quarell gan he make,
> Cause that he wolde of Inglisshmen be take.
>
> Heeld hem but smal of reputacioun,
> In his report man may his writing see;
> His fantasie nor his oppynioun
> Stood in that caas of noon auctorite:
> Ther kyng was take; ther knihtis dide flee;
> Where was Bochas to help at such a neede?
> Sauff with his penne he made no man to bleede.
>
> (IX, 3166–86)

A further dimension of the fifteenth-century nationalism was the
interest which many writers felt in the origins and past of the
English nation. Since Nennius and Geoffrey of Monmouth, the
English, by a false etymology and a disregard of historical fact,
had considered the Trojans as their heroic ancestors through
Brutus, the great-grandson of Aeneas. A noble beginning was seem-
ingly a prerequisite in the history of a proud nation. Early in his
Troy Book (1412–20) Lydgate explains how the nation was
founded by

> Brute, so passyngly famus
> After whom, yif I schal nat feyne,
> Whilom þis lond called was Bretayne:

For he of geauntys þoruȝ his manhood wan
Þis noble yle, and it first began.

(I, 832–6)

And this notion not only appears in romances and legends but also in histories. One version of a very popular poem listing the kings of England, attributed to Lydgate, actually begins with Brutus.[8] These beliefs naturally gave the Troy story a particular emotional appeal to the English and this had a marked effect on its treatment by English authors. Lydgate, for example, begins his *Troy Book* by accusing Homer of inaccuracy and partiality, in much the same way as he had Boccaccio, because he was 'with Grekis . . . allied' and therefore 'to hem favourable/In myche thyng' (Prologue 280–2), and he proceeds, as Renoir has pointed out, to attempt to correct this false emphasis. The fall of Troy was not due, in Lydgate's version, to any deficiency in Trojan fighting ability and still less to any outstanding qualities shown by the Greeks, but simply to the treachery of Antenor, the desertion of Calchas, and the implacable malice of the God Mars. The Trojan princes, particularly Hector, appear as the patterns of chivalry and knightly virtue, and the Greeks, particularly Achilles, are decided villains. In Lydgate's opinion, Homer's praise of Achilles 'Entriked is with fraude and with fallas'. He kills Hector in a cowardly fashion when he is unprepared and unarmed 'Through necligence . . . of his sheelde' (III, 5399), but his own particularly treacherous betrayal and brutal death are something done 'rightfully, of resoun as it sit' (III, 3195). One gets the impression that Lydgate would have liked to have rewritten the whole story.

Not only was England's legendary past invoked, but its historical past was also ransacked for evidence of the nation's greatness. The author of *The Libelle of Englyshe Polycye* (1436), for example, finds in Ailred of Rievaulx the story of the pre-Conquest English King Edgar who, as a sign of his supremacy, was rowed on the river Dee by eight tributary kings. In the author's opinion, this king, 'so commendable/To Englysshe men', ought to be honoured by the English as a national hero no less than Cyrus was honoured by the Persians, or Charlemagne by the French or Romulus by

the Romans. Among later kings, fifteenth-century Englishmen were
still attracted to Richard I, or at least to the long and often overtly
nationalistic romance about him which continued to be copied and
modified throughout these years. Later accounts of Edward I, also,
emphasize his greatness as a conqueror in Wales and Scotland and
the occasional thirteenth-century song deriding his enemies was
still known, in modified form, in the fifteenth century.[9] But most
captivating of all were the exploits of more recent kings, particularly
Edward III. Lydgate remembers him for his victories abroad:

> At Scluse he hent a grete navy
> At Cressy he faught agayn
> The Kyng of Beme ther was slayn
> And the Kynge of Fraunce put to flight
> No lenger ther durst he fight.
> (*Minor Poems*, II, 51, 124–8)

The author of *The Libelle of Englyshe Polycye* says that his exploits
on both land and sea were so well known ('ye knowe his worthy-
nesse') that there is no need to repeat them. Nevertheless, he
manages, incidentally, by means of an adroitly maintained
occupatio to give an account of the siege of Calais of 1347 and to
allude also to the triumphs at Sluys and Crécy. Earlier in this same
poem, the author had praised Edward III for his protection of
English merchants. As an example he cites an incident he has read
about 'in a scrowe', which is maintained as truth 'bothe wyth hygh
and lowe', about how Edward III had once avenged Breton piracy
in the Channel by firm retaliatory action: without any 'grete tary'
he caused to be fortified three English towns 'Dertmouth,
Plymouth, the thyrde it is Foweye' and 'gaffe hem helpe and notable
puissance' so that they could make war upon 'the Pety Bretagne'
(*Libelle*, 214–20). Strangely, no incident in Edward III's reign is
known which approximates to this. Indeed, it looks as though this
author has used, and suitably embellished, similar events which
took place in 1403 under Henry IV. But the nationalistic Englishman of the fifteenth century looked back on the days of Edward
III as a splendid era of military success, and it is hardly surprising

that factual accuracy should suffer a little through the need to maintain him as a hero.

It was not long before fifteenth-century writers had contemporary heroes. Shortly after the accession of Henry V war again broke out with France. At the beginning of the century the French political scene was one of extreme disorder. The central rule of Charles VI, who suffered from fits of insanity, was weak, and the princes of the royal family, his uncles, brothers and nephews, vied for authority in the court. Chief among these were Louis, Duke of Orléans, and John the Fearless, Duke of Burgundy, whose wide domains also included Flanders and Artois. They differed on practically every aspect of policy, including their attitudes towards the English, for Louis of Orléans was in favour of military operations to drive the English out of Gascony and Calais, but John the Fearless, conscious of the importance of the English wool trade for the economic prosperity of Flanders, was more conciliatory. Matters came to a head in 1407, when John the Fearless had Louis murdered in the streets of Paris by paid agents. Thereafter the conflict escalated into a bloody civil war and both sides sought English help. The English themselves must have known that these internal dissensions were favourable to their cause, but their reaction to these events was restrained. The author of the poems in MS Digby 102 thought that the murder of Louis of Orléans was discreditable:

> Eche man destroyȝe his best frend:
> So dede Flaundres: how dede it wende?
> Of noblay þey han lore þe sown.
>
> (XII, 84–6)

But he does not dwell upon it. It may be that the English, who were used to thinking in terms of 'gallicana duplicitas', were not surprised by French treachery to each other. Others, usually retrospectively, simply saw the French situation as an example of what trouble civil disorder could cause in a kingdom which was badly led:

> Take hede how synne hath chastysyd frauns,
> Whan he was in hys fayrest kynde,

How þat flaundrys hath myschaunys,
ffor cause þe bysom ledyth þe blynde.

(*HP*, 49, 69–72)

But there was also some awareness of their predicament. Thomas Hoccleve, writing in 1412, recognises the serious effects of the civil war on France: 'Thi self manaseth þi self for to dye', and he continues by saying that he feels sorry though he is an enemy to France and knows that the English will derive political advantage from her disorders:

I am an Englyssh-man & am þi foo,
ffor þou a foo art vnto myn lygeance;
And yit myn herte stuffid is with woo
To see þyn vnkyndly disseueraunce:
Accordeth yow! girdeþ yow with suffraunce!
Ye greue god, and your-self harme & shame,
And your foos thereof han disport & game.

(*Regement*, 5307–13)

Humane and essentially peace-loving, Hoccleve is in favour of negotiations and the sealing of a peace between France and England through a marriage between Prince Henry and the Princess Katherine.

There were negotiations, of course, but nothing much came out of them. Henry V had, before he came to the throne, shown some interest in French affairs. But he had shown a preference for a military rather than a negotiated settlement, and the expedition of 1411 in support of John the Fearless had been partially due to his influence in the Council. After his accession he pursued three policies simultaneously: he showed himself ready to negotiate with Charles VI and enter the French royal house by a marriage with the Princess Katherine; he was prepared to form an alliance with John the Fearless; and at the same time he made preparations for war. The negotiations were protracted. The talks between the English and Burgundian ambassadors at Leicester in May 1414 got as far as an agreement to attack the lands of the Orléanists, but no agreement could be reached on what should be done if Charles VI or the Dauphin intervened. At a later meeting at Ypres, the

English asked that the definition of their common enemy should include Charles VI and the Dauphin, but John was reluctant to agree to this as the King of France was his feudal overlord. He promised a definite answer at St Omer in September, but none came. At the same time, Henry V had been negotiating with Charles VI. In August 1414 the English ambassadors had met with the French in Paris. They reminded the French of Henry V's claim to the French throne, of his rightful possessions in France, of the French disregard of previous treaties, and of money still owed to the English for the ransom of King John II who had been captured at Poitiers. Nevertheless, they agreed to talk about a marriage between Henry and Katherine. Nothing was settled at this or at subsequent meetings: the French refused to recognise Henry's claim to the crown, his territorial demands got nowhere, King John's ransom was not paid, and even the dowry of Katherine was argued about—the English demanded two million crowns but came down to one million, the French offered six hundred thousand initially but went up to eight hundred and fifty thousand. By the time the last negotiations were being conducted, however, Henry had concluded they were pointless and his last memorandum complained of evasion of his demands by the French. He decided on a military solution.

Public opinion was moving in this direction also. There were plenty of propagandists who were ready to support the dynastic claims of Henry V in France, and no lack of support for the view that military activity was the best means to acquire and hold what was thought to be rightfully English. One of the more interesting examples comes from the MS Digby 102 author in a poem dated 1414. Henry V is urged to unite his own land, make secure his borders and get control of the sea before he turns his mind to foreign projects:

> Whanne ȝe han made pes wiþ-ynne,
> All ȝoure reme in vynte,
> Vttere-more ȝe mot bygynne;
> Strengþe ȝoure marche, and kepe þe see.
>
> (XIII, 105–8)

The author then reminds Henry that God is on his side, that his claim to the French throne is a just one, and recalls that Edward III, who had the same valid claim, had sought to repossess his territories and rights by military action:

> To ffraunce, kyng Edward had queryle,
> Hit was his kynde heritage;
> And ȝe han þe same style,
> Wiþ armes of þe selue parage.
>
> (113–16)

This writer particularly distrusts negotiations with the French: no war, he says, was ever ended by words and treaties: 'Wiþ word of wynd, mad neuere werre ende' (127). Henry's enemies are the only ones who profit by treating for peace:

> Ȝoure enemys han þat eure in hord,
> Þat þey wynne wiþ word,
>
> (156–7)

and by continuing to negotiate he is depriving himself of his possessions and allowing the enemy time to prepare:

> Als ofte as ȝe trete,
> Ȝoure enemys, ordynaunce þey diȝt.
> While ȝe trete, ay þey gete.
> Ȝe trete ȝoure self out of ȝoure riȝt.
>
> (137–40)

The only way for Henry to reclaim his possessions is through military force:

> And þat ȝe wynne, ȝe wynne wiþ sword.
> Þerfore wiþ swerd do ȝoure dede.
>
> (159–60)

And this poet was not alone in his advice, for as Kail has demonstrated, the sentiments of his verses, and even some of his phrases, echo the Chancellor's speech before the Leicester parliament of 1414. The author of another poem, *The Crowned King* (1415), written while Henry was still at Southampton, also urges him on to military prowess: 'For he þat armes shall haunte, in youþe he must begynne' (*HP*, 95, 123). Perhaps the author of the MS Harley 565 version of *Henry V's Invasion of France* was not being too fanciful when he showed the King receiving the good wishes of all as he embarked on his expedition.[10]

Most verses on foreign affairs relate to specific events and the first substantial group concern Henry V's campaign of 1415. After the failure of negotiations early in this year, war was inevitable. Bishop Beaufort, the Chancellor, had announced on 16 April before the Council that Henry had decided to recover his heritage by force of arms, but it was not until 11 August that he set sail. By this time nine thousand men had been mustered, and fifteen hundred ships collected to transport them, their horses, weapons, heavy siege equipment and supplies. A large amount of money had been raised in loans and taxes to pay for the expedition. By this time too, various items of anti-French propaganda had begun to circulate. One such blames the French for breaking off negotiations and insulting Henry by sending him a gift of tennis balls. As E. F. Jacob has pointed out, this story most probably originated in misunderstood court gossip, but it proved attractive to the popular imagination and was often retold and embellished.[11] Perhaps its first literary occurrence is in the contemporary verses on *Henry V's Invasion of France* from BM MS Harley 565, which deal with the whole campaign of 1415. After the conventional opening prayers for the well-being of the King, the author goes on to explain his just claim to the throne of France, and relates how ambassadors were sent to claim Henry's rights. The Dauphin's reply is insulting:

> 'Me thinke youre Kyng he is nought old
> No werrys for to maynteyn;
> Grete well youre Kyng', he seyde, 'so yonge
> That is bothe gentill and small,
> A tonne of tenys ballys I shall hym sende
> For to pleye hym with all.'
>
> (Nicolas, p. 302)

Henry receives the taunt grimly and predicts his vengeance:

'Swyche tenys ballys I schal hym sende
As schall tere the roof all of his all.'

The poet then turns to Henry's determination to repossess Normandy, which was his 'Be right of eritage', his preparations for
transporting 'Hyse gret gonnys and engynes stronge', his departure
from London and arrival at Southampton to his ships with their
'riche sayles and heye top castell'. The poet's only interest is
Henry's foreign campaign: the plot on the King's life at Southampton is dismissed in a few lines, and his imagination is caught again
only when the English 'pyght there tentys a down' before Harfleur.
Here Henry V remembers his prediction:

> My gonnys shall lyn upon this grene,
> For they shall play with Harflete
> A game of tynes as y wene
>
> (pp. 307–8)

and proceeds with the bombardment. Eventually, 'The houses of
Harfleur they all to rent'. The English breached the walls and the
French were forced to negotiate a surrender:

> It is best now that we therefore,
> That we beseche the Kyng of grace
> That he asayle us now no more
> For to dystroye us in this place;
> For but the Dolfyn us rescewe,
> This toun to delivere wyl we sikerly.
>
> (p. 311)

Despite his anger at the inhabitants for keeping what Henry took
to be his own, he allowed them to inform the Dauphin of their
plight and gave him until 22 September to relieve the town. But no
relief came and at the appointed time the citizens of Harfleur duly
surrendered. The first passus of this poems ends with Henry's
consolidation of his position in the town. The English occupied it:

> let stuffe the town overall
> Wyth Englysshmen therinne to be,
>
> (p. 314)

and he also enforced a partial evacuation of the French inhabitants.

Although the author of these verses follows broadly the events of the campaign, his interests are not those of the impartial chronicler. The poem principally glorifies Henry V, who is shown not only as brave and resolute but also as merciful and pious. It exults in the discomfiture of the enemy, particularly that of the Dauphin and his friends, who are shown as too afraid to attempt to relieve the town:

> The Kyng of Ingelond is fers as lyon
> We wil noughte mete hym in the felde.
> (p. 313)

There is no hint here of the considerable difficulty the English had at the siege (though the defending force was small): the walls were strongly built and well defended; Henry's miners were not very effective; communications among the English were hampered by local flooding, and dysentery had severely reduced the troops. This author sees only the glory of the English victory, as indeed do others among his contemporaries.

> He sette a sege, þe sothe for to say,
> To harflu tovne with ryal aray;
> Þat tovne he wan & made afray,
> Þat fraunce shal rywe tyl domesday
> (*HP*, 32, 5–8)

writes the author of *The Agincourt Carol*, and, naturally enough, later writers remember only the triumph. So, in 1429 John Audelay recalls how Henry V 'taȝt franchemen to plai at þe ball' before Harfleur and how the bombardment so frightened the inhabitants that they thought it was 'þe fynd þat mad þat fray' (*HP*, 41, 20).

Although Harfleur was an English triumph to be remembered and celebrated, Agincourt was more so and several English poems relate to this battle. After the capitulation of Harfleur Henry's forces were considerably depleted: some had been killed in the siege; more had died of dysentery; twelve hundred were needed to garrison the town. Thus it was with only five or six thousand men that Henry set out to march the hundred and fifty miles through Normandy to the safety of Calais. He marched along the coast but when he came to the Somme he found the bridges down, the fords staked and the enemy waiting in force on the other side. Forced to march up river, the English eventually managed to cross at Béthancourt and Voyennes on 19 October. The French chose to engage the English in battle on the 25th at Agincourt, and with superior numbers and fresher men held considerable advantages. But Henry induced them to attack over marshy ground and on a narrow front, conditions which were unfavourable to the heavily armoured French infantry and cavalry, and, as at Crécy and Poitiers earlier, the lightly armed English archers slaughtered the enemy in large numbers. The second passus of *Henry V's Invasion of France* broadly follows the events of the campaign: the author remarks on the journey how 'Toward Caleys full faire they yede', and on the destroyed bridges 'that over the water he myght nought ryde', but he concentrates on the events of the battle itself. Not that the details of the battle are at all fully reported, but he does have a few lines on the effectiveness of the English archers:

> Oure archiers shotte full hertyly,
> And made Frensshmen faste to blede:
> There arwes went full good sped,
> Oure enemyes therwith doun gon falle,
> Thorugh bresplate, habirion and bassonet yede,
> Slayn there were xj thousand on a rowe alle.
>
> (Nicolas, p. 322)

What interests him most are personalities. He ironically sets out the boasts of the French aristocracy before the battle: the Duke of Orléans predicts the capture of Henry V 'the Kynge of Ingelond with us shall byde'; the Duke of Brabant thinks that the French have more than enough men to win the battle 'Alas, he seyde, what nedith us alle'; the Duke of Bourbon looks forward to selling off the English archers cheaply into captivity; and the Duke of Berry 'full mochell of pryde' urges that they ought to win the battle quickly so as to be home in time for dinner. Many of these nobles, the poet points out, were either captured or killed in the subsequent defeat. Among the English, the exploits of the Duke of York, the Duke of Gloucester, and the Earls of Huntingdon, Oxford and

Devonshire are remarked upon. But the real hero is predictably
the King himself who encourages his soldiers:

> He bad alle men blithe to be
> And seyde, 'Felas well shall we spede',
> (p. 320)

disposes his battle:

> He batailyd hym ful rially
> Stakes he hewe doun in a wood
> Beforn our archers pyght them on hy,
> (p. 319)

prays to God for victory in his rightful cause:

> This day hold over me thin holy hond,
> And spede we well in al my right,
> (p. 320)

and finally fights bravely in person:

> That day he faught withe his owne hond,
> He sparyed nother heigh no lowe
> There was no man his dynt myght stond.
> (p. 323)

No hero of romance could have acquitted himself better. Henry
V's nationalistic fervour, his personal bravery, his piety and his
concern for his soldiers all impressed this poet. The author of the
fragmentary *Battle of Agincourt*, from BM MS Cotton Cleopatra
C iv, stresses the same points. Evidently a chronicler began to use
the poem as source material for his account of the battle, and much
of the beginning is lost in the chronicler's paraphrase. But, even
so, it is clear that the earlier part of the poem comprised a stirring
speech by the King. Henry resolves to forgo the possibility of being
ransomed 'for as I am a trew kynge & knyght for me þis day schall
neuer Inglond rawnsome pay', encourages his soldiers, particularly the archers, to 'be englysshemen, þat neuer wold fle at no
batelle', and finally exhorts them to put all their trust in God. There
follows a fine alliterative stanza on the battle and particularly on
Henry's part in it:

> Stedes þer stumbelyd in þat stownde,
> Þat stod stere stuffed vnder stele;
> With gronyng grete þei felle to grownde,
> Here sydes federed whan þei gone fele.
> Owre lord þe kynge he foght ryght wele,
> Scharpliche on hem his spere he spent,
> Many on seke he made þat sele,
> Thorow myght of god omnipotent.
>
> (*HP*, 27, 1–8)

The rest follows the same lines as the previous poem: it praises the English heroes and lists some of the more important French killed or captured. The final stanza reviles the Flemish, who, under the orders of John the Fearless, failed to support the English cause at the battle.

Henry's triumphant return after his victorious campaign was the signal for much English rejoicing. The King himself had said that he wanted no poems made in his praise, but, nonetheless, some have survived. The third passus of *Henry V's Invasion of France* is, like the previous two, factual; it describes the crowds who welcomed Henry, the Lord Mayor of London's speeches, the pageants and the decorations. But, as in the previous passus, the author's patriotism is obvious. He puts an astonishing speech into the mouths of 'the lordes of Fraunce' (presumably Henry V's French prisoners) in praise of the energy and fighting ability of the English:

> Inglond is nought as we wen,
> It farith be these Englishmen
> As it doth be a swarm of ben;
> Ingland is like an hive withinne,
> There fleere makith us full evell to wryng,
> Tho ben there arrowes sharpe and kene,
> Thorugh oure harnys they do us styng.
>
> (p. 327)

He also adds his own voice to the chorus of praise and good wishes for Henry V:

> Crist that is oure hevene Kyng,
> His body and soule save and se;

Now all Ingelond may say and syng,
'Blyssyd mote be the Trinite'.

(p. 329)

Along with contemporary prose accounts of Henry's return, this
poem mentions the fact that many songs were sung during his
procession through London. It is possible that either of two surviving political songs dated 1415 were composed for this occasion,
but it is impossible to be certain. Both are in the 'carol' form, with
short stanzas and a refrain, and the music of one—the so-called
Agincourt Carol—has survived. The title is slightly misleading, for
the poet casts his mind back over the whole campaign from
Harfleur to Agincourt, and on to the contemporary situation when
the French prisoners 'were ladde in-to lundone', but it is principally
a prayer of thanks for the English successes:

> Owre kynge went forth to normandy
> with grace & myȝt of chyualry;
> ther god for hym wrouȝt mervelusly
> wherfore Englonde may calle & cry,
> Deo gracias.

(*HP*, 32, 1–5)

The second poem, *The Rose on Branch*,—called 'A Carolle for
Crystmasse' in BM MS Additional 31042—does not appear initially
to bear any political significance. The first stanza seems to be no
more than a panegyric on the 'rose' which 'es þe fairest flour', but
the second suggests that the 'rose' is to be interpreted as a symbol
of England when it is contrasted with the 'flour-de-lyse' which has
obvious connotations with France:

> me thynke þe flour-de-lyse
> Sholde wirchipe þe rose of ryse,
> And bene his thralle.

(*HP*, 33, 9–11)

The final stanza reveals the full political significance of the poem
though it maintains the use of the flower imagery:

> Many a knyghte with spere & launce
> ffelowade þat rose to his plesance;

When þe rose betyde a chaunce
þan ffadide alle þe floures of fraunce
And chaungyde hewe,
In plesance of þe rose so trewe.
(13–18)

Although this is another song of triumph, the author's partiality is restrained by the formality of the poem's structure and the elaboration of its central conceit.

Henry V did not return immediately to France but sought to consolidate his position by diplomatic means, when the Emperor Sigismund visited England for talks on 1 May 1416. Both religious and political problems were involved. At the Council of Constance, which had begun in 1414, Sigismund was attempting to resolve the vexed question of the papal schism. Europe had been divided in its support of the rival popes since 1378 and divisions on this question tended to follow the alliances which were the result of the Hundred Years War. England and her allies favoured the Roman Pope, France and hers the Avignonese. Sigismund rightly divined that national animosities were the crucial obstacle to healing the schism and part of his strategy was to try to reconcile France and England. He met the French in Paris on 1 March 1416, but the council was hopelessly divided and Sigismund transferred negotiations to England. He was lavishly entertained and talks, to which the French sent representatives, soon got under way. But the usual stalemate was reached before long: Henry V refused to moderate his demands and the French were evasive. Moreover, it soon became clear that the French were using the talks as a device to cover military preparations, and, when they began to blockade Harfleur, Henry felt he had to reply with force. Both Henry and Sigismund felt they had been badly betrayed by the French, and the result of this was an alliance of friendship signed at Canterbury. In the same document, Sigismund reviewed the progress of negotiations between England and France since he had landed in England. It is effectively an indictment of French duplicity and ill will: Charles VI is termed a lover of discord who has done his best to sabotage negotiations for the unity of the Church, and the French are accused of making depredations on the Empire and of treating cynically Sigismund's efforts to restore Henry V's just rights. Under the terms of the treaty Henry V, Sigismund and their successors were to have a perpetual treaty of friendship; merchants and craftsmen of either country were to have free access to the other; neither country would harbour the other's traitors; and each was to assist the other in the recovery of their just rights in France. In England, at least, this treaty made a deep impression, and Sigismund, when he eventually left, was given a fine sendoff. He replied by causing 'his servauntis for to throwe billis be the wey' which, according to Capgrave, bore the following complimentary verses:

> Farewell, with glorious victory,
> Blessid Inglond, ful of melody,
> Thou may be cleped of Angel nature
> Thou servist God so with bysy cure.
> We leve with the this praising,
> Whech we schul evir sey and sing.[12]

The verses are very ordinary, and even the play on 'Angle' and 'angel' is an old one, but Sigismund's generosity, his optimism and firmly pro-English stance impressed the English. Later, in 1429, in his verses on the coronation of Henry VI, Lydgate remembers him as 'worthy Sygesmound', and in 1436 the author of *The Libelle of Englyshe Polycye* recalls his good advice to Henry V.[13] But it is doubtful if much of lasting value was achieved by Sigismund's visit or the resulting treaty of Canterbury: it still further alienated the French and sharpened rather than reconciled the national divisions at the Council of Constance. It was, however, a great propagandist triumph for Henry V.

Even the military successes in France had not achieved much of lasting importance. As Perroy writes: 'The campaign of Agincourt meant nothing decisive. It was only one more raid after so many like it.'[14] But Henry determined, according to a contemporary chronicler, 'to cross the Channel the following summer in order to break the obstinate and more than adamantine hardness of the French'. During the winter of 1416–17 he raised loans and organ-ized supplies. In July 1417 about twelve thousand men crossed from

Southampton. Henry's plan was to seize lower Normandy and then to march up the Seine valley to Paris. Caen fell early in September, then Argentan, Verneuil and Alençon. On 16 November 1417 Anjou, Brittany and Maine made a separate truce with Henry, who afterwards besieged Falaise, which finally capitulated on 1 February 1418. Throughout the spring of this year, key towns were subdued by a series of English expeditions and Henry began to push forward towards Paris. Up to this point Henry had been partially supported by John of Burgundy whose military activity around Paris had tied down Charles VI's forces. But John had been alarmed at Henry's progress in Normandy and he saw himself threatened. Accordingly he consulted his own security. He had always had supporters in Paris, notably Isabel of Bavaria, Charles VI's Queen, who, in November 1417, joined John at Chartres, and a little later, at Troyes, proclaimed herself 'Queen of France, having on behalf of our lord the King, government and administration of the kingdom'. On 29 May 1418 the Parisian supporters of John of Burgundy revolted and opened the gates of the city to him. There-after for a short time the whole of northern France was under his domination. His policy from then onwards was one of containing Henry V's advances, and he sought to rally both his own supporters and those of Charles VI to this end. A temporary agreement was made at St Maur-des-Fossées under which John of Burgundy and the Dauphin were to co-ordinate their efforts against Henry V. The English object in the summer of 1418 was Rouen, the Norman capital, and John of Burgundy made efforts to save it. He had rein-forced the city with soldiers from Paris and had exhorted its defenders to hold out against the English until he could organize relief.

The siege of Rouen began on 30 June 1418 and lasted until 19 January 1419. Among the English was a certain John Page whose remarkable poem in short couplets is perhaps the best English account of the siege.[15] The extant poem is presumably his revised version based on notes he made at the siege itself:

> Thys procesce made John Page
> Alle in raffe and not in ryme,

By cause of space he hadde no tyme.
But whenne thys werre ys at a nende,
And he have lyffe and space he wylle hit amende.

(pp. 45–6)

But he is careful to assure the listener or reader of the accuracy of the factual details and of his credentials for writing such an account: 'For at that sege with the kyng I lay.' He begins with the expedition of Thomas Beaufort, Duke of Exeter, who went to the city in order to negotiate a surrender, or, if this was not possible, to get some idea of the terrain around the city so that he could advise on the disposition of the siege:

To loke yf that they yolden wolde be
And alle soo for to se that grounde
That was aboute the cytte rounde.

(p. 2)

The French made it very clear that they did not intend to give up the city, and on both sides preparations went ahead for the siege. According to Page, Rouen was well fortified and the defence was conducted by able soldiers under good commanders, some of whose names he gives. The English commanders and the disposition of their troops are also described in detail before he passes on to the fighting. The defenders were not by any means passive. Artillery fire from the walls and raiding parties caused the English some trouble:

Hyt was grete lykyng hem to hede;
To counter hem hyt was grete drede,
For the fensce of hem nought at alle,
For moche of the drede come fro the walle;
For schot of goonne and quarelle bothe
Sawe I nevyr gretter wothe.
Evyr as they yssuyd oute and made afray
There wolde be schot I dar welle say
A hundryd govnnys at wallys and tourys
Within the mount of ij halfe hourys.

(p. 15)

The defenders of Rouen hoped that eventually the Duke of Burgundy would organize relief, but none came and by Christmas 1418 'mete and drynke and othyr vytayle' were in short supply. Prices began to rise steeply and the inhabitants were forced to eat practically anything:

> They etete doggys, they ete cattys;
> They ete mysse, horse and rattys.
> For an hors quarter, lene or fatte,
> At Cs hyt was atte.
> A horsse hedde for halfe a pound;
> A dogge for þe same mony round;
> For xxxd went a ratte
> For ij noblys went a catte.
>
> (p. 18)

Inevitably it was not long before the famine began to take its toll and the pride of the citizens was replaced by sorrow.

> Thenne to dye they dyd begynne
> Alle that ryche citte withyn.
> They dyde faster every day
> Then men myght them in erthe lay.
> There as was pryde in ray before,
> Thenn was hyt put in sorowe fulle soore.
>
> (p. 19)

The situation in Rouen had been aggravated by the fact that people from the devastated suburbs and from the surrounding countryside had been admitted inside the walls. As the food shortage became ever more acute the captain, Guy le Boutellier, was forced to eject many of the 'bouches inutiles', that is, the aged, or very young, or women, who were not directly concerned in the defence of the city. Since Henry V would not let them pass through the English lines, they had to remain in the ditch surrounding the city where many of them died a slow death from starvation. It was no real surprise, when on 31 December 1418, the citizens asked to negotiate a surrender. Their request was first heard by Gilbert d'Umfraville (in whose service John Page may have been) who, with due formality, informed his commanders. Henry V consented to see a deputation. D'Umfraville warned the men of Rouen to weigh their words carefully when they came to negotiate:

> For one worde wrong and owte of warde
> Myght cause you alle to fare fulle harde.
>
> (p. 27)

This was sensible advice, for their bargaining position was weak in the extreme.

The rest of John Page's poem deals with the negotiations for the surrender of Rouen, and so far as may be determined, the poet's accuracy here measures up to that of his account of the fighting. The talks got off to a bad start. The Rouen representatives asked Henry to have pity on the starving people ejected from the town:

> Consydyr ye the charyte
> The pore pepylle that ben with owte
> In youre dychys rounde aboute,
> That ben there and lacke mete and brede,
> For hunger many on ben dede.
>
> (p. 29)

Henry, apparently, replied that he was not responsible for their predicament:

> I putte them not there, and þat wote ye
> Nothyr hyt was not myn ordynaunce,
>
> (p. 30)

and added that they had brought their troubles upon themselves by denying to him his rightful possession of the city:

> Ye have offendyd me with mysse,
> And fro me i-kepte my cytte,
> That ys myn herrytage so fre,
> And ye shalle be my lege men.
>
> (p. 30)

The question of allegiance and the rightful possession of the city, to which Page shows himself sensitive, was a vexed one. Henry insisted that the city was his by right, that he was seeking only to reclaim what was his own, and that the citizens owed allegiance to him. The French argued that, in defending the city, they were only doing what they had been ordered to do by the King of France, Charles VI, and John of Burgundy:

> That us betoke oure soverayne lege,
> For to defende from saute and sege.
> We ben hys lege men ibore
> And also we have to hym swore
> Also to the Duke of Burgayne fre.
>
> (*Ibid.*)

They obviously still hoped for relief and asked Henry's permission to send messengers to inform Charles VI and John of Burgundy of their position. Page has Henry reply that they knew all about the siege and had done so since it started, for he himself had sent messengers. To send more, he maintained, would be pointless:

> To sende them message newe and newe
> Hyt were to me but novylte,
> To us but superfluyte.
>
> (p. 31)

This was the brutal truth. Despite the intentions of the agreement of St Maur, neither the French nor the Burgundians were prepared to attempt to raise the siege. Henry informed the men of the city that he intended to have Rouen, by force if necessary, but consented to negotiate. The talks were protracted. According to Page:

> We than chalengyde and accused,
> And they answeryd and excusyd.
> We askyt moche and they profered smalle,
> That was ylle to corde with alle.
> So they tretyd a forghtnyght,
> And yet accorde they ne myght.
>
> (p. 36)

The refusal of the representatives of Rouen to surrender was not popular among the poorer people of the city who were most severely hit by the food shortage. According to Page, the poorer citizens attributed the failure of negotiations to the selfishness of their rich representatives who, of course, stood to lose their possessions if Henry V entered the city:

> But for youre goode that ye hyde,
> Youre pompe and youre grete pryde.
>
> (p. 38)

According to one version of *The Siege of Rouen*, that incorporated in the *Brut*, the poorer citizens threatened to kill the richer negotiators unless they allowed the city to surrender. The MS Egerton 1995 version is particularly graphic at this point:

> Youre styffe gatys that ye steke
> We shall them bren and up breke.
> We shalle lat hym in to hys ryght;
> If ye defende we shalle fyght,
> Levyr then thys to byde here
> And dy for hunger alle in fere.
>
> (*Ibid.*)

Page makes the citizens willing to accept Henry V as their rightful King, but it is doubtful if this was a strong motive in their behaviour. Their situation was hopeless as they well knew. Once the townspeople had made plain their determination to overrule their negotiators it was clear that the siege would soon end. Henry Chichele, Archbishop of Canterbury, mediated with the clergy of Rouen and discussions went on for another four days. Henry V allowed the citizens of Rouen to communicate formally with Charles VI and John of Burgundy '. . . in what degre they stode and howe Bydyng on them to have rescowe' (p. 40). If no rescue came by 19 January, Rouen was to be surrendered. The city was to pay Henry V fifty thousand pounds in war indemnity and within half a year to build him a castle on the Seine. In return, the city was to be allowed the privileges 'By fore as hyt was wounte to be', that is, before the reign of Philip VI. These terms were communicated to the French and Burgundians but they sent no help, and on the agreed date Henry V received the keys of the city. He wasted no time. The Duke of Exeter occupied the city that night and

c

Henry himself rode in next day, receiving, according to Page, a fine welcome from the citizens:

> Alle the pepylle of that cytte,
> They sayde, 'Welcome, oure lege so fre,
> Welcome in to youre oune ryght,
> As hyt ys the wylle of God Almyght.'
> With that they cryde alle 'Nowewelle',
> Al so schyrle as eny belle.
>
> (pp. 44–5)

It is difficult to be persuaded that the people of Rouen, or any of the captured Norman towns for that matter, were whole-hearted about welcoming Henry, or about acknowledging his rightful claim to the city. But no doubt they were glad that the siege was over and that food was once again available, and most must have been ready enough to pay homage.

Though *The Siege of Rouen* is notable for its factual accuracy, and though the compiler of the *Brut* chronicle included a version, it has already been seen that the poem is much more than a chronicle of events. How John Page himself regarded the poem is more difficult to say. But a clue may be afforded by the opening where the author draws attention to stories

> of travalyle,
> Of saute, sege, and of grete batayle,
> Bothe in romans and in ryme,
> What hathe ben done before thys tyme.
>
> (p. 1)

His own story, he implies, is comparable to legends of the past:

> A more solempne sege was nevyr sette
> Syn Jerusalem and Troy was gotte.
>
> (*Ibid.*)

From the analogies he cites it is clear that, consciously or unconsciously, Page regarded his poem as a romance, a modern story of heroism and chivalry. And perhaps because of this he allows himself no sentiments unworthy of such a poem. There is very

little anti-French or anti-Burgundian feeling. The only criticism of
Charles VI and John of Burgundy is implied by the fact that they
failed to relieve the city. Page respects the inhabitants of Rouen and
allows them the virtues of bravery and resilience. He takes them to
task only for the 'cursyde deede' of destroying the suburbs outside
the city wall—churches, houses, streets—'And made hyt as bare as
my honde', and also for ejecting the 'bouches inutiles' from the
city:

> The cytte wolde not lete them yn,
> There of I wote they dyd grete syn.
> For many one there dyde for colde
> That warmythe of howese savyd wolde.
>
> (p. 20)

Of course, he considers the French wrong to have opposed Henry
'agayne ryght' and he does not doubt their cruelty when things
were going well for them:

> when hyt lay in there lotte
> They were fulle cruelle, God hyt wote,
> And marcy wolde they non have.
>
> (p. 36)

But his natural harshness towards the enemy softens to pity at the
sight of the sufferings of the 'bouches inutiles' outside the city and
of the starving defenders within:

> Moche of the folke that were thereyn,
> They were but bonys and bare skyn,
> With holowe yeen and vysage sharpe,
> Unnethe they myght brethe or carpe;
> With wan color as the lede,
> Unlyke to lyvys men but unto dede.
>
> (p. 43)

Nonetheless, although Page treats the enemy generously, he is
also proud to be an Englishman fighting with his King in what he
considers a significant engagement. He warms to the splendour and
the pageantry, the purposeful bustle of activity about the English

camp. He delights in listing the names of the English leaders and commending them. All behave with dignity, propriety and bravery. And, predictably, he is most concerned with the personage of the King. In the poet's opinion, Henry V is 'Of alle worschyppe . . . a welle' but the most concerted passage of praise is a speech he puts into the mouths of the French negotiators after their first encounter with him:

> They sayde, 'He ys, at oure avyse,
> Of alle erthely prynces the pryce,
> Takyng rewarde of hys chere,
> And to hys countenaunce so clere;
> To hys person in propyrte;
> To hys fetowrys and hys beute,
> And to hys depe dyscrecyon,
> That he hathe in possessyon,
> And to hys passyng pryncehode
> And to hys mykylle manhode.
> And he ys marcyfulle in myght
> And askysse no thynge but hys ryght.
> Thes vertuys ys a grete thynge
> To be withyn an erdely kynge.
> Howe shulde he but wyn honowre?
> Howe shulde he be but a conquerowre?
> Welle we wote withowtyn wene,
> God hym lovys, and that ys sene.'

(p. 33)

Though praise of Henry V among contemporary Frenchmen was not unknown, such hyperbole obviously belongs to John Page. Elsewhere he finds occasion for more specific praise. Henry appears in the negotiations for this city as so sternly insistent on his rights and so firm in his resolves that the French 'were adradde'. Yet in victory he is merciful: on Christmas day he offered food and drink to the starving poor of the city and those in the ditches outside, so that, according to Page, they gave thanks for the 'tendyr hertys' of the Englishmen and affirmed that Henry himself had had upon them '. . . more compassyon/Thenn hathe oure owne nacyon'

(p. 22). He appears as the pattern of knighthood in all that he does. John Page draws attention to the propriety of his action in allowing the citizens of Rouen to inform Charles VI and John of Burgundy of their plight by stressing it was 'a poynt of chevalrye'. Henry's piety is also stressed. The Rouen negotiators have to wait until he comes from Mass before they can speak with him and his first action on entering Rouen is to hear Mass. It is only afterwards that he takes possession of the city:

> Masse he hyrde and offyrde thoo
> Sethen unto the castelle he dydyn goo.
>
> (p. 45)

Probably no other English King has ever received this kind of adulation or has ever inspired such national pride.

With the fall of Rouen the way to Paris was open. While he contemplated the final campaign, Henry V reduced the fortresses in the Caux region, invaded Vexin and in July 1419 took Pontoise despite Burgundian resistance. The only hope for the French was a concerted campaign by the combined Burgundian and Dauphinist forces, but, despite the agreement of St Maur, the deep rivalries between the factions persisted. They came to a head on 10 September 1419 when, after an acrimonious meeting on the bridge at Montereau, an armed scuffle broke out between the two parties. The Dauphin escaped unhurt, but John the Fearless was killed. The English had no reason to be sorry about this. He had been, at best, an unreliable ally, and his murder ensured a continuance of the split between the Dauphinists and the Burgundians on which English success in France depended. They derived what propagandist advantages they could from the incident, for the murder served to discredit the Dauphin in the eyes of practically the whole of northern France, where Burgundian influence was strong. *The Remembrance of Fifty Two Follies* from MS Digby 102 is a critical and moralizing review of the career of John the Fearless. According to this author, John had been too ready to listen to flatterers, too improvident and over-ambitious, and had brought the once rich land of Flanders into war and sorrow:

Flaundres was þe richest land, and meriest to mynne;
Now is it wrappid in wo, and moche welþe raft.

(XVI, 57–8)

He remembers with disapproval the murder of Louis of Orléans
twelve years back and John the Fearless' brazen defence of this
action:

Of mannys deþ haue no rouþe,
But hate hem þat tellen hym trouþe,
Loue hym þat cherische hym in synne.

(37–9)

He also apparently criticises him for taking up arms against
Charles VI on behalf of Henry V:

... of his neyȝebour his enemy make
For a straunge mannys dede.

(33–4)

Such an action was morally reprehensible since the French King
was John's feudal overlord to whom he owed loyalty, but it is,
nonetheless, an odd sentiment to come from a poet usually so
prejudiced in favour of England. Nevertheless, he is most critical
of the Duke for his defection from the English cause and his
alliance with the Dauphin:

A gret fool, y holde þat man
þat of his enemys haþ no drede.
þurgh such foly, Flaundres be-gan,
of after perile þey tok non hede.
Hit is worthy, he ete bred of bran,
þat wiþ floure his foo wil fede.

(45–50)

A man so consistently treacherous and foolish was clearly not, in
this author's opinion, deserving of much sympathy.

John of Burgundy's son, Philip the Good, had no alternative but
to re-negotiate an Anglo-Burgundian alliance and, once secure in
this, Henry V was easily able to impose his own terms on the aged

Charles VI. The result of this, the Treaty of Troyes of 1420, represented the peak of English fortunes in France in the fifteenth century. The terms of this treaty provided for a partnership between France and England. Upon the death of Charles VI there was to be a single dynasty—the Lancastrians—and the French crown would belong to Henry V and his heirs forever. This agreement was to be sealed by the marriage of Katherine, daughter of Charles VI, with Henry V. It cut the Dauphin out of the succession. Other clauses dealt with the administration of the two realms, Katherine's dowry, and plans for military activity against the Dauphin, who, needless to say, did not accept the treaty. More clauses were added later, but without substantially altering the main intentions, so that, on the deaths of both Henry V and Charles VI in 1422, the infant son of Henry and Katherine was the heir to both crowns. English writers were enthusiastic, but it is clear that some of their celebration of Henry VI's dual kingship was prompted by royal officials. In 1423 John, Duke of Bedford, who was appointed Regent in France, commissioned verses in French by Laurence Calot which justified Henry VI's claim to both thrones. Four years later Richard Beauchamp, Earl of Warwick, had Lydgate translate them. Doubtless the fact that Henry VI was still a child worried the Council, and the opening of Lydgate's verses attempts to allay any disquiet about the problem:

> Trouble hertis to sette in quyete,
> And make folkys their language for to lette,
> Which disputen in their opynyons
> Touching the ligne of two regions,
> The right, I mene, of Inglond and of Fraunce.
> (*Minor Poems*, II, 28, 1–5)

But the Prologue apart, Lydgate follows Calot's arguments fairly closely. Before Henry VI's claim is justified, the Dauphin's claim is declared invalid because he has caused strife and bloody war through his murder of John the Fearless:

> the grete confusioun
> Of both reames, by devisioun

> Thurgh feyned falshed causid cursidly
> By the Dolphyn, that so horribly
> Made sleen withoute drede or shame,
> At Monstreux, a toun of grete fame,
> Iohn due of Burgoyne . . .
>
> (81–7)

W. F. Schirmer sees in this treatment of the Dauphin Bedford's pro-Burgundian policy and it may be that the Regent did suggest this attitude,[16] but Calot himself was a Burgundian sympathiser and the sentiments would have come naturally enough from him. Henry VI's claim is justified in terms of his genealogy. In place of the Dauphin, Lydgate continues, God has sent us Henry VI, whose claim is sanctioned by a solemn treaty 'sworn and assured by full besy peyn' at Troyes, and by the fact that he unites the English and the French royal lines:

> For to possede by enheritaunce
> crownes two of Englond & of Fraunce
> By true title . . .
>
> (228–30)

And Lydgate stresses the validity of his title not only because he is the son of Henry V and grandson of Charles VI, but also because he is descended on both sides of his family from the French King St Louis IX '. . . of the stok and blode of Seint Lowys'. The poem is skilfully angled, extremely explicit, and insistent.

Nowhere is there a more detailed justification in English verse, though the fact that Henry VI was King of both countries is mentioned frequently: as by Lydgate himself in his *Roundel on the Coronation of Henry VI* (1429):

> Reioice, ye reames of Englond & of Fraunce,
> A braunche þat sprang oute of the floure-de-lys,
> Blode of Seint Edward and Seint Lowys,
> God hath this day sent in gouernaunce,
>
> (*Minor Poems*, II, 29, 1–4)

or in the elaborate *Ballade to King Henry VI on his Coronation* (1429) where the same image reappears:

Royal braunche descendid frome twoo lynes
Of Saynt Edward and of Saynt Lowys,
(*Minor Poems*, II, 31, 9–10)

or again in the very popular *Kings of England sithen William Conqueror:*

The sext Herry, brouht foorth in al vertu,
Bi iust title, born bi enheritaunce.
Afforn provided, bi grace of Crist Ihesu,
To wer too crownys in Yngland & in Fraunce.
(*Minor Poems*, II, 51, 204–7)

One would expect dynastic propaganda from Lydgate, who by this time had assumed a sort of unofficial laureateship. But other authors, such as John Audelay, were also moved to celebrate Henry VI's accession to the dual monarchy:

Þus was his fader a conqueroure
& wan his moder with gret onoure;
Now may þe kyng bere þe floure
of kyngis & kyngdams in vche cuntre.
(*HP*, 41, 41–4)

If an unworldly Shropshire priest, far from the capital and the elaborate celebrations associated with Henry VI's coronation, could be provoked to write in this way nationalistic feeling in England must have been running high. It looked as though the long war had finally come to an end, and on terms very favourable to the English.

Verses were sometimes used to accompany visual propaganda for the dual monarchy. It is obvious from Laurence Calot's poem that a picture is meant to accompany it:

Et qu'il soit vray, veez, je vous supplie
Ceste figure de genealogie,

and other contemporary sources confirm that Calot was commissioned to produce a picture in the form of a genealogy in 1423. This picture was apparently hung alongside the poem in Notre Dame in Paris, and B. J. H. Rowe has shown that it is likely that the genealogy preserved in BM MS Royal 15 E vi f.3 is a copy of Calot's original.[17] This ingeniously shows, in pictorial terms, Henry VI's twofold claim to the crown of France. The genealogist is also careful to demonstrate that the Lancastrian claim to the English throne was a just one, and thus he shows both Edward the Black Prince and John of Gaunt as sons of Edward III and equal descendants of St Louis IX. This makes it easy for him to show Richard II and Henry IV as similarly equal in their degree of descent. The genealogist does not trouble himself with the claims of the Dauphin, as both Calot and Lydgate had done, but omits him entirely. A picture shows Henry VI as a child to whom two angels, one from the French line and one from the English, present crowns to symbolize his claim to both thrones. It is clear that Lydgate's version of Calot was also accompanied by a similar pictorial genealogy:

> Verily, liche as ye may se
> The pee-degree doth hit specifie,
> The figure, lo, of the genelagye
> (123–5)

and a few lines later 'This ffigure makith clere demonstracioun . . .' (129). But other information is lacking. A sketch copy of just such a genealogy does survive in CUL MS Ll. v. 20 f.34, but this is to be dated 1444.

Lydgate wrote other 'pictorial' poems on the same subject. Banquets and celebrations were eagerly seized upon as opportunities for emphasizing Henry VI's claims to the thrones of England and France. At his English coronation banquet in 1429, the three courses were each accompanied by a 'soteltie', or miniature decorative tableau, the significance of which Lydgate explained in verse. The 'soteltie' to the first course showed St Edward and St Louis escorting Henry VI, all 'armed in cote amours' and the verses read:

> Loo here twoo kynges righte perfit and right good,
> Holy Seint Edwarde and Seint Lowes:
> And see the braunch borne of here blessid blode;

Live, among Cristen moost souereigne of price,
Enheretour of the floure de lice!
(*Minor Poems*, II, 30, 1–5)

The second 'soteltie' showed Henry VI being escorted by his father
and the Emperor Sigismund and enjoined him to follow their
example in suppressing heretics, and the third showed him accompanied by St George and St Denis, who are presenting him to the
Virgin and Child. The verses again emphasize his just title to the
crowns of England and France:

O blessid Lady, Cristes moder dere,
And thou seint George, þat callid art his knight;
Holy Seint Denyse, O martir moost entier,
The sixt Henry here present in your sight,
Shewith of grace on hym your hevenly light,
His tendre yougth with vertue doth avaunce,
Bore by discent and by title of right
Iustly to reigne in England and in Fraunce.
(17–24)

As J. W. McKenna points out, this last 'soteltie' is very similar to
the scene depicted in BM MS Cotton Domitian A xvii f.50, a
psalter of Henry VI, which shows him being presented by St Louis
IX to the Virgin and Child. No opportunity was lost to emphasize
the right of Henry's claim. Even the coinage issued in France in
1422 stressed the dual monarchy.[18]

In fact, the political situation in France in the 1420s was by no
means as favourable to the English as their celebratory verses
suggested. The Dauphin did not accept the Treaty of Troyes and
his disinheritance, nor, except for Gascony, did central and
southern France. The Dauphin's supporters had had to give up
Paris as their capital, and set up their court and administration at
Bourges. The English and Burgundians controlled the greater part
of northern France. According to the treaty, Henry VI was King of
England and the whole of France, but the conquest necessary to give
the title a reality had still to be made. Henry V, in the short time
between the Treaty of Troyes and his death, had shown no great

hurry to advance into the Dauphin's territory, preferring to consolidate his positions in the north. On his deathbed Henry V had instructed John, Duke of Bedford, who was to be Regent in France, in the basic points of his policy: to be friendly towards Burgundy; to attempt to hold Paris but if this was impossible to fall back upon Normandy; and to effect an energetic attack on the Dauphin. But Bedford, for a variety of reasons, was unable to carry the attack into the Dauphin's territories. In the first place, the territory under English rule was far from completely pacified, for the peasants and certain country landowners remained hostile. This meant that some English soldiers were forced to remain in the north. Secondly, Bedford was short of money, for the taxes of the French territories did not yield a great deal, and he found it impossible to pay for reinforcements from England.

Fortunately for Bedford the Dauphin was not in a position to exploit the English and Burgundian weaknesses. The kingdom of Bourges was certainly richer in resources than those parts of France under English and Burgundian control, but though he levied high taxes he too was perpetually short of money. The administration of his territory seems frequently to have been corrupt and inefficient. The Dauphin's advisers were often more concerned with their own interests than with his. He himself was not an inspiring leader either, being by nature somewhat diffident, apathetic and indolent. Nevertheless he persisted in proclaiming the justness of his cause, had himself proclaimed Charles VII, and constantly sought to achieve a reconciliation with the Burgundians, which he saw as his only means of getting the English out of France. It may be, as Perroy suggests, that 'he had no faith in victory by force of arms' and, certainly, between the Treaty of Troyes and the siege of Orléans of 1428 the military engagements were sporadic and inconclusive.[19] Here and there cities were attacked and small expeditions were organized, but, though the English chroniclers diligently note these engagements, contemporary poets are, for the most part, silent. There were no victories spectacular enough, it seems, to catch the imagination. An odd exception, however, was the Battle of Verneuil of 1424. The Dauphin's supporters had collected a large army of about fifteen thousand men, including a large contingent of Scots and some Italian mercenaries, with the intention of capturing English-held towns on the borders of Normandy. On the road between Verneuil and Damville, they were opposed by an English army under Bedford and the Earl of Salisbury numbering about eight thousand men. The battle was on the Agincourt pattern, and the English archers again reduced the effectiveness of the French cavalry. The French army, and particularly the Scottish contingent of it, suffered heavily.

An hitherto unpublished poem from BM MS Lansdowne 762 seems to refer to this battle,[20] though not directly, for it is set out in the terms of a prophecy:

> When a m cccc togyther be knett
> and xxiiij with them be mett
> as merlyon sayith in his story of bryttayne
> of kynge henry of englond certayne
> And thempoure & the kynge of ffraunce & flaunders also
> and other lordis many moo
> by trew prophecy that sholde befall
> of meruelous amonge them all.
>
> (1–8)

There is a slight doubt about the date of the piece, for the manuscript reads 'a m ccccc', giving a date of 1524. But since the poem mentions 'kynge henry' and 'the kynge of ffraunce' and since the rhymed 'key' prefixed to the text of the prophecy specifically refers to 'the duke of f[l]aunders p. burgeyn' (that is, Philip of Burgundy), it is clear that the 1524 date is a mistake, probably for 1424. The prophecy itself is of the well-known 'the lion, the lily and the son of man' type, and is not infrequently used in political contexts: some fourteenth-century versions, for example, seem to refer to Edward III. Here, it appears, the prophecy is updated to refer to the 1424 situation. Like all political prophecies it pretends to predict events, but may have been written later simply using the prophecy form as a literary device. Briefly, it predicts how the King of France (according to the 'key' represented by 'the lylie that faire flowre') will prosper for some years before he attempts to invade the possessions of the Duke of Burgundy:

> ffirst the lylie that faire flowre
> that many yeres shall kepe his color
> After that he shall sprede into lyons landis.
> (11–13)

He will be opposed by 'a mans son' (who, according to the 'key' 'is the kynge of inglonde'):

> After that a mans son shall mete with the mone
> bryngyng in his armes bests many oon
> Thus mannys son all nacions hym shall drede
> Above all the worlde in euery stede.
> (15–18)

(The 'key' further tells us that 'the londe of the mone' is 'englonde walis and Irelond'.) The King of England, the author continues, will receive help of various sorts and will carry all before him until he wins the French crown:

> ffirst many a castell they shall ouerthrow
> With pillers and towres that shall be full low
> Also in one parte of the lyons londe
> Shalbe a grete battaile I vnderstonde
> for many kynge shall fight their foo
> That of rede blod a grete flode shall goo
> There shall the lylie lose his crowne so gay
> With the which the mans son schalbe crowned par fay.
> (27–34)

There are, though, some inconsistencies if this does indeed refer to the events of 1424. In the first place the 'grete battaile' mentioned in this poem is supposed to have taken place in 'one parte of the lyons londe' which the 'key' tells us is 'fflaundres', whereas Verneuil is on the border of Normandy. Again, the poem tells us that the English King was supported by 'an egill oute from the east', which, according to the 'key', signifies 'the nobyll emperour'. Sigismund, who was still Emperor at this date, had in England the reputation of being pro-English but had nothing to do with the battle of Verneuil. Finally, the last fourteen lines, as often in this type of prophecy, predict a crusade by the English King, of which, in 1424, there was not the remotest possibility. What appears to have happened is that the author of this poem has not sufficiently modified the version of the prophecy that he knew so that it fitted the 1424 situation at all points. The result, as often in verse prophecies, is confused and unsatisfactory. Nonetheless, like this author, other Englishmen thought Verneuil to be significant: Lydgate, for example, three years later in a eulogistic passage on the Duke of Bedford, recalls among his triumphs '. . . þe grete high victory/which that he had in Venoill in Perche' (*Minor Poems*, II, 28, 42–3).

Verneuil was the last opportunity for the nationalistic poet to rejoice for many years. The defeat virtually destroyed the Dauphin's army and a push into the territory south of the Loire at this point might have brought the English considerable gains. But for a variety of reasons the attack was delayed. Bedford wanted to put down all resistance north of the Loire, to conquer Anjou and Maine and to capture Mont St Michel. There was also danger in Brittany, where Duke John V had made an alliance with the Dauphin. In order to counter these threats the English army had to be divided among various commanders. Bedford himself was needed back in England from 1425 to 1427, and Philip of Burgundy had withdrawn his troops to the Low Countries. So it was not until 1428 that a concerted attack could be organized. The target was Orléans. At first things went well for the English, except for the fact that the Earl of Salisbury was killed by a chance crossbow shot. The Dauphinist strongholds around Orléans—Janville, Meung, Beaugency and Jargeau—were efficiently taken. But by this time a relieving Dauphinist force, inspired by Joan of Arc and led by the Duke of Alençon, had been organized. The swiftness and confidence of the French counter-attack surprised the English. They never had time to make much impression on Orléans and, in the summer of 1429, the formerly captured Dauphinist strongholds all fell back into French hands. The English retreated to Patay but were again defeated and Sir John Talbot was captured. Incited to do so by

Joan, the French pushed on to Rheims, where on 18 July the Dauphin was crowned Charles VII. It was not immediately apparent, however, that 1429 was to be a turning point. Though the Dauphin's army had protected its own towns and had inflicted defeats on the English it was not powerful enough to do significant damage in the north. The attack on Paris in September 1429 failed and the army was eventually taken back south of the Loire and disbanded. Nor, outside the Loire district, does Joan of Arc appear to have impressed her contemporaries. No contemporary English political verses mention her or the events in which she was concerned, and she only rates a brief mention in contemporary chronicles where she is predictably treated as a 'witch'. The following account of her capture on 24 May 1430 at Compiègne is typical:

> And at that same Journey was take the wicche of Fraunce that was callid the 'Pusshell'; and she was take alle armyd as a man of armys; and by her crafte of sorserie alle the Frensshe men and her compeny trystid for to have ovyrcome alle the Engelisshe pepull. But God was lord and maistir of that victorie and scomfiture, and so she was take, and brought and kept in hold bi the Kynge and his counseill all tymes at his comaundement and will.[21]

Her significance, however, was not unappreciated by the Burgundians or the English leaders in France. Philip of Burgundy said at her capture that he was 'more delighted than if the king had fallen into his hands'. After she had been sold to the English for 10,000 gold crowns, she was put on trial as a witch and a sorceress and burned in 1431.

As has been suggested by several historians, 'proving' that Joan of Arc had used 'magic' and 'sorcery' was one way of explaining away the English defeats.[22] But the great upsurge of French morale resulting from the victories of 1429 and from Charles VII's unhampered march to Rheims and his coronation there also had to be countered. In order to flaunt Henry VI as the rightful King, according to the Treaty of Troyes, Bedford had him brought to Paris in April 1430 to be crowned. Two ornate verse prayers, dating from this year, provide evidence of the anxiety which some Englishmen felt at the prospect of their eight-year-old King's journey to a hostile country. The first, *Speed Our King on his Journey*, from Lambeth MS 344, is basically a prayer for Henry VI's safety. In each stanza saints are asked to intercede with God to 'kepe oure kynge from all myscheve' (*RL XV*, 130, 68) or to ensure more particularly that 'In enemyes fortune ... he never falle' (31), and the Latin refrain 'Salvum fac regem domine' reiterates the same point. The poem is not primarily concerned with political questions, but the author alludes to the motive of the journey when he asks Saint Anne to

> speed oure kyng in his yournay,
> That he may well speed yn hys vaye
> And kepe ys ryght as yt shold be.
> (20–2)

The second poem, *Mary Take in Your Hand this Dread Voyage*, from Arundel MS 249, is more unusual in that it is supposedly spoken by the young King himself before he embarked for France. Again it is basically a prayer for a safe voyage, but in the stanza to St George appears an allusion to the recent English reverses in France and hope for better military success in future:

> þow fortune hath cast vs late be-hynde,
> Yet fayle vs nat whan þat we crye thi name,
> ffor with thyn helpe we hope recure gode fame.
> (*RL XV*, 131, 50–2)

As it transpired, the King's journey was safe enough but his French coronation did not win the enthusiasm of the French, as Bedford had hoped.

He remained in France until the beginning of 1432 when he returned to a triumphant welcome in London on 21 February, celebrated by Lydgate in his best public manner. Henry VI's return to England has, he says, dispelled both his people's unhappiness and the winter weather:

> The stormy reyne off alle theyre hevynesse
> Were passed away and alle her olde grevaunce,

> For the vjte Herry, roote of here gladnesse,
> Theyre hertis ioye, theyre worldis suffisaunce
> By trewe dissent crovynd kyng of Fraunce,
> The hevene reioysyng the day off his repayre
> Made his komyng the wedir to be so ffayre.
>
> (*Minor Poems*, II, 32, 8–14)

For the most part, the poem is an expression of pious hopes for the boy King's future and a description of the pageantry of his welcome. The question of the dual monarchy is touched upon in the Mayor of London's welcoming speech which Lydgate quotes:

> Sovereyn Lorde and noble Kyng, ye be welcome out off youre Reeme of Fraunce into this your blessed Reeme off Englond . . .

As for his English coronation of 1429, the dual monarchy was emphasized in the tableaux, one near St Paul's being described by Lydgate:

> Twoo green treen ther grewe vp-ariht,
> Fro Seint Edward and ffro Seint Lowys,
> The roote y-take palpable to the siht,
> Conveyed by lynes be kyngis off grete prys;
> Some bare leopardes, and some bare fflouredelys,
> In nouther armes ffounde was there no lak,
> Which the sixte Henry may now bere on his bak.
>
> (398–404)

To a considerable extent Henry VI's London welcome was an exercise in public relations. No pains were spared to persuade the English of the reality of the dual monarchy. Meanwhile, in France, despite Bedford's efforts, it was becoming increasingly clear that the implementation of the Treaty of Troyes was impossible.

A new threat to the English position was emerging. On his deathbed, it will be recalled, Henry V had impressed upon Bedford that at all costs he was to seek to maintain the Anglo-Burgundian alliance and Bedford had done all in his power to carry out this policy. But there were predictable strains in the alliance. One of the more serious occurred in 1424–5 when Bedford's impetuous younger brother Humphrey of Gloucester, in seeking to reclaim territories in the Low Countries belonging to his wife Jacqueline of Hainault, was actually involved in military activities against Philip of Burgundy. On this occasion Bedford bought off Philip's resentment with the counties of Mâcon and Auxterre. But from 1423 onwards there were negotiations between Philip and Charles VII. They came to nothing for many years, for the divisions were deep: Philip was not going to put his trust too readily in the man who had killed his father, and moreover, the anti-Burgundian faction among Charles VII's courtiers was initially quite powerful. Still, the contacts remained, and it is clear that from 1429 onwards Philip was seriously considering a peace with the French. Before the crucial conference at Arras in 1435, the Burgundians and the French had worked out, in principle if not in detail, an acceptable final settlement. It is difficult to imagine that a negotiated peace between the English and the French at Arras was ever a remote possibility. The basis of the English position was that the dual monarchy established by the Treaty of Troyes should stand: if Charles of Valois, as they termed him, were allowed to keep the lands over which he had control (and this was their best offer) he would have to pay homage to Henry VI for them. On their part, the French insisted that Henry VI should renounce the throne of France and give up all occupied territories; anything granted in return for this should be held in homage to Charles VII. There was clearly no possibility of reconciliation, and on 6 September 1435 the English delegation left the conference. Philip felt able to hold the English responsible for the breakdown of negotiations and free to conclude a separate peace with Charles VII. In return for his recognition of Charles as the rightful King of France, he received territorial concessions in the north, an apology for the murder of his father John the Fearless, and an exemption for life from paying homage to Charles. Papal legates were conveniently on hand to absolve him from oaths sworn at the Treaty of Troyes, and his sixteen years' alliance with England thus ended.

The English were naturally indignant and various reprisals were organized against Flemish merchants. But their rage knew no bounds when in the following year, 1436, Philip, with a large Flemish army, attacked and besieged Calais. A contemporary

author in verses entitled *Scorn of the Duke of Burgundy* (1436)
adequately represents English feelings in his opening lines:

> O thou Phelippe, fonder of new falshede,
> Distourber of pees, Capiteine of cowardise,
> Sower of discorde, Repref of al kynghthode,
> Whiche of al burgoigne (that is so grete of pryse)
> Thou clepist thiself due . . .
>
> (*HP*, 30, 1–5)

The English considered his behaviour treacherous. On the assassination of his father in 1419, he had been glad enough to come to terms with Henry V (22) and on his own initiative had ratified the Treaty of Troyes:

> To kyng henry the fyft by thyn ovne assent,
> Withoute his desire, thou madest a solempne vow,
> Vsyng goddes body the holy sacrament,
> To become trev ligeman with gode entent
> To hym and to his heires without variance.
>
> (26–30)

He had also, the poet reminds him, paid homage to Henry VI by proxy in Paris 'By suffisant warrant'. The English, for their part, had assisted him loyally against the Dauphinists:

> Remembre the, Phelippe, how peple of England
> Haue been to the euer gentil and trew,
> ffor whan thou were beseged with many a thousand
> Of Armynakes, thay did the rescewe.
>
> (41–4)

If this refers to a specific event it is probably the siege of Crevant of 1423. The poet then turns to the ways in which Philip had failed to fulfil his obligations to the English. He had avoided Henry VI when he was in France: 'Thou absent thiself with feyned contenance, (54). At Arras he had broken 'Bothe of thyn avow and othes with all'. And in addition he

did provow charles, rightwis king of france,
fforsaking thy ligelord and frend moste special.

(62–3)

The poet even casts doubts on the validity of Philip's absolution from his oaths:

Thou shewedest thyself assoilled by a cardinal
The which was withoute power papall.

(60–1)

The treachery of the attack on Calais is then discussed and Philip's flight before the English relieving forces. The final stanza is as censorious as the first:

Conteyne thiself, Phelipp, rightwisly shamed,
Vnderstonde thiself nothing availlable;
See thurgh cowardise thy knyghthod defamed,
To werre ayenst god, thenk thou art not able.

(105–8)

Nevertheless, the poet ends with a plea to Philip to reconsider his position and to re-negotiate the Anglo-Burgundian alliance.

Fforsake thy frowardnes and become stable,
Be trew of promesse and sadde of gouernaunce,
Obey thy ligelord, and be not variable
Lest thou be destroied and ende with myschance.

(109–12)

This poet recognized that England needed the support of Burgundy, but few contemporary authors were so far sighted. The author of the *Ballade in Despyte of the Flemynges* (1436), sometimes said to be Lydgate, restricts himself to a brief review of Anglo-Burgundian relations and a denunciation of Philip's 'fraudulent falsnesse', 'fals decepcioun' and 'fals collusioun'. He gives an additional reason why Philip should be grateful to the English by reminding him of Henry V's reburial of his father, John the Fearless:

How Herry the Fyfthe, of knyghtly gentylnesse,
Had of his dethe manly compassioun
Leete digge hym vp . . .

(*Minor Poems*, II, 25, 11–13)

He ends with the expected sneer at Philip's defeat at Calais.

The failure of the siege of Calais provoked a considerable amount of verse. Some has certainly been lost, but what does survive covers the incident and English attitudes to it very fully. Much is made of the treachery of the attack and of the cruelty of the Flemish to the inhabitants of neighbouring fortresses:

> And eke the castel of Oye whan thou haddest brent,
> The people thou henge by cruel Iugement;
> And thus thou began werre with treson and vengeance.
>
> (*HP*, 30, 76–8)

But for the most part the authors concentrate on English military successes and Flemish failures. The siege was begun on 2 July 1436, but it was not well organized and there were dissensions among the besiegers even from the beginning. The Flemish were highly nervous of the English relieving force which had gathered at Sandwich under Humphrey, Duke of Gloucester, but even before he arrived on 2 August the siege had been abandoned. The defenders of Calais were by no means passive and made frequent and successful raids into West Flanders. As he was returning from one such raid, the Earl of Morton was attacked by the townspeople of Gravelines, whose 'exploits' are the object of the sardonic humour of the author of *Mockery of the Flemings* (1436). He relates how these 'bold' men attacked the English with the ferocity of sheep ('fersli as lyons of Cotteswold'), in their old-fashioned and make-shift armour of 'straunge wise', and with such effectiveness that by the end of the fight three hundred Flemings had been killed, but the English had not lost a single man:

> Ye laid vpon þ'englisshmen so myghtily with your handes,
> Til of you iij hundrid lay strecchid on the sandes.
> Ye fled þen in-to Grauenyng and wold no lenger bide,
> And gaue þe erle leue to passe ouer that same tyde
> In saafte with his prisoners, & lost neuer a man.
> This was þe first wurship of Caleys that ye wan.
>
> (*HP*, 29, 15–20)

In the same vein of mockery attention is drawn to the great number of Flemish involved at the siege and the fact that their threats failed to frighten the inhabitants of the city:

> And yette for al youre gret host, erly nothir late,
> Caleis was so ferd of you þey shitte neuer a gate.
>
> (25–6)

Nothing went right for the besiegers. Their attempt to blockade the harbour of Calais, by sinking six ships filled with stones, failed because:

> þe calisers hem brake the next day,
> When it was lawe watir, and bare hem clene away—
> Euery stikke & stone, & lafte not ther one log.
>
> (29–31)

The author then ridicules the shortcomings of the separate contingents of Flemings. He reminds the men of Bruges how easily their attacks were beaten off and how they were overcome and captured by the Calais soldiers:

> how sone the Calisers made you to turn agayn,
> And ouerthrew you sodeynly, or euer that ye wist,
> And brought you in-to Caleis tyed fastly by the fist.
>
> (38–40)

But this is nothing to the scorn heaped upon the men of Ghent who mistook the landing of a small party of English one night for that of the full English relief force under Gloucester and hurriedly quit the siege:

> & ye that same night
> Ffled ouer Grauenyng watir, but go þat go myght;
> And youre lord with you, for dreed and for fere
> Of the duyk of Gloucester—& yette was he not þer!
>
> (43–6)

It was out of a similar groundless fear, he reminds the Picard contingent, that they fled the siege of Guisnes when the citizens of the town rang the alarum bells. In conclusion he advises the Flemish to 'Sette ye stille & bith in pees' because they are good only at fighting with words. The crude sarcasm and the heavy scorn of the defeated enemy recall some of the less attractive aspects of Laurence Minot's poems of a century earlier.

The fullest and most accurate verse account of this incident is *The Siege of Calais* (1436). The author treats events in rough chronological order, beginning with how the Duke of Burgundy 'made grete assemble in landes wide' taking men from Flanders, Brabant, Burgundy, Picardy, Hainault and Holland. Numbering more than a hundred and fifty thousand, he says, they pitched camp before the city:

> Stately tentes anon they pight
> Large, longe and of gret hight,
> It was a riall rowte.
> (*HP*, 28, 34–6)

They were well supplied, according to the poet, with guns and military equipment. For much of the poem the author dwells on the failure of the siege: how the enemy attacked on the first day 'But countred they were anon' (99); how the artillery bombardment damaged houses but 'hurt neither man, woman, ne childe' (104); how because of the accuracy of the Calais artillery the Duke of Burgundy had to move his tents; how the attempt to blockade the harbour 'with bulged shippes' failed; how the English counterattacks were very effective and how finally the besiegers abandoned the attack one night:

> The next nyght, or it was day,
> Erly the duc fled away;
> With hym they of Gaunt;
> And after Bruges and Ipre bothe,
> To folow hym were they not lothe.
> Thus kept thay thaire avaunt.
> (151–6)

But apart from the irony of the last line this poet does not spend much of his time on the shortcomings of the Flemish. Instead he celebrates the deeds of the English. Naturally enough he singles out the leaders for special mention. The Earl of Morton was confident of their success from the beginning:

> I trust to god to see that day,
> That for al thaire proude aray
> fful low that they shul lowte;
>
> (52–4)

Sir John Ratcliff 'kept full gode governaunce'; the Baron Dudley 'made full gode ordenance'; Lord Camoys, Sir William Ashton and Sir Geoffrey Warburton all fought well. But no rank of society is allowed to go without its special mention:

> Þe trew soudeours, bothe day and nyght,
> Lay on the walle in armes bright
> It was thaire hous and kirk.
>
> (76–8)

The mayor and burgesses were ready 'fforto defende thaire possession'; the common people had made preparations for withstanding the siege by filling the town 'with godes and vitaille'; even the women played a part in the defence:

> The women, bothe yonge and olde,
> With stones stuffed euery scaffolde,
> They spared no swete ne swynk.
>
> (91–3)

Among others whose deeds he celebrated were an Irishman mounted 'on his hoby', and also a dog:

> an hounde that hight goby,
> That longed to the waterbailly,
> fful swiftly wolde he renne.
> At euery skirmyssh to trauaille,
> Man and horse he wolde assaille,
> fful wel he cowde hem kenne.
>
> (127–32)

In style and sentiment this looks like popular verse. The facts (even that about Goby the water-bailiff's dog) can be corroborated elsewhere in contemporary verse and prose, and appear to have been part of a common tradition. But neither his stock material nor his evident pride in the English successes at the siege blinded this author to the real reason for the Flemish withdrawal:

> ffor thay had verray knowyng
> of the duc of Gloucester commyng
> Calais to rescowe.
>
> (157–9)

Nor is he unaware of the reasons for Philip of Burgundy's particular choice of Calais for his attack. Important English exports went through Calais:

> The wolles and the merchandise
> And other godes of grete emprise,
>
> (25–6)

and this author knows that the commercial jealousy of the Flemish in part provoked the siege. He recognises, too, the crucial importance of the retention of Calais by the English:

> O oonly god, in whom is all,
> Save Calais the tovn riall,
> That euer it mot wel cheve
> Vnto the crown of England.
>
> (163–6)

The scribe of the copy of these verses in MS Cotton Galba E ix has even added a four-line tag to the final stanza:

> Lytelle wote the fool,
> Who myȝth ches
> What harm yt wer
> God caleys to lese.
>
> (*PPS*, II, p. 156)

These lines, and the sentiment they embody, appear to have been popular, for they reappear only slightly changed in *The Libelle of Englyshe Polycye* (1436) lines 826–7, along with other injunctions to 'cherishe ye Caleise better than it is' (819).

The Libelle of Englyshe Polycye is among the most remarkable poems to have survived from the fifteenth century. Many of the author's attitudes are predictable: he is passionately nationalistic, suspicious of foreigners, fearful lest England be encircled by hostile enemies, and contemptuous of Philip of Burgundy and the Flemish, whose flight from Calais he recalls with a scornful satisfaction:

> For fere they turned bake and hyede faste,
> Milorde of Gloucestre made hem so agaste
> Wyth his commynge . . .
>
> (294–6)

But this author is also politically informed and sophisticated to a degree that is rare. He does not simply celebrate the English success at Calais, but attempts to persuade the King's Council to accept the coherent set of policies his poem expounds. As G. A. Holmes points out, the poem 'expresses very much the discontents, especially about Calais and naval defence, which were represented in the parliament of January 1437 . . . it stands roughly for the point of view of the Duke of Gloucester, the staplers and the cloth exporters against the opposite policy pursued by the council.'[23]

The Council had reacted to the new alliance between France and Burgundy by putting massive armed reinforcements into France, with the result that Calais was neglected and the English navy remained virtually non-existent. This author seeks to get the policy reversed. In one section, he urges

> for the love of God and of his blisse
> Cherishe ye Caleise better than it is,
>
> (818–19)

and reinforces this plea by reminding the Council how the Emperor Sigismund had rejoiced 'That Caleise was soget unto Englyssh coste', and recalling with what difficulty Calais had been won in the first place:

> Loke well how harde it was at firste to gete.
> And by my counsell lyghtly be it not lete.
>
> (838–9)

He also urges even more strongly the need for a good navy and for the English to control the Channel. Historical precedents are quoted to substantiate the argument. The pre-conquest King Edgar controlled the sea; Edward III took firm action against Breton piracy in the Channel; and the Emperor Sigismund had given Henry V good advice on keeping naval superiority in the narrow seas particularly between Calais and Dover:

> 'Kepe these too townes sure to your mageste
> As youre tweyne eyne to kepe the narowe see.'
> (20–1)

He recalls at length how Henry V had built great ships:

> The Trinite, the Grace Dieu, the Holy Goste
> And other moo, whiche as now be loste,
> (1014–15)

and points out that his intention in this was to be 'Lorde rounde aboute environ of the see' (1019). He demonstrates the usefulness of this navy by reference to the relief of Harfleur by John, Duke of Bedford, in August 1416. This involved a sea battle against a French fleet, supported by 'carikkys orible, grete and stoute' (1021) from Genoa and some ships from Spain, in which the English were successful because they had a powerful navy:

> My lorde of Bedeforde came one and had the cure;
> Destroyde they were by that discomfiture.
> (1024–5)

The point of laying so much stress on England's naval strength under Henry V was to throw into relief the lack of a navy in 1436–7. No effective force had existed, in fact, for ten years or so, and while this situation was acceptable enough when England and its allies controlled most of the western seaboard of northern France and Flanders, with the defection of Burgundy this situation had changed. England now had enemies across the Channel and still no navy as a defence. Hence the urgency of this author's warning:

> Kepe than the see abought in speciall,
> Whiche of England is the rounde wall,

> As thoughe England were lykened to a cite
> And the wall environ were the see.
> Kepe than the see, that is the wall of Englond.
>
> (1092–6)

Without a navy, he implies, England was as exposed as a town without its defensive wall.

But though the proposals this author makes for controlling the Channel are motivated to some extent by defensive considerations, the opportunity such control would give for embarrassing Flanders is not lost to him. He understands in considerable detail the working of the Flemish economy—that it depended basically on imports of food and raw materials, and exports of cloth made principally from the wool imported from England. Because Flanders had few natural resources its economy was vulnerable, for

> all that groweth in Flaundres, greyn and sede,
> May not a moneth fynde hem mete of brede.
>
> (118–19)

Above all, Flanders needed English wool, and if this was withheld, argues the author, the Flemish economy would be ruined:

> They may not lyven to mayntene there degrees
> Wythoughten oure Englysshe commodytees,
> Wolle and tynne, for the wolle of Englonde
> Susteyneth the comons Flemmynges I understonde.
>
> (88–91)

In fact, Philip of Burgundy himself had already in 1436 forbidden the entry of English merchants and merchandise into Flanders; this had had an adverse effect on the economy, but he hoped to obtain wool from other sources, principally Spain. This, says the author, would do him no good, since Spanish wool was of poor quality 'But if it be tosed and menged well/Amonges Englysse wolle'. Anyway, the Flemish would not be able to import Spanish commodities, nor venture in their own ships

> Into the Rochell to feche the fumose wyne,
> Nere into Britounse bay for salt so fyne,
>
> (112–13)

nor would the Spaniards be able to carry from Flanders

> Fyne clothe of Ipre, that named is better than oures,
> Cloothe of Curtryke, fyne cloothe of all colours,
> Moche fustyane and also lynene cloothe,
>
> (74–6)

simply because this trade had to pass 'By the costes . . . of oure Englonde/Betwyxt Dover and Caleys', and if the English controlled the sea it could easily be stopped. He reviews the commercial relations between Flanders and other countries in this light also. The Portuguese, though friendly to the English, 'schulde not be suffrede' to pass the English coasts to Flanders, nor would the Bretons with their 'Salt and wynes, crestclothe and canvasse' (153). In the same way, he says, the commodities of Scotland 'felles, hydes and of wolle the fleesse' (247) which were exported to the Flemish towns of Poperinghe and Bailleul had to 'passe by oure Englysshe costes' and could be intercepted, and so too could the trade of the Italians, who bought wool in England and shipped it to Flanders:

> they be charged wyth woll ageyne, I wene,
> And wollene clothe of owres of colours all.
> And they aventure, as ofte it dothe byfall,
> Into Flaundres wyth suche thynge as they bye;
> That is here cheffe staple sykerlye.
> And if they wold be oure full ennemyse,
> They shulde not passe oure stremez with marchaundyse.
>
> (337–43)

At the time this poem was written the English were particularly resentful of the activities of Italian merchants, whose business had increased greatly as a result of Philip of Burgundy's ban on the English, and this author proposes to restrict what he considers to be the over-favourable conditions of trading they enjoy. About the direct trade between the Germans and the Flemish he accepts that little can be done. But he is aware that the German merchants go to Bourgneuf for salt and contemplates the disruption of this trade if they fail to co-operate in a boycott of trade with Flanders:

> Thus, if they wolde not oure frendys bee,
> Wee myght lyghtlye stope hem in the see.
>
> (326–7)

It is even possible, he thinks, to disrupt the land-based trade in Brabant, Zeeland and Hainault if English merchants stay away from the markets and fairs, for

> yff the Englysshe be not in the martis,
> They bene febell and as noughte bene here partes;
> For they bye more and more fro purse put oute
> For marchaundy than all the othere route.
>
> (534–7)

The effect of this, he adds, would be as great as if 'wee sent into the londe of Fraunce/Tenne thousande peple, men of gode puissaunce'. This author is supremely confident about his proposals. If England controls the trade routes, he reasons, it follows that her enemies must either come to terms, or face economic ruin:

> they muste dresse hem to pease in haste,
> Or ellis there thrifte to standen and to waste.
>
> (1076–7)

He predicts that Flanders will soon feel the need for 'unite/And pease wyth us' and that her ambassadors 'wolde bene here sone to trete for ther socours' (1087).

Judging from the eighteen different manuscript copies of this poem which have survived it was fairly popular. Furthermore the 1436–7 version appears to have been revised and reissued a few years later. But despite this the Council ignored its proposals. Such policies would certainly have harmed Flanders. But to blockade the Channel properly would have been difficult and enormously costly; it would have antagonized England's allies; and also have further disrupted England's own trade.

These poems on the siege of Calais and its aftermath are almost the last examples of nationalist verse in the period in question. After the Treaty of Arras the English were in an extremely unfavourable position in France and the nationalistic poet had very little to celebrate. The immediate result of the siege, though, was a punitive expedition by Humphrey of Gloucester into Flanders. He met with little resistance and returned triumphant and laden with plunder. This was one more reason for a sneer at Philip of Burgundy and his policies:

> Beholde duc humfray with knyghtly desire
> To meve thy courage the felde forto take;
> He soght the in flaundres with swerd and with fyre,
> Nyne daies brennyng, no pees did he make.
> Where art thou, Phelippe, whan wiltow thy swerd shake?
> Where is thy strong power and grete alliance?
> Thy land is distroied, and thou dar not awake.
> Thus endith thy purpos with sorow and myschance.

> > (*HP*, 30, 97–104)

But for the most part the tide of war was moving against the English. In 1435 John, Duke of Bedford, their most able commander, died. In the next year the English had to evacuate Paris. The weakness of the French meant that they could not press their advantage, for Charles VII's court was still not free of plots and internal dissentions. Nevertheless, the French campaign of 1442 was fairly successful and the English counter-offensive under Edmund Beaufort, Duke of Somerset, failed dismally, so the English were ready enough to agree to negotiations. In May 1444 at Tours it was found that a general peace was impossible but a truce was arranged, and, more hopefully, Henry VI was betrothed to the French Princess Margaret, daughter of René of Anjou. In 1445 Lydgate was moved to express the hope that

> Twixt the Reawmes two Englande and ffraunce
> Pees shal approche

as a result of the marriage.[24] But as a political solution its success was very limited. The truce was more or less observed for five years before hostilities again broke out. In 1449 the French advanced into Normandy and the English garrisons quickly fell, including, on 9 October 1449, the capital Rouen. A relief expedition under Sir Thomas Kyriel landed at Cherbourg on 15 March 1450 and had a few successes, but a month later at Formigny it was crushingly defeated.

At about this time must have been written the verses from MS Cotton Rolls ii 23 to which Wright gives the title *On the Popular Discontent at the Disasters in France*. By means of reference to their badges or cognizances, explained in the manuscript by an interlinear gloss, the author at the outset laments the passing of those English war leaders who had fought effectively in France:

> The Rote is ded, the Swanne is goone,
> The firy Cressett hath lost his lyght;
> Therfore Inglond may make gret mone,
> Were not the helpe of Godde almyght.

> The castelle is wonne where care begowne
> The Portecoleys is leyde adowne;
> Iclosed we have oure welevette hatte
> That keveryd us from mony stormys browne.

> The White Lioun is leyde to slepe,
> Thorouʒ the envy of the Ape clogge;
> And he is bownden that oure dore shuld kepe,
> That is Talbott oure goode dogge.

> The Fisshere hathe lost his hangulhooke;
> Gete theym agayne when it wolle be.
> Oure Mylle-Saylle wille not abowte
> Hit hath no longe goone emptye.
>
> (*PPS*, II, pp. 221–2)

The poem is certainly to be dated after November 1449 since it refers to the loss of Rouen in line 5. It is difficult to explain the reference to Edmund, Earl of Somerset ('Portecoleys'), here. By 'leyde adowne' the poet perhaps alludes to his recall from France after the fall of Rouen and Caen in 1449, but Somerset was extremely unpopular at this time as a result of these defeats and it

D

is difficult to imagine why he should be mentioned along with the other English leaders. For the rest, with the exception of Cardinal Beaufort ('oure welevette hatte'), were of some military renown. Bedford ('The Rote') had been Regent in France for the period of greatest English success; Humphrey of Gloucester ('The Swanne') had the relief of Calais to his credit and was popular because of his war policy; John Holland, Duke of Exeter ('The firy Cressett'), who died in 1447, and John Mowbray, Duke of Norfolk ('The White Lioun'), who died in 1432, had both fought on Henry V's victorious campaigns; William Neville, Lord Fauconberg ('hangulhooke'), and Robert, Lord Willoughby ('oure Mylle-Saylle'), had both served with distinction in France and John Talbot, Earl of Shrewsbury, was perhaps the most experienced English military leader living. All these fine leaders, laments the poet, are now dead, or, like Talbot, recalled from active service. Much of the blame for the English failures in France was attributed to the policy of William de la Pole, Duke of Suffolk ('the Ape Clogge'). He was held responsible for the initiation of Henry VI's unpopular marriage with Margaret of Anjou; for the murder of Humphrey of Gloucester; and for the breaking of the truce with France in 1449 and thus the loss of the English possessions there. This author does not restrict himself to foreign affairs though. Much of the rest of the poem accuses the Lancastrian court party of mismanagement of home affairs and is not relevant in this chapter, but the inference is inescapable that the domestic discontent and the failures of the French war were not disconnected in the popular mind.

This was not the end of English disasters. In 1451–2 the French turned their attention to Gascony and one by one the English fortresses fell. An expedition under Talbot in the autumn of 1452, coupled with pro-English risings in the Gascon towns, threw off French rule for about a year, but in 1453 another French army marched against the fief and defeated the English at Castillon on 17 July. Bordeaux was besieged, and, with no prospect of relief, surrendered on 19 October 1453. These later reverses find no mention in contemporary English verse, unless the opening lines of a complaint from Cambridge University Library MS Hh ii 6 refer to them:

Nowe is Englond perisshed in fight,
With moche people & consciens light,
Many knyghtes & lytyll myght,
Many lawys & lityll right . . .

(HP, 62, 1–4)

But even if these verses were written in 1453 or slightly later, as R. H. Robbins suggests, it is clear that the writer is not so much concerned about foreign affairs as with the degeneration of England, for the rest of the poem is a fairly conventional 'evils of the age' piece complaining principally about upstart courtiers, extravagant fashions, and irreligious and immoral behaviour in general. To all intents and purposes the war with France was over, and from this time most political verses deal with domestic affairs.

Throughout the war with France there were a few witnesses who, contrary to the general trend, spoke out in favour of peace. Written just after Henry IV's accession, John Gower's elaborate address to him urges that he strive for peace in Christendom:

Noght only to my king of pes y write,
Bot to these othre princes cristene alle,
That ech of hem his oghne herte endite,
And sese the werre er more meschiefe falle.

(PPS, II, p. 15)

However, the new King did not continue Richard II's policy of peace with France, but ended the truce and declared war in 1401. In 1412, still three years before the Agincourt campaign, Thomas Hoccleve, in the final section of his *Regement of Princes*, which was written for Prince Henry, similarly urged an end to hostilities:

Allas! what peple haþ your werre slayn!
What cornes wast, and doune trode & schent!
How many a wif and maide haþ be by layn!
Castels doun bette, and tymbred houses brent,
And drawen downe, and al to-torne and rent!
The harm ne may not rekened be, ne told;
This werre wexiþ al to hoor and old.

(Regement, 5335–41)

He suggests that Prince Henry should be betrothed to Princes Katherine so that 'By matrimoigne pees and vnite/Ben had . . .' and adds that peace should be made among Christian princes in order that they might wage a just crusading war upon the infidel 'And hem vnto the feith of crist to brynge' (5434). Hoccleve, who died in about 1426, lived to see his advice thoroughly disregarded and to witness the military triumphs of Henry V, but, so far as is known, never added his voice to those who praised his achievements. Lydgate, on the other hand, as has been shown, defended the Lancastrian right to the throne of France often and at length, but at the same time he not infrequently wrote in favour of peace. At the end of his *Troy Book*, which had been commissioned by Prince Henry in 1412 and was finished in 1420, Lydgate asserts the justice of his patron's attainment by force of the throne of France, but looks forward also to the settlement of the Treaty of Troyes to usher in a time of peace:

> I mene þus, þat Yngelond and Fraunce
> May be al oon, withowte variaunce,
> Oute of hertis old rancour to enchase. . . .
> (V, 3411–13)

Like Hoccleve he has hopes that the marriage of Katherine will result in a peaceful stability:

> And alliaunce of þe blod royal,
> Þat is knet vp by bonde of mariage,
> Of werre shal voide aweie þe rage,
> To make pes with briȝte bemys shyne.
> (V, 3420–3)

Particularly notable is the statement in favour of peace in the closing lines of *The Siege of Thebes*, written between 1420 and 1422:

> But the venym and the violence
> Of strif, of werre, of contek, and debat,
> That makeþ londys bare and desolat
> Shal be proscript and voyded out of place,
> And Martys swerd shal no more manace,

Nor his spere, greuous to sustene,
Shal now no more whettyd be so kene,
Nor he no more shal his hauberk shake.
But loue and pees in hertys shal awake,
And charite, both in length and brede,
Of newe shal her bryghte beemys sprede
Thorgh grace only in dyuers naciouns,
Forto reforme a twixe Regyouns
Pees and quyet concord and vnyte.

(4690–703)

As W. F. Schirmer points out, this poem was written outside the patronage system, and, if he is right that here Lydgate 'speaks his own mind', it is demonstrable what faith he had in the settlement of 1420, for both the opening and closing lines of this quotation seem to echo actual clauses of the Treaty of Troyes.[25]

Subsequent to the heady years of military success under Henry V, even the most militantly nationalistic of writers were prepared to settle for a peace which safeguarded England's interests and which was ostensibly honourable. The author of *The Libelle of Englyshe Polycye* (1436), for all his recommendation of a trade embargo and a naval blockade of Flanders, sees a settlement as ultimately desirable:

And thus shuld everi lande, one with another,
Entrecomen as brother wyth his brother,
And live togedre werreles in unite
Wythoute rancoure in verry charite,
In reste and pese to Cristis grete plesaunce,
Wythouten striffe, debate and variaunce.
Whiche pease men shulde enserche with besinesse
And knytt it sadely, holdyng in holynesse

(1100–7)

and he substantiates his case by a series of biblical references. Perhaps only a short time after this, if R. H. Robbins' dating of 1437–40 is correct, comes a poem which voices the gladness which many Englishmen must have felt at the gradual closing of the war:

Hyt wer grete nede to prey for pes,
And fro all sich folys hus defende;
for, loke, sython warus began to ses!
how feire insampuls god has hus sende:
þo sesonabulst wedur, withowtyn leyse,
þat euer mon sawe dryven tyl a nende,
And feyr on gronde kon kornus incres,
And lyke þoro grace þat þo worde schuld mende.

(HP, 99, 49–56)

Later poems written by Lydgate too show that the bias towards peace so evident in the verses written about 1420 was maintained. Perhaps the best expression of his later ideas appears in the *Praise of Peace*, though W. F. Schirmer would date it around 1422. It is certainly to be dated after Henry V's death to which it refers, and it may be considerably later: Thomas Wright suggested it might refer to the peace negotiations of 1443.[26] The poem is elaborate and learned: Lydgate plays on the letters of the word 'pax', cites 'the four daughters of God' and 'seven daughters of the Holy Ghost' as favourers of peace, quotes from Diogenes and Socrates, reviews the disruptive influences of war from Old Testament to contemporary time, and ends with the hope that England and France may be reconciled in peace:

Al werre is dreedful, vertuous pees is good,
Striff is hatful, pees douhtir of plesaunce,
In Charlys tyme there was shad gret blood,
God sende vs pees twen Ynglond and Fraunce.

(Minor Poems, II, 64, 169–72)

Perhaps dating from the later stages of the wars, and sharing some of Lydgate's sentiments, comes a short carol which deplores in fairly general terms the viciousness of the world but which ends with a reference to the French war and a plea for peace:

Fortewn is a mervelous chaunce,
And envy causyth gret distaunce
Both in Englond and in Fraunce:
Exylyd is benyngnyte.

> Now lett us pray, both on and all,
> And specyally vpon God call
> To send love and peace among us all,
> Among all men in Christente.
>
> (*EEC*, 386, stanzas 5–6)

It is impossible to estimate the contemporary support for this feeling, but by the middle of the century there cannot have been too many who seriously believed in the advisability of an aggressive military policy against France.

None the less, no treaty marked the English defeats of 1453 and subsequent English kings still formally claimed the throne of France. In his *Active Policy of a Prince* (*c.* 1470), George Ashby stresses Prince Edward's English and French ancestry in much the same way as Lydgate had done for his father Henry VI:

> Seintes of youre noble blode ye may knowe,
> Diuers many that lyued blessedly
> Both of this England and Fraunce ynowe.
>
> (*Poems*, II, 141–3)

It is doubtful, though, whether the Lancastrian Ashby would have supported the use of force for the recovery of Edward's inheritance, for later in the same poem he specifically warns against ill-considered agression:

> I wold fain ye wolde kepe in remembrance
> To be right wele aduised by goode sadnesse,
> By discrete prudence & feithful constance
> Er ye begynne werre for any richesse,
> Or of fantesie or of symplenesse.
> For werre may be lightly commensed
> Doubt is how it shal be recompensed.
>
> (674–80)

Less cautious is the author of the carol *Edward, Dei Gratia*, a Yorkist celebration of Edward IV's accession probably written about 1461 but in any case before 1464. The new King is here urged to claim not only the throne of France, but that of Spain also, and to recover them by force:

> Rex Anglie & francia, y say,
> hit is thine owne—why saist þou nay?
> And so is spayne, that faire contrey,
> Edwardis, dai gracia.
>
> ffy on slowtfull contenewaunce,
> where conquest is a noble plesance,
> And regesterd in olde rememberance
> Edwardes, day Gracia.
>
> (*HP*, 92, 21–8)

The Yorkists were more keen on attempting to recover the English possessions in France than Henry VI's Lancastrian supporters. The French, in fact, usually supported the Lancastrians. Charles VII's sympathies naturally lay with his niece Margaret of Anjou, to whom he sent advisers and to whose followers he gave refuge. His successor Louis XI was in large part responsible for the reconciliation between Margaret and Warwick and the subsequent Lancastrian recovery which resulted in the brief restoration of Henry VI in 1470. But the Dukes of Burgundy, both Philip the Good and his successor Charles the Bold, supported the Yorkists in general, and frequently it must have seemed likely that an Anglo-Burgundian alliance against Louis XI would revive the old conflict. There were preparations in England for war with France in 1461, again in 1468, and in 1475 Edward IV actually crossed with twenty thousand men. On this last occasion Louis XI bought off the English with substantial grants of money, but the English did not renounce their claim to the throne of France and Edward IV was preparing another expedition at the time of his death in 1483. Even with the coming of a new dynasty, the claim to France remained. There were rumours of a landing in Gascony in 1487 and English forces fought in Brittany in 1489. Henry VII did actually invade France in 1492 and a contemporary poet, using the conventional red rose imagery to refer to him could still speak of the recovery of 'hys ryȝth':

> Thys apryll schowyres, wyche are ful swet,
> Hathe bownd thys rosse not ȝet ful blown;

In france he woll hys levys schote—
hys ryȝth to conquer, hys henmyes to knowe.

Thys Rosse þat is of color rede
Wyll sseke hys henmys, bothe fare & wyde,
And wyth hys bemys he woll frensse lyth—
Sent Iorge protector, be hys good gyd.

(*HP*, 36, 5–12)

It was by no means a large-scale expedition and Henry VII was ready enough to settle for a cash indemnity and peace with honour. He could scarcely have expected to recover any territory. The invasion was a tactical gesture, as empty almost as the title to France which English kings continued to bear.

NOTES

[1] *The Libelle of Englyshe Polycye* ed. Sir George Warner, lines 802, 332, 344, 505.

[2] *Hardyng's Chronicle* ed. H. Ellis, 1812, pp. 422, 429.

[3] *Translation:* 'The duke of Burgundy and the Scottish king plot treachery, but the English king and the people are masters over them. England rules kingdoms, Burgundy purchases shame, France in weakness trembles, having been conquered Scotland groans. On all sides stands a conspiracy and England rough and bear-like. England then roars, the surrounding countries flee.'

[4] See Margaret Aston, *The Fifteenth Century: the Prospect of Europe*, 1968, p. 41 for a fuller treatment.

[5] *The Governance of England* ed. C. Plummer, Oxford 1885, p. 141.

[6] *Libelle, op. cit.*, lines 390, 391, 734.

[7] 'Treatyse of a Gallant' in F. J. Furnivall ed. *Ballads from Manuscripts*, 1868–72, I, 445–53.

[8] *Minor Poems* ed. H. N. MacCracken, II, 51, lines 1–3. On Lydgate's use of the idea of the Trojan founding of Britain see A. Renoir, *The Poetry of John Lydgate*, 1967, pp. 96–101.

[9] See R. M. Wilson, *The Lost Literature of Medieval England*, 1952, p. 208, who cites occurrences of this song in *The Brut* ed. W. F. D. Brie, EETS OS 131, 136, 1906–8, p. 189; and Fabyan's *New Chronicles of England and France* ed. H. Ellis, 1811, p. 398.

[10] In N. H. Nicolas ed. *History of the Battle of Agincourt*, 1832, pp. 301–29.

[11] *Henry V and the Invasion of France*, 1947, pp. 71–3.

[12] *Chronicle of England* ed. F. C. Hingeston, Rolls Series 1, 1858, p. 314.

[13] *Minor Poems, op. cit.*, II, 31, 83; and *Libelle of Englyshe Polycye, op. cit.*, lines 8–21.

[14] *The Hundred Years War*, 1965, p. 239.

[15] John Page's *Siege of Rouen* ed. J. Gairdner in *Collections of a London Citizen*, Camden Society 1876, pp. 1–46.

[16] *John Lydgate*, translated by Ann E. Keep 1961, p. 119.

[17] 'King Henry VI's claim to France: in Picture and Poem', *The Library*, 4th Series, 13, 1933, pp. 77–88 for details, including a text of Calot's poem from which I quote. *Translation*: 'And to show that this is true, look, I pray you at this genealogical chart.'

[18] For details see the article of J. W. McKenna, 'Henry VI of England and the Dual Monarchy' *JWCI* 28, 1965, pp. 145–62.

[19] *The Hundred Years War*, *op. cit.*, p. 264.

[20] See Appendix A.

[21] *The Brut* ed. W. F. D. Brie, EETS OS 131, 136, 1906–8, p. 439.

[22] See E. F. Jacob, *The Fifteenth Century*, Oxford 1961, pp. 248–52 for an account of the trial.

[23] *EHR* 76, 1961, pp. 193–216.

[24] These lines are taken from the verses written by Lydgate to welcome Margaret of Anjou to London. See Carleton Brown *MLR* 7, 1912, pp. 225–34 and R. Withington, *Mod. Phil.* 13, 1916, pp. 53–7.

[25] *John Lydgate*, *op. cit.*, p. 65.

[26] *Ibid.*, pp. 88–9 for a discussion of the date.

4 : Domestic Affairs I : 1399-1422

ALTHOUGH England's foreign affairs concerned fifteenth-century poets a good deal, domestic affairs predictably concerned them more, and more poems are extant. Domestic problems were also treated in greater detail and complexity. Though a few writers questioned the wisdom of English foreign policy in the fifteenth century, the great majority take up fairly predictable and strictly nationalistic attitudes: an uncritical assumption of the rightness of the English cause and an unswerving support for those leaders who carried out firm nationalist policies. Poems on domestic affairs, on the other hand, are more frequently critical of the regime. They tend to be more personal and represent more points of view. As was the case with poems dealing with foreign affairs, however, these verses tend naturally to concern the more sensational and dramatic (though not necessarily the most important) events. And in the period 1399–1422 there was certainly no lack of such incidents: the usurpation of Richard II, the frequent rebellions against Henry IV, his financial and parliamentary difficulties, and the rebellions (complicated by the factor of Lollardy) which disturbed the reign of Henry V.

The events surrounding the deposition of Richard II and the establishment of Henry IV in 1399 had far-reaching consequences, but the volume of English verse they provoked is surprisingly small. Perhaps because it was essentially a struggle between magnates, it did not arouse a great deal of vocal popular feeling. The most important poem on these events consists of two substantial alliterative fragments which probably belong together and are usually entitled *Mum and the Sothsegger*. The first fragment must have been begun after August 1399 (since it mentions the release of Thomas Beauchamp, Earl of Warwick, from his exile in the Isle of Man) but before February 1400 (since it alludes to Richard as still alive). The second fragment was written some years later and does not concern the deposition. Not much can be deduced about the author. Since the poem is written in a south-west Midland dialect and opens in Bristol it may be that he was a Bristol man. He was certainly well-informed about contemporary affairs, but because of the fragmentary nature of the text, the purpose and disposition of the poem are not easy to establish. It looks as though the author conceived the poem originally as one of advice to Richard II. In the Prologue he explains that he has thought 'many tyme and ofte' of writing a poem of advice to Richard II 'to meuve him of mysserewle/hys mynde to reffresshe'. But immediately after this he broadens his scope:

> euery Cristen kyng/þat ony croune bereth
> So he were lerned on þe langage . . .
>
> (42–3)

will be able to profit from his advice. In the context this is almost certainly a reminder to Henry IV not to fall into the same political errors as Richard II, and, indeed, the second fragment of the poem is directed towards Henry IV only. But though the poem is nominally advice, and though the author was sorry for Richard II:

> I had pete of his passion þat prince was of Walis
> And eke oure crouned kynge . . .
>
> (Prologue, 23–4)

the first fragment is, for the most part, a criticism of Richard's political behaviour and policies and an approving welcome for Henry IV.

In the last year of his reign criticism of Richard II was not uncommon, but what makes this poem unusual is the precision of the criticism. The poem confirms the impression given by contemporary chroniclers that the style of Richard II's government was offensive to a great many people. The courtiers the King chose to have about him, says the poet, were too young, inexperienced and low-born. They cared more for comfort and self-advancement than for guiding the destinies of the kingdom:

> But walwed in her willis/forweyned in here youthe,
> þey sawe no maner siȝth/saff solas and ese,
> And cowde no mysse amende/when mysscheff was vp,
> but sorwed for her lustus/of lordschipe þey hadde,
> And neuere for her trespas/oo tere wolde þey lete.
>
> (I, 27–31)

He also complains of the numerous liveried retainers the King employed. Anyone who travelled about England would have seen 'mo þan ynowe' of these men wearing the King's white hart badge, but who benefited the country not at all. They were expensive to maintain and arrogant towards the common people. Because they were liveried retainers in the King's service, they regarded themselves exempt from any redress for the wrongs of which they were guilty:

> For þey acombrede þe contre/and many curse seruid,
> And carped to þe comounes/with þe kynges mouþe,
> Or with þe lordis/þer þey belefte were,
> That no renke shulde rise/reson to schewe.
> Þey plucked þe plomayle/from þe pore skynnes,
> And schewed her signes/for men shulde drede
> To axe ony mendis/for her mysdedis.
>
> (II, 28–34)

Liveried retainers were never very popular, whether they served the King or other lords, and from the early fourteenth century onwards vernacular poems contain complaints against them. But Richard II seems to have been especially badly served by the tactlessness of his men. They seem to have offended most of the chroniclers, and this poet also, by their interference in the processes of law and their cruelty in carrying out Richard's often arbitrary decisions:

> Þey constrewed quarellis/to quenche þe peple,
> And pletid with pollaxis/and poyntis of swerdis,

> And at þe dome-ȝeuynge/drowe out þe bladis,
> And lente men leuere/of her longe battis.
> Þey lacked alle vertues/þat a juge shulde haue.
>
> (III, 327–31)

This probably alludes to the interference in local courts by the King's retainers when he was on progresses, but it may refer in particular to the behaviour of the Cheshire archers at the trial of the Earl of Arundel in 1397, when, according to the Monk of Evesham, some two thousand of them guarded the parliament building and actually shot arrows at the public to keep them away.

Nor were Richard's ministers, in the popular mind, very happily chosen. Three in particular—Sir John Bushy, Sir Henry Green and Sir William Bagot—incurred the scorn of more than one contemporary writer. Bushy, a Lancastrian official and speaker in the parliaments of 1393-4, 1397 and 1398, and Green, also a Lancastrian and member of parliament but one of Richard's household knights, had been recruited by the King from among the lesser aristocracy. Bagot, also a member of parliament, probably came into the King's service through the influence of Thomas Mowbray, Earl of Nottingham, who had been an opponent of Richard's in the crisis of 1387-8 but had later become one of his chief supporters. Bushy, Green and Bagot were loyal to the King and closely involved with his affairs: Bushy and Green were on the committee of eighteen to which the parliament of 1398 delegated its duties, and all three, together with Sir William Scrope, chamberlain in the King's household, had effective charge of the country under the Regent Edmund Langley, Duke of York, when Richard was in Ireland. If contemporary verses convey a true impression it was at this time that their unpopularity was at its height:

> The busch is bare and waxus sere;
> Hit may no lengur leves bere.
> Now stont hit in no styde.
> Ywys I con no nodur bote
> But hewe hit downe crop and rote
> And to the toun hit lede.

The long gras, that semeth grene,
Hit is roton alle bydene;
Hit is non best mete.
Til the roton be dynged ouȝt,
Our lene bestes schul not rouȝt
Hur liflode to gete.

The grete bage is so ytoren
Hit nyl holde neyther mele ne corne;
Hong hit up to drye.
When hit is drye, then schalt thou se
ȝyf hit wil amended be,
A beger for to bye.

(*PPS*, I, pp. 365–6)

So writes an anonymous author in 1399, but his fanciful images do not hide his real contempt and hatred: these ministers are corrupt and of no use; therefore, they should be removed. And the violence of his language ('hewe hit downe crop and rote', 'dynged', 'Hong hit up to drye') leaves no doubt that he advocated force. What caused this extreme unpopularity is not always clear: but in this poem the ministers are accused of being involved in Richard's plots. More often, though, the belief that they were low-born upstarts was enough to provoke a general resentment.

Although his ministers were unpopular, many of Richard II's policies and decisions were even more so. After he regained power from the Lords Appellant in 1389, he had steadily acquired support among a group of court knights as well as among the gentry in the country. By 1397 he felt his position to be sufficiently secure and set about avenging himself on his former masters. In July 1397, the King invited the three principal appellants, Richard Fitzalan, Earl of Arundel, Thomas Woodstock, Duke of Gloucester, and Thomas Beauchamp, Earl of Warwick, to a banquet. Only Warwick came, and he was immediately arrested. Shortly afterwards Arundel was put under restraint and Gloucester was detained and shipped out of the way to Calais. Referring to the principals by means of their cognizances the author of *Mum and the Sothsegger* demonstrates his disapproval of these actions:

This is clerlie hir kynde/coltis not to greue,
Ne to hurlle with haras/ne hors well atamed,
Ne to stryue with swan/þouʒ it sholle werre,
Ne to bayten on þe bere/ne bynde him noþer . . .

(III, 26–9)

The passage refers to proper nature of 'hertis' (a clear allusion to Richard II and his supporters who wore the badge of the white hart) which should not, says the poet, attack the 'hors' (Arundel's badge was a white horse), or the 'swan' (Gloucester's badge) or the 'bere' (the black bear being the badge of Warwick). Basing his comments on fabulous material in Pliny,[2] the poet says that it is the proper nature of 'hertis' to catch adders 'þat armen/alle hende bestes'; that is, the King and his supporters should strive to remove evil influences from the kingdom, and not those, like Arundel, Gloucester and Warwick, who are beneficial to the country. But Richard II was set on asserting himself: he wanted to be freed from the few remaining restraints on his authority; he wanted revenge for the Lords Appellants' exile of his friends Michael de la Pole and Edward de Vere and for their executions of Nicholas Brembre and Simon Burley his old tutor; he also wanted their lands. Against Arundel, Gloucester and Warwick he used their own instrument of appeal. A council of eight magnates at Nottingham agreed to accuse them of treason. At the suitably cowed parliament of 17 September at Westminster, Warwick confessed and was exiled to the Isle of Man and Arundel, after an outspoken defence, was executed. At this parliament it was reported that Gloucester had died in Calais confessing his guilt, and it seems almost certain he was murdered. The author of the verses *On King Richard's Ministers* implicated Bushy, Green and Bagot in these affairs, punning on their names and using the same system of reference by badges for Gloucester, Arundel and Warwick as the author of *Mum and the Sothsegger*. Bushy helped to kill Gloucester ('Thorw the busch a swan was sclayn'), Green was responsible for the death of Arundel (the 'strong steed'), and Bagot had betrayed Warwick, who had earlier shown favour to him ('thorwe the bag the bereward is taken'). Of course responsibility was not as particular or as simple as this, but in broad terms the poet is not far from the truth, for these ministers certainly acted on behalf of the King in the parliament and Bushy was especially vigorous in his demands for Arundel's execution as a traitor. In some of his statements, Arundel himself implied that the parliament had been rigged to secure a verdict favourable to the King.

This was almost certainly the case in subsequent parliaments. That of 17 January 1398 at Shrewsbury was entirely subservient to the King's will. It confirmed all the decisions of the previous year and granted him generous subsidies besides. A committee of eighteen, which the King controlled and manipulated for his own ends, was formed to carry on the business of parliament. His prerogative rights thus effectively restored, the King's authoritarianism and arbitrariness increased. He enforced loans, he fined the commons of those shires which had not supported him against the Lords Appellant in 1387, and he sought to manipulate local government by influencing the election of sheriffs. By these means he succeeded in increasing his power and wealth, but many sections of opinion were offended. His financial measures were particularly resented and the author of *Mum and the Sothsegger* voices what were probably fairly typical contemporary views. The expense of maintaining such an extravagant household of courtiers and retainers, says the poet, kept the King perpetually in debt, and not

> alle his fynys for fauȝtis/ne his fee-fermes,
> Ne for-feyturis fele/þat felle in his daies,
> Ne þe nownagis/þat newed him euere,
> As Marche and Moubray/and many mo oþer,
> Ne alle þe issues of court/þat to þe kyng longid,
> Ne sellynge, þat sowkid/siluer rith faste,
> Ne alle þe prophete of þe lond/þat þe prince owed,
> Whane þe countis were caste/with þe custum of wullus . . .
>
> (IV, 4–11)

could offset this. New loans and grants had to be arranged, he continues, through cynically rigged parliaments. If the views expressed here were at all representative, it is not difficult to see why support for Richard II in the crisis of 1399 was so meagre.

But the discontent was not focussed until in 1398 he banished Henry Bolingbroke and followed this in February 1399 with the confiscation of the extensive Lancastrian estates inherited from John of Gaunt. By these ill-judged actions he gave the discontent a point of reference. To Bolingbroke he gave a cause, and by setting out for Ireland in May 1399 and leaving the country in the incompetent hands of Edmund Langley, Duke of York, an opportunity also.

What Bolingbroke's intentions were when he landed at Ravenspur in Yorkshire a few weeks later is difficult to know. He said he had come to claim his own. At Doncaster he told the Percies, who had joined him, that he intended to regain the inheritance of which he had been unjustly deprived by his cousin the King and to insist on good government. It is interesting to see that the author of *Mum and the Sothsegger* describes the invasion in much the same terms, justifying it on the grounds Bolingbroke himself had chosen. In one place Bolingbroke, who is referred to as the 'egle' throughout the first fragment, is said to have 'entrid his owen' (III, 69) by invading the country. In another, the common people, who are described as the offspring of the eagle and under his protection, complain

> how þei bete were,
> And tenyd with twiggis/two and twenty ȝeris
> (III, 78–9)

that is, for the whole of Richard II's reign, and how they were 'well ny yworwid/with a wronge ledir'. According to the poet, it is for these sound and justifiable reasons that the people defected from the cause of Richard II 'þe leder/þat hem wrong ladde' (III, 80) and associated themselves with Bolingbroke 'And followid him fersly/to fighte for þe wrongis' (II, 77). Assured of support of this kind and of the comparative weakness of the King's position, Bolingbroke was able to dispose of Bushy, Green and Scrope, to the evident delight of this poet who plays on their names in the familiar punning way:

> Thus baterid þis bred/on busshes abouȝte,
> And gaderid gomes on grene/þer as þey walkyd,

Þat all þe schroff and schroup/sondrid from oþir.

(II, 152–4)

Sir William Bagot escaped to Ireland to warn Richard of the invasion and was not captured until later. But the warning was in vain, and by the time he landed from Ireland at Conway, Richard's cause was hopeless. When Bolingbroke entered London on 2 September he had met with hardly any resistance.

By this time it was fairly clear that the crown was Bolingbroke's object. Since the King's arbitrary and misguided rule had caused him to forfeit the support of the majority of his people, and since his few supporters had been hopelessly outmanoeuvred, it was relatively easy to depose him. Indeed he seems to have been prepared to abdicate readily enough and did so on 29 September. It was much more difficult, however, to present Bolingbroke's right to the crown convincingly. Nevertheless, the day after his abdication, in order presumably to give a semblance of legality to the proceedings, Richard II was formally deposed on a variety of charges before a hastily summoned assembly at Westminster. The status of this assembly is much argued about.[3] It was not the properly constituted 'parliament' the coronation roll speaks of, but through this assembly Bolingbroke's claim to the throne was accepted and he was elected Henry IV.

There is little evidence that his accession was widely celebrated. The account of the author of *Mum and the Sothsegger* would doubtless have been approving but the section of the poem in which he presumably dealt with this has been lost. Chaucer, however, referred to Henry IV's accession in a poem addressed to him:

> O conqueror of Brutes Albyon
> Which that by lyne and free eleccion
> Been verray kyng . . .,
> (*Complaint to his Purse*, 22–4)

as did Gower:

> The high god, of his justice allone,
> The right which longeth to thi regalie
> Declared hath to stonde in thi persone,

And more than God may no man justifie.
Thi title is knowe uppon thin ancestrie,
The londes folk hath ek thi riht affermed;
So stant thi regne of god and man confermed.

(PPS, II, p. 4)

Chaucer is not markedly enthusiastic in tone, and it is likely he was mainly concerned with the continuation of his royal grants, but, none the less, it is interesting to see that both he and Gower echo and accept Henry's threefold claim to the throne—that he was descended from Henry III, that he had been elected King by the assembly of 30 September 1399, and that the success of his conquest indicated divine favour. At best the case was weak: the claim of descent from Henry III was absurd, and the assembly of 30 September did not strictly have the legal authority to do the things it did. The conquest was real enough, though, and the majority seem to have accepted the fact, hoping, like Chaucer, that Henry IV would 'alle oure harmes amende', or, like Gower, that he would be the 'comfort of ous alle'.

It soon became amply clear, however, that Henry IV was not going to be the solution to all England's problems. As the sharp resentment against Richard II faded, disillusionment with Henry and his government increased. The earlier part of his reign saw the most violent manifestations of this in the frequent and open rebellions against his authority. As early as 1400, the author of the verses in MS Digby 102 urged him to be firm with such opposition:

kepe ȝow euere fro suche myscheue;
And chastise hem that matere meue:
Make othere take ensaumple treuth to hede.

(I, 76–8)

Only a few months after Henry IV's accession a conspiracy by four of Richard II's supporters almost succeeded in surprising him at Windsor. Though these men were captured and executed, attempts continued to be made on his life. The most serious challenge came initially from the Welsh, who, motivated by various social grievances and a vague nationalism and led by the skilful Owen

Glyndwr, rose against their English overlords in the Marches. The Digby MS 102 author was again quick to warn Henry of the danger:

> What kyngdom werreþ hym-self wiþ-ynne
> Distroyeþ hym-self and no mo.
>
> (III, 113–14)

But the revolt spread quickly and military success was immediate. Many of the castles of the King and the Marcher lords fell into Welsh hands and three expeditions led by Henry IV himself failed to reverse these successes. On one expedition in 1402 the Welsh captured Sir Edmund Mortimer, and this indirectly caused the rebellion to escalate. Henry IV refused to ransom Mortimer who, disgruntled, threw in his lot with Glyndwr. He was joined in 1403 by an alliance of the powerful Percy family and the Scots they had defeated earlier at Homildon Hill. In 1399 the Percies had supported Bolingbroke but now they had several reasons to resent him: he owed them money which he could not or would not repay; he had made them, against their will, give up the Scottish prisoners captured at Homildon Hill; and Mortimer, whom Henry IV would not ransom, was Harry Hotspur's brother-in-law. By 1403 this combined threat to Henry IV was serious. It would seem from the ban which he imposed on the Welsh bards for writing prophecies, 'the cause of the insurrection and rebellion in Wales', that the rebels fomented their cause by means of verse, but little of this is now extant.

Fragmentary as the information is, however, it would not be true to say as C. L. Kingsford does that 'of the Welsh war no English poems have survived'.[4] A more precise notion of the literature which the rebels used to encourage themselves and their supporters may be derived from a story preserved by Hall '. . . howe a certayne writer writeth that this earle of Marche, the Lorde Percy and Owen Glendor wer vnwisely made believe by a Welsh Prophecier, that King Henry was the Moldewarpe, cursed of Goddes owne mouth, and that they thre were the Dragon, the Lion and the Wolffe, which shoulde devide this realme betwene them, by the deviacion and not divination of that mawmet Merlin.'[5] This can only refer to a section from the popular 'six kings to follow John' prophecy which existed in prose and poetical versions in Latin, French and English, most of which are very hostile to Henry IV. Particularly interesting is the couplet version in MS Cotton Galba E ix, since its optimism about the possibility of Henry IV's overthrow suggests to its editor it may have been written before the Battle of Shrewsbury in 1403—but it may equally well refer to 1405.[6] The correspondence between the animals mentioned in the prophecy and the historical figures is not the same here as that in Hall's story, or as that in similar prophecies, but the message is the same. Not only does the author deride Henry IV as the mole who is a 'swith grete wretche' and 'Weried with Goddes mowth', but he predicts also that Henry IV will 'be casten down with sin & with pride' by 'a dragon ful fell & ful scharp' (which seems to refer to Percy but is usually Glyndwr) and a 'wolf þat sall cum out of the west' (which seems here to be Glyndwr). Prophecies are usually very generalized, but on occasions this poem is curiously precise. For example, lines 237–8:

> Out of Yreland þan sall cum a liown
> And hold with þe wolf and with þe dragown

make it clear that the writer expected the rebels to be supported by the Irish. Glyndwr had, in fact, requested such help in 1401 and used as one of his inducements the fact that Merlin had foretold that the Irish would join the Welsh and the Scots against Henry IV. The poet also alludes to the tripartite division of England proposed by the rebels after their hoped-for victory:

> Þan sall all Ingland on wonder wise
> Be euyn partid in thre parties.
>
> (271–2)

So, in the normal way, he rewrote the traditional source prophecy in his own terms, inserting various particular pieces of information which seemed appropriate. A final point of interest is the dialect of the poem, which is northern and indicates that the author was from the region where the Percies had their main support. Versions of this same prophecy are also found in manuscripts written in Wales. The literary opposition to Henry IV derives from those areas where the actual rebellion was strongest.

The victory of the royalist forces at Shrewsbury in 1403 did not end the rebellion. Though Hotspur was killed and Worcester executed, Northumberland averred his innocence and was pardoned on condition that he surrendered his castles. It was his plotting with Glyndwr which brought on the rising of 1405, which, through the implication of Richard Scrope, Archbishop of York, appeared to have the support of the clergy. This was not the first occasion on which clerics had been implicated in plots against Henry IV. A plan for murdering him in 1400 had been developed at meetings held at the lodgings of the Abbot of Westminster. In 1401 several priests and friars were executed for treason against the King and in 1402 the Franciscans were instrumental in spreading rumours that Richard II was still alive. But Scrope was a much more influential figure and also much more direct in his methods, for though he had not protested against the usurpation, nor been an active supporter of the rebellion of 1403, he now joined his kinsmen in armed revolt. The rebels' grievances were 'made be written in English' by the Archbishop 'and were set on the yatis of the cite, and sent to curatis of the tovnes aboute, for to be prechid openli'.[7] Some of these grievances show evidence of clerical discontent, particularly those complaining of the impossible burden of taxation borne by the clergy. Other complaints are that the government was inefficient and interfering, and that the nobility and merchants were excessively penalised by taxes, which were too high in general. Money raised by such taxes was being misappropriated, it is stated, by the King's ministers. But, despite the influence of Scrope and widespread support from the northern areas under Percy influence, the rebel forces were confronted by the Earl of Westmorland at Shipton Moor and their leaders tricked and captured. Henry IV was determined to make an example of the rebel leaders, particularly Scrope. Despite the opposition of the chief justice, Gascoigne, and of Arundel, Archbishop of Canterbury, the King packed a tribunal to ensure a capital sentence on Scrope, who was summarily executed at Clementhorpe just outside

York. This was the first time a secular court had sentenced a prelate to death.

Scrope, in his death, attracted much sympathy. In York particularly he was regarded as a martyr. Miracles were supposed to have been worked at his tomb in the minster, and pilgrimages were made there. Shortly after his death this veneration reached such proportions that orders were issued by the King forbidding it. The decree was not totally effective, however, for poems lamenting the death of the archbishop appeared. Most, no doubt, were written by clerics. One poem, in Latin, laments at some length the hasty indignity of his trial and execution:

> Judex praepotens, nulla dilatio,
> Nulla negotii examinatio,
> Gravis sententiae praeceps probatio,
> Progressus temerarius.[8]
> (*PPS*, II, p. 115)

The calm manner of Scrope's acceptance of his death seems also to have impressed his contemporaries, particularly the chroniclers, and also the author of the English carol *On the Death of Archbishop Scrope* (1405):

> When he was brought vnto the hyll,
> he held hym both mylde and styll;
> he toke his deth with full gode wyll.
> (5–7)

This man relates the moving story of how Scrope forgave the executioner his death and asked for five strokes of the axe because Christ suffered five wounds for mankind:

> Here I wyll the commende,
> Þou gyff me fyve strokys with thy hende
> And then my wayes þou latt me wende.
> (*HP*, 31, 13–15)

It is from such stories that legends grow, and Scrope's popularity continued among Yorkists throughout the century. As late as 1459, a York lawyer John Dawtry bequeathed to William Langton, a clerk, a book which 'the blessed Richard Scrope had and bore it in his breast at the time of his beheading'.[9] With such veneration accorded to Scrope, it is little wonder that Henry IV's responsibility for his death was a matter of constant accusation. It was popularly supposed that he was punished for this action by a loathsome disease, said to be leprosy, which shortened his life. This too was remembered, along with Scrope's saintliness. A Yorkist poet reviewing the century's history can still recall on the one hand that

> Holy bisshope Scrope, the blyssed confessour,
> In þat quarel toke hys deth ful paciently,
> That all the world spak of þat gret langoure
> (*HP*, 93, 14–16)

and on the other that

> God smote the said henry for hys gret fersnesse
> With a lepre holdyng hym to hys end fynally.
> (25–6)

And these verses date from as late as 1462.

After the rising of 1405, the Earl of Northumberland once again escaped the King's vengeance, and it was not until 19 February 1408 that his forces were finally defeated at Bramham Moor. After this Henry IV was relatively secure against rebellions. The French, who had earlier supported Glyndwr, now had serious troubles in their own kingdom, and the Welsh revolt was diminishing in effectiveness. The Scottish king fell into English hands in 1406 and so trouble was avoided from that quarter also. But contemporary discontent at Henry IV's rule did not disappear with the crushing of the rebellions. It is true that Henry IV is sometimes lavishly praised:

> he hymsilf is souurayn, and so mote he longe,
> And þe graciousist guyer goyng vppon erthe,
> Witti and wise, worthy of deedes,
> Y-kidde and y-knowe and cunnyng of werre,
> Feers for to fighte, þe felde euer kepith,
> And trusteth on þe Trinite, þat trouthe shal hym helpe:

> A doughtful doer in deedes of armes
> And a comely knight y-come of þe grettist,
> Ful of al vertue þat to a kyng longeth . . .
>
> (*M*, 211–19)

But in other passages such praise is modified by a sharp sense of disappointment at his failure to live up to the expectations which were aroused when he came to the throne.

The grievances which find expression in surviving contemporary verse are fairly predictable. Henry IV's main problem was finance. His income as King was smaller than Richard II's had been and his expenses were greater. In the early years of his reign money was needed for the campaigns against Glyndwr and the Percies, Ireland and Scotland had to be pacified, and abroad Calais had to be garrisoned and Gascony recovered. The Commons were rarely eager to agree to increases in taxation. It is obvious also from the contemporary poem in MS Digby 102 that they were acquiring a sense of their own financial importance:

> A kyngdom in comouns lys,
> Alle profytes, and alle myscheues.
> Lordis wet neuere what comouns greues
> Til here rentis bigynne to ses.
> Þere lordis ere, pore comons releues,
> And mayntene hem in werre and pes.
>
> (III, 99–104)

So it is hardly surprising that constant wrangles over money are a feature of the parliaments of this reign. The persistence of the Commons was only partly matched by the King's adroitness at circumventing the restrictions they sought to place upon his expenditure: when in 1406, for example, the Commons asked that the treasurers, Sir John Pelham and Thomas Neville, Lord Furnivall, should submit their account, Henry retorted that 'kings were not wont to render account' but, nevertheless, conceded the point. On the other hand he usually got the grants he requested, with the result that taxation was high and among the people there was, as one chronicler put it, a 'grete grucching'.[10] Something of this feeling comes out in the second part of *Mum and the Sothsegger* which amongst other things advises Henry to be careful to see that his financial advisers were efficient and trustworthy:

> Leste vncunnyng comyn caste vp þe halter
> And crie on your cunseil for coigne þat ye lacke,
> For þay shal smaicche of þe smoke and smerte þereafter
> When collectours comen to caicche what þay habben.
>
> (M, 5–8)

He adds later that the King should live within his means '. . . of his owen' (M 1667), that is, that the normal revenues of the crown should be sufficient for the ordinary expenses of the royal household—a theory the Commons never tired of repeating. And in order to do this the King should retain control of the revenues from his possessions 'Alle hoole in his hande þat he haue oughte' (M 1682) rather than grant them away to favourites—a recommendation specifically made at the Coventry parliament of 1404. But in spite of such advice, Henry IV's finances were frequently in difficulties. He was forced to borrow heavily, especially from lords and rich merchants, and frequently had trouble with the repayments. The situation was so bad that in 1404 the payment of annuities and pensions was stopped. This, amongst other complaints, provoked the earliest 'begging poem' from the improvident Privy Seal clerk Thomas Hoccleve who asks the treasurer Lord Furnivall:

> To paie me þat due is for þis year
> Of my yeerly x li in theschequer.
>
> (MP, III, 420–1)

But Henry's purse, like Hoccleve's, was 'alle voide and empty' and in this year, and sometimes in the years that followed, civil servants such as Hoccleve went unpaid or were paid late. The situation improved only slowly. As late as 1411–12 the same poet is complaining that he would be comfortably off if he received his annuity more regularly, but 'paiement is hard to gete adayes'.

The other main problem concerned the Council of advisers through which Henry governed the country. He recognized the importance of control of the Council and in the early years of his reign ensured that it was dominated by his own trusted friends under Thomas Arundel, Archbishop of Canterbury. But to some this seemed to be a reversion to the favouritism which had flourished under Richard II and there was much parliamentary disapproval. The Commons blamed the incompetence of the Council and the extravagance of the King's household for his financial troubles and constantly sought, with some degree of success, to obtain some control over both. In 1404, for example, the King acceded to the Commons' requests to remove four individuals from his household, and in 1406 he was forced to nominate his Council according to the wishes of the Commons. Such disapproval was not confined to parliament. In contemporary verse it predictably takes the form of bitter attacks on the 'flatterers' and 'evil councillors' who surrounded the King. The flattering evil councillor was a literary type, familiar in sermons and miracle plays. Often he is contrasted with the true councillor, as in Chaucer's figures of Placebo and Justinius, and in this way the 'sothsegger' of *Mum and the Sothsegger* contrasts himself with those who deceive by concealing the truth. Moreover, in this poem and in some of the verses from MS Digby 102, flattering evil councillors are demonstrated to be politically as well as morally undesirable. They diminish the King's revenues because they care more for acquiring wealth than for giving good advice:

> muche more for þe mede to make þaym–selfe riche
> Thenne to cunseille þe king of þe comune wele
> Or for any deue dome or defence of þe royaulme
> This same cursid custume oure coroune hath a-payred.
>
> (M, 1659–62)

When only evil councillors and flatterers have access to the King the truth about the state of the country is never revealed fully to him:

> þe king ne his cunseil may hit not knowe
> What is þe comune clamour ne þe crye nother,
> For þere is no man of þe meenye, more noþer lasse,
> That wol wisse þaym any worde . . .
>
> (M, 156–9)

Similarly, according to the Digby MS 102 poet, nothing is worse for a kingdom than 'glozers' and 'ȝong counseil', with a care only for 'syngulere profit'. The MS Digby 102 poet appears always to speak in general terms, but if, as J. Kail the editor thinks,[11] the poems quoted date from around 1404 there is no mistaking the specific objects of the criticism: he too was troubled by the composition and powers of Henry IV's Council.

From the latter part of the reign hardly any political verse has survived. This is not because the King no longer had problems: his financial difficulties remained, there were predictable differences of opinion within the Council, and parliament was often critical of his policies. But there were no more rebellions and Henry's position as King was no longer seriously threatened. Under him England achieved some sort of stability, even a measure of prosperity. Perhaps the temper of popular interest in politics during these later years is accurately indicated by some verses from MS Digby 102. The author castigates those who debase the coinage:

> That clippen money, þey have þe curs
> ffoure tymes in þe ȝere,
>
> (IX, 49–50)

or who use false weights and measures:

> Here waȝtes, þat þey waye þe wors,
> ȝerde or elne, fer or nere;
> Wheþer þey selle good chep or dere:
> But þey þe full mesure mete,
> Hit semeþ in skornyng þat it were.
>
> (51–5)

There are strictures on those who pervert justice for their own ends:

> Auyse ȝow þat leden lawe,
> ffor drede of lordschipe or for mede
> Holde no pore men in awe
> To storble here ryȝt or lette here nede,
>
> (57–60)

on soldiers who are excessively brutal in putting down disturbances:

> Caste þe not to couetys,
> 3e þat ry3twys werryours be,
> But loke where ri3t querel lys;
> Chastise þe rebell in charyte,
>
> (137–40)

and on clerics who neglect their duties. As Kail demonstrates, these are all problems which concern the Parliament of 1410 and the poem probably dates from this year. The attention given to these minor grievances would suggest that most of the major ones had ceased to seem important.

Henry IV died at Westminster on 20 March 1413. From 1408 onwards the records show that he was often in ill health, and it had probably been felt for some years before he died that the bright hopes with which his reign had started had become dimmed. Certainly, later poets recall the mixed fortunes of his reign: one remembers him as 'A famous knyht and of greet seemlynesse', another how 'all Englone made solas' at his coronation, but they do not forget either that he 'Travailed aftir with werr & gret siknesse'.[12] In the latter part of his reign the burden of government had been entrusted increasingly to the Council, thus giving opportunities to the ambitions of his son Henry, Prince of Wales. Along with the King's half-brothers John, Henry and Thomas Beaufort, the Prince sought to win dominance of the Council and control of its policies, particularly its foreign policy. This had the immediate effect of alienating him from his father, who was worried at the Prince's ambition. But it also gave the Prince valuable political experience, so that, when he came to the throne at the age of twenty-five, he knew fairly clearly what had to be done and also, in broad terms, what his policies were to be. He intended to restore order and unity in England and assert his right to the French throne. His accession was greeted with enthusiasm by most contemporary poets: The MS Digby 102 author entreats

> god, kepe in þy gouernance
> Oure comely kyng, and saue þe crowne!
>
> (XII, 151–2)

And Thomas Hoccleve elaborates on the same sentiment:

> The Kyng of Kynges regnyng oueral,
> Which stablisshid hath in eternitee
> His hy might þat nat varie he may ne shal,
> So constant is his blisful deitee,
> My lige lord this grace yow graunte he,
> That your estaat rial which þat this day
> Haath maad me lige to your sovereyntee,
> In reule vertuous continue may.
>
> (*MP*, IV, 1–8)

Nevertheless, there was some immediate criticism. From a Latin poem written in 1413, it is plain that Henry V and his policies were not universally popular. Its author, Thomas of Elmham, a monk, begins by warning the King that he should correct the mistakes of his government:

> Errores solitos quos nunc tua curia mittit
> Corrige.
>
> (*PPS*, II, p. 119)

In particular he complains about Henry V's overbearing soldiery ('cervicata cohors') and their disorderly behaviour in England which apparently so alienated the King from his people's affections that they were glad when he and his soldiers went abroad and sorry when they returned:

> Nam tuus adventus cunctis tristis perhibetur
> Jocundus tuus est exitus a patria.[13]

Also criticised are his grasping ministers ('avari . . . ministri'). But Elmham's is a single and muted voice. It was not until somewhat later in his reign, when the full weight of the heavy taxation necessary for financing the campaigns in France had been felt, that criticisms of Henry's rule were raised again. To a greater extent than probably any other medieval King he had the uncritical approval of his people.

Henry V immediately sought to unify the country by composing the troubles of the former reign. He restored the earldom of

Northumberland to Henry Percy, Hotspur's son. Richard of York, the son of Edmund Langley, who had plotted against Henry IV, was made Earl of Cambridge. Most notably, in December 1413, he had the body of Richard II brought from King's Langley to be buried in Westminster Abbey—a popular move and praised by Thomas Hoccleve in a poem of this year:

> See eek how our Kynges benignitee
> And louyng herte his vertu can bywreye.
> Our kyng Richard þat was yee may wel see,
> Is nat fled from his remembrancc awcyc.
> My wit souffysith nat to peyse and weye
> With what honour he broght is to this toun,
> And with his queene at Westmynstre in thabbeye
> Solempnely in Toumbe leid adoun.
>
> (MP, VIII, 33–40)

Nevertheless, there were a few small-scale conspiracies in the earlier part of his reign. In 1413, shortly after his accession, a conspiracy organized by a certain John Wightlock, once a groom in the household of Richard II, was discovered. He and his accomplices excited disorders against Henry V, as they had done against his father, and spread the rumour that Richard II was still alive and would return to claim the throne. It is probably with this conspiracy in mind that the MS Digby 102 author writes:

> Among oure self, god sende vs pes!
> Þerto eche man be boun:
> To letten fooles of here res,
> Stonde wiþ þe kyng, mayntene þe croun.
>
> (XII, 5–8)

The plot was ill-judged and absurd. It had little support and was easily detected. It did show, however, that there were a few people still who, for one reason or another, refused to accept the Lancastrian dynasty. This is implicit too in the much more serious Southampton plot of 1415. This was organized by Sir Thomas Grey, Richard, Earl of Cambridge, and Henry, Lord Scrope, Henry V's treasurer, who were to assassinate the King before he embarked to France. Henry Percy, the Earl of Northumberland, was to raise the north and either Richard II or the Earl of March was to be proclaimed King. But again this plot had little support and was betrayed and easily crushed. Contemporary writers hardly deal with it at all. A more momentous event was about to take place—the invasion of France, and the author of some contemporary verses in MS Cotton Vitellius D xii can spare it a few lines only:

> Lordes of thys lond oure Kyng gan sell
> For a mylyon of golde, as I here say.
> Therefore here travell was quyte ful well,
> They wold have made a quent affray.
> The Erle of Marche, the sothe to say,
> That ys grasyos in all degre,
> He warned the Kyng, that ys no naye,
> Ho he was solde certenly.
>
> (Nicolas, p. 306)

After the discovery of the plot the poet has a couplet on the justice of Henry's summary treatment of the conspirators:

> They that had hym sold, they song, wela way!
> Here lyves they lost full sone a none,

and then passes on to the more important topic of the invasion. The author of the verses on the same subject in BM MS Harley 565 treats the plot even more briefly.

The greatest domestic threat at this time came from the Lollard Rising of 1414. Why the Lollards should have rebelled at this particular juncture is not easy to appreciate. It may have been due, at least in part, to the increasing pressure brought to bear on unorthodoxy by the authorities. Lollards had been under attack for many years. In 1381, Wycliffe's teachings of the Eucharist were condemned at Oxford. In 1382 twenty-four propositions from his writings were condemned at Blackfriars by a council convened by the Archbishop of Canterbury, William Courtenay. Many of the Oxford Lollards recanted, but the heresy continued. In 1401 was enacted the statute 'of the burning of heretics'. In 1411 Thomas

E

Arundel, Courtenay's successor, visited the university of Oxford to make sure that it fully accepted the condemnation of Wycliffe's views. And the King fully supported Arundel's harsh thoroughness. This was not only because he appreciated the political advantage of Arundel's support, or because he feared the divisive nature of Lollardy. He was himself orthodox by conviction and took more than a usual monarch's interest in religious matters. He kept a close supervision over the details of services at his chapels, chose his bishops and confessors with care, honoured particular saints, visited recluses and shrines, and concerned himself with general moral and theological questions. Lollardy was a denial of much that he held most sacred. Contemporary writers celebrated his piety, urged him to suppress heresy and praised him for doing so:

> O verray sustenour
> And piler of our feith, and werreyour
> Ageyn the heresies bittir galle
> (*MP*, V, 12–14)

wrote Hoccleve in one place, and in another urges the English:

> God thanke, & for thy cristen Prince preye,
> Syn he, fo is to this Rebellioun:
> He, of thy soules helthe, is lok and keye.
> (*MP*, VIII, 22–4)

But the King found himself in a difficult position in 1413 when his personal friend, Sir John Oldcastle, was faced with charges of heresy which were backed by incontrovertible proof. Throughout Oldcastle's trial Arundel appears to have kept in close touch with Henry, who allowed the law to take its course but delayed proceedings in the hope that the Herefordshire knight would recant. This was normal treatment for convicted heretics. According to Hoccleve, Henry, while still Prince of Wales, had himself offered the same opportunity to the heretic Worcestershire tailor John Badby, who was burned at Smithfield in March 1410:

> My lorde þe prince—god him saue & blesse—
> Was at his deedly castigacioun,
> And of his soule hadde grete tendernesse,

Thristynge sore his sauacioun:
Grete was his pitous lamentacioun,
Whan þat þis renegat not wolde blynne
Of þe stynkyng errour þat he was inne.
(Regement, 295–301)

Oldcastle was naturally more generously treated than Badby. Henry even offered him a respite of forty days after his conviction in order that he could think things over, but Oldcastle, like Badby, had no intention of recanting. On 19 October 1413, assisted by a few friends, Oldcastle escaped from the Tower, where he had been imprisoned during his stay of execution, and immediately set about the organization of an armed rebellion.

Oldcastle had support in various parts of the country. Most of it derived from the artisan classes, but one or two knights and several clerics helped in the organization of the rising. This was timed for the night of Tuesday 9 January 1414 when the various bands of insurgents, who had been organized on a county to county basis, were to converge on London. The response to Oldcastle's call to arms was pitifully small, and those who answered it were easily intercepted by Henry's forces, which had been carefully deployed outside the capital. There was very little fighting. Most of the rebels managed to escape and made their ways back to the shires, but many were captured. The King, after his dilatoriness over Oldcastle, now acted quickly. On Wednesday 10 January a commission was appointed to look into the disturbance, and by 12 January sixty-nine prisoners had been found guilty. Next day, thirty-eight of these were executed. On 11 January a commission had been appointed to draw up lists of suspected fugitive Lollards and stay-at-home sympathizers. But, despite the swiftness of these counter-measures, Oldcastle himself escaped and was hidden and protected so well, first in London and then in various parts of the midlands and the west of England, that he eluded capture. How much the rising of 1414 was motivated by religious and how much by political considerations is not clear. It may not have been too clear even to the participants and certainly in the public enquiries which followed the rising the categories were blurred. Some of the charges brought against the captured rebels were political: they had plotted the death of the King and the overthrow of the nobility, attempted to subvert the Catholic faith and to destroy monasteries and churches. But others were specifically theological and related to Lollard denials of the efficacy of pilgrimages, the worship of images and the like. The manner of the executions also varied: all the convicted rebels were hanged as traitors, but some were also burned as heretics.

There is no evidence of support for Oldcastle among contemporary poets but their disapproval varies. As one would expect, criticism of Oldcastle often involves doctrinal as well as political questions. The dating of the anonymous *Defend Us From All Lollardy* from MS Cotton Vespasian B xvi has provoked some disagreement. But, from the forthright and harshly vengeful attitudes it embodies, it would be reasonable to assume that it was composed very shortly after the rising in 1414, when feelings against the Lollards ran highest. The author ridicules some characteristic Lollard attitudes—on pilgrimages and on the veneration of images —but really feels that the religious aspect of the rising was just a convenient pretext for the rebels:

> vnder colour of suiche lollynge,
> To shape sodeyn surreccion
> Agaynst oure liege lord kynge.
> *(HP, 64, 137–9)*

He considers the main supporters of the rebellion to have been the poor and socially alienated who saw it as an opportunity to redress social and political grievances:

> When beggars mow neþer bake ne brewe,
> ne have wherwith to borrow ne bie,
> þan mot riot robbe or reve,
> Vnder þe colour of lollardie.
>
> (61–4)

He regards Oldcastle simply as a traitor:

> Þat rereth riot for to ride
> Agayns þe kynge & his clergie,
> (37–8)

and, playing on his name, blames him for considerable political damage:

> An old castle draw al don
> hit is ful hard to rere hit newe.
> (57–8)

The poem urges firm action. Lollardy must be destroyed and the rebels punished. Of course, he exaggerates the seriousness of the situation, but in the early months of 1414 he was not alone in this.

The feeling of crisis soon passed. The King had modified his harshly repressive policy by 28 March 1414 when pardons were offered to all the rebels except for a dozen named traitors and those who were already in custody or on bail. Oldcastle, of course, headed this list of exceptions and large rewards were offered for his capture. But by 9 December 1414 the King was ready to pardon even him, if he surrendered himself. What determined the change of policy is not clear. It may be that he still hoped to win Oldcastle back to orthodoxy, but it was more likely dictated by political expediency. Henry was preparing to invade France and clearly did not want to have to worry about what Oldcastle may have been plotting in his absence. The offer was renewed on 18 February 1415 but met with no response, and Henry had to embark in August with the knowledge that the rebel leader was still at large. While Henry was in France Hoccleve wrote his long poem *To Sir John Oldcastle* which reflects the King's offer of pardon in that it seeks with all persuasion—learned references to the Roman emperors Theodosius, Constantine and Justinian, and quotations from St Augustine—to bring the Lollard leader to repentance and reconcilement with God and Henry V. Hoccleve shares the then fairly general opinion that the Lollards were a spent force, and reminds Oldcastle of it: 'Come on, whan yow list, yee shul reewe it deere' (*MP* II, 467). Nevertheless he takes his usual orthodox stand against heresy. Some of the doctrinal positions assumed by Lollard propagandists—questions on the moral position of the sinful priest, on Church property, the efficacy of auricular confession, pilgrimages and image worship—are discussed and refuted, at least to Hoccleve's satisfaction. Oldcastle himself is not presented here as vicious or wicked, but rather as tragically deluded and deceived by the 'sly coloured arguments' (281) of the heretics. Because of their promptings he has separated himself from God, become an enemy to Holy Church and stirred up rebellion against the King. But what seems to have been Hoccleve's most serious appeal was to Oldcastle's sense of duty as a knight, and his greatest regret is that Oldcastle has compromised his integrity by engaging in activities which are unfitting to a man of his social position. The MS Cotton Vespasian B xvi poet had said as much: 'hit is no gentel mannes game' (76) and Hoccleve elaborates on it. Knights should read books of chivalry, not engage in religious matters:

> Bewar Oldcastel & for Crystes sake
> Clymbe no more in holy writ so hie!
> Rede the storie of Lancelot de Lake,
> Or Vegece of the aart of Chiualrie,
> The Seege of Troie or Thebes thee applie
> To thynge þat may to thordre of knyght longe.
>
> (193–8)

By his activities he has alienated himself from his class:

> no man with thee holdith,
> Sauf cursid caitifs, heires of dirknesse.
>
> (14–15)

He neglects his real knightly duty which was to support the King in the French wars:

> Looke how our cristen Prince, our lige lord,
> With many a lord & knyght beyond the See,
> Laboure in armes & thow hydest thee!
> And darst nat come & shewe thy visage!
> O, fy, for shame how can a knyght be
> Out of thonur of this rial viage.
>
> (499–504)

But Oldcastle was as impervious to Hoccleve's persuasion as he was to the King's offers of pardon, and was not caught until 1417.

Henry V's premature death at Bois de Vincennes on 1 September 1422 came as a considerable shock to the English. His contemporaries thought of him as an impressive ruler. One chronicler considered him a 'noble prince and victoriouse kynge, flour in his tyme of Cristen chivalrie', another compared him to heroes of antiquity, and even the normally anti-English chronicler Chastellain feels able to commend his justness and impartiality.[14] Much the same impression is derived from contemporary verses. According to Lydgate he was

> of knyhthod loodesterr,
> Wis and riht manly, pleynly to termyne,
> Riht fortunat preevid in pes & werr,
> Gretly expert in marcial disciplyne,
> Able to stonde among the Worthi Nyne.
> *(Minor Poems*, II, 51, 197–201)

Elsewhere he speaks of Henry's 'worthiness', 'governaunce' and 'hy prowesse' but singles out his achievement as a 'worthi conqueror' of France:

> Iustly to bring worthi reames twayn
> Vndir oo crowne by descynt of lyne.
> *(Minor Poems*, II, 28, 215–16)

This was commonly the way in which he was remembered. But his domestic achievements—his firm action against Oldcastle and the Lollards and his religious foundations—did not go uncelebrated:

> Att his begyning, verament,
> He destroyed Lollards, and hem shent.
> Aftur he made religions at Shene,
> Syon, Ierusalem, and eke Bedleme.
> *(Minor Poems*, II, 51, 161–4)

John Hardyng, writing some years later, recalls the fact that he had administered the law with firmness and impartiality:

> Above all things he kept the law and peace
> Through all England, that no insurrection
> Nor riots then were . . .

Even when he was away in France, continues Hardyng, his reputation was so influential that England was safe and peaceful.[15] The English felt his loss severely and almost everyone must have looked to the future with some trepidation.

NOTES

[1] *Vita Ricardi* II ed. T. Hearne, 1729, pp. 133–4.

[2] *Historia Naturalis* viii, 32 and xxviii, 9.

[3] See E. F. Jacob, *The Fifteenth Century*, Oxford 1961, pp. 10–17 for a summary of the evidence and references.

[4] *English History in Contemporary Poetry*, 1913, p. 6.

[5] Quoted by Mabel Day and R. Steele ed. *Mum and the Sothsegger*, EETS OS 199, 1936, p. xxiii.

[6] Ed. J. Hall, *Poems of Laurence Minot*, Oxford 1897, p. 101.

[7] *English Chronicle* ed. J. S. Davies, London 1874, p. 32.

[8] *Translation*: 'The very mighty judge, no delay, no examination of the business, the hasty proving of the heavy sentence, a fearful sequence of events.'

[9] *Testamenta Eboracensia* ii, 231 quoted by Jacob, *op. cit.*, p. 62.

[10] See V. H. H. Green, *The Later Plantagenets*, 1955, pp. 258, 256.

[11] *Twenty Six Political and Other Poems*, EETS OS, 124, 1904, pp. xiii–xiv.

[12] *The Minor Poems of John Lydgate* ed. H. N. MacCracken, EETS OS, 192, 1934, II, 51, i, 190–6 and also 51, ii, 149–58.

[13] *Translations*: 'Correct the accustomed errors which now your court puts forth' . . . 'For your arrival is considered sad by everyone, your going from the country joyful.'

[14] For contemporary judgments of Henry V and references see Jacob, *op. cit.*, pp. 121–7.

[15] C. L. Kingsford ed. 'Extracts from the First Version of John Hardyng's Chronicle', *EHR* 27, 1912, p. 744. See also his article, *ibid.*, pp. 462–82.

5 : Domestic Affairs II : 1422-1455

THE thirty-three years from the death of Henry V in 1422 to the beginning of the civil wars in 1455 were if anything less disturbed than the previous twenty-three, yet a considerable amount of political verse was produced. Its concerns, however, are somewhat different. Whereas in the earlier period the personality and rule of Richard II, Henry IV and Henry V provided the main subject matter, in the later period Henry VI (partly because of his youth and partly through natural diffidence) played a comparatively unimportant role. His accession, coronation and marriage to Margaret of Anjou were perfunctorily celebrated by contemporary poets, but their main attention in these years was focussed upon the leading men of the Council—Cardinal Henry Beaufort, Humphrey, Duke of Gloucester, William de la Pole, Duke of Suffolk, and Richard, Duke of York.

Henry was less than a year old at his father's death. Difficulties began immediately, for the question of the rule of the country during his minority was a disputed one. The dangers facing any country ruled by a child were, at this period, almost proverbial. It represented a disruption of the natural order of things:

> Þere childe is kynge
> & clerke bysshop,
> And chorle reue
> all is greue.[1]

It is apparent that Henry V was aware of the dangers that his early death could produce, for during his last illness he strove to define the pattern of rule after him. The English-held part of France, except for Normandy which was to be controlled by John, Duke of

Bedford, were to be ruled during the minority by Philip, Duke of Burgundy, or, if Philip declined this (which he did), by Bedford. On his other brother, Humphrey, Duke of Gloucester, Henry V appears to have intended to confer some sort of regency in England. But the magnates suspected and distrusted the ambitions of Humphrey, and seem from the first to have been determined to limit his powers. In 1422 Humphrey claimed the governance of England 'as wel by the mene of birth as be the last wylle of the kyng that was'. He also claimed the custody of Henry VI. But the Council refused to allow this and declared, after much learned argument and searching for precedents, all his claims invalid. It was realized, however, that he had to have a high position. His title was to be Protector and Defender of the Realm and Church of England, but he was to assume this position only when Bedford was out of the country. His authority was also to be dependent on the Council, for though it was admitted he was 'chief of the Kynges Council' his appointment as Protector was not necessarily for the whole of the minority but could be terminated at any time by the Council.[2] The rule during Henry VI's minority was to be conciliar, but from the first there were latent, if not actual, divisions, for Humphrey never really accepted the restrictions placed on his power and sought constantly to break them.

Fears about the potential divisiveness of this situation possibly caused Lydgate to produce what is accepted as his only prose work. There is some dispute about the date of *The Serpent of Division*.[3] On the basis of one manuscript it has been ascribed to 1400, but the balance of evidence supports the more generally held view that it was composed shortly after the death of Henry V, perhaps in December 1422. It has been suggested that the piece was commissioned by Humphrey of Gloucester but there is no proof of this, and, in view of the theme of the tract, it is not likely. The piece is an account of the events leading up to the Roman civil war between Pompey and Julius Caesar, and beyond it to Caesar's death. It is based on a number of sources, principally a lost French version of Lucan's *Pharsalia* and chapters of Vincent of Beauvais' *Speculum Historiale*, but the emphasis of the story is Lydgate's own. As W. F. Schirmer has pointed out, it is not 'a humanistic vita of Caesar' but 'political propaganda developing out of what is in spirit and form a sermon'. The theme is conventional enough, but one to which Lydgate constantly returns: a kingdom is strong while united, but weak when divided. After a brief survey of Roman history as far as the dictators, Lydgate states his theme in unambiguous terms:

> And thus all þe while they weren of oon herte and of oon assente, and voide of variaunce withinne hemself, the noblesse of Rome flovred in prosperite; but als sone as fals covitise broughte Inne pride and vayne ambicion, the contagious serpent of Division eclipsed and appalled theire worthiness; concluding sothely as in sentence that every kingdome be division be conveied to his distruccion. (pp. 49–50)

Shortly after this he seeks to establish why the decline of a nation is inevitable. He isolates three reasons. A decline from prosperity to destruction is 'necessarie' because all things in nature live but for a time and then die, 'consuetudinarie' because Fortune's gifts may be enjoyed only for a time and 'voluntarie' because the sinful and misguided wills of men are in part the causes of their own misfortunes. The metaphysical aspects of mankind's inevitable suffering are not long dwelt upon. What interests Lydgate are the 'voluntarie' aspects of civil discord, and he emphatically attributes to the misguided wills of the dictators their own deaths and the ruin of Rome.

> And lete þe wise gouernours of euery londe and region make a merowre in here mynde of þis manly man Iulius and consideren in þer hertis þe contagious damages & þe importable harmes of devision, and lete hem seen avisely and take example how þe ambicious pride of Iulius, and þe fretynge envie of Pompeyus, and þe vnstawncheable gredy covetise of Marcus Crassus were chefe and primordiall cause firste of hire owne distruccion execute and complissched bi cruell deþe, and not onely þat þese þre abhomynable vices were cause of here owne deþe but occasion for many a þowsande oþer mo þan I can tell, the cite of Rome not onely made bare and bareyn of

þe olde richesis and spoiled of here tresowre on þe too side, but destitute and desolate bi deþe of here knitʒthod on þe toþer side, which me semyth owte Inow suffise to exemplifie what hit is to begynne a werre & specially to considre þe irrecuperable harmes of division. (pp. 65–6)

Lydgate is explicit as to his theme. He leaves no doubt either as to the particular audience he seeks to address. The opening words of the last quotation stress that he has the rulers and governers of lands in mind and catches up the earlier suggestion that 'all prudent prynces whiche have governaunce in provynces and regions schulde take ensample whate harme and damage is and how finale a destruccion is to bene devyded amonge hemselfe' (p. 58). In some manuscripts, three eight-line stanzas follow the prose to stress to 'lordes and prynces of renowne' that they should

> eschewe stryf and dissencion
> Within yowreself beth not contrarious,
> (p. 67)

but should make a 'merowre' of the story told in the prose. *The Serpent of Division* is, then, a 'mirror for princes' of a particular kind: a generalized warning that they should at all costs avoid the danger of civil dissension. Nothing overtly links it with the situation in England at the end of 1422, but, none the less, such a link may be assumed. And Lydgate's intention to stress the relevance of his theme to the English situation emerges from one significant alteration to his source. It is likely that the French translation which he used simply followed Lucan in briefly listing Britain as one of Julius Caesar's conquests. But Lydgate seems both to have expanded the reference and to have made his expansion relevant to his theme, for he attributes the subjugation of the Britons to internal dissentions between the King and the Duke of Cornwall. Caesar had been resisted until:

this manly King Cassibolan & Androgius the Duce of Cornewaile felle at debate among hemselfe; whereby I may conclude that whiles vnite & acorde stode vndefowled & vndividid in the bondis of Bretayne, þe myʒti conqueroure

Iulius was vnable and impotente to venquische hem. By whiche
example ȝe may evidently consideren & seen þat devision, liche
as is specified to forne, is original cause in prouynces &
regions of all destrucioun.   (pp. 50–1)

The emphatic repetition of this point about the disastrous consequences of dissent would suggest that Lydgate thought discord a
distinct possibility.

Surprisingly, the Council began well and the routine matters of
finance and administration seem to have been dealt with efficiently.
But it was not long before serious trouble broke out between
Humphrey, Duke of Gloucester, and Henry Beaufort, Bishop of
Winchester, a man who was probably the most powerful in the
Council, and who was certainly largely responsible for the con-
straints placed upon Humphrey as Protector. As early as 1425,
the armed adherents of these two councillors were facing each
other in the capital and John, Duke of Bedford, had to be called
back from France to reconcile them. There were genuine differences
of policy, particularly in the matter of the French war: Humphrey
was convinced of the efficacy of military activity but Beaufort
favoured a policy of peace. Basically, however, it was a struggle
for personal power, for each in his own way was a very ambitious
man. Though they clashed principally over domestic affairs both
had ambitions outside England. In 1424 Humphrey sought to
increase his wealth and acquire a foothold in Europe, by his
marriage to Jacqueline of Hainault and through an expedition to
the Low Counties to recover her lands. Though this expedition
proved a fiasco it does not appear to have damaged irrevocably
his prestige in England. Afterwards he confined himself principally
to domestic affairs. Beaufort had somewhat better success in
Europe, but his ambitions were related to ecclesiastical politics.
He became a cardinal in 1426, and in 1428–9 was given the task of
preaching the Bohemian crusade and raising forces in England.
When these forces, on the orders of the Council, were diverted
from the crusade to help reinforce the English in France, Beaufort
must have lost considerable prestige at the papal court, and the
death of Pope Matin V in 1431 saw a real end to his ambitions

outside England. Thereafter he turned his full attention back to English affairs. The Beauforts were the legitimized progeny of John of Gaunt and his mistress Catherine Swynford whom he had married in 1396. They were an extremely influential family in fifteenth-century politics. By 1422 Henry Beaufort had considerable political experience, having been Chancellor as early as 1404. He also possessed vast wealth, acquired from a varied assortment of ecclesiastical positions, particularly the bishopric of Winchester which he had held since 1405. During the minority of Henry VI, he was perhaps the richest man in England and the Crown was constantly in his debt. In addition, he was a much more astute politician than Humphrey and exploited to the full his advantages. Thus it was the Beaufort faction in the Council which usually dominated.

Henry Beaufort, however, seems to have claimed little of the attention of those contemporaries who treated the events of Henry VI's reign in verse. He is mentioned, somewhat incongruously, among the English heroes of the French wars, in a poem written shortly after his death, but he appears to have been of only casual interest to this writer.[4] On the other hand, the personality and achievements of Humphrey of Gloucester received enormous attention in contemporary poetry. There are a number of possible reasons for this. His affable personality and forthright nationalistic policies apparently endeared him to many, in particular the common people of the capital. His exploits tended to be of the sensational kind. But he also undoubtedly profited from his generous literary patronage. That his interest in learning and literature was genuine is beyond doubt. His encouragement of Italian scholars and his assiduous collecting of books make him one of the most important figures in the spread of humanistic learning in England. This, and his generosity to English authors won for him fulsome tributes, such as Lydgate's:

> Off hih lettrure I dar eek off hym telle
> And treuli deeme that he doth excelle
>
> In vndirstondyng, alle othir off his age,
> And hath gret ioie with clerkis to comune,

And no man is mor expert off language,
Stable in study alwey he doth contune,
Settyng a-side alle chaungis of Fortune;
And wher he loueth, yiff I shal not tarie
Withoute cause ful loth he is to varie.

Duc of Gloucestre men this prynce calle,
And nat withstandyng his staat & dignite,
His corage never dothe appalle
To studie in bookis off antiquite,
Therin he hath so gret felicitie
Vertuously hymsilff to ocupie,
Off vicious slouthe to haue the maistrie.

(Fall of Princes, I, 384–99)

It may be, however, that Humphrey was not unaware of the political benefits of the patronage of writers. It was a frequent claim of humanist authors that their art could confer immediate glory and lasting reputation on their patrons. And it may be, as Roberto Weiss suggests, that Humphrey's motives in his patronage were in part dictated by a desire for self aggrandisement and political advantage.[5] It has been suggested that he also commissioned Frulovisi's *Vita Henrici Quinti* to support his war policy by recalling the glorious campaigns of his brother's reign. It is possible, too, that in his patronage of Lydgate, the premier English poet of the age, Humphrey was seeking to procure for himself contemporary glory through literature.

Whatever the reason, the triumphs and failures of Humphrey's varied political career were a frequent subject for contemporary verse writers, not all of whom were patronized by him. For the most part he was handsomely treated. His deeds at Agincourt, which perhaps first brought him into public prominence, were celebrated by the author of *Henry V's Invasion of France* (1415):

The Duk of Gloucestre, that is no nay,
That day full worthyly he wroughte,
On every syde he made good way
The Frensshemen faste to grounde he brought,

(Nicolas p. 323)

and also by the author of the fragmentary verses on *The Battle of Agincourt* (1415):

> The Duke of glowcestre also þat tyde
> Manfully, with his mayne,
> Wondes he wrought þer wondere wyde.
>
> (*HP*, 27, 9–11)

On Henry V's second expedition he seems to have been no less successful and in 1422 Hoccleve calls to mind his deeds of valour: how in 1417 'Of Constantyn he wan the cloos and yle', how in 1418 he performed well at the siege of Cherbourg and in 1419 at Rouen. It is impossible, says Hoccleve, taking refuge in a conventional modesty formula, to relate all Humphrey's military achievements:

> ffor to reherce or tell in special
> Euery act þat his swerd/in steel wroot there,
> And many a place/elles I woot nat al;
> And thogh euery act come had to myn ere,
> To yepresse hem my spirit wolde han fere,
> Lest I his thank par chaunce mighte abregge
> Thurgh vnkonnynge if I hem sholde allegge.
>
> (*MP*, xxi, 582–8)

He finds further evidence for Humphrey's distinction in an elaborate bilingual pun on his name. Hoccleve imagines that his name was given to him by the god Mars ('Humphrey' is equivalent to the French 'Homme ferai' which Hoccleve glosses 'Man make I shal, in englissh is to seye' 597) in token that he should become a man noted for 'martial' achievements. In fact, Hoccleve continues, he is so pre-eminently the epitome of knightly valour that his deeds ought to be set down as examples to others:

> To cronicle his actes wer a good deede
> ffor they ensaumple mighte, and encorage
> fful many a man/for to taken heede
> How for to gouerne hem in the vsage
> Of armes. . . .
>
> (*Ibid.*, 603–7)

Implicitly these stanzas suggest that Humphrey's achievement was limited: Hoccleve speaks only of military glory. None the less, the praise is lavish. But what Hoccleve says should be weighed against what he reveals about his relationship to Humphrey:

> Next our lord lige, our kyng victorious,
> In al this wyde world/lord is ther noon
> Vnto me so good ne so gracious,
> And haath been swich/yeeres ful many oon.
>
> (554–7)

In what ways Humphrey had been 'good' and 'gracious' is not now clear. But it is probable that he had at some time extended his patronage to Hoccleve. In fact, the poem in question may have been written for him (lines 701–14) and clearly his patronage is an important factor.

The other major court poet of this time, John Lydgate, was even more closely involved with Humphrey. In 1422 he wrote a poem celebrating the Duke's approaching marriage with Jacqueline of Hainault. That such a union was not politically well advised and was almost certain to cause serious trouble between Philip of Burgundy and the English cannot have escaped Lydgate. Nor can he have been unaware that Jacqueline, in the opinion of many, was guilty of bigamy, for her husband John of Brabant was still living and the annulment of their marriage, of which there is much mention, does not seem to have been valid. None the less, the poem dexterously avoids all controversial topics and is flatteringly favourable. Lydgate hopes that the match may bring together England and the lands belonging to Jacqueline:

> Þat Duchye of Holand by hool affeccoun
> May beo allyed with Brutus Albyoun,
> (*Minor Poems*, II, 26, 55–6)

and cites instances of other marriages which have produced friendship and unity between two countries. He continues by praising, in extravagant terms, the physical beauty and moral virtue of Jacqueline and by equating her with heroines of antiquity. Humphrey comes in for similar treatment:

> Thoroughe al þis worlde oon þe best knyght,
> And best pourveyed of manhood and of might,
> In pees and werre thoroughe his excellence,
> And is also of wisdam and prudence
> Most renommed.
>
> (123-7)

His love of religion, philosophy and poetry is mentioned and he is also compared with a list of heroes of antiquity. There is no evidence to prove that this poem was commissioned by Humphrey, but it would be surprising if it were not.

There seems to have been, none the less, some genuine public affection in England for Jacqueline. This became apparent in 1428. At this time she was held a prisoner by Philip of Burgundy, and though Humphrey had not entirely abandoned his attempts to win Hainault, his enthusiasm for the project appeared markedly diminished. In 1427 money was raised to equip a force to recover Hainault. Both the Council and public opinion were in favour of the project but Humphrey withdrew at the last minute, under pressure from his brother John of Bedford, who was sensitive to the damage it would do to the precarious Anglo-Burgundian alliance. Humphrey, in any case, had for the previous few years been consoling himself with Eleanor Cobham, once a lady-in-waiting to Jacqueline and now his mistress. After the Pope had issued a bull, on 9 January 1428, declaring the marriage of Jacqueline and John of Brabant valid and any other marriage contracted by the former in the lifetime of the latter to have been invalid, Humphrey found himself free of any ties and could legalize his own relations with Eleanor.

His conduct of the whole affair offended contemporary opinion and he became the object of much censure. Several contemporary chroniclers voiced their disapproval. So, by implication, did the mayor and aldermen of London, who appeared before Parliament with letters from Jacqueline requesting their aid. They declared that the nation ought to rescue her, and offered to do what they could to help. At about the same time a deputation of London women also appeared before Parliament, censuring the Duke for neglecting his wife, for allowing her to remain in captivity and for living in adultery with another woman 'to the ruin of himself, the kingdom and the marital bond'.[6] A contemporary author, perhaps Lydgate, added his own voice to these protests in a poem entitled *Complaint for my Lady of Gloucester* (1428). Here he stresses how

> Ryche and pore of al þis reme
> With hole hert and al lownesse
> Hem recomaunden to þat pryncesse
> (*Minor Poems*, II, 27, 115–17)

because 'She is beloued so entierely/Thorughe al þe londe' (123–4). Perhaps he is alluding to the petition of the women of London by revealing that he has

> Herde in alle citees and alle townes,
> Howe wymmen made þeyre orysouns
> Desyrouse þat pryncesse to see,
> And for hire comyng raunsoned to be.
> (81–4)

He repeats the frequently reiterated charge of witchcraft against Eleanor Cobham and her entourage, who are depicted as a mermaid and witches:

> Þey were of courage serpentyne
> By apparence of looke and sight
> Besy to bowe and tenclyne,
> With al þeyre power and þeyre might,
> Þe prynces hert ageynst al right,
> His noblesse night and day to trouble
> His hert in love to make hit double.
> (50–6)

This does not look like the product of the patronage system. It is altogether a very circumspect performance and mentions no names, though its intentions are clear enough. It is possible that W. F. Schirmer is right in thinking that Lydgate had the poem circulated anonymously.[7] Certainly it is not ascribed to Lydgate in contemporary manuscripts, and is probably not his.

This unpopularity was followed in the next year by Humphrey's loss of his title of Protector. On 5 November 1429, Henry VI was crowned King of England at Westminster Abbey. Indirectly, events in France made this coronation necessary. The Dauphinist forces had recently succeeded in the relief of Orléans and had won a victory at Patay. Public opinion in France, moreover, was moving in favour of Charles VII who had been crowned at Rheims on 18 July. John of Bedford needed a propagandist counterweight to these successes, something which emphasized the reality of the Lancastrian dual monarchy, and he decided that Henry VI should be taken to France and crowned there. The English coronation was thus somewhat hastily arranged, but nevertheless, as contemporary descriptions show, it was the usual splendid affair. Some celebration verses were produced but they are, for the most part, the uneasy performances one would expect. The situation abroad was serious and it would be some years before Henry VI, who was only seven years old, could exert any real influence. So it was with anxious glances at events in France and frequent regretful thoughts of the glorious reign of Henry V, that contemporary poets wrote. Typical are the opening lines of some indifferent verses from British Museum MS Lansdowne 285:

> Holde up oure yong kyng, *ave benigna*,
> And sende us peas in oure londe, *ave regina*.
> *Mater, nunc* bright bee thy beamys,
> Moodir of mercy, save bothe reamys;
> See to oure innocent, oure crowne may be gladder,
> Holde up oure lorde that nevir sigh his ffadir,
> Ne the fadir his sone reynyng in his londes;
> Grete nede have we to kepe peas amonge us.
>
> (*PPS*, II, p. 146)

Lydgate, in his many productions of this year, sounds a similar note. His *Ballade to King Henry VI upon his Coronation* (1429) initially stresses the young King's lineage:

> Royal braunche descendid from twoo lynes
> Of Saynt Edward and of Saynt Lowys . . .
>
> (*Minor Poems*, II, 31, 9–10)

—part of Lydgate's normal justification of the dual monarchy. Lydgate continues to advise him 'Heretykes and Lollardes for to oppresse' (82), and to hope that he will attain to the chivalric and personal qualities of a whole list of heroes of antiquity. He urges him above all to seek to emulate his father, 'myrrour of manhede', and his 'blessid moder';

> With him in knyghthode to haue excellence,
> Lyke þy moder in vertuous goodnesse;
> And lyche hem booþe grounde þy conscyence
> To love þy Lord in parfyte stabulnesse,
> Goode lyve and longe alle vyces to represse,
> Love of þy lieges, pees and obeyssaunce,
> With alle vertues þat longe to gentylnesse
> Þy right reioyssing of England and of Fraunce.
>
> (113–20)

The most popular and perhaps the most appropriate way of celebrating his coronation took the form of a prayer for the future well-being of the young King. Lydgate contributed the grave and stately *Prayer for King, Queen and People* (?1429), the Envoy of which mentions the King specifically:

> A lorde! Amonge haue a Remembraunce
> On sixt Henry, thyn oone chose knyght,
> Born tenheryte the Regioun of Fraunce,
> By trew discent and by title of ryght,
> Now good lorde conserve him thurgh thy myght,
> And ay preserve under thy myghty honde,
> Him and his moder, thy peple and thy londe.
>
> (*Minor Poems*, I, 41, 57–63)

Most of the verses on Henry VI's coronation appear to have been exercises in propaganda. Since Humphrey of Gloucester was responsible for making the arrangements for the coronation, it may be supposed that some were commissioned by him. It is difficult to estimate how realistic the pious hopes expressed in these verses were felt to be. Few, presumably, would have shared the optimism of the Shropshire priest John Audelay:

> On him schal fal þe prophece
> Þat haþ ben sayd of kyng herre;
> Þe hole cros wyn or he dye,
> Þat crist halud on goodfryday.
>
> Al wo & werres he schal acese,
> & set all reams in rest & pese,
> & turne to cristyndam al heþynes—
> Now grawnt him hit so be may.
>
> Pray we þat lord is lord of all,
> To saue our kyng, his reme ryal;
> & let neuer myschip vppon him falle
> Ne false traytoure him to betray.
>
> (HP, 41, 45–56)

Medieval political prophecies were not notable for their accuracy, but the extent to which this one was mistaken might have amazed even the most pessimistic of Audelay's contemporaries.

Humphrey of Gloucester's prestige in England recovered from the setbacks of 1428 and 1429, when the absence of the King and Beaufort's interest in papal affairs gave him his chance. During his period as Regent he enhanced his reputation by firm action against all who threatened the peace of the realm, particularly Lollards. Just how much his stock had improved may be deduced from the praise of him in Lydgate's *Fall of Princes* (1431–8), though it must be remembered that this was commissioned by Humphrey himself. The political aspect of Lydgate's eulogy covers both Humphrey's energetic and able government of the country:

> Eek in this land, I dar afferme a thyng:
> There is a prynce ful myhti off puissaunce,
> A kyngis sone and vncle to the kyng
> Henry the Sexte, which is now in Fraunce,
> And is lieftenant, and hath the gouernaunce
> Off our Bretayne, thoruh whos discrecioun
> He hath conserued in this regioun,
>
> Duryng his tyme, off ful hih prudence,
> Pees and quiete and sustened riht;

> Yit natwithstandyng his noble prouidence,
> He is in deede proued a goode knyght
> Eied as Argus with resoun and forsiht,
>> (*Fall of Princes*, I, 372–83)

and also his firm suppression of heretics:

> hooli chirche meyntenyng in deed
> That in this land no Lollard dar abide.
>> (I, 402–3)

He is also praised for his love of learning and books. Perhaps nowhere was Humphrey's patronage of letters more successful. This work appears to have been extremely popular, for more than thirty manuscripts, some of them highly decorated, have survived. But probably his greatest triumph was the relief of Calais in 1436 and the punitive expedition into Flanders which followed it. Though the chronicler Hardyng belittles the achievement:

> The protectour with his flete at Calys then
> Did lande, and rode in Flaunders a little waye
> And little did to counte a manly man,[8]

most contemporary poets celebrate his decisive action, skill and bravery. One writer considers that the Flemish raised the siege of Calais because 'thay had verray knowyng' that Humphrey was coming to relieve the town (*HP* 28, 157). Another sets his bravery against the cowardice of Philip of Burgundy:

> He soght the in flandres with swerd and with fyre,
> Nyne daies brennyng, no pees did he make.
> Where art thou, Phelippe, whan wiltow þy swerd shake.
>> (*HP*, 30, 99–101)

So great was the fear that Humphrey caused, says another poet, that the enemies of England hid themselves and did not dare to oppose him:

> For fere they turned bake and hyede faste,
> Milorde of Gloucestre made hem so agaste
> Wyth his commynge and sought hem in here londe

> And brente and slowe as he hadde take on honde,
> So that oure enmyse durste not byde nor stere;
> They fledde to mewe, they durste no more appere.
>
> (*Libelle*, 294–9)

Never again was Humphrey to achieve such a spectacular success. On his victorious return to London he was given a splendid reception. He had not only made Calais safe, but, more important in the minds of the English, he had exacted some sort of vengeance for the unforgiveable treachery of the Flemish.

After his success of 1436, Humphrey seems to have taken less part in political affairs. Certainly, over the next few years his influence in the King's Council considerably declined, though he was still honoured and treated respectfully by his contemporaries. In 1441, however, there occurred an event which was to taint his whole reputation and finally disgrace and discredit him. On 16 July of this year two obscure clerics—an Oxford priest, Roger Bolingbroke, and a canon of St Stephen's Westminster, Thomas Southwell—were imprisoned in the Tower accused of using necromancy to procure the death of Henry VI. It was, ostensibly, an event of no great political importance, but under examination it emerged that Eleanor Cobham, Duchess of Gloucester, had been the instigator of their necromancy. From then on it was no longer a simple question of heresy. Despite two attempts to avoid arrest, Eleanor was brought to trial and found guilty, on various charges of heresy and witchcraft, which she refused to attempt to disprove, and of treason, which she denied. It seems probable that she did indeed interest herself in necromancy: her connection with Bolingbroke, who certainly did, was proved; and it had been widely said that she had used magical arts to win Humphrey's affections in the first place. That her activities were treasonable is more difficult to believe, but, to contemporaries, it seems, these charges were credible.

Eleanor, before her marriage to Humphrey, had been of no great social standing, but afterwards she had become ambitious and proud. She was, at this time, first lady of the kingdom and, had the young Henry VI died, Humphrey would have succeeded to the throne and Eleanor would have been Queen. There was some public sympathy for her, but most contemporary authors saw her fall as due to overweening pride and ambition. According to one:

> Thys ladye was soo proude & highe of harte
> that she hur-selffe thought pereles of estate,
> And yet higher fayn she wold haue starte
> Butt sodenlye she fell, as was hur fate.
>
> (*HP*, 74, 25–8)

And the anonymous author of the remarkable *Lament of the Duchess of Gloucester* (1441) puts a similar admission into her own mouth:

> 'With welth, wele, and worthinesse,
> I was be-sett on euery syde;
> of glowcestre I was duchesse,
> of all men I was magnifyed.
> As lucifer fell downe for pride,
> So fell I from felicite.'
>
> (*HP*, 72, 25–30)

To the author of these verses, Eleanor's was an example of a 'wheel of fortune' tragedy ('who may the whele of Fortune trowe?' 21) and, in accordance with this theory, he interprets her career. She tells of her former humble origins ('I that was browght up of noght' 11), her prosperity as Humphrey of Gloucester's wife ('That had all thyng vndyr my cure' 43) and finally of the circumstances of her fall and her present wretchedness ('ffor now am I worst of all' 47). The author was aware of the details of her trial and penance, for he makes her speak of how she had to appear 'Byfore the counsell of thys lond/At westmynster vpon a day' (73–4), and how she was saved from death only by the intervention of Henry VI:

> 'The law wold I had ben slayne,
> And sum men dyd ther diligence.
> That worthi prynce of hys prudence
> Of my persone had pyte.'
>
> (83–6)

She then 'cam byfore the spiritualte' who 'examynd me of all my lyfe' (92), ordered her to do penance 'Thorow-owt london in many a strete' (97) and finally imprisoned her for life. But the lasting impression left by the poem is of pity for Eleanor's 'dulfull destiny'. She relates herself how she has lost not only all her possessions and her social position, but also all happiness ('All erthly ioy is fro me gone' 4) and all her companions ('all my frendys fro me thei flee' 6). Whether or not the author of the verses shared this pity is difficult to estimate. The poem is certainly not vindictive, but it does include, in the Cambridge University Library MS Hh. iv 12 version hitherto quoted, three stanzas in which Eleanor admits that she 'gef credence' to a cleric and 'wrowght agayne all course of kynd' (53) by trying to kill the King:

> 'Owre souerayn lord and kyng with crowne
> Hym to distroye was owre entent.'
>
> (59–60)

This reverses the denial of treason made during her trial ('I wroght treson' 65). These stanzas are omitted, along with another in which she admits to cruelty to the poor ('Of poore men I had no pite' 38), from the later version of the poem preserved in Balliol College MS 354, the commonplace book of the London grocer, Richard Hill. R. H. Robbins thinks that 'the variations are not important'.[9] But they can scarcely be the accidental omissions of a careless copyist, and it looks as though the Balliol College MS 354 text is the product of a certain amount of editing by someone who considered Eleanor innocent both of treason and of the oppression of the poor.

The conviction of his wife, and particularly her public disgrace, hastened the political ruin of Humphrey of Gloucester. His opponents did not engineer the affair, but they exploited it, knowing that by striking at Eleanor they were also discrediting her husband. One chronicler involves him in the affair in the following way:

> But then he fell into a foul error
> Moved by his wife Eleanor Cobham
> To truste her so men thought he was to blame.[10]

Nowhere is there any formal suggestion that Humphrey was

directly implicated and he was careful to involve himself as little as possible. Henry VI himself, it appears, showed some kindness to Eleanor in mitigating her punishment, but the affair inevitably alienated Humphrey from him. Thus, when in 1443 the question of arranging for Henry VI's marriage arose, it was settled without Humphrey's advice. In charge of the negotiations was William de la Pole, Earl and later Duke of Suffolk. The object was Margaret, daughter of King René of Anjou who was also titular King of Naples, Sicily and Jerusalem. By this match, Suffolk hoped to procure a peace settlement with France. It is difficult to estimate how popular the marriage was when, in 1445, Margaret arrived with her entourage in England. There seem to have been few dissenting voices, but this might simply indicate a general lack of interest. There are some 'official' verses by Lydgate, which were doubtless commissioned, written to accompany the pageants and tableaux set up in London to welcome Margaret.[11] They express the wish that

> Twixt the Reawmes two Englande and ffraunce
> Pees shal approche Rest and Vnite
> Mars sette aside with alle hys cruelte
> Which to longe hath troubled the Reawmes tweyne,
> (10–13)

but for the most part they consist of elaborate praise for the young Princess, and offer a hopeful welcome:

> Moost cristen Princesse by influence of grace
> Doughter of Iherusalem oure plesaunce
> And ioie welcome as euere princesse was
> With hert entier and hool affiaunce
> Causer of Welth ioie and abundaunce
> Youre cite youre poeple youre subgites alle
> Welcome welcome welcom vn-to you calle.
> (1–7)

At the time Suffolk derived great credit from the negotiations but, in retrospect, feelings on the matter were very different. Margaret did not prove to be a popular Queen, and none of the expected political advantages of the match materialized. Some twenty years later one chronicler could call it 'A dere mariage for þe reame of Englond; ffor it is knowen verely þat, for to haue hir was delyuered þe Duchie of Angeo & þe Erldome of Maign, which was þe key to Normandie, for þe French men tentre. And Above þis, þe said Marquys of Southfolk axed in playn parlement A fyftenth & an half for to feche hir out of Fraunce.'[12]

After her marriage, Margaret naturally associated herself with the court faction led by Suffolk, and, if H. N. MacCracken's conjecture is right,[13] she may even have been the recipient of one of Suffolk's elegant verses declaring his allegiance to 'þe floure' (perhaps with a pun on 'Margaret' and 'Marguerite'):

> Myn hert ys set, and all myn hole entent,
> To serve this floure in my most humble wyse
> As faythfully as can be thought or ment,
> Wyth out feynyng or slouthe in my servyse.
>
> (1–4)

The court faction was supported by former Beaufort adherents and predictably clashed over foreign policy with Humphrey of Gloucester. By this time he could have been little more than an irritant to them, but none the less the Suffolk faction planned to overthrow and destroy him through fabricated charges of treason. By 1447 they had succeeded in stripping Humphrey of most of his power and influence. He was alienated from the King, who denied him access to the court, and he was removed from the Privy Council. At the parliament of Bury in 1447, Suffolk laid charges against Humphrey, who was arrested before he had a chance to answer them. He died in captivity shortly afterwards on 23 February 1447, perhaps from natural causes, though there is a suspicion, shared by many contemporary writers, that he was murdered. The immediate reaction seems to have been that he died from natural causes: that the grief and shock occasioned by his arrest and disgrace overthrew an already weakened constitution. As one contemporary poet put it:

> For shame and angwishe off which, Ieloussye
> I-toke hym sone after, & soo lowe brought hym downe
> That In short while after I-caused hym to dye.
>
> (*HP*, 74, 63–5)

Certainly there is no hint of suspicion that Humphrey may have been murdered in the *Epitaph for the Duke of Gloucester* (1447), sometimes attributed to Lydgate. If the poem is not by Lydgate, it certainly follows Lydgate's usual line in its praise of Humphrey's various achievements: his strong foreign policy;

> He hath with his wisdom, while hym lasted breth,
> And with his richesse made the grete hete
> Of oure enemyes to kele, wold they werre or trete,
> (*HP*, 73, 19–21)

his firm but just administration at home:

> Neuer man had more 3ele, as I vndrestond,
> Ne redyer to redresse alle transgressis by and by;
> I dare wele say it sat his hert so ny,
> (75–7)

and his piety and anti-heretical activities:

> Behold of thy chirche the myghti piler stronge,
> Euer to withstande and redy to bataile;
> Ageyne the chirche, enemys he wold suffre no wronge
> Vnto hir to be done, whiles he myght aught availe.
> (81–4)

For the rest it is a lament for his death and a plea for Christ and Mary to intercede for his soul. R. H. Robbins thinks that the refrain 'have mercy on hym buryed in this sepulture' indicates that a copy of the verses was hung on Humphrey's tomb.[14] It is certainly a highly formal and decorous performance and more of a prayer than a political document.

The question of Humphrey's death, however, came up again a few years later, in 1450. Complicity in Humphrey's murder was one of the accusations levelled against the by then unpopular court party and its leader William de la Pole, Duke of Suffolk. In 1447 Humphrey's enemies had taken what steps they could to persuade public opinion that he had died from natural causes: stories were circulated to this effect, and his body was publicly exposed so that all could see it was uninjured. But in 1450, Suffolk was impeached

before Henry VI as the 'cause and laborer of the arrest, empris-
onyng and fynall destruction of the most noble valliant true Prince,
your right obeisant uncle the Duke of Gloucester'. Public opinion
had moved in this direction also. The commons of Kent, who
marched to London with Jack Cade in the same year, demanded,
amongst other things, the punishment of those traitors who had
'counterfeytyd and imagyned' Humphrey's death.[15] In contemporary
verses too, the fact that Humphrey had been murdered is more than
hinted at. One author, exultant at Suffolk's fall, blames him
directly for the death of Humphrey (who is referred to by his
cognizance). He also alludes to Suffolk's treatment of Humphrey's
supporters, who were arrested with him and taken to Tyburn to
be hanged, but were pardoned at the last moment:

> Þis fox at bury slowe oure grete gandere;
> Þerfore at tyborn mony mon on hym wondere.
>
> (HP, 75, 17–18)

In the Lambeth MS 306 version of another poem of this year, The
Death of the Duke of Suffolk, there appear some lines which even
name Humphrey's murderers and allude to the manner of his
death:

> Pulford and Hanley that drownyd ye Duke of Glocestar
> As two traytors.[16]

Another poem of about the same date On Bishop Boothe also
alludes to this suspicion. This author gives the story a curiously
appropriate expression by punning on Suffolk's family surname
Pole as meaning 'pool':

> Hit is a shrewde pole, pounde or a welle,
> That drownythe the dowghty, and bryngethe hem abeere.
> And alle is for the lordane lovithe no pere.
>
> (PPS, II, 228–9)

Here the word 'Abeere' probably means 'on their bier' and if so,
the allusion is certainly to the exposing of Humphrey's body after
his death. Later in 1462, the author of A Political Retrospect
includes among the 'myschyefȝ' of the reign of Henry VI, Humphrey's supposed murder:

The good duc of gloucestre in the season
Of the parlement at Bury beyng,
Was put to deth; and ay sith gret mornyng
Hath ben in Ingeland, with mony a scharp schoure,
ffalshode, myschyef, secret synne upholdyng,
Which hath caused in Engeland endele3 langoure.

(*HP*, 93, 35–40)

Whether he was murdered or not, it was in some sense true that Suffolk had caused him to die. And Humphrey's death helped to bring down Suffolk and the court party.

William de la Pole, Duke of Suffolk, had had control of the ruling faction since before the death of Henry Beaufort. By 1450 he was extremely unpopular in the country at large though still trusted implicitly by both Henry VI and Queen Margaret. The reasons for his unpopularity are complex. He was certainly a grasping and self-seeking politician. He had inherited extensive lands in East Anglia and, in his own lifetime, added considerably to his wealth and influence. Between 1445 and 1450 he had become Chamberlain of England, Captain of Calais, Warden of the Cinque Ports, Constable of Dover Castle, chief justice of Chester, Flint and North Wales, chief steward of the duchy of Lancaster north of the Trent, steward and surveyor of mines over all England. In handling the local administration of his estates and in his relations with his neighbours, he appears often to have employed dubious methods. In 1455 Sir John Fastolf set down how he had been

vexed and troubled seth he came last into this lande by the myght and power of the Duke of Suffolk and by the labour of his counseill and servaunts in divers wyses, and in gret oppressions, grevous and outrageous amerciemants and manye grete horrible extorcions . . .   (*Paston Letters*, No. 309)

and the correspondence of the Paston family gives ample illustration of these charges. To many, Suffolk was an upstart who had enriched himself too quickly and by dubious means. Nor was his foreign policy popular. He himself had served with some distinction in the French wars yet his policy, like Henry Beaufort's, was one of conciliation. He had attempted to seal a peace by organizing the marriage of Henry VI and Margaret. This came to be looked upon as a mistake. He had also ceded large territories in France to her impoverished father René, which offended English patriotic feeling. Had his policy worked, Suffolk might have survived. But despite his efforts a final peace was never settled, and when, in 1449, the truce with France was broken by an English attack on Fougères and the wars reopened with disastrous English losses in Normandy Suffolk was largely held responsible.

Suffolk's sensational fall from power and his brutal death predictably aroused much public interest. Contemporary poets show themselves to have been interested in various aspects of the affair but are uniformly hostile to Suffolk. In the poem *On the Popular Discontent at the Disasters in France* (1449), mentioned in a previous chapter, it is implied that Suffolk was in part responsible for the losses in France since he had failed to give Sir John Talbot, Earl of Shrewsbury, the necessary financial support:

> he is bownden that oure dore shuld kepe—
> That is Talbot oure goode dogge.
>
> (*PPS*, II, 222)

Another poem, perhaps written in the early months of 1450 and mainly concerned with attacking William Booth, Bishop of Coventry and Lichfield, also expresses misgivings about Suffolk:

> God kepe oure kyng ay, and gide hym by grace,
> Save hym fro Southefolkes, and frome his foois alle.
>
> (*PPS*, II, 228)

It also blames him for the murder of Humphrey of Gloucester. Dating from about the same time are some tail-rhyme verses from Cotton Rolls ii 23, written in the form of a 'bill', which urge the King to assert himself and advise him and his council to beware of the treachery of Suffolk and his followers:

> Be ware, kyng henre, how þou doos;
> Let no lenger þy traitours go loos—
> þey will neuer be trewe.
>
> (*HP*, 86, 43–5)

The author seems to have been a commoner and his political impotence against the court faction ('We can do them no griffe' 21) sharpens his sense of frustration at the way the country was ruled. The King's advisers, he says, do not tell him the truth about the state of England:

> Trowth and pore men ben appressed,
> And myscheff is nothyng redressed;
> þe kyng knowith not all.
> (13–15)

He is disturbed too about the poverty of the King in comparison with the wealth of his ministers and lords:

> So pore a kyng was neuer seen
> Nor richere lordes all by-dene
> (25–6)

—a common enough complaint at this time, for as a contemporary chronicler put it '. . . alle the possessyons and lordeshyppes that perteyned to the croune the kyng had yeve awey, some to lordes and some to other simple persones so that he had almoste noughte to lefe onne.'[17] For this state of affairs he blames specific members of the court faction and, most of all, Suffolk himself. Here are the familiar charges that Suffolk had been responsible for the loss of English possessions in France and for the reopening of the war:

> Suffolk normandy hath swold.
> to get hyt agayn he is bold.
> how acordeth þese to in on?
> (31–3)

Here too are the familiar suspicions of Suffolk's ambition:

> But yif the commyns of Englond
> Helpe þe kyng in his fond,
> Suffolk woll bere þe crown
> (40–2)

—though it was usually said that he wanted the crown not for himself but for his son.

The commons laid formal charges against Suffolk on 7 February.

F

Mostly they related to his foreign policy. It was said that he had conspired with the French for the invasion of England; plotted to remove Henry VI and set his own son John on the throne; incited Charles VII to reopen the war; ceded Maine and Anjou to the French; given them information about England's defences; and withheld money to enable English armies to fight in France. Some of these charges were also appearing on contemporary verses. Suffolk's arrest and committal in the Tower prompted some exultant verses preserved in Cotton Rolls ii 23 entitled *Arrest of the Duke of Suffolk* (1450). The poem is unusual in that its basic imagery is taken from hunting. There is also reference to Suffolk's cognizance. Sometimes he appears as a trapped fox ('Now is the fox drevin to hole!' *HP* 75, 1), and at others as 'Iack napys' after his badge, which was a clog and chain of the sort attached to tame apes. The result is a not very well integrated artistic whole. Suffolk's arrest by John, Lord Beaumont, is celebrated in a mixture of the two images:

> Wherefore Beaumownt, þat gentill rache,
> Hath brought Iack napis in an evill cache
> (21–2)

—'rache' meaning a kind of hunting dog. The familiar charges are made against him by means of either image: he had caused the death of Humphrey of Gloucester ('þis fox at bury slowe oure grete gander' 17), and had hindered the activities of Sir John Talbot in France:

> Iack napys, with his clogge,
> Hath tied talbot oure gentill dogge.
> (19–20)

Despite the confusion of his imagery, this author's intentions are plain enough: he is concerned lest Suffolk be allowed to escape the charges laid against him 'ffor and he crepe out, he will yow alle vndo' (2). He adds a specific warning for Henry VI:

> God saue þe kyng, and god forbede
> Þat he suche apes any mo fede.
> (27–8)

What worries this poet is that Suffolk still has friends at court as yet unexposed ('Many mo þer ben, and we kowd hem knowe' 13) who secretly sympathize with him ('Sum of yow holdith with the fox' 5). There were grounds for these fears. The King was reluctant to sacrifice Suffolk and shortly after the impeachment he ordered that he himself would decide the case. There were rumours of a reconciliation. On 12 March 1450, Margaret Paston sent the latest gossip she knew to John Paston:

> Wyllyam Rutt, the whiche is wyth Sere Jon Heuenyngham kom hom from London yesterday; and he seyd pleynly to his mayster and to many othere folkys that the Duke of Suffolk is pardonyd and hath his men ayen waytyng upon hym, and is rytgh wel at ese and mery, and is in the Kyngys gode grase and in the gode conseyt of all the lordys as well as ever he was.

Such rumours may have prompted the warnings against a lenient treatment of Suffolk which appear at this time, as for example in the so-called *Advice to the Court* I:

> Let ffolke accused excuse theym-selff, and þey can;
> Reseyue no good, let soche bribry be;
> Support not theym this wo by-gan,
> And let theym suche clothis as þey span,
> And take fro þeym þer wages and þer fee,
> Or, by god and sent Anne,
> Som must go hens, hit may non othere weys be,
> And els is lost all þis lond and we.
>
> (*HP*, 85, 6–13)

These verses, like others relating to this affair, are anonymous. The author clearly thought of himself as a representative of majority opinion for he urges that the King and his councillors should follow his advice and 'Loose not the loue of alle þe commynalte' (2).

Publicly, Suffolk made a strenuous denial of the charges against him. A more intimate reaction is possibly contained in one of the poems, usually attributed to him, which are preserved in Bodleian MS Fairfax 16.[18] H. N. MacCracken thinks that No. XVIII could 'refer to political misunderstandings such as often over took Suffolk in his chequered career'. The second stanza of the poem seems most apposite. In it the author laments the ingratitude of the world and the change in his fortunes this has produced:

> And as I went, I gan remembre me
> how long I had contynude my servyse
> Wyth carefull thought, and gret adversyte,
> And guerdonless, lo sych was myn offyse;
> The world ys straunge, and now yt ys the guyse
> who that doth best aqwythe hym in hys trouthe
> shall sunnest be forgot, and that ys routhe.
>
> (6–14)

Elsewhere in the same poem he remarks that 'Wyllyngly I never dyd trespace' (16) and fears that 'in thys lyfe I may noght long endure' (17) for 'what I do yt ys gret dysplesaunce' (21). The MS Fairfax 16 poems are usually about love and the sadness of this poem is so generalized that it could refer to the poet's lack of success with his lady. But if MacCracken is right, the first line of the poem, in which the author reveals it was written 'Not far fro Marche in the ende of feberyere', might indicate it referred to the troubles of early 1450. Certainly this was just the time of the year when Suffolk was out of royal favour. If the poem is Suffolk's and if it does refer to the 1450 situation, the pessimism it expresses was amply justified, for on 9 March the Commons laid various additional charges against him. These related to domestic maladministration, embezzlement and misappropriation. Suffolk denied these charges, as he had denied the earlier ones, but the Commons would almost certainly have found him guilty had the King allowed him to come to trial. To save his life Henry VI was forced to banish him for five years dating from May 1450. This was not the end of the affair, however, for on 3 May, as he was travelling towards France, Suffolk's ship was attacked by another English ship the *Nicholas of the Tower* whose sailors captured Suffolk and next morning beheaded him.

His murder aroused little sympathy. Most contemporaries appear to have been pleased, as is the author of the savagely amusing

Death of the Duke of Suffolk (1450) which is preserved in three manuscript versions. The 'seasonal' opening leads the reader to expect a very different kind of poem:

> In the moneth of May when gresse groweþ grene,
> fflagrant in her floures with swete sauour . . .
>
> *(HP,* 76, 1–2)

but the story is not one of love or chivalry but about the death of 'Iac Napes' who, in this particular month of May

> wolde on the see a maryner to ben,
> With his clog & his cheyn, to seke more tresour.
> Suych a payn prikked hym, he asked a confessour.
> Nicolas said, 'I am redi thi confessour to be.'
> He was holden so that he ne passed that hour.
> For Iac Napes soule, Placebo et dirige.
>
> (3–8)

The author deliberately misrepresents the nature of Suffolk's journey, by implying it was a voluntary voyage 'to seke moore tresour'. He alludes to Suffolk's murder ('payn') as though it were a natural illness. He also urges, with apparent sincerity, that the Office of the Dead should be sung for Suffolk's soul. The author maintains the pose of wishing Suffolk well for a few more lines by bidding all ranks of society to pray for his soul, but then abandons this ironic pose: he is glad that Suffolk is dead and does not mind very much if he is in heaven because this, at least, means that he no longer inhabits the earth ('let neuer suych another come after this' 13). He follows this by calling down a blessing on those men who had killed him:

> His interfectours blessed might thei be,
> And graunte them for ther dede to regne with angelis.
>
> (14–15)

The rest of the poem is an attack on Suffolk's supporters who are made to sing the various parts of his funeral rites.

A previous poem had intimated that there were others of the court faction who needed to be eliminated once Suffolk's power had been broken ('won must begyn þe daunce, and all com arowe' *HP* 75, 14), and around this time there was a considerable amount of propaganda against those who had been his supporters. Adam Moleyns, Keeper of the Privy Seal in 1450, Bishop of Chichester and a notable Suffolk adherent, had been murdered earlier by sailors at Portsmouth because of a wage dispute: 'And so it happid that with boisteȝ languge, and also for abriggyng of thair wages, he fil with variaunce with thaym, and thay fil on him, and cruelli there kilde him.'[19] It is clear from contemporary verses, that just after Suffolk's death three royal officials were hated in particular: Sir James Fiennes, Lord Say and Sele, who was treasurer in 1450, John Trevelyan, a Cornishman who was a member of Henry VI's household, and Thomas Daniel, a Cheshire man who was knight of the shire for Buckinghamshire and another member of the royal household. All three were suspected of corruption and maladministration on a large scale. Lord Say and Daniel are urged in some verses of 1450 to restore Henry VI's franchises to him:

> Tom of Say, and Daniel both,
> to begyn be not to loth,
> þen shall ye haue no shame.
>
> (*HP*, 86, 7-9)

In some verses of the previous year Daniel, referred to by his badge of 'þe lily', and Trevelyan ('The Cornysshe chawgh') are both accused, along with John Norris ('The Coundite'), one of Henry VI's officers, of misleading the King ('oure Egulle'):

> Þe lily is both faire and grene;
> The Coundite rennyth not, as I wene.
> The Cornysshe chawgh offt with his trayne
> Hath made oure Egulle blynde.
>
> (*HP*, 84, 21-4)

All three are mentioned among those who help to sing Suffolk's funeral service in the poem *On the Death of the Duke of Suffolk*. Punishment was demanded for all three by the Kentish rebels under Jack Cade in 1450. Another victim of the disturbances of this year was William Ayscough, Bishop of Salisbury. On 29 June, he was dragged from the chancel of his church at Edington, where he was saying Mass, and murdered on a nearby hill. He was well known to be a friend of Suffolk and had been associated with him and Lord Say in a lampoon of 1448 'set upon the gates of powles' in London:

> But Suthfolke, Salesbery and Say
> Be don to deathe in May
> Englond may synge well away.
> *(Lost Lit.*, p. 199)

A more comprehensive indictment of Suffolk's supporters appears in the MS Cotton Vespasian B xvi version of the poem *On the Death of the Duke of Suffolk.* Among the list of his supposed mourners, along with those already mentioned, appear the names of John Sutton, Lord Dudley, and a whole list of unpopular clerics, including Walter Liard, Bishop of Norwich, Reginald Bowlers, Abbot of St Peter's Gloucester, and William Booth, Bishop of Coventry and Lichfield. This version, according to R. H. Robbins, must have been written after 3 May 1450, when Suffolk was murdered, and before 29 June, the date of Ayscough's death. But it was evidently revised somewhat later, for the MS Lambeth 306 version omits the final two stanzas of the Cotton Vespasian B xvi version and adds seven new stanzas.[20] The chronicler John Stow terms the MS Lambeth 306 version 'a dyrge made by the comons of Kent in the tyme of ther rysynge, when Jack Cade was theyr capitayn' and this may be so. But the additional stanzas do not materially change the character of the poem. The organization by reference to the Office of the Dead is preserved. The MS Lambeth 306 reviser, it seems, wished only to add more names, as, for example, in the following stanza:

> Expectans expectaui, seyth Sir Thomas Hoo,
> Complaceat tibi, begynneth Iohn Hampton;
> Beatus qui intelligit, and dredit also,
> Seyth Iohn Fortescu, all this fals treson.
> Sana, domine, owre wittes with reson,
> The Lorde Sudeley devoutly prayth.

> Quem ad modum, desiderat ye Lord Stowrton,
> Situit anima mea, for hym lyeth.
> The Lord Ryvers all onely seythe,
> Requiem eternam, God grawnt vs to se;
> A pater nostar ther must be in feyth,
> For Jake Napis sowle placebo and dirige.

Four of the people mentioned here—Sir Thomas Hoo, John Hampton, Sir John Fortescue and Richard Woodville, Lord Rivers—and also several others mentioned in these additional stanzas are cited in a petition by the Commons which listed those who should be removed from the royal presence. This petition dates from the parliament of 6 November 1450.[21] It may be that the MS Lambeth 306 version dates from about the same time, when the people mentioned in its additional stanzas were particularly unpopular. If this is the case, it looks as though the reviser, like the author of the original, closely reflected public opinion.

Though the two versions of this poem cite many names, and though the antagonism of both the original author and the reviser towards Suffolk and his supporters is very marked, no specific accusations are made. This is not the case with the alliterative verses *On Bishop Boothe* in MS Cotton Rolls ii 23. This poem must have been composed after 1447 when William Booth became Bishop of Coventry and Lichfield, popularly known as the bishopric of Chester. But it must be before the death of Suffolk in 1450, since Suffolk is referred to as if he were still alive. Here the author makes specific charges against Booth. One was that he had achieved his position through simony:

> Thy goode and thy catelle made the to mete
> With the churche of Chester, which crieth, alas!
> That to such a mafflarde marryede she was.
>
> (PPS, p. 225)

A few lines further on, punning on Booth's name, the poet accuses him of usury also—

> Thow hast getyne gret goode, thou wost welle how,
> By symoni and usure bilde is thy bothe.
>
> (p. 226)

But the attack is not confined to Booth. The author mentions Trevelyan and Suffolk also and accuses the whole faction either of plotting treason or of misappropriating money. He assures them, whichever is true, that people are aware of their misdoings:

> Men seyne that youre secte is opynly knowyne and asspiede,
> Concludede in conciens wonne of the tweyne,
> That ye be ychone with tresoun aliede,
> Or els hit is lucre that maketh you to leyne
>
> (p. 228)

and the last stanza contains a warning to Booth and his associates that they should restrain their ambitions:

> Bridelle yow, bysshope, and be not to bolde,
> And biddeth yowre beawperes se to the same.
> (p. 229)

In this author's opinion the country was being ruined by the cupidity of its ruling faction, who cared only for amassing private wealth and nothing for the public good. Using the conventional 'evils of the age' formula he draws attention to the situation in Rome before its fall:

> Justice ne was egaly execute,
> Fredome was forfarene for lak of liberte,
> Right was repraysede and fonde for no repute . . .
> (p. 227)

and he invites a comparison with the state of contemporary England. The poem ends with the conventional prayer to God 'for his mercy alle this reme gyde' and elsewhere the author asks 'god save the kyng, his lawe, and his londe', but he does not seem very confident of a secure future for England.

The failure of the Beaufort party and the fall of Suffolk had the effect of giving Richard, Duke of York, an opportunity to assert himself in English politics. He was an important figure, by his lineage heir to all the claims of the Mortimer family, and by his marriage into the Neville family one of the richest and most influential men in the kingdom. His early career had been military rather than political, and concerned with foreign rather than domestic affairs. He was appointed to the lieutenancy of France in February 1436 and again in July 1440. It was during his second term that he first found himself opposed to the Beaufort faction, first over the appointment of Edmund Beaufort, Duke of Somerset, as lieutenant and captain-general in Gascony in 1443 and secondly over finances, for York claimed on his return in 1445 that he had been kept short of money by the Council. Serious recriminations in the Council followed and Adam Moleyns, Bishop of Chichester, accused him of having defrauded the Norman garrisons of their pay. York's defence and counter-accusations were more than adequate, and the Council found it awkward to have the heir to the throne (as York now was) as an opponent. It was no doubt to get him away from the country that he was appointed lieutenant in Ireland in December 1447. Though he did not take up this post for about two years, it was from Ireland that he witnessed the momentous events of 1450. There was some support for his recall to England. In 1449 one contemporary poet, referring to him by his badge, had regretted he was out of England just when some strong influence was needed:

> The Fawkoun fleyth and hath no rest
> Tille he witte where to bigge his nest.
> (*PPS*, II, p. 223)

York's recall had also been mentioned in the propaganda of Jack Cade.

When York returned in August 1450 it was at the head of an army of four thousand men. He presented himself as a reformer of the government, but the majority of the lords suspected that he wished to challenge the throne. York assured Henry VI of his loyalty and made certain suggestions for reforming the government, but the fears of a usurpation remained and Somerset was recalled from France and made Constable of England. Thereafter, the political struggle was between York and Somerset. As early as 1452, an army of York's supporters and the royal army had faced each other at Blackheath and a battle was only averted when Henry VI agreed that Somerset should be made to answer charges that York had brought against him. But Somerset and the Beaufort party remained in power. With Queen Margaret lending them considerable support, they even succeeded for a time in denying York a place in the Council. In March 1454, though, Henry VI fell temporarily insane and, despite an attempt by Margaret to have the government of the kingdom put in her hands, York was elected Protecter and Defender. He received much the same powers as Humphrey of Gloucester had been given in Henry VI's minority. York lost no time in consolidating his position: he had his lieutenancy of Ireland confirmed, made himself captain of Calais in place of Somerset, who was imprisoned, and had his brother-in-law Richard Neville, Earl of Salisbury, made Chancellor. His success was not to last for very long. In February 1455, Henry VI recovered his senses and again took over the government. York's men were removed from office and Somerset was released. Since 1454 Somerset had been mustering forces in London and after Henry VI's recovery it was clear to York that it was not safe for him to attend Council meetings unprotected. He fled to the north to join the Earls of Salisbury and Warwick, and only came back when accompanied by a large army. When this met with the King's army at St Albans, York was adamant that he intended no harm to Henry VI but wished only that his complaints against Somerset be heard. This was denied him and armed conflict—the first battle of the civil war—became inevitable.

This turn of events cannot have surprised many. It is interesting to note that Charles of Orléans, in a *ballade* written in 1453, had predicted just such an outcome. His twenty-five years imprisonment in England had no doubt provided him with some insight into the workings of English politics and, though his poem concerns itself principally with the successful French military reoccupation of Normandy and Gascony, he sees clearly enough the disorganized and factional state of contemporary England and the weakness of the Crown:

> N'ont pas Anglois souvent leurs rois trays?
> Certes ouyl, tous en ont congnoissance.
> Et encore le roy de leur pays

Est maintenant en doubteuse balance;
D'en parler mal chascun Anglois s'avance;
Assez monstrent, par leur mauvais langaige,
Que volontiers lui feroient oultraige.
Qui sera Roy entr'eux est grant desbat. . . .[22]

How Charles knew about the state of English affairs is a matter for speculation. But whatever his source, it is clear that his assessment of the situation was both acute and prophetic.

NOTES

[1] Ed. W. A. Pantin, 'A Medieval Collection of Latin and English Proverbs and Riddles from Rylands Latin MS 394', *Bulletin of the John Rylands Library*, 14, 1930, p. 102.

[2] See E. F. Jacob, *The Fifteenth Century*, Oxford 1961, p. 215.

[3] Ed. H. N. MacCracken, 1910. For a summary of views on the date of the piece see W. F. Schirmer, *John Lydgate* translated by Ann E. Keep 1961, pp. 82–3.

[4] *Political Poems and Songs* II, p. 221.

[5] *Humanism in England during the Fifteenth Century*, 3rd edition 1967, p. 41.

[6] *Annales a Johanne Amundesham* ed. H. T. Riley, Rolls Series 28, 1870, p. 20.

[7] *John Lydgate, op. cit.*, 115.

[8] *Chronicle* ed. H. Ellis, 1812, p. 396.

[9] *Historical Poems of the Fourteenth and Fifteenth Centuries*, New York 1959, p. 344.

[10] Hardyng, *op. cit.*, p. 400.

[11] Ed. Carleton Brown *MLR* 7, 1912, pp. 225–34 and by R. Withington *Mod. Phil.* 13, 1916, pp. 53–7.

[12] See *The Brut* ed. W. F. D. Brie, EETS OS 131, 136, 1906–8, pp. 511–12 for the view that Henry VI's troubles stemmed from his marriage to Margaret of Anjou.

[13] *PMLA* 26, 168–171 for a text of the poem, and pp. 149–50 for his comments.

[14] *Historical Poems, op. cit.*, p. xxxix.

[15] See E. F. Jacob, pp. 491–5 for details of the charges against Suffolk.

[16] *Political Religious and Love Poems*, ed. F. J. Furnivall, EETS OS 15 1866, p. 11.

[17] *English Chronicle* ed. J. S. Davies, Camden Society 64, 1856, p. 79.

[18] See MacCracken, *op. cit.*, for this poem.

[19] *English Chronicle, op. cit.*, p. 64.

[20] *Political Religious and Love Poems, op. cit.*, p. 11.

[21] See *Political Poems and Songs, op. cit.*, II, lvi–lvii for this document.

[22] On this poem see particularly Enid McLeod, *Charles of Orleans*, 1969, pp. 326–7. *Translation*: 'Have not the English always betrayed their kings? Certainly, everyone knows of it. And once again their king is now in a precarious position. Each Englishman pushes himself forward by speaking ill of him. They show sufficiently by their evil words that they would readily do him injury. There is a great dispute among them about who will be king . . .'

6 : Domestic Affairs III : 1455-1485

DURING the years 1455 to 1485 the civil war provides English political writers with their main body of material. That there is so much interest is surprising, however, for the war directly affected only a minority of the population and even then by no means continuously. No great religious or political issues were involved. The war was little more than a thinly disguised power struggle between the leading members of a politically irresponsible nobility. It took the form of sporadic outbreaks of bitter violence punctuated by long periods of comparative peace and stability. Perhaps what chiefly evoked the interest of contemporary political writers was the alarming prospect of any civil war in England. But verse was also consciously exploited, by both sides, as propaganda.

The civil wars began against a background of considerable discontent. By the early 1450s, the losses in France were causing nationwide dissatisfaction; the rule of Henry VI was extremely weak; the Council was seriously divided within itself; and there was widespread discontent with the way in which the country was governed. The notion that England was badly served by its ruling faction lay behind many of the complaints of the Kentishmen who rebelled with Jack Cade in 1450, and contemporary documents frequently testify to a similar discontent. A petition from John Paston to Henry VI, dating from the beginning of 1450 and referring in particular to his own forcible expulsion from his house at Gresham, goes beyond his personal troubles to stress the need for firm government and the impartial administration of the law:

> if this gret insurreccyon, ryottis, and wrongis, and dayly
> continuans ther of so heynosly don a geyn your crowne,

dignite and peas, shuld not be your hye myght be duly punysshed, it shall gefe gret boldnesse to them, and alle other mysdoers to make congregacyons and conventicles riottously, on abille to be sesyd, to the subversyon and finall distruccyon of your liege peple and lawes. (*Paston Letters*, No. 102)

Later in the same year, a 'bill' from Richard, Duke of York, urges Henry VI

tendirly to consider the grett grutchyng and romer that is universaly in this your reame of that justice is nouth dewly ministred to such as trespas and offende a yens your lawes. . . .

(*Ibid.*, No. 143)

More often the complaints are confined to local matters. In October 1450 James Gresham mentions in a letter to John Paston 'how the cuntre of Norfolk and Suffolk stonde right wildly' (*Ibid.*, No. 146) and a measure of the lawlessness there can be gauged from the petition from the town of Swaffham in 1451, which complains of the 'trespasez, offencez, wronges, extorcyons, mayntenauncez, imbraceryes, oppressions, and perjuryes' (*Ibid.*, No. 185) of Sir Thomas Tuddenham and his supporters in the locality. Another petition, of 1452, to Cardinal Kemp, Archbishop of York and Chancellor of England, complains of one Roger Cherche and his supporters and the

divers riottes, extorciouns, forsibil entreys and unlawfull disherytauns of gentilmen and other of the Kynges liege peple in the seid shire [*i.e.* Norfolk] that thei dayly use, which riottes, extorcions, as wele as the seid untrewe diffamaciouns, causyth gret grudgyng, trobill, and comocyon in the seid shire.

(*Ibid.*, No. 218)

Even allowing for the fact that it was in the interests of these writers to exaggerate the extent of the disturbances, that at most periods in the Middle Ages there was some measure of local disorder, and that the documents quoted here all relate to a single area of England, it is difficult to escape the conclusion that, at the outbreak of the civil wars, the country was more than usually disturbed and disordered. It is clear too that contemporary writers felt this to be so.

It is necessary to stress all this because similar expressions of political discontent are also to be found in verse dating from this time. Traditionally, scholars have attributed many generalized political verses to these disturbed years. But few may be precisely dated. An exception is *The Bisson Leads the Blind* which refers to the political situation in 1456. For the most part, the poem is an indictment, using the generalized terminology of 'abuses of the age' verses, of the moral corruption and political instability of England in the 1450s. But towards the end of the poem the reference becomes more specific and the author's fear of a continuation of the civil divisions (which had showed themselves a year previously at the first Battle of St Albans of 1455) is very clear. He warns the English nobility of the dangers of civil war by reminding them of the unhappy situation such a conflict produced in France and Flanders in the earlier part of the century, and recommends that they reconcile themselves:

> Take hede how synne hath chastysyd frauns
> Whan he was in hys fayrest kynde,
> How þat flaundrys hath myschaunys
> ffor cause þe bysom ledyth þe blynde.
>
> Þerfor euery lord odur avauns
> And styfly stond yn ych a stoure
> Among ȝou make no dystaunce
> But, lordys, buskys ȝou out of boure,
> ffor to hold up þis londus honour.
>
> (*HP*, 49, 69–77)

But perhaps the most striking description of the lawlessness of the times comes from the conclusion of John Hardyng's *Chronicle* in the MS Lansdowne 204 version which was finished in 1457:

> In euery shire with Iakkes and Salades clene
> Myssereule doth ryse and maketh neyghbours werre;
> The wayker gothe benethe, as ofte ys sene,
> The myghtyest his quarell wyll preferre,

That pore mennes cause er putte on bakke full ferr;
Whiche thrugh the pese and law wele conserued
Myght bene amende, and thanke of god deserued.

Thay kyll your men alway by one and one,
And who say ought he shall be bette doutlesse;
For in your Reme Iustyse of pese bene none
That darr ought now the contekours oppresse;
Suche sekenesse now hath take thaym and accesse,
Thay wyll noght wytte of Ryot ne debate,
So comon is it now in eche estate.

Like the author of the poem previously quoted, Hardyng thinks
that Henry VI should act quickly to put an end to the lawlessness
and dissention before it increases: 'Withstonde, gode lorde,
begynnyng of debate.' The King should also consider the lessons
of past history:

> your auncetry
> In welthe and hele regned of hiegh recorde
> That keped pese and law contynuly.

He warns Henry that those kings who 'kept nayther law ne pese . . .
distroyed wer, right as thay had deserved'. The only way in which
it would be possible for Henry VI to win back the crown of
France and to conquer Scotland is for him first to ensure that his
'Reme stonde hole in vnyte/Conserved wele in pese and equyte'.
Failure to impose peace at home and to put an end to the prevalent
lawlessness will, Hardyng says, speaking directly to Henry VI,
cause to 'fall the fayrest flours/of your coroune and noble monarchy'.[1]

The warnings set out in these poems were timely, but the
situation was already, at least for Henry VI, beyond solution. The
first Battle of St Albans in 1455 was a brief but bloody affair at
which the leaders of Henry VI's party—Edmund Beaufort, Duke
of Somerset, Northumberland, Clifford and the Earl of Stafford—
were all killed. This had the effect of allowing the Yorkists to take
charge of the key roles in the government. Richard of York took
over Somerset's old position as Constable of England, and at the

end of the year was again given the Protectorate. Richard Neville, Earl of Warwick, became captain of Calais, York's brother-in-law, Henry Viscount Bourchier, was made treasurer. There were those in the late 1450s who looked to Richard of York as the only man capable of restoring England to good rule. In the proem to the second version of his chronicle, John Hardyng addresses him as the ruler, or at least the potential ruler, of England. He stresses the uses of history, a study of which, he says, will make York a wiser leader:

> By whiche knowledge your discrete sapience
> All vyce evermore destroye maye and reprove,
> By vertuous and blessedfull dilygence,
> And vertue love, that maye not ought greve
> How ye shall rule your subiectes, while ye lyve,
> In lawe, and peace, and all tranquyllite,
> Whiche been the floures of all regalyte.

Throughout the earlier part of his narrative he inserts personal observations and advice. After his account of how the Britons were conquered by 'Gurmound', Hardyng warns York that civil disorders might weaken the country and enable a foreign enemy to invade it:

> O worthy prince! O duke of York I meane,
> Discendid downe of highest bloodde royall.
> Se to such ryotes that none sustene
> And specially that alyens none at all
> Inhabite not with power greate ne small,
> That maye this lande ought trouble or over ride,
> For twies it was so wonne with muche pride.

Again addressing York directly, he makes a similar point after his account of the reign of Cadwalader, urging York 'over all thyng se there be no devisyon' but instead 'reste and peace'. He concludes with the moral that 'where a realme or a cyte is devyded/It may not stand' and draws York's attention to the falls of Carthage and Rome and to the more recent disasters in France due to civil war. It is difficult to know for certain when Hardyng composed these passages. The version of his *Chronicle* from which they are taken was presented to Edward IV in 1464. But since these passages refer to Richard of York as living they must have been composed before his death at Wakefield on 30 December 1460.[2]

York was by no means universally popular. Dating certainly from 1456 come some interesting verses evidently written by a Lancastrian supporter who lived in London. Supposedly spoken by servants who had been sacrificed to his ambitions, these verses are forthright in their condemnation of York:

> My mayster ys cruell and can no curtesye,
> ffor whos offence here am y pyghte.
> hyt ys no reson þat y shulde dye
> ffor hys trespace, & he go quyte
>
> (*HP*, 77, 1–4)

or again

> Wat planet compellyd me, or what signe
> To serue þat man that all men hate?
> Y wolde hys hede were here for myne
> ffor he hathe caused all þe debate.
>
> (13–16)

The directness of these verses and the particularly sensational way in which their author chose to publicise them show that he had the objective of discrediting York in the public mind,[3] whereas Hardyng's intention seems to have been to commend himself to York, presumably with the object of acquiring his patronage.

Early in 1456 Henry VI restored himself to power and for a few years an uneasy truce was maintained. Some of the Yorkists who had been installed in key positions after the first Battle of St Albans were replaced, but Richard of York himself remained the most influential figure in the Council and Warwick retained the captaincy of Calais. Outwardly it must have seemed that the civil divisions, which had seriously threatened the kingdom in 1455, were being healed. An amicable meeting between the two factions in 1458 ended with a public demonstration of their reconciliation in the form of a procession to St Paul's London, which according to one chronicler 'made all men so gladd'.[4] A contemporary poet was moved to celebrate the same event in much the same way: 'Reioise, Anglond, in concorde & vnite.' He sees the procession as a sign that 'peas is made there was diuision':

> In Yorke, In Somerset, as I vnderstonde,
> In Warrewik also is loue & charite,
> In Sarisbury eke, & in Northumbrelande,
> That euery man may reioise in concord & vnite.
>
> Egremown and Clifford, with other forsaide,
> Ben set in the same opynyon.
> In euery quarter love is thus laide;
> Grace & wisdom hath thus the dominacion.
>
> (*HP*, 79, 21–8)

The author was evidently a Londoner who witnessed the procession and who was impressed by the demeanour of Henry VI, Margaret and the lords:

> There was bytwyn hem lovely contynaunce
> Whiche was gret ioy to all that ther were;
> That long tyme hadden be in variaunce,
> As frendes for euer that had be in fere.
>
> (41–4)

It is difficult to be persuaded, however, that this friendship was anything but superficial. The reconciliation and procession took place on 25 March but within six months brawls were breaking out among the supporters of the two factions in Westminster, and on 11 October of the same year Warwick narrowly escaped an attempt on his life. More seriously both parties were intriguing for allies outside England: Margaret in Scotland, and Warwick in Burgundy and France.

These conflicting loyalties are apparent in contemporary verse. The Lancastrians had more cause to be pleased by the reconciliation than the Yorkists. At least it appeared to re-establish Henry VI as the ruler of a united England. There is a hint of Lancastrian partiality in the author of *The Reconciliation of Henry VI and the*

Yorkists who is more concerned for Henry VI than for the other leaders: 'Oure Soueraigne lord kyng, god kepe alwey.' Similar, but more emphatic, Lancastrian sentiments appear in *The Ship of State*, which a Latin note in Trinity College Dublin MS 516 dates as 'Anno domini ml cccc o lviij o'. In the first stanza of this Henry VI is compared to a ship:

> This noble shyp made of good tree
> Oure souerayne lord, kynge henry,
> God gyde hym from aduersyte,
> Where þat he go or ryde
> *(HP*, 78, 5–8)

and the rest develops this figure by equating the principal Lancastrian supporters with parts of the ship: Prince Edward is compared to the mast, Henry Holland, Duke of Exeter, with the ship's light, Henry Beaufort, third Duke of Somerset, with the rudder and so on. This figure is readily to be found elsewhere. Most noteworthy is the tone of unqualified approval for all these leaders who are always 'fayre', 'well good', 'full good and sure', 'hole and sounde' and so on. The image of the ship, in which all parts are interdependent, itself suggests harmony and purpose among the Lancastrian leaders. In view of this the confidence of the final stanza is not unexpected:

> Now help, saynt George, oure lady knyght,
> And be oure lode-sterre day & nyght,
> To strengthe oure kynge and england ryght
> And fell oure fomenus pryde.
> Now is oure shype dressed in hys kynde,
> With hys taklynge be-for and be-hynde;
> Whoso loue it not, god make hym blynde
> In peynes to a-byde.
> (73–80)

Nor should one be surprised by its uncompromising attitude to the Yorkists, who are almost certainly referred to as those who 'love . . . not' Henry VI and whose 'pryde' is to be destroyed.

The Yorkists gained little from the reconciliation of 1458 but their cause was not weakened. A poem entitled *Take Good Heed* expresses advice and anxiety for the Yorkists, who were obviously expected to make another bid for power. Various dates have been suggested for the poem: February 1454, May 1455, or late 1460. But R. H. Robbins, following a suggestion by Brotanek, is probably correct in attributing it to the period shortly after the reconciliation. These verses, which are plain and forthright, may have been written by a lower-class Yorkist partisan, perhaps one of 'þe comyns', who he assures the Yorkist lords 'ben youres, euer at youre nede'. Whoever he is, the author's concern is for the safety of the leaders of his faction (to whom he refers by their cognizances):

> But pray we al to god þat died on a spere
> To saue þe rose, þe lyon, þe egle, & þe bere
> (*HP*, 87, 45–6)

—that is, Richard of York, John Mowbray, Duke of Norfolk, the Earl of Salisbury and Warwick. He urges them not to trust the outwardly friendly Lancastrians, who, he says, have not significantly changed their basic attitudes:

> ffor som that speke ful fayre, þei wolde ȝour evil spede;
> Þouȝ þei pere in your presence with a fayre face,
> And her tunge chaunged, þe hert is as it was.
> (2–4)

The author seems to have no specific political knowledge with which to substantiate his allegations, but relies on the resonance of popular tags such as 'two fases in a hode is neuer to tryst' (20). He is particularly emphatic that the Yorkist lords should preserve what political advantages they have, and that in any negotiations substantial concessions should be demanded from the Lancastrians: 'lat not ȝoure sauegardes be to liberalle/To your foos . . .'. They ought not to be too open about their own positions: 'Of youre disposicion telliþ not euery man.' The author himself, it appears, is an admirable example of the restraint he urges in the Yorkist leaders: 'Miche is in my mynde, no more is in my penne' (43). He is wary of being betrayed, and conscious that the very existence of his verses jeopardises his safety: 'ffor þis shuld I be shent, might som men it kenne' (44). A writer of partisan political verses always exposed himself to some sort of risk, but the fact is used here to reinforce the warning of danger to the Yorkist leaders.

The mutual suspicion of the two parties and their constant intriguing were not long in producing a new outbreak of violence. In the summer of 1459 Queen Margaret, who had by this time gained considerable authority within the Lancastrian faction, decided to move against the Yorkists and if possible to remove the troublesome Warwick from his captaincy of Calais. The Yorkists mobilised what forces they could and a contingent under Richard Neville, Earl of Salisbury, actually defeated a Lancastrian force at Blore Heath on 22 September 1459. But any hopes of a successful rebellion were dashed on 12 October when the Yorkists were routed at Ludford Bridge. This victory was not decisive, however, for York escaped to Ireland and Warwick to Calais, from which positions the Lancastrians found it impossible to dislodge them. None the less, the Lancastrians had complete control of the government and were able to consolidate their military gains. At a parliament at Coventry on 20 November, the Yorkist lords were attainted in their absence, and their known supporters in England were persecuted. Those present at the parliament were asked to take an oath of loyalty to Henry VI and his son Prince Edward, and to swear to protect and support Queen Margaret. But the Lancastrians did little that was constructive. The problem of widespread lawlessness, about which Hardyng and others had earlier complained, was as serious as ever, and frequent commissions of array and demands for money did little to enhance Lancastrian popularity. The Yorkists exploited this discontent with manifestoes. Once certain of the extent of their public support, Warwick, his father Salisbury and Edward, Earl of March (the future Edward IV) landed at Sandwich in Kent, on 26 June 1460, with their supporters. They marched through Kent and on to London.

A surviving example of versified Yorkist propaganda associated with the invasion is *The Ballade Set on the Gates of Canterbury* (1460) preserved in the John Speed Davies MS version of the

English Chronicle. Brotanek suggests that the author of this poem was a Canterbury cleric who had Yorkist sympathies, and that the chronicler 'may have copied this Yorkist effusion from the city gates'.[5] This may be true, but certain features of the verses distinguish them from the typical 'bill' set up in a public place to win popular support. The typical 'bill' is brief, direct and simple but this poem is fairly long, consisting as it does of ten eight-line stanzas and a six-line coda. It is also far from simple, using frequent biblical quotations in Latin, together with other Latin phrases, and having in general a highly aureate English vocabulary. The author asserts that England is decadent:

A planta pedis, fro the pore tylyer of the lond
Ad verticem of spiritualle eke temporalle ennoynted crown,
Grace ys withdrawe and Goddys mercyfulle hand;
Exalted ys falsehod, trowthe ys layde adoune;
Euery reame cryeth owte of Engelondes treson.

(HP, 88, 17–21)

Referring to the Bible as his 'authority' he predicts the destruction of the kingdom: 'Omne regnum in se divisum . . . shall be desolate. . . . And now is Englond in lyk reputacione.' Yet there is no evidence in this poem of any move to replace Henry VI as King:

No prynce, alle thyng consydered, wythe honoure
In alle thyng requysyte to a kynges excellence
Better may lyue . . .

(73–5)

Rather the writer feels that Henry VI has allowed himself to be dominated by incompetent councillors, and by dissociating himself from the Yorkist leaders, 'His trew bloode hathe flemed bothe be swerde and exyle' (34). Two other charges frequently cited in Yorkist propaganda also appear. The impoverishment of the King by his councillors is implied in the lines:

What prynce by thys rewle may haue long endurying,
That also in moste pouert hath be long whyle?

(35–6)

and the phrases 'fals wedlok' and 'Fals heyres fostred' hint at the suspicion, encouraged by the Yorkists, that the heir to the throne, Prince Edward, was not really Henry VI's son. Having stressed some of the shortcomings of the ruling faction in England, the author proceeds to the need for reforms:

> Tempus ys come falshede to dystroy,
> Tempus eradicandi the wedes fro the corne,
> Tempus cremandi the breres that trees noye,
> Tempus evellendi the fals hunter with his horne,
> Tempus miserendi on por alle to torne,
> Tempus ponendi falsnes in perpetuelle absence. . . .
>
> (49–54)

He ends by commending the qualities of the Yorkist leaders Edward, Earl of March, Richard, Earl of Salisbury, Richard, Earl of Warwick, William, Lord Fauconberg and particularly Richard, Duke of York, who the writer hopes will be restored to his former high position in the Council: 'Sette hym ut sedeat in principibus, as he dyd before' (62). How much effect this poem had is impossible to determine, but it apparently was well enough known among Yorkist supporters for lines from it to be taken over and used in later partisan verses.

After the landing of the Earls, events moved swiftly. When they arrived in London on 2 July 1460 the Yorkists split their forces. Richard, Earl of Salisbury, remained to besiege the Tower which Lord Scales and other Lancastrian supporters would not surrender. Meanwhile the main force under Edward, Earl of March, followed the Lancastrians to Northampton and on 10 July defeated them and captured Henry VI. At some time between this date and the return from Ireland of Richard, Duke of York, must have been written the verses on *The Battle of Northampton* preserved in Trinity College Dublin MS 432. These are basically a celebration of the Yorkist successes of 1460. The author uses the familiar methods of referring to those involved in the major events by means of puns on their names, or by references to either their badges or to features of their coats of arms. In addition the Battle of Northampton is described in terms of an extended metaphor of a hunt in which the 'bere' (Richard, Earl of Warwick) and the 'bereward' (Edward, Earl of March) defeat the Lancastrian 'dogges' (John Talbot, second Earl of Shrewsbury, John, Viscount Beaumont and Thomas Percy, Lord Egremont) and kill the 'buk' (Humphrey Stafford, first Duke of Buckingham):

> The bereward asked no questioun why,
> But on þe dogges he set full rounde;
> Þe bere made the dogges to cry,
> And with his pawme cast þeyme to grounde.
> The game was done in a litel stounde,
> Þe buk was slayne, & borne away;
> Agayne þe bere þan was none hounde,
> But he might sporte and take his play.
>
> (*HP*, 89, 49–56)

The events in London are treated in a similar way except that in these stanzas the metaphor is changed to one of fishing. The 'egle' (Richard, Earl of Salisbury) is seeking to catch the 'fisshe' (Lord Scales) whose unfortunate death (he escaped his besiegers at the Tower but was recognized by a Thames boatmen, killed and laid naked in St Mary Overy's churchyard) as well as his name lends itself very well to the author's imagery:

> All þei had scaped vpon a nyght
> Saue þeire skales were plucked away;
> Þan had þe fissh lost all here might,
> And litel ioy in watyr to play.
>
> (137–40)

But the poem is more than a clever celebration of the Yorkist victory. It is also shrewdly aimed propaganda. The poet says that the Earls invaded England because they were aware of 'þe falshode in euery place' and heard 'þe peple crying for mercye'. Even more obviously designed to win public support for the Yorkists is this author's account of their meeting with Henry VI to whom he refers as 'þe hunt' ('the huntsman'). Edward, Earl of March, ('þe huntes frende') and Warwick are presented as treating Henry VI with kindness and deference ('He lowted downe, & at his fote lay'). Their intention was merely to rescue Henry VI from the Lancastrian 'dogges' and 'þe buk', and to clear themselves of malicious and unfounded charges made against them by their enemies:

> We haue desired to com to your presence;
> To oure excuse we myght not answere;
> All þinges were hyd from your audience.
>
> (65–7)

Furthermore, in a long speech given to him Henry VI admits that the Lancastrians

> wrought agayne all kynde
> Þei labored to bryng me in distresse.
>
> (82–3)

They were responsible for his unhappiness and lack of success ('In no place game kowde I fynde' 87). They had also impoverished him ('They lapped awey the fatte me fro' 95). Evidently this author's intention was to emphasize the reconciliation between the Earls and the King and to establish the Yorkists as the King's natural councillors. He may even have hoped to reassure public opinion that no move to replace Henry VI was contemplated. It is impossible to estimate how representative this author is of Yorkist opinion, but it is clear enough that he himself is well disposed towards Henry VI ('oure noble kyng') for whom he prays in his concluding stanza: 'Saue þe kyng & his ryalte' (158). He urges the return from Ireland of 'þat noble prynce' Richard, Duke of York

> whom treson ne falshod neuer dyd shame,
> But euer obedient to his sovereigne
>
> (146–7)

but there is not the slightest hint here that York would be anything more than a prominent member of the Council.

Subsequent events must have surprised this author considerably, for, on his return to England, Richard of York pressed his claim to the throne by inheritance and conquest. The lords were reluctant to grant this and after some negotiation a compromise was reached whereby it was proclaimed, on 8 November 1460, that Henry VI was to remain King for life, and York and his heirs were to succeed thereafter. This obviously strengthened the Yorkist position. But Lancastrian forces were still operating in the north, where Richard of York's own tenants were being attacked, and it was on an expedition to quell these troubles that the newly-made heir apparent lost his life. He badly underestimated the strength of the Lancastrians and was defeated at the Battle of Wakefield on 30 December 1460. A poem lamenting his death evidently written by 'Chester the Herald' has survived. It is fairly predictable in its position. Richard of York is praised for his personal qualities 'saige, vaillant, vertueux en sa vie' and for his record in political affairs:

> Sy fut roygent et gouverneur de France,
> Normandie il garda d'encombrance,
> Sur Pontaysse la ryviere passa,
> Le roy Francoyez et son doulfin chassa.
> En Erllande mist tel gouvernement,
> Tout le pais rygla paisiblement.
> D'Engleterre fut long temps prottetur,
> Le peuple ama, et fut leur deffendeur.
> (*PPS*, II, p. 257)

The author also mentions the Westminster agreement of 8 November and stresses that Richard was the rightful heir to the English crown:

> Droyt heritier, prouvé en mainte terre
> Des couronnez de France et d'Engleterre.
> (p. 256)

The only surprising thing about the poem is that it is written in French, which at this time was probably little understood in England.[6]

Following the death of York the Lancastrians were successful in other engagements. Queen Margaret sought to consolidate the advantage by negotiating for help in Scotland. A marriage was arranged between Princess Mary, the sister of James III, and Edward, Prince of Wales, and as part of the settlement Margaret promised to cede Berwick to the Scots. Charles VII of France was prepared to help also, and allowed Margaret's supporters to use the harbours of the Normandy coasts. Once sure of support in these two areas, the Lancastrians made a two-pronged attack on the Yorkist-held southern areas of England, and the Yorkist leaders, to counter this, had to divide their forces. Those under Edward, Earl of March, marched west to intercept the forces of the Earls of Pembroke and Wiltshire who, supported by Frenchmen, Bretons and Irishmen, had landed and intended to join with Margaret. At Mortimer's Cross on 3 February 1461 the Yorkists were victorious, but on 16 February at St Albans Margaret's Lancastrian forces overcame Warwick's army and recaptured Henry VI. This was an important victory, but for various reasons did not prove decisive. For one thing Warwick himself, and a substantial part of his army, were able to escape in reasonably good order and join Edward's forces in the Cotswolds. For another, the Lancastrians were unable to consolidate their position, the populace of the south being suspicious of their supporters. They had good grounds, for Margaret's forces had ransacked and pillaged both the town of St Albans and the monastery where they had been entertained after the battle. In the course of a review, in Latin verse, of the events of the civil war, John Whethamstede, a monk of St Albans, has a long passage on the deplorable conduct of these 'northern men':

> Gens Boriae gens perfidiae, gens prompta rapinae,
> Gens est centimano raptu similis Briareae,
> Et Tityo jecore, Sisypho saxoque ruente;
> Et licet ulterius societur Tantalus istis,
> Non portat metrum, mos est his pejor eorum,
> Diripiunt, rapiunt, post se vix saxa relinquit
> Gens Boreae, gens nequitiae, gens absque pietate,
> Et sine lege veris vindex, sine judice juris.
> Decisor quia vi vult cuncta regi gladiali,
> Moreve barbarico, licitum foret in spoliando,
> Ut fierent propriae per raptum res alienae.
> Friguit aut caluit nimis id quod tollere nollet.
> Gens Boreae, gens vipereae pellis generisque,

Mordet et emordet, rodit, corrodit, et urget
Matris ad interitum, male sicut tendat ad ortum.[7]

(PPS, II, pp. 262–3)

More crucially, the people of London were also ill-disposed toward the Lancastrian forces. A deputation of ladies was sent to the Queen's forces to say that they would only be allowed to enter the capital if they refrained from pillaging. But though arrangements satisfactory to both sets of negotiators were settled, the citizens of London refused, against the wishes of the Mayor and aldermen, to open the gates. A couplet preserved in Gregory's *Chronicle* summarizes their determination not to accept Henry VI back among them:

> He that had Londyn for sake
> Wolde no more to hem take.

Their sympathies were made plain in sayings reported by Gregory: 'Lette us walke in a newe wyne yerde, and lette us make us a gay gardon in the monythe of Marche with thys fayre whyte ros and herbe, the Erle of Marche.'[8]

It was clear to the Yorkists (to whom London opened its gates on 27 February 1461) that they had to depose Henry VI, since they no longer had any control over him. On 1 March the Earl of March was acclaimed Edward IV by the 'populus' (in this case his soldiers) in St John's Fields. In the days following, his claim to the throne was recognized formally by the citizens of London at St Pauls. He took his oath at Westminster Hall, was installed in his seat and, after outlining his hereditary claim to the throne, received the acclamation of his subjects and their homage at Westminster Abbey. This was not a formal coronation, but simply a recognition of his title. His next problem was to give the title reality. The Yorkists were conscious that Henry VI, his Queen and a substantial Lancastrian army were at large in the north, and immediately turned their attention to confronting them. The Battle of Towton, fought on 29 March 1461 in a snowstorm, was among the more decisive, as well as the most bloody, engagements of the civil war. It established a Yorkist King and destroyed Lancastrian hopes for many years. It did not end the struggle, however, for Henry VI and Margaret escaped to Scotland, where, in safety, Margaret continued to plot ways of recovering the English throne.

None the less the Yorkists were undisputed masters in all except the far north of England, and the joy of their supporters was predictably great. It sometimes took the form of celebratory verses, as in *The Battle of Towton* (1461) from the collection of pro-Yorkist items in Trinity College Dublin MS 432. This account, written in the carol form, is not notable for its factual accuracy. To say that 'many man gan blede' at the second Battle of St Albans is a gross exaggeration, as is the statement that the Lancastrian casualties at Towton numbered 'XXVII thousand'. However, the basic purpose of the poem is to praise the achievements of Edward IV, 'the rose of Rone' (so called because his badge was the rose, and because he was born at Rouen):

> Almighti ihesu save þe rose & geue hym his blessyng,
> And al þe reme of englond ioy of his crownyng,
> Þat we may blesse þe tyme þat euer god sprad þe floure
>
> (*HP*, 90, 73–5)

and the other Yorkist leaders are referred to in the same way by means of their cognizances. Perhaps the most significant aspect of the poem is the author's implicit concern with the geographical basis of Yorkist support. He alludes to the arms of some of the cities, such as Bristol ('þe white ship'), Coventry ('þe blak ram') and Northampton ('The wild kat'), from which Edward IV derived support. He also sees the Yorkist triumph as essentially that of the south (with support from Calais):

> ffor to saue al englond þe rose did his entent,
> With Calys & with loue London, with Essex & with Kent,
> And al þe south of englond vnto þe watyr of trent.
>
> (26–8)

A corollary to this is his hatred of the 'northern men', who, he says, had boasted 'We wol dwelle in þe south cuntrey & take al þat we nede', and from whose depredations he sees Edward IV as having saved the people of the south:

Now may þe housbond in the south dwell in his owne place—
His wif & eke his faire doughtre & al þe goode he has.
Soche menys haþ the rose made by vertu & by grace.

(67–9)

The tone here is not as harsh as in Whethamstede's Latin verses,
but, like Whethamstede, the author conceives the struggle not
simply as one between rival aristocratic factions, but as a conflict
between north and south. None of the Lancastrians, for example,
are referred to specifically: they are simply 'þe lordes of þe northe',
'The northern men', or 'The northern party' which is in many ways
a misrepresentation of the situation, but which was, none the less,
the way in which many contemporaries thought of it.

Edward IV's coronation on 28 June 1464 was the signal for more
celebratory verses. The political attitudes embodied in the so-called
Twelve Letters to Save England are predictable enough, but the form
of the poem is unusual. It opens like a normal *chanson d'aventure*: as
the poet wanders out one morning 'in chepe-syde' he sees a 'gentyl-
woman . . . wirkyng upon a vestiment' which she decorated with
'xij letteris' in the following order W, three Rs, Ʒ, E, R, E, M, S, R
and F. Using the technique of the Sibylline type of prophecy the
author proceeds to expound the significance of these letters which
comprise the initials of the names, titles and badges of the four
principal Yorkist heroes: Edward, Earl of March ('þe feturlok), his
father Richard, Duke of York ('Ʒorke', 'þe rose'), Richard, Earl of
Warwick ('þe ragged staf'), and his father Richard, Earl of
Salisbury ('þe egle'). This poem is usually dated 1461, since it refers
to Edward as 'kyng', but if this is accepted, it presents certain
problems. At this date both York and Salisbury were dead, yet the
more reliable text of this poem, Trinity College Dublin MS 432,
refers to them in the present tense as if they were alive. However,
one passage of the poem:

Þouʒ þei be disseverid, þe olde from þe yinge,
Þeire entent & purpos corden all in oone

(*HP*, 91, 63–4)

has been interpreted by R. H. Robbins to imply that York and

Salisbury were dead. And this may be the case. Yet the poem has what seem to be verbal echoes of the earlier *Ballade Set on the Gates of Canterbury* which was dated 1460, and both that poem and that on the *Battle of Northampton*, also dated 1460, are notable for their concentration on the same four Yorkist heroes as the *Twelve Letters to Save England*. It is possible that what we have here is a not very completely updated version of a poem whose original version was written in 1460. In the early part of July 1460, when they were on the way to Northampton, 'þe yinge' Edward of March and Richard of Warwick could have been said to be 'disseverid' from 'þe olde' Richard of Salisbury, who was in London, and Richard of York, who was in Ireland. But this is speculative and both versions of the poem now extant certainly refer to a period after Edward IV's assumption of the throne and are concerned principally with declaring support for him:

> to destroy treson, & make a tryall
> of hem þat be fauty, & hurten full sore.
> ffor þe wylle of edward, kyng most ryall,
> That is þe moste purpos þat we labor fore.
>
> (65–8)

The Trinity College Dublin MS 432 version ends with a prayer that the Yorkists' 'entent & purpos may last & endure' for, he claims, 'þe welfare of vs alle'.

The young King was evidently very popular. The author of the carol *Edward, Dei Gratia*, which was probably written some time after his coronation but before his marriage in 1464, recognizes Edward as King by right of a divinely assisted conquest ('god hathe chose þe to be his kny3t'). It also alludes to the justness of his claim through his hereditary title ('Oute of þe stoke that longe lay dede') and hopes that he will remain as King ('God save thy contenewaunce'). It urges him to press the English claim to the thrones of France and Spain:

> Remember þe subdeue of þis regaly
> Of Englond, fraunce & spayn trewely.
>
> (*HP*, 92, 30–1)

This last was advice Edward did well to ignore: he made peace treaties with Henry of Castile and John of Aragon in 1465, and though he claimed the French crown and actually invaded France in 1475, he quickly settled for a lucrative peace. Between 1461 and 1464 he was, in any case, too preoccupied with reducing the Lancastrian strongholds in the north to entertain expansionist notions of this sort. Outside the northern areas, however, Edward's accession was generally welcomed. At Bristol in 1461, for example, there was pageantry and verse:

First atte the comyng ynne atte temple gate there stode
Wylliam conquerour with iij lordis, and these were his wordis
> Well-come Edwarde, our son of high degre!
> Many yeeris hast þou lakkyd oute of this londe,
> I am thy fore fader, Wylliam of Normandye,
> To see thy welefare here thrugh goddys sonde.
Over the same gate stondyng a greet Gyaunt delyueryng the keyes.

At the Temple Cross there was another tableau, this time of St George and the dragon.[9]

  These celebratory poems assume implicitly that Edward IV's accession had restored the rightful line of English kings which had been interrupted by the usurping Lancastrians. This is explicitly stated in *A Political Retrospect* (1462) which is at once a review of the

> gret wrongys doon of oold antiquitey,
> Unrightful heyres by wrong alyaunce
> Usurpyng this Royaume . . .
> > *(HP*, 93, 2–4)

and praise and thanks for the achievements of Edward IV. There is no attempt at objectivity: the poem is skilfully partisan. Richard II is totally rehabilitated:

> Kyng Richard the secounde, high of dignytee,
> Whiche of Ingeland was Rightful enheritoure,
> In whos tyme ther was habundaunce with plentee
> Of welthe & erthely Ioye withouȝt langoure
> > (5–8)

G

—a remarkable contrast to the descriptions of authors writing in the last years of the fourteenth century. The author does not forget those who had suffered under the Lancastrians ('Many a trew lord then put to mortil fyne') and mentions specifically Richard Scrope, Archbishop of York, 'the blessed confessour', who was beheaded in 1405, and Humphrey 'The good duc of gloucestre' who died, probably murdered, in 1447—significantly figures whose deaths had provoked a good deal of public sympathy. These men were regarded almost as martyrs. Of the Lancastrian kings, Henry IV predictably comes in for the harshest treatment: not only was he guilty of Scrope's death (for which, says the poet, repeating the common Yorkist story, he was struck with leprosy) but he also 'in prison put perpetuelly' the rightful King and usurped the kingdom 'by force & myght' and 'undir the colour of fals periury'. The author is forced to allow Henry V some credit, but makes the point that he did not possess the crown by right:

> henry the fyfte, of knyghtly prowesse,
> Named the best of þat lyne & progeny;
> How-be-it he regned unrightfully,
> ʒit he upheld in Ingeland the honnour.
>
> (27–30)

But, like the skilful propagandist he is, the author turns even this grudging and qualified praise to the discredit of Henry VI in the next two lines:

> Henry, hys sone, of Wyndsore, by gret foly,
> All hath retourned unto huge langoure.
>
> (31–2)

His reign has been marked by 'gret mornyng', 'many a scharp schoure', 'ffalshode, myschyef, secret synne upholdyng' all of which has caused 'endeleʒ langoure' in England. It is, says the author, 'Noo mervail þough engeland hath ben unhappy' and he substantiates this by citing three proverbs which predict dire consequences: firstly for those who hold inheritance wrongly ('heritage holdyn wrongfully/schal never cheve'); secondly for the country which has an inexperienced leader ('woo be to þat Regyon/

where ys a kyng unwyse or Innocent'); and thirdly for a country
which is ruled by a woman ('. . . it ys Right a gret abusion/A
womman of a land to be regent').

Having thus established the disastrous effects of the usurping
Lancastrian dynasty, the author summarises his argument with a
memorable and resonant image, and shifts attention to Edward IV:

> Wherfore, I lykken England to a gardayne,
> Which þat hath ben ouergrowen many yere
> With wedys, which must be mowen doune playne,
> And þan schul the pleasant swete herbes appere.
> Wherfore all trewe englyssh peuple, pray yn fere
> ffor kyng Edward or Rouen, oure comfortoure,
> That he kepe Iustice and make wedis clere,
> Avoydyng the blak cloudys of langoure.
>
> (73–80)

From this the author moves easily into praise for Edward IV which
takes up most of the rest of the poem. He recalls Edward's past
victories at Northampton, Mortimer's Cross and Towton, and
sees the fact that he has always put his enemies to flight as an
indication of God's favour. On this basis he predicts future
successes:

> he it ys þat schal wynne castell, toune, and toure;
> Alle Rebellyous undyr he shal hem brynge.
>
> (94–5)

The 'Rebellyous' can only refer to the continuing activities of the
Lancastrian remnants in the north of England who were proving
difficult to subdue, and it is perhaps some slight anxiety on this
point which provoked the poem. The object of this retrospective
survey is to consolidate Edward IV's position in England by discrediting his enemies, and by inspiring public confidence in the
justness of his title and in his abilities.

A Political Retrospect also embodies interesting attitudes to
Henry VI and his wife. Queen Margaret had never been particularly well liked by the English, but the reasons for this seldom
appear in contemporary verse. Here, however, the author un-

equivocally blames her ambition ('þat ever hath ment/To gouerne all engeland with myght and poure') and the cruelty of her followers:

> Sche and here wykked affynite certayne
> Entende uttyrly to destroye thys regioun;
> ffor with theym ys but Deth & distruccioun,
> Robberye & vengeaunce with all Rygour.
>
> (59–62)

Margaret was also frequently criticised for the way in which she dominated Henry VI particularly with regard to the composition of his Council. In the poem *God Amend Wicked Counsel* (a lament supposedly made by Henry VI and overheard by the poet) which R. H. Robbins dates as 1464, the King himself blames her for his misfortunes:

> Sum tyme lordis of thys lond sette me at gret pris,
> Swiche a prynse in this rem was þer neuer non;
> I weddyd a wyf at my devyse,
> That was the cause of all my mon.
>
> Thyll her intente seyd I neuer naye;
> Ther-for I morne & no thynge am mery.
>
> (*HP*, 81, 13–18)

More specifically, in the following lines, Margaret is held responsible, through the agency of Lord Say, for the death of Humphrey of Gloucester:

> Whan sche ded syen the lorde saye
> The duke of Gloucester was sclayn at Bery.
>
> (19–20)

The criticism of Margaret appears to have had the effect of drawing attention away from the deficiences of Henry VI's rule, but does not save him entirely.

Henry VI's opponents did not usually see him as wicked or vicious, rather as ineffectual and misguided. But increasingly his weakness is held blameworthy. Whethamstede, with a hint of contempt, had compared him unfavourably with Edward IV ('Hector novus, alter Achilles'):

> Hic fuit in verbis rex mitis, rex pietatis,
> Attamen in factis nimiae vir simplicitatis.
> Hinc postquam triginta novem rex praefuit annis,
> Caeca suam fortuna rotam, quasi fortis in armis
> Volverat, et regimen rapiebat regis, eundem
> Compulit ac subito sic dicere, 'sum sine regno'.[10]
>
> (*PPS*, II, pp. 265–6)

The author of *God Amend Wicked Counsel* makes the King admit that the civil wars were the result of his ineffectual rule:

> Many a man for me hath be slayn
> With bowe and axe and swerde I-drawe;
> And thate I wite myn own brayn
> I-helde nowth my lordys under awe.
>
> (*HP*, 81, 33–6)

Authors are rarely more precise than this, but in one place the King is accused of having unnaturally used foreign assistance to establish his position in England (thus risking foreign domination):

> O, it ys gretly agayne kynde and nature,
> An englyssh man to corrumpe hys owne nacion—
> Willyng straungiers for to Recure,
> And in Engeland to have the domynacion.
>
> (*HP*, 93, 65–8)

The author is apparently referring to the help received by the Lancastrians from the Scottish King and Pierre de Brézé, seneschal of Normandy. It is a little unjust that Henry VI should have been attacked for this since the policy was organized principally by Margaret.

After the final fall of the Northumbrian castles in 1464, Lancastrian resistance in England seemed to have been crushed, and when Henry VI was captured in Lincolnshire in 1465 Edward IV appeared totally secure as King. Margaret was still intriguing in France. But it seems certain that her efforts would have come to nothing had it not been for the break between Edward IV and his former principal supporter Richard Neville, Earl of Warwick. Until the late 1460s, Warwick's loyalty had never been in doubt. It had been partly due to his efforts that Edward IV had achieved the throne in the first place. Warwick was popular with Yorkist supporters and is always mentioned by contemporary propagandists among their heroes. In 1462, for example, one poet addressed him as follows:

> Richard, the Erl of Warwyk, of knyghthode
> Lodesterre, borne of a stok þat evyr schalbe trewe,
> Havyng the name of prowes & manhode,
> Hath ben Redy to helpe and Resskewe
> Kyng Edward, in hys right hym to endewe.
>
> (*HP*, 93, 97–101)

What precisely caused Warwick's defection is not clear. It seems, however, that Edward consciously set out to free himself and his policies from Neville domination. In his foreign policy he allowed Warwick to negotiate alliances with Louis XI on his behalf, but at the same time himself worked for treaties with Charles the Bold, Duke of Burgundy. Warwick, not unnaturally, was vexed at this rather cynical slighting of his efforts. Nor did he take kindly to Edward's promotion and favour of the Woodville and Rivers families, who were related to Queen Elizabeth, especially when this involved a clash with Neville interests. Warwick's initial moves against Edward in 1469 seem to have been motivated only by a desire to change the power structure around the King. When he and George, Duke of Clarence, invaded the country they said they had come to ask the King to remove evil councillors from around him, to lower the taxes on his subjects and to take the advice of the lords of his blood. Such forces as could be mustered on Edward's behalf were defeated at Edgecot and he himself fell into Warwick's hands. For some months the composition of the government was controlled by Warwick.

This situation did not last. Though there was, for a time, ostensible amity between Edward IV and Warwick, it began to emerge that neither could really trust the other. Though Edward behaved affably towards Warwick and complied with all his requests, he had been organizing support among nobles loyal to himself. The inevitable break came as the aftermath of a rising in Lincolnshire and Yorkshire which was organized by Sir Robert Welles. It became known to Edward that Warwick and Clarence had been involved. Branded as 'great rebels' and 'traitors' they were forced to flee the country and seek refuge in the only place available to them—the France of Louis XI. It is difficult to know how far, at this stage, Warwick was committed to attempting to reinstate Henry VI as King. Sir Robert Welles' connections were Lancastrian and the chroniclers say that he ordered his men to shout for King Henry VI. But his confession, no doubt extracted under duress, indicated that the plan was to depose Edward and to make his younger brother Clarence King. It seems likely that Warwick had thoughts only of replacing Edward IV and that the *rapprochement* with Queen Margaret and the exiled Lancastrians was largely organized by Louis XI. At any event, when Warwick and his two thousand supporters landed unopposed at Dartmouth on 25 September 1470 he declared himself publicly in favour of Henry VI. It must have been shortly after this that a contemporary Lancastrian carol writer celebrated him as the restorer of England's rightful King:

> Nowell, nowell, nowell, nowell!
> & cryst saue mery ynglon & sped yt welle!
>
> Tyll home sull wylekyn, þis Ioly gentyl schep,
> all to houre combely kyng hary þis cnat ys knyt;
> þer-fore let vs all syng nowel.
> (*HP*, 82, refrain and lines 1–3)

Warwick is here referred to as 'wylekyn' and the 'cnat' (knot) probably indicates his reconciliation with the Lancastrians. The ship imagery is fairly common in political verses and is continued in the other stanzas of the poem which celebrate Warwick's prospective joining with Edward, Prince of Wales ('my lorde prynce'), John Neville, Marquess of Montagu ('my lorde chamberlayne'), and with 'my lorde fueryn' who has so far resisted identification.

For once Edward IV was caught unprepared. He had under-estimated Warwick and in any case thought he would land in Yorkshire where Neville support was strong. The King had insufficient troops (especially after the desertion of John Neville, Marquess of Montagu to the Lancastrians) to risk facing Warwick in battle, and on 2 October 1470 he sailed from King's Lynn for the safety of his brother-in-law's duchy of Burgundy. Without a blow being struck, Warwick and the Lancastrians had regained the kingdom. There seems to have been little public enthusiasm for the reconquest and no poems of joy at the Lancastrian restoration have come down to us. Warwick was never entirely trusted by the Lancastrians, who could not forget his past career. The French alliance he sought to establish was disliked especially among the commercial men, for, after Edward's deposition, the lucrative trade with Burgundy was soon hit. Queen Margaret was no great favourite in England, and Henry VI (a broken and pathetic figure after his five years in the Tower) inspired no confidence as King. None the less, when Edward IV sailed from Burgundy in ships supplied by merchants of the Hanse and accompanied by fifteen hundred men paid for by Charles, Duke of Burgundy, he seemed to have little chance of regaining the kingdom. When he landed at Ravenspur in March 1471 he was greeted very warily. Some towns, such as Kingston-upon-Hull, shut their gates upon him. His support did not, at first, increase dramatically. On the Lancastrian side, Warwick raised an army at Coventry; George, Duke of Clarence, was in charge of another in the south west; the Duke of Exeter, the Earl of Oxford and Viscount Bourchier were with their forces in the east midlands; the Bastard of Fauconberg had a fleet in the Channel; and Queen Margaret was expected with supporters from France. There was some reluctance to rally to the combined Neville and Lancastrian cause. But their support ought to have been sufficient to crush Edward if they had engaged him early. However, indecisiveness allowed Edward to muster support, to move about fairly freely, even to besiege Warwick and his army in Coventry, and on Thursday 11 April 1471 he entered London. Edward's brother George, Duke of Clarence, had already defected from the Lancastrian cause, and when Warwick realized that he had about as much support as he could hope for (Queen Margaret had still not arrived from France) he marched his forces south. On Sunday 14 April, just north of Barnet, Edward IV defeated the Lancastrians in a bitter, confused battle in which Warwick lost his life.

The events of 1471 from the time of Edward's landing at Ravenspur to his victory at Barnet are treated in a pro-Yorkist fashion in the first part of a fairly long poem *On the Recovery of the Throne by Edward IV* from British Museum MS Reg. 17D xv. Among the most notable features are the way in which the poet stresses Edward's difficulties and the privations he suffered (which he seems to think were a divine punishment 'for wickyd lyvyng'), and the way in which the pathos of Edward's situation is emphasized. This is clear from the beginning of the poem:

> At his londyng in Holdyrnes he hadde grett payne;
> His subjectes and people wolde not hym obey,
> Off hym and his people thay had grett disdayne.
> There schewid hym unkyndnes, and answerid him playne
>
> (*PPS*, II, p. 272)

and the poet follows this by a reference to the way in which 'this nobille prynce' and his followers were 'trowbelid' by the magistrates at York who first warned them off before eventually allowing them 'into the cite'. The poet then turns to Edward's march south, past Pomfret Castle and the Marquess of Montagu who 'Wyth the prince . . . durste not mete', and on to Coventry where he prepared his army:

> To fyght with Warwicke and all his meny.
> But he was affrayed, and his people also.
>
> (p. 272)

Again the poet stresses how Edward was 'trowblid mervelously' by lack of 'mete, dryncke and logynge'. Clarence's change to his brother's side is attributed to the force of natural affection between them ('Nature hath compellid hem agayne togere go') and the Duke's motives are further flattered by the poet's statement that he had only been separated from Edward's cause by a trick ('a sotell meane'). After this the poet alludes briefly to Edward's further efforts to bring Warwick to battle ('Dayly he prophered batayle, his enmys durst not fyghte'). He also describes how Edward had to leave Coventry for 'lacke of logynge and vitayle', and then how he 'passid to Londone'. There is a fuller treatment of later events, from the time Edward entered the capital 'with a company of men trew'. The poet wittily portrays the discomfiture of Edward's enemies in London ('Thayre red colowrus chaungid to pale hewe') and touches on the re-imprisonment of Henry VI, before describing in greater detail the ceremony at Westminster which reinstated Edward as King. But what really catches his imagination is the King's reunion with his wife and children (who had been in sanctuary in Westminster for the previous year):

> The kyng comfortid the quene, and other ladyes eke;
> His swete babis full tendurly he did kys;
> The yonge priynce he behelde, and in his armys did bere.
> Thus his bale turnyd hym to blis.
>
> (p. 274)

Several stanzas are devoted to the Battle of Barnet, but the author appears to have no detailed knowledge of it. His description is impressionistic, but made particularly effective through the judicious use of alliterative phrases: 'hewyng of harnes', 'tremelyng and turnyng', 'rorynge and rumbelynge' and so on. He is aware that the battle was confused—

> There was rydynge and rennyng: sum cryed 'Wayleaway!'
> Unknowyng to many man who the better hadde.
> Sum souȝte thayre masters, sum hit thaym that day
>
> (p. 276)

—because it was fought in a thick mist. But most notable is the pity this author reveals for the dead and wounded at the battle:

> Sum hurte, sum slayne, sum cryinge 'Alas!'
> Gretter multitude than I con telle.
> Sum waloyng in blood, sum pale, sum wan.
> Sum sekyng thayre frendis in care and in wo.
>
> (p. 277)

Though this is a partisan poem, the author's pity extends to all. There is no exultation at the defeated enemies of Edward: he simply remarks of Warwick and Montagu that they 'were slayne in fere'. Nor does he treat Edward as a great conqueror. He fights 'stidfastly and worshypfully' in the battle, but though the victory is his it is achieved very much 'throw Goddes myȝte'. The author stresses the divine favour which is shown to Edward: on his march south an 'ymage wiche was closid brake opyn sodenly' at Daventry as a 'tokyn of victory', and before Barnet there 'shone a star over his hede full bryȝte'. In fact he almost removes Edward's reconquest from the human sphere, so much is it 'paste mannys resoun and mynde'. But, says the poet, God has disposed things in this way and it is beyond the power of mankind to alter them 'What may man-hode do agaynst Goddes myȝte' (p. 271).

From the emphasis in the first part of the poem on events which took place in London (Edward's meeting with his wife, his rein-statement as King) and the lack of detailed knowledge about events which took place elsewhere one may deduce that the author was a Londoner. This is borne out by the way in which the poem continues, for there is no mention of how, soon after Barnet, Edward had to march his army west to meet the threat of Queen Margaret. She had landed at Weymouth on the day Barnet was fought and had raised forces in the south-west. Margaret then crossed into Wales to join up with Jasper Tudor but was caught and defeated at Tewkesbury on 4 May 1471. This was a crucial battle, for it effectively ended large-scale Lancastrian resistance. The author of *The Recovery of the Throne by Edward IV*, however, deals with events which took place in London while Edward was away, and describes at some length the unsuccessful attack on the city by the Bastard of Fauconberg and the Kentishmen. Though this part of the poem follows, without a break, that on the events leading up to the Battle of Barnet, it is of a different character. Because the author experiences these later events more immedi-ately, he writes about them with more knowledge and involvement. He is precise about the details of the fighting:

> At Londone brygge thay made asawte, sham to see,
> The utter gate on the brygge thay seth on fyre
> Into Londone shott arows withowte pete.

> (p. 277)

And when this attack was beaten off they made another:

> Wyth gunpowdir and wildefire and straw eke;
> Fro the gate to the drawbrygge thay brent down playne,
> That x myle men myȝte se the smeke.

(p. 278)

When this failed 'Thay brente fayre howsis' in Aldgate. The author feels a good deal of hatred for 'these false men' who did 'opyn tresoun' with their 'myschevus dedis' and caused 'Moche sorow and shame'. He allies this with a contemptuous derision at their defeat and flight:

> Like maysterles men away thay wente,
> Erly in the mornyng, or it were day,
> Throw halkys and hegges resortid into Kent.
> Thay vanysshyd away as thayre tayles had be brente,
> Remembrynge thayre false tresoun, in hertes woo.

(p. 279)

And although, in his refrain, the author reiterates that the defeat of Fauconberg's forces happened in accordance with God's will ('Thus the wille of God in every thynge is doo'), he is more disposed, in this part of the poem, to recognize the human agency through which it was performed. He duly praises the Earl of Essex and the city aldermen who 'sewde out like manly men' on the rebels, and also Earl Rivers 'that gentill knyȝte' who 'Throw his enmyes that day did ... passe' thereby gaining 'grett love of the comyns'.

The rest of the poem presents few problems. There is a notable expression of sympathy for the 'langowr and angwiche' the Queen experienced:

> When hir lorde and sovereyn was in adversite
> To here of hir wepyng it was grett pete.

(p. 281)

But for the most part, it celebrates in a straightforward way the Yorkist heroes who returned in triumph to London after their successful campaigns. There is praise in general for the 'nobill lordis of grett renowne' and the 'many other kny3tes and yomen' who rode in the triumphal procession to St Paul's, and special tribute is paid to the loyalty of William, Lord Hastings:

> The lord chambirlayne, that gentill kny3te,
> Whiche failid his mayster nother in storme ne stoure.
>
> (p. 280)

But predictably the author's attention is focussed on Edward IV and his brothers: Clarence is an 'honorabill kny3te' and Richard, Duke of Gloucester (later Richard III), who is 'yonge of age and victorius in batayle', might achieve 'the honoure of Ectour'. No conqueror in the history of the world, says the poet, was more splendidly accompanied than Edward IV on this occasion:

> Nothur Alisaunder ne Artur, ne no conquerouere
> No better were acompenyd with nobill men.
> Like none of the rounde tabull were beseyn,
> Ryally horsid and aparelde in the fere of thayre foo.
> Thus victoriusly he come. Goddes wille was soo.
>
> (p. 279)

Much the same type of praise by comparison appears in another poem written at about this time—the so-called *Battle of Barnet* from Trinity College Cambridge MS 601:

> Of a more famous knyght I neuer rad
> Syn the tyme of Artors dayes;
> He that loueth hym nat, I holde hym mad.
>
> (*HP*, 94, 21–3)

In fact the battle itself is not treated in any detail here: the poet simply remarks that it took place 'Uppon Ester day' and that 'Many a man hys lyfe lost in that mornyng' including Warwick 'that louyd dyuysion'. The intention here is propagandist. The author seeks to establish Edward IV's position as King by stressing his twofold claim to the title: by line of descent, and through a divinely assisted conquest:

> now regneth ryghtwysly oure souerayn,
> Trew enherytour to the crowne, hys quarell preueth so,

Edward the fourth, by grace to attayn,
With the crowne of England on vs to rayn,
By iust tytle of hys descendyng. . . .

(2–7)

He seems to be trying to persuade the common people in particular (among whom Warwick had been popular) to accept Edward IV as their rightful ruler. Hence probably the insistence on Warwick's death ('Mortuus est, ther can no man hym se') and the refrain: 'Conuertimini, ye comons, & drede your kyng.'

The remaining twelve years of Edward IV's reign were perhaps as peaceful and prosperous as any England knew in the fifteenth century. After the battles of 1471, the Lancastrian opposition was innocuous, even if not completely destroyed. On the day Edward returned to London from Tewkesbury, Henry VI died in the Tower, probably murdered. His only son Edward had been killed at Tewkesbury, and Queen Margaret was in captivity, where she remained until 1476 when Louis XI ransomed her. In 1473, John de Vere, Earl of Oxford, who had escaped from Barnet, captured St Michael's Mount in Cornwall, but this rising petered out and he surrendered on 1 February 1474. The only danger at home, in fact, came from the discontented Clarence who continued to intrigue in a petty way against Edward. He was finally attainted for treason in 1477 and executed in the Tower on 18 February 1478. Troubles on the Scottish border were handled effectively by Richard, Duke of Gloucester, and abroad Edward was not to be drawn into a war such as had drained the country's resources earlier in the century. In 1475 he did take a large and well-equipped army to France, but settled at Picquigny for a lucrative peace. With the money that Louis XI paid him and with what he raised through reorganized royal finances at home, Edward made the Crown richer than it had been throughout the century. He freed himself from a dependence on parliamentary grants. With peace and relative stability trade revived and prosperity increased. Edward himself made money as a wool merchant. When he died at the age of forty in 1483, the Yorkist dynasty still looked secure.

Perhaps because of his successful rule, his martial valour and his general affability, Edward IV was a popular King and two sets of contemporary verses on his death are extant. The ten rhyme-royal stanzas entitled *The Death of Edward IV* (1483) have a refrain which stresses that 'All men of Englond ar bounde for hym to praye', and consist initially of pure adulation, particularly on the subject of his military achievements:

> this Prynce that conquered his right
> Within Ingland, master of all his ffoon;
> And after ffraunce, be very force & myght,
> Without stroke, and afterward cam hoom;
> Made Scotlond to yelde, and Berwyk wan he from.
>
> (*HP*, 42, 1–5)

Strictly speaking, Edward can hardly be said to have 'conquered' France, and the success in Scotland and the winning of Berwick were due to Richard, Duke of Gloucester. None the less, all of this is made to contribute to the achievement of the King who was 'the dowthiest, the worthiest, without comparison', who was the 'well of knyghthode', the 'lode-sterre' of all earthly princes, and the 'lanterne & the light' of his people. These are frequently used comparisons in eulogistic verse, and the poet also presses into service Yorkist badges ('the sonne', 'the rose', 'the sonne-beme') to provide himself with further ways of praising Edward. From using another eulogistic device—the comparison with heroes of history and legend—the poet disqualifies himself, for the simple reason that Edward was incomparable:

> In gestis, in romansis, in Chronicles, nygh & ferre,
> Well knowen it is, þer can no man it deferre,
> Perelees he was. . . .
>
> (32–4)

What appears to strike the poet most deeply, however, is the suddenness of Edward's death at the height of his prosperity, a point which is emphasized in the frequently repeated half line 'he was here yestirday', and the significance of the poem is deepened in the last two stanzas. It is clear from the earlier questions 'Wher is this Prynce . . .?' (1) and 'Where is he now . . .?' (15) that this

is in some sense an 'ubi sunt' poem, and the author seeks to incul-
cate the usual moral of this sort of poem—that worldly prosperity
is temporary, and that no trust should be placed upon it:

> Ye wofull men that shall this writyng rede,
> Remembre well here is no dwellyng place.
> Se howe this prince is from vs goon, and dede,
> And we shall aftir hym sue the trace.
> Ther is no choise, there is noon other grace;
> This knowe ye well—he was here yestirday.
>
> (64–9)

Edward IV is an example here of the inevitable mutability of all
earthly things, and the splendour of his achievements and the
suddenness of his death are meant to sharpen the reader's sense of
this.

The second poem, *The Lament for the Soul of Edward IV*, is
attributed in British Museum MS Additional 29729 f.8r to Lydgate
(an impossibility since he died in 1450) but someone else, probably
John Stow (to whom the manuscript belonged), has crossed this
attribution through and has substituted 'Skelton'. Between 1542
and 1548 this poem was printed, with five others, by Richard
Lant and again attributed to Skelton, but it is not certainly his. It
is written in an elaborate twelve-line stanza with a Latin refrain
'ecce nunc in pulvere dormio' ('behold now I sleep in dust').
Supposedly spoken by Edward himself, it prays to God for grace
and to people of England that they should pray for his soul:

> In manus tuas, domine, my spryte vp I yeld;
> Humbley I besech the off thy grace!
> And ye, corteys commyners, with your hert vnbrace
> Benyngly to pray for me also.
>
> (*RL XV*, 159, 91–4)

It has much in common with the previous poem, but here the 'ubi
sunt' element is more fully articulated:

> Where is my gret conquest & vyctory?
> Where is my Rentis & my Rally aray?

1 Richard II yields the Crown to Bolingbroke (*see page* 115)

2 The author and his patron I:
Thomas Hoccleve presents his
Regement of Princes to Henry,
Prince of Wales (*see page* 16)

3 The author and his patron II: John Lydgate presents his *Troy Book* to
Henry V (*see page* 16)

4 Henry V marries Katherine
(*see page* 71)

5 The siege of Calais (1436).
"Here shows how Philip of
Burgundy besieged Calais and
Humphrey Duke of Gloucester,
Richard Earl of Warwick
and Humphrey Earl of
Stafford, with a great
multitude, went over the sea
and followed the Duke, he
ever fleeing before them."
(*See page* 83)

6 Henry VI

7 Edward IV

8 Richard III

9 Henry VII

10 Perpendicular Churches I: Lavenham, Suffolk (*see page* 219)

11 Perpendicular Churches II:
the south porch of
Northleach, Gloucestershire
(*see page* 219)

From Brasses and Brass Rubbing, *Clare Gittings Blandford, 1970*

12 The memorial brass of John Fortey, Northleach (*see page* 220)

13 William Grevel's house at Chipping Campden, Gloucestershire (*see page* 220)

National Monuments Record

14 Women's headdresses; the birth of St Edmund from Lydgate's *Life of St Edmund* (*see page* 341)

15 Friars with a devil on their backs (*see page* 236)

16 The court of the King's Bench (*see page* 323)

> Where by my coursors & my horsys so hy?
> Where is my grett plesure, solas & play?
> As vanite to nouȝte all ys gon away.
>
> (61–5)

And the poet continues in the traditional way by making the King recall other great men who have been laid low by death—Alexander, Samson, Solomon and Absalom. Most notable, though, is the implied criticism of Edward. He is made to admit that his reign had not satisfied everyone: 'Som men to plesoure, and som men nott to lykyng' (8). Furthermore, the poet attributes Edward's acquisition of splendid buildings to avarice and pride:

> I had Inogthe, I hyld nott me content,
> With-outt Remembraunce that I schuld dy,
> More to encresse was myne entent.
>
> (49–51)

In the previous stanza, moreover, there had appeared a forthright condemnation of his accumulation of money:

> I stored hucches, cofers and chyst
> With tresore takyng off my commynalte—
> ffore there tresore that I toke there prayers I myst.
>
> (41–3)

Edward IV was criticized for his avarice in the latter part of his reign, but some people it seems, preferred to forget this. In Lant's print the stanza containing these lines was omitted—clearly expunged by someone who wanted the poem to present as favourable a picture of Edward as possible.

Had Edward V been older, the disastrous events of the next two years which destroyed the Yorkist dynasty might never have occurred. But Edward IV's early death meant there would be quite a long minority. This in itself practically guaranteed a power struggle within the ruling clique. Throughout his brother's life, Richard, Duke of Gloucester, had been undeviatingly loyal, but, immediately on hearing of Edward IV's death, he moved against the Queen's relatives: Anthony Woodville, Earl Rivers, Sir Richard

Grey and Sir Thomas Vaughan. He took custody of Edward V on 30 April 1483 at Stony Stratford. It is doubtful if Richard had immediate designs on the crown. Perhaps he simply wished to ensure that his just claim to the Protectorate was implemented, or perhaps he simply wished to prevent the Woodvilles (with whom he had no sympathy) from overmuch influencing his nephew. But once he had begun to make his position secure it seems he had to continue to the logical end—the crown. There is probably some truth in the hypothesis of Sir William Cornwallis who, in 1603, said that for Richard 'there was no safety but in sovereignty'.[11] Certainly he felt himself threatened, for by June he was writing to York for armed men to be sent to assist him. From this point events moved quickly. On 13 June William, Lord Hastings, who had been intriguing with those Woodvilles still free, was arrested and killed. On 16 June Richard of York, Edward V's nine-year-old brother, was taken from his mother's care and the sanctuary of Westminster to be put with the young King in the Tower. By 22 June stories were being circulated that the Princes were illegitimate (on the grounds that Edward was pre-contracted to Lady Eleanor Butler at the time he married Elizabeth Woodville) and so disqualified from the succession. On 26 June Richard, Duke of Gloucester, was presented with a petition asking him to assume the crown, as its rightful heir by the election of the three estates. He accepted and became King. A sumptuous coronation followed on 5 July.

But Richard III's hold on the crown was never secure. In October 1483 Henry Stafford, Duke of Buckingham, who had been hitherto his principal ally, revolted against him, albeit unsuccessfully. In April 1484 his only son, and heir to the throne, died, and not long afterwards his Queen, Ann. He was more isolated than ever. Those about him could not be trusted, and it was the disaffection of a large part of his army under Sir William Stanley to the side of Henry Tudor, Earl of Richmond, at the Battle of Bosworth on 22 August 1485, which finally caused his downfall. Except in the north, Richard III was never very popular. But neither, to his contemporaries, was he the evil monster that later Tudor historians made him. In 1484 Wyllyam Collyngbourne did deride him and his supporters in a punning and allusive couplet nailed to the door of St Paul's London:

> The Cat, the Rat and Lovel our dog
> Rule all England under a hog,

and if the Tudor chroniclers are to be believed verses such as

> Jack of Norfolk, be not too bold
> For Dickon thy master is bought and sold

were circulated before Bosworth, designed to isolate Richard from his supporters.[12] This one was nailed to the gate of John, Duke of Norfolk.

The events of Richard III's reign seem to have been almost totally ignored by contemporary poets. An exception was the author of the hitherto unpublished prophecy in BM MS Lansdowne 762 f. 63v.[13] The opening lines refer to 1483, and allude to the death of Edward IV and to Buckingham's rebellion:

> The yere of our lorde m cccc lxxx iij
> betuext the departyng of Aprell and not fer from may
> The bull shall departe & passe away
> The same yere shalbe moche adoo
> Walles shall bere armys and to Albion goo
> Which shall cause men to sofer moch woo.
>
> (1–6)

Though the poet uses the future tense the events he refers to belong to the past. His account, as far as it goes, is accurate: Edward IV did die at the end of April, and Buckingham did derive support from Wales. The rest of the poem, however, cannot be so precisely interpreted, but some of it appears to allude to Henry of Richmond's invasion. He is perhaps the man, who in 'The yere of our lorde m cccc lxxx iiij' (11), will claim the throne ('The crowne to opteyne he will chalenge by name' 14). He may be the 'banysshed man . . . far be yonde the see' (22). But the prophecy seems to have no coherent pattern. Other people, difficult to identify for certain, are alluded to by means of their badges or the initial letters of their names. Scraps of other prophecies are worked into this poem with no precise relevance. The author repeats himself without any obvious point. However, he fairly consistently predicts trouble in England:

> Then mene shall aryse one ageyne another
> And fare as men that were all wood
> The son shall slee the father the broder the broder
> That the stretes of London shall ron all on blod,
>
> (39–42)

and it seems to be the object of the poem to stir up discontent by prophesying it. In the usual way, he seeks to give authority to his verses by referring some of his prophecies to 'Seint Bede' (17) and 'Merlin' (127).

Tudor chroniclers saw Henry VII's victory at Bosworth as a momentous turning point in history. In 1485, however, nobody thought of it in this way. Yorkist sympathizers were still free, and Henry VII still had battles to fight before his crown was secure. Nor was there any sense of relief that the civil wars were virtually over, though there had been, through the years, signs that those not closely involved were tired of the instability. Writing in the turbulent years about 1470, George Ashby comments on the greed of the contemporary nobility and the trouble it has caused:

> Ther hath be in late daies right grete change
> Of high estates and grete diuision,
> Right meruelous, wonderful & eke strange
> To myche folk unportable punicion,
> Sorouful, peineful, and tribulacion
> Whiche might haue be eschewed. . . .
>
> (*Poems*, II, 169–74)

Dating from about the same time comes a memorable passage in which Sir Thomas Malory abandons his narrative in order to make a comparison between the civil war in Arthur's kingdom, and the propensity of the English for revolting against their kings:

> Lo ye all Englysshemen, se ye nat what a myschyff here was? For he that was the moste kynge and nobelyst knyght of the worlde, and moste loved the felyshyp of noble knyghtes, and

by hym they all were upholdyn, and yet myght nat thes Englyshemen holde them contente with hym. Lo thus was the olde custom and usayges of thys londe, and men say that we of thys londe have nat yet loste that custom. Alas! thys ys a greate defaughte of us Englysshemen, for there may no thynge us please no terme.[14]

In 1485, though, the first preoccupation of the new King and his supporters must have been the establishment and the justification of his conquest. For this purpose verse and pageantry were used. When he entered his capital on 3 September 1485 some Latin verses in his honour were sung by the blind poet Bernardus Andreas:

> Ergo jucundis hodie camoenis
> Gaudeat late regio tumultu
> Tota, nec post metuat tenente
> Rege coronam.[15]

In some of the cities through which Henry VII passed on his first progress, pageants were organized and verses to welcome him were sometimes written. As Sydney Anglo has pointed out, it was very necessary for the people of Worcester to make their peace with Henry because there had been opposition to him earlier.[16] A character in the welcoming pageant apologizes for this, and explains that the local citizens had been led astray by

> A Gentilman detected with Riottours
> Making Suggestion agenst you and youres. . . .

There follows fulsome praise of Henry from the character Janitor who finally yields up the keys of the city to him:

> And now welcome our noble Souveraigne Lorde,
> Better welcome was never Prince to us.

Possibly a similar need to ensure that the city be reconciled with the new King lies behind the deference with which the character Ebrauke (the supposed founder of York) symbolically delivers up the city to Henry:

> I pray for compasion;
> And to mynd how this Citie of old and pure affecion

> Gladdith an injoith your high grace and commyng,
> With oon concent, knowing you ther Sufferaine and King.

It was from York, of course, that Richard III had received so much assistance.

The preoccupations of early Tudor propaganda also emerge from these pageants and from verses written at about this time. Henry VII's claim to the throne by right of conquest was incontestable, but he had no legitimate hereditary claim, and early Tudor apologists are uneasy on this point. Occasionally, something is made of his Welsh descent, as when the writer of the Worcester pageant presents him as a descendant of Cadwalader, whose progeny (it was prophesied) would come once again to rule England:

> Cadwaladers Blodde lynyally descending,
> Longe hathe bee towlde of such a Prince comyng.
> Wherfor Frendes, if that I shal not lye,
> This same is the Fulfiller of the Profecye.

More often, something was made of Henry VII's connection with Henry VI (Henry VII's father was half-brother to Henry VI). In the Worcester pageant a figure representing the last Lancastrian King welcomes him:

> I am Henry VIth, sobre and sad,
> Thy great Uncle, sumtyme of England King.
> Full XXXIX yeres this Realme myself I had,
> And of the people had the Governyng.
> Slaine was I, Martir by great Tormenting. . . .

For reasons which were basically propagandist the memory of Henry VI was rehabilitated in these years. He is presented as a saint and martyr. In the typical treatment of the Franciscan James Ryman, probably written in 1492, he is said to have been 'Full of mercy without vengeaunce', 'meke & benigne' and utterly without worldly vanity:

> In thy gesture thou were like Iobe
> Stedfast of feith & myelde of mode,

Not prowde of vesture ne of roobe,
Ne auarous of worldely goode,
Ne sumptuous of carnall foode;
Wherefore in blisse the king of grace
Hath graunted the A ioyefull place.
(*HP*, 83, 36–42)

For obvious reasons, all reference to his insanity and incompetence are suppressed.

But it was Henry VII's marriage to Elizabeth, daughter of Edward IV, that provided Tudor propagandists with their most effective image—the red and white rose which symbolically reconciled the Yorkist and Lancastrian factions. The white rose was frequently used as a badge by the Yorkists, and it is probably Elizabeth of York who is celebrated in a song from BM MS Additional 5464 entitled *The Lily White Rose:*

þe white rose is most trewe
This garden to rule, by ryȝtwis lawe.
(*HP*, 34, 11–12)

It has been suggested that this was written in 1461 when Edward IV was proclaimed King in London, but R. H. Robbins is probably right in dating it 1486. It is most likely a celebration of Elizabeth's suitability as Henry VII's Queen. The red rose had not been used much as a Lancastrian badge until late in this period, but Henry VII was greeted in the Bristol pageant as the 'delicate Rose of this your Brytaigne',[17] and the symbolism of the red and white roses is used in the York pageant to welcome Henry VII:

at the entrie of the Citie and first Bar of the same, shalbe craftely conceyved a place in maner of a heven, of grete joy and anglicall armony; under the heven shalbe a world desolate, full of treys and floures, in the which shall spryng up a roiall rich rede rose convaide by viace, unto the which rose shall appeyre another rich white rose, unto whome so being togedre all other floures shall lowte and evidently yeve suffrantie, shewing the rose to be principall of all floures. . . .

The same symbolism is used for a similar purpose in the final stanza of a three part song called *The Roses Entwined*, which probably dates from 1486:

> 'I loue the rose both red & white.'
> 'Is that your pure perfite appetite?'
> 'to here talke of them is my delite!'
> 'Ioyed may we be,
> oure prince to se
> & rosys thre.'
>
> (*HP*, 35, 31–6)

The last three lines seem to refer to the birth of an heir to Henry VII.

Beyond the establishment of Henry VII on the English throne this chapter does not go. The civil wars of the latter part of the fifteenth century were fought with words as well as with guns, bows and swords. It is plain, also, from the use of propaganda by Henry VII, that the written word was to continue, under the Tudors, to be an important political weapon.

NOTES

[1] C. L. Kingsford ed. 'Extracts from the First Version of Hardyng's Chronicle' *EHR* 27, 1912, pp. 749–50.

[2] *Hardyng's Chronicle* ed. H. Ellis, 1812, p. 155.

[3] See above, Chapter 2.

[4] *Three Books of Polydore Vergil's English History* ed. H. Ellis, Camden Society 29, 1844, p. 101.

[5] *Mittelenglische Dichtungen*, Halle 1940, p. 204.

[6] *Translations:* 'He was regent and governor of France; he guarded Normandy from danger; he crossed the river at Pontoise; he put to flight the King of France and his son. In Ireland he established such government that he ruled all the land in peace. He was for a long time Protector of England. He loved the people and defended them.'

'Rightful heir, proved in many a land, to the crowns of France and England.'

[7] *Translation:* 'Northern people, treacherous people ready for plunder, people like Briareus in one hundred handed spoliation, in liver like Tityus, in rolling a stone like Sisyphus, and one may further associate Tantulus with those, their habit observes no measure, it is worse than that of those, they destroy, they plunder, they scarcely leave a stone after them, Northern people, a worthless people, a people without piety, and without law protectors of honour and without justice protectors of the right. Because the arbitrator wished all things to be ruled by force of the sword, by barbarian custom, it will be permitted in spoliation that one's own property should become the

property of others, through plunder. That which they did not take away was either too hot or too cold. Northern people, people of the appearance and character of the snake, they bite, and eat up, they consume, and eat away, and burden their mothers to destruction as if striving wickedly to be born.'

[8] *The Historical Collections of a Citizen of London*, ed. J. Gairdner, Camden Society 17, 1876, p. 215.

[9] *Political Religious and Love Poems* ed. F. J. Furnivall, EETS OS 15 1866, p. 5.

[10] *Translation:* 'This was in words a mild king, a king of piety, but yet in actions a man of excessive simplicity. This man reigned as king for thirty nine years, then blind fortune, as if strong in arms, had turned her wheel and had taken away the king's power, had compelled him suddenly to say thus: "I am without a kingdom." '

[11] Quoted by S. B. Chrimes, *Lancastrians Yorkists and Henry VII*, 2nd edition 1966, p. 134.

[12] For these couplets see Fabyan's *New Chronicles of England and Scotland* ed. H. Ellis, 1811, p. 672 and *Holinshed's Chronicles*, 1808, III, 444.

[13] See Appendix B.

[14] *The Works of Malory* ed. E. Vinaver, Oxford 1947, III, 1229.

[15] *Memorials of Henry VII* ed. J. Gairdner, 1858, pp. 35–6. *Translation:* 'Therefore today, with pleasant songs, let the whole country far and wide enjoy festivity, nor afterwards be afraid while the king wears the crown.'

[16] *Spectacle Pageant and Early Tudor Policy*, Oxford 1969, pp. 28–31 from which the following extracts from the Worcester pageant are taken. The York verses appear in *York Civic Records* ed. Angelo Raine, Yorkshire Archaeological Society 1939.

[17] For an account of the Bristol pageant see Sydney Anglo, *op. cit.*, p. 34. For the red and white rose symbolism at York see *York Civic Records*, *op. cit.*

7 : Religion and the Clergy

RELIGION permeated fifteenth-century life. About a fifth of the land of England was owned by the Church and its wealth was increasing. The Church largely controlled education and the hospitals, and in most towns and villages the finest buildings were churches. Moreover, the arts were almost exclusively religious: the majority of poetry and prose was on religious subjects; almost all drama was religious; and the most obvious outlet for a painter's skill was the adorning of churches or the illumination of psalters and books of hours. All the media were used to transmit Christian doctrine, and Christian morality, but their effectiveness varied. Popular sermons, which were in English, were informative and entertaining, but most of the average church congregation could not follow the services in any detail, since they were in Latin, and even the iconography of the stained glass, which the richest churches had, was sometimes incomprehensible to the unlearned.

The Pardoner and þe Miller, and oþir lewde sotes,
Souȝt hem selfen in the Chirch, riȝt as lewde gotes;
Pyrid fast, and pourid, hiȝe oppon the glase,
Countirfeting gentilmen, þe armys for to blase,
Diskyueryng fast the peyntour, and for the story mourned,
And a red it also right as wolde Rammys hornyd
'He berith a balstaff', quod the toon, 'and els a rakis ende.'
'Thow faillist', quod the Miller, 'þowe hast not wel þy mynde;
It is a spere yf thowe canst se, right with a prik to-fore
To bussh adown his enmy, and þurh the Sholdir bore.'
'Pese!' quod the hoost of Southwork, 'let stond þe wyndow glasid!
Goith vp, and doith yeur offerynge! yee semeth half amasid.'

So writes the anonymous author of *The Tale of Beryn*, a pseudo-Chaucerian continuation of the *Canterbury Tales*.[1] But, fully understood or not, religion was a central factor in fifteenth-century life.

In this century no sensational changes occurred in the doctrine or institution of the Church. Such changes as did take place were gradual. The pattern of building altered somewhat. With the notable exceptions of Syon Abbey, founded by Henry V in 1414 for the Brigettine nuns, and the Carthusian house at Sheen, there were no new monastic foundations in this century. Nor was it a great age of cathedral building—though there was some rebuilding, especially of towers, as at Gloucester. Money was devoted to other things. The rich nobility and the higher clergy sometimes founded schools and colleges to train the clergy: Henry VI, for example, founded Eton in 1440, and King's College, Cambridge, in the following year; Margaret of Anjou began Queens' College in 1448; Henry Chichele started All Souls in 1438. Others founded chantries in existing institutions to perpetuate their memories and to ensure that Masses were said continually for their souls. Thus, Richard Beauchamp, Earl of Warwick, in his will of 1435, provided for the foundation of a chapel in St Mary's Warwick:

> when it liketh to God, that my soule depart out of this world, my body be enterred within the Church Collegiate of Our Lady in Warwick, where I will that in such place as I have devised ther be made a Chappell of Our Lady, well, faire and goodly built, within the middle of which Chappell I will that my Tombe be made . . . Also I will that there be said every day, during the Worlde, in the aforesaid Chappell . . . three masses.[2]

Persons other than the nobility and the clergy frequently bestowed their wealth upon parish churches. Hence from the fifteenth century date many handsome perpendicular churches built on the money of the local community. Particularly notable are those in East Anglia (such as Dedham, Long Melford, Cavendish and Lavenham) and those in the Cotswolds (such as Chipping Campden, Fairford and Northleach), regions both made rich by the wool and cloth trade. Tradition ascribes the building of Chipping

Campden to the great benefactions of William Grevel 'the flower of the wool merchants of all England', Fairford was rebuilt between about 1490 and 1500 by John Tame, another wool merchant, and to yet another, John Fortey, Northleach owes its clerestory. At Northleach a set of memorial brasses emphasize the connections between various merchants and their local church.

But neither the changes in endowment, nor those changes in patterns of devotion which put more emphasis on a personal rather than an institutionalized religion, had the effect of significantly disrupting the English Church so as to provoke comment. Heresy, particularly around the time of Oldcastle's rebellion, frightened the orthodox and prompted some anti-Lollard literature. But, for the most part, fifteenth-century poets concentrate on the perennial topics of the materialism, inefficiency and immorality of the Church and the clergy. Their concern is almost exclusively with English problems and there is little of the violently anti-papal literature characteristic of the previous century.

In fact, fifteenth-century poets were surprisingly little interested in papal affairs. Even the great schism of the West which divided the Church for forty years from 1378 received little attention, except in Gower's *Address to Henry IV* written in about 1400. He regrets that the schism has diminished papal authority. Because 'holy chirche is in hir silf divided' a lot of lesser problems went unsettled: 'No wonder is thogh it stonde out of reule.' What concerns him most is the absence of the traditional papal mediation between warring Christian princes. The divisions in the Church had come to reflect political divisions, with England and its allies supporting the Roman popes and the French the Avignonese. Gower urges that secular rulers ought to attempt to settle their problems among themselves in the absence of papal initiatives:

> These kynges oughten of here rightwissnesse
> Here oghne cause among hem self redresse;
> Thogh Peters schip as now hath lost his stiere,
> It lith in hem that barge for to stiere.
>
> (*PPS*, II, p. 10)

In the last stanza he urges Henry IV to 'sette ek the rightful pope uppon his stalle', but who, in his opinion, this was, or how it was to be done, he does not say. The division got worse in 1409 when the Council at Pisa elected a third pope, and it was not until the Council of Constance (1414–18) that the matter was settled. This receives no attention in English verse, however, nor do any of the later councils, except that at Basle in 1433. This seems to be referred to in a rather garbled prophecy, hitherto unpublished, from National Library of Wales MS Peniarth 50 f. 126r.[3] After a fairly conventional spring opening, a mysterious lady appears to the poet:

> Scho seyd 'Y shal say þe soþ surly & none oþer.
> Þe pope schal be poysned & put out of Rome
> & þe were shal be Veroncle & Wainer deprived
> Then shal clerly þe clergy comyn to gedre
> In þe bourgh of Basyl & byde many a day.
> But Basyl þe burgh shal be broght to grond
> ffor þe falsnes of freckes þat be broght þerin.'
>
> (26–32)

But it is difficult to be certain of the 'soþ' of this. In what sense Basle shall be destroyed ('broght to grond') is not clear—perhaps this line simply alludes to the failure of the Council in its attempt to give general councils of the Church an authority over the Pope. If this is the case, it may be that the expulsion of the Pope from Rome refers to the flight of Eugenius IV after the riots and the proclamation of a republic in May and June 1434. But such a reading of these lines is not by any means certain, and the rest of the poem, which predicts wars, pestilence and famine all over Europe, does not afford further clues.

The only other aspect of the international Church which received the attention of English poets was that of crusades. In the years during which Gower and Hoccleve wrote, the threat of the infidel to Europe was felt to be considerable. Alarmed earlier by the progress of the Turks to the Bulgarian town of Vidin on the Danube in 1390, the powers of the west had organized a large force under John, Count of Nevers, to throw back this invasion. After a few early successes the crusaders were disastrously defeated by the forces of the Sultan Bayezit at Nicopolis in 1396. This defeat left the Turks on the Danube, on the shores of the Adriatic, and in Hungary. Rhodes was still Christian, as was Cyprus, but these were exposed outposts, and Constantinople held out only because Bayezit possessed neither artillery powerful enough to reduce it by direct attack nor enough ships to blockade it successfully. The expedition to Nicopolis was to be the last great international crusade.[4] But contemporaries were unaware of this, and in the early years of the fifteenth century there was talk of another. Ideas for a crusade were current at the time of the visit of the Byzantine Emperor Manuel II to Europe. He came to London in the winter of 1400–1401. Gower, writing perhaps a little before this, laments that the rulers of western countries are too concerned with their own wars against each other to fight the infidel:

> The worldes cause is waited over al,
> Ther ben the werres redi to the fulle,
> Bot Cristes oghne cause in special,
> Ther ben the swerdes and the speres dulle;
> And with the sentence of the popes bulle,
> As for to do the folk paien obeie,
> The chirche is turned al another weie.
>
> (*PPS*, II, p. 10)

He urges them, if they wish to fight, to do so in a just war against the enemies of Christ:

> And if men scholde algate wexe wrothe,
> The Sarazins, which unto Crist be lothe,
> Let men ben armed aȝein hem to fighte
> So mai the knight his dede of armes righte.
>
> (p. 11)

In about 1412 Hoccleve makes much the same point, after urging a settlement of the war between England and France based on a marriage between Prince Henry and Katherine:

> Vppon þe mescreantys to make werre,
> And hem vnto the feith of crist to brynge,

Good were; therynne may ye no thyng erre,
That were a meritorye werrying;
That is the wey vn-to the conqueryng
Of hevenes blysse, that is endeles,
To which yow brynge the auctour of pees.

(Regement, 5433–9)

Both Henry IV and Henry V did, in fact, speak of undertaking crusades. But they were never a practical possibility during the earlier part of the fifteenth century. Later came the disastrous expedition to Varna led by John Hunyadi in 1444 and the pathetic attempt of Pius II in 1464. But in neither of these were the English significantly involved and, after the early years of the century, crusades are hardly mentioned in political literature.

To most English writers papal matters must have seemed remote. Much more pressing were those problems of the Church in England which could scarcely have escaped notice. In the fifteenth century, the Church was organized on a diocesan and parochial basis. The bishop's activities tended to be administrative, advisory and legal rather than pastoral. A contemporary said his duties should be to '. . . overse that the louȝer curatis fulfille her chargis, to here the complayntis maad vpon the louȝer curatis and for to helpe amende hem, to gadir togyder the louȝer clergy forto determyne doutis reised in thi lawe of kynde and of feith, and to devise what counseil may be gouun to pryncis and potestatis.'[5] This last duty seems to have taken up most of the time of many bishops: the critical Thomas Gascoigne pointed out that Archbishop Kemp (who held five dioceses during his life) only stayed in these dioceses for periods of two or three weeks at intervals of ten or a dozen years; Archbishop Chichele in 1433 admitted that he had been absent from meetings of the Royal Council for only thirty-three days in eleven years; Thomas Bourchier (later Archbishop of Canterbury) is said to have been in his diocese of Ely only on the day of his installation. Not all bishops were such persistent absentees, but many were. The absentee's episcopal functions were carried out by deputies. His religious functions might be carried out by a suffragan; the vicar general was his deputy in administrative matters; another official usually presided over the diocesan consistory court; an archdeacon was supposed to carry out yearly visitations to parishes within his jurisdiction. These parishes differed greatly in size, wealth and organization. The normal benefice was the rectory from which the incumbent had the whole tithe. The rector normally had cure of souls, but if the rectory had been appropriated to some corporate body such as a religious house, or a college, or a cathedral (as increasingly happened in the fifteenth century) a vicar was appointed who carried out the rector's parochial duties. In such circumstances the vicar originally kept the small tithes and offerings (while the rector kept the great tithe of hay and corn), but later he came to be paid a fixed annual sum (while the rector kept the difference between this and the total value of the living). If an individual rector was non-resident his work might be done for some (usually small) financial consideration by a chaplain. It was not a very satisfactory system. Holders of benefices were frequently non-resident; pluralism was common, partly because the incomes of the parish clergy were so low; there was some neglect of parochial duties because the clergy had to spend time making a living at something else; the parish priest was frequently poor and not very well educated. There was cause for complaint and complaint was frequent.

Much of it is to be found in contemporary sermons, particularly those of the mendicants, which denounce memorably the vices of the secular clergy. But contemporary verse writers also express their dissatisfaction. Hoccleve is concerned that the best men should be appointed as bishops. He warns Prince Henry that 'no smal charche is the soules cure/Of al a diocese' (*Regement* 2932–3) and begs him to make sure that he does not use his influence in appointing bishops to promote the wrong men:

> Lokith þat þe man haue abilite
> Þat shal resseyue þat hy dignite
> Þat is to seyn, he be clene of lyuyng
> Discrete, iust, and of suffisant konnyng.
>
> (2916–19)

Furthermore he urges the Prince to recognize the 'laweful liberte' of the 'chapitre of a chirche Cathedral' in electing bishops, and to support their nominations:

> Writeþ vnto þe pope in hir fauour,
> Bisekyng humblely of his fadirhede
> It to conferme,
>
> (2910–12)

rather than replacing them with his own men. What happened normally, however, was that the King, after consultation with the Council, would nominate a candidate to the Pope, who, if he agreed to the nomination, would formally 'provide' him. The cathedral chapter would then be told who to 'elect'. Thus, because the appointment of bishops was virtually in the hands of the King and the government, it often came about that those elected had political and administrative rather than religious abilities. The author of *Mum and the Sothsegger* tacitly admits that the advisory function of the higher clergy is a legitimate one, and accuses them of failing to restrain the nobility:

> The grucchingz of grete þat shuld vs gouuerne
> Han y-shourid sharpely þorough suffrance of clercz,
> That lightly with labour y-lettid þay mighte,
> The conseil of clergie yf þay had caste for hit.
>
> (*M*, 759–62)

He doubtless had in mind the trouble provoked by the deposition of Richard II and the Percy rebellions. In the same way the author of the poems in MS Digby 102 complains that the clergy fail (either through bribery or because of fear) in their duty to criticize the faults of the powerful:

> Thouȝ holy chirche shulde fawtes mende,
> Sumee put hem of for mede;
> And summe wiþ maystriȝe hem defende,
> That holy chirche stant of hem drede.
>
> (IV, 137–40)

This looks as if it is a fairly general criticism, but J. Kail thinks that the author refers specifically to one of Henry IV's confessors who

H

was expelled from court in 1404. He dates another poem as 1410 on the grounds that the complaints the author makes are similar to those brought forward in parliament that year.[6] Some deal with the negligence of the clergy, and the author reminds bishops, with the appropriate imagery, of their pastoral duties to protect their charges and to preach to them:

> To kepe his shep fro helle tike,
> In folde go, amonge hem blete.
>
> (IX, 157–8)

Predictably the higher clergy are criticized for their worldliness. The author of *Mum and the Sothsegger* complains that they do not care about the truth, but think only of eating until they almost burst:

> euer kepte þaym cloos to cracche and to mangier
> And fedde so þe foule flesh þat þe velle ne might
> Vnethe kepe þe caroigne but yf hit cleue shuld.
>
> (*M*, 560–2)

Their other concerns are fine clothes, such as 'gurdell of good gold or gilte atte leste' (569), and money. In 1413–14 Margery Kempe, the mystic from Lynn, noted among Archbishop Thomas Arundel's retinue 'many of þe Erchebysshoppys clerkys & oþer rekles men boþe swyers & ȝemen whech sworyn many gret oþis & spokyn many rekles wordys'. She rebuked the Archbishop for the worldliness of his household and reminded him of his duty to 'correctyn hem or ellys put hem owt of ȝowr seruyse' because 'God hath not ȝon ȝow ȝowyr benefys & gret goodys of þe world to maynten wyth hys tretowrys & hem þat slen hym euery day be gret othys sweryng'.[7]

The parish clergy, whose activities brought them into contact with the majority of people, provoke more comment. Writing in about 1400, John Mirk, an Austin Canon of Lilleshall, Shropshire, makes the point that most contemporary priests 'beth blynde in goddis lawe' and provides a book instructing them in the proper performance of their office.[8] There was no lack of critics who said much more than this. 'Jack Upland' accuses priests of forsaking their parishes '. . . to do lewid mennes office' although they still take incomes from them '. . . as offringis and tiþis and oþere possessiouns dowid for almes' (*JU* 23–5). He says they fail to perform their services properly and sell the sacraments 'or els gete no man noon' (26–7). They do not 'studie in Goddis law' but in 'oþere dyuers lawis for þe more wynnynge' (28–9). The falling away by contemporary priests from their ideals of conduct is the subject of a clever 'punctuation' poem from Pembroke College Cambridge MS 307:

> Trvsty; seldom/to their ffrendys vniust;/
> Gladd for to helpp; no Crysten creator/
> Wyllyng to greve; settyng all þeir ioy & lust/
> Only in þe plesour of god; havyng no cvre/
> Who is most riche; with them þey wyl be sewer/
> Wher nede is; gevyng neyther reward nor ffee/
> Vnresonably; Thus lyve prestys parde./
> (*SL XIV and XV*, 110, 1–7)

This may be read in two ways. Punctuated by means of the semi-colons it commends the proper behaviour of priests; but punctuated by means of the / sign it exposes their faults. The author of some verses from BM MS Harley 372 objects strongly to the secularization of clerical dress:

> Yee poopeholy prestis fulle of presomcioun,
> With your wyde furryd hodes voyd of discrecioun,
> Unto your owyn prechyng of contrary condicioun,
> Wheche causithe the people to have lesse devocioun,
> (*PPS*, II, p. 251)

and in the next stanza urges them to devote themselves less to worldly ornament and more to their roles as priests, 'Make schorter your taylis and broder your crounys.' This criticism of the worldliness of the clergy is taken up again in *Mum and the Soth-segger*. In one place the author points out that the contemporary clergy are interested only in taking their ease, in advancement in the Church, and in making money:

so vsid to ease erly and late
That þay cunne no crafte saue kepe þaym warme.
Thay bisien more for benefices þenne bibles to reede,
And been as worldly wise and wynners eeke
As man vppon molde. . . .

(*M*, 667–71)

In another he contrasts the simplicity and the piety of the early martyrs of the Church with the 'worldly workes' of his contemporaries who dress themselves in 'royal raye' and spend their time in 'service of souuerayns', or by acquiring money through 'rente' when they are not 'drynkyng of dollid wyne' (*M*, 643–51). What seems to concern this author most, however, is the way in which the parish clergy fail to make the proper use of the tithes they collect. He describes how he went to church and heard a priest ask for the lesser tithe:

He taughte þaym by tyme þaire tithing to bringe
Of al manier grene þat groweth vppon erthe,
Of fructe and of floxe in feldes and in homes,
Of polaille and of peris, of apples and of plummes,
Of grapes and of garlik, of gees and of pigges . . .,

(*M*, 600–4)

and how he waited to hear 'How hooly churche goodes shuld be y-spendid' (*M*, 614), but recalls that the priest said no word of this. The author points out that one third of the tithes and offerings should be for the sustenance of the priest, another third for the upkeep of the fabric of the church, and the rest to the poor, but the fact is, he concludes, the priest keeps his own share and the other 'two dooles' as well (*M*, 666).

The most frequent complaints, however, were about the non-residence of the beneficed clergy. The author of the poems in MS Digby 102 speaks out against those who hire others to perform their duties:

Worldis good nes not holichirche;
Richesse and worscheþ y ʒow forbede.
Þe folkis cherche, in hem ʒe worche;

Here noo oþer to don þy dede.
(VIII, 25–8)

In the same poem he stresses that the priest with cure of souls had a duty to preach to his parishioners and to instruct them, and that to take a benefice simply for the income it provided was displeasing to God:

Who ressayueþ benefys for richesse and ese
To haue hys lyuyng in sykernes
Raþere þan serue god to plese,
He ressayueþ hit o mys.

(33–6)

In this author's opinion a poor priest is more likely to serve his parishioners well than one who has many benefices:

A symple prest wole synge his masse
While his lyuyng is but smal.
As summe encrese, serue god þe lasse.
(XIV, 25–7)

In the Prologue to Hoccleve's *Regement of Princes* the Beggar draws attention to the fact that courtiers covet benefices for their income ('Only for muk, þou ȝernest soules cure' 1407) and that this is wrong 'ffor þat conceyte nat to presthode longeþ' (1414). He deplores the absentee pluralist:

A-dayes now, my sone, as men may se,
O chirche vn-to a man may not suffise;
But algate he mote han pluralite,
Elles he can not lyuen in no wyse.
(1415–18)

Such a man deserts his parishes and does not perform church services but 'kepith his seruise/In courte' (1418–19). He neglects the fabric of his church, not caring

Thogh þat his chauncel roof be al to-torn,
And on þe hye auter it reyne or snewe.
(1422–3)

Nor does he preach to his parishioners, for either he is too ignorant ('so threde bare of konnynge' 1431) or, if he has the ability, he may lack the inclination ('may not his herte bende/þer-to' 1433–4). Absentee priests, says the Beggar, think only of dressing themselves in secular clothes that are 'nyce, fressh, and gay' and not at all fitting for priests who ought to be 'mirours of sadnesse' (1441). The Beggar admits finally that many priests perform their duties properly ('many of hem gye hem as hem oghte' 1444), but the attention he devotes to their shortcomings suggests that they were widespread. Later in the poem, Hoccleve points out that men with high academic qualifications were not given good positions in the Church:

> Alas, so manny a worthi clerk famouse,
> In Oxinford, and in Cambrigge also,
> Stonde vn-avanced. . . .
>
> (5272–4)

When Hoccleve makes such criticisms one must bear in mind that his own hopes of advancement in the Church had been disappointed: he had 'waytid faste/After some benefice' but 'non cam' (1451–2). In this case though, his analysis is supported by the facts: parish priests were often deplorably ignorant and, though matters improved somewhat over the fifteenth century, the improvement was slow.

Distinct from the secular clergy were the regulars—monks, canons, nuns and friars—whose task was not so much to minister to the spiritual needs of the laity but to live the religious life of prayer and meditation for its own sake. Monasticism in the fifteenth century was not the force it had been earlier. It is difficult to be sure about the reasons for its decline. There seems to have been no lack of monks. It is true that the Black Death had seriously reduced the population of monasteries, but this was not a disaster from which they failed to recover. Throughout the fifteenth century the numbers rose. Nor, in general, were monasteries impoverished, though a few undoubtedly were. Benefactions were not as numerous in this century as previously, for the fashion ran to the foundation of colleges and chantries. Moreover, taxes on monasteries during the French war were high. But once the religious houses had modernized the management of their estates, so that they had a steady income from leases, they suffered no undue economic hardship. In fact, though some foundations were in a delapidated state, it was the opulence of the greater monasteries which impressed the Venetian envoy in 1497, '. . . more like baronial palaces than religious houses'.[9] However, monastic expenditure increased because the monks allowed themselves a somewhat easier mode of life than in former centuries: from monastic accounts it appears that large quantities of food were eaten; living quarters tended to become more sumptuous; clothes became finer and more secularized in style; and it is clear that some people in orders came to possess personal property. This last fact contravenes the rule of personal poverty, and other examples of laxity are not difficult to find: it is obvious from the visitation records of fifteenth-century bishops that apostasy, insubordination, immorality and vice sometimes occurred. There were, of course, many serious monastics in the fifteenth century, and among them a few great men, but the conclusion is inevitable that the monastic ideal had been eroded, and that there was in England a fatal lack of enthusiasm and vitality in the movement.

No fifteenth-century poems deal exclusively with the behaviour of monks, but, there are various incidental comments. In the later fragment of *Mum and the Sothsegger*, written after 1402, attention is drawn to the richness of the monasteries, the selfishness of the monks and their lack of concern for the poor:

> Thay koueiten no comers but yf þay cunne helpe
> Forto amende þaire mynstre and to maynteyne þaire rente,
> Or in worke or in worde waite þaire profit
> Or elles entreth he not til þay haue y-sopid.
> Thus thaire portier for my pourete putt me þens.
>
> (*M*, 546–50)

Perhaps dating from around the same time comes a paragraph criticizing monastics in 'Jack Upland's' rhythmical, alliterative prose. He believes that monks, because they are cloistered, are of no benefit to the rest of society; that they are idle and think only of eating and wearing expensive clothes; and that they are hypocritical:

> And herto haþ he made anoþer oost aȝens Cristis ordinaunce,
> & closid hem as fro þe world in wallis of stoon, cloistris & sellis;
> & þereas þei schulden haue labourid in þe world in help of alle
> þre partis of Cristis chirche, wiþ meke loue & leue lijflode, now
> þei schulen lyue in idil lijf & sikir fro al pouert, & al men
> schulen help hem & þei neuer no man aftir, but lyue in
> mamelynge of mete and many wast cloþis, & þouȝ þei weren
> þe heire & þe hood, euer enuy is her cauce at eueri melis mete.
> & þes hidde jpocritis ben in þe myddilward of Antecristis bateil.
>
> (*JU*, 60–8)

Sometimes the criticism is less outspoken. That in the verses from
Bodleian MS Digby 102 entitled *The Declaryng of Religioun* is
implicit, for the poem is overtly one which offers various pieces of
advice to monks. J. Kail dated the poem 1421 on the grounds that
it was perhaps suggested by the complaint made to Henry V in that
year 'that the Benedictine monks had deviated from the rules of
their first institution'.[10] In the following year a Provincial Capitulary was made to reform the monks and most of its ordinances
sought to counteract their worldliness. *The Declaryng of Religioun*
touches on various topics both general and particular. The author
stresses that the condition of a cloistered religious is 'þe hiȝest lyf of
spiritualte' (8), and that the rule of the order should be strictly
observed, but he also warns that the trappings of the religious do
not prove a man devout:

> Tonsure, abyte, ne no wede,
> Nes no cause of religeon,
> Ne wakyng, ne fastyng, ne almesdede,
> Ne prayer ne oreson.
>
> (Digby 102, XVIII, 161–4)

The greatest threats to those in orders, he says, are secular ambition
and worldliness:

> To religeon they don a gret defence
> Þat bryngen hem to werkis temperale.
> (151–2)

Monks should not engage in trade:

> Byȝe no thyng to selle and wynne.
> Marchaunt and religeous on mot be forbore,
> (138–9)

or have costly possessions—'Gret hors ne iewel, ne browded hood' (155). They should not seek to achieve high positions: 'Resceyue no worship, ne hyȝe sete' (99). They should cut themselves off from the affairs of the world, from receiving news, from reading unserious books, and from receiving and writing unnecessary letters:

> To herkene tydynges, not ȝe wende,
> Ne bokes of vanyte, not ȝe rede.
> Resceyue no lettere, ne non out sende,
> But hit be for ȝoure hous nede,
> Oþer to kyn or certeyn frende,
> In goodnes ȝoure erande for to spede.
> (107–12)

There should be, he says, no physical contact with women, not even at leavetaking: 'When ȝe take leue, loke not ȝe kys' (84), and handshaking is forbidden too. He also warns against over-indulgence in food and drink:

> War for dronkenesse of drynkes grete
> Fro glotry of metes of gret deynte.
> (103–4)

The poem is not openly critical of monks. The author only restates, in fairly simple terms, the ascetic ideal: 'Fro hard to hardere ȝoure lyf to lede' (124). But the context of the poem and the mere fact that such obvious advice needs to be given at all suggests that there had been some falling away in monastic ideals. Perhaps standards of discipline had slipped too, for he also stresses that monks should not be too heavily punished for lapses from their rule lest they regret having entered orders:

> non wiþ other be to harde,
> þat ben professed in ȝoure couent;
> þey myȝte for-þenke it afterward
> þey toke þe abyte, and wolde repente.
>
> (43–6)

From John Lydgate, himself a Benedictine monk at the abbey of
Bury St Edmunds, comes some confirmation of the laxity that
might occur in a monastery. In his *Testament*, which was probably
written late in his life, Lydgate recalls how, as a young monk, he
talked too much 'Rekeles to kepe my lyppes in silence' (714), spent
his time in 'ryot and dronkenesse' (719), grumbled about his food,
loved pleasure more than the monastic services,

> One with the firste to take my disporte
> Last that aros to come to the quere,
> (*Minor Poems*, I, 68, 726–7)

preferred 'veyn fables' to 'holy histories', and resented criticism:
'Geyn my correctiouns, answered frowardly' (735). This is, of
course, presented not as a criticism of monks, only of Lydgate
himself, and he characterises his superiors in the monastery as
'vertuous men, religious and sad/Ful wel experte, discrete, prudent
and wyse' (686–7). But these shortcomings are not likely to be his
alone. From comparison with what can be derived from visitation
records, they appear to be a selection of typical failings. It is
essential, in fact, that the faults Lydgate mentions should not be
particular, for the poem is exemplary and his rejection (at the age of
fifteen, he tells us) of these failings is meant to encourage others to
reject them.

On nuns in the fifteenth century there is very little comment.
This is perhaps not surprising, since most nunneries tended to be
poor and small; less than two thousand nuns peopled some one
hundred and thirty houses. It goes without saying that many of
these nuns were devout and had the necessary sense of vocation.
But nunneries also provided a career for many girls—these usually
the unmarriageable daughters of upper-class or middle-class
parents (those, that is, who could afford the dowry nunneries were
not supposed to accept). For some older women, usually widows,

the nunnery provided a refuge in which they could spend a peaceful old age. For a few (usually young girls who had been put into nunneries against their wills) it was a prison. This being the case it is hardly surprising that in some nunneries the rule was only partially observed: the visitation records speak of quarrels, apostasy, immorality, nuns having personal possessions, wearing fine clothes, keeping pets and so on.

But the only poem principally concerned with nunneries is a longish fragment from British Museum Cotton Vespasian D ix which its editor F. J. Furnivall entitles *Why I Can't be a Nun*.[11] The poem is supposedly spoken by a young girl Katherine whose father, without explanation, has forbidden her to enter a nunnery. She is grief-stricken, until one day, in a dream, Dame Experience appears to her and says she will show her 'An howse of wommen reguler'. The greater part of the poem consists of an exposition by Katherine of what she saw in the convent 'that to religion schulde not long'. The characteristic moral failings of nuns are personified by the inmates of the house: 'a lady that hyȝt dame pride', 'Dame ypocryte', 'dame slowthe and dame veyne glory',

> dame envy was there dwellyng
> The whyche can sethe stryfe in every state.

The sexual immorality of nuns is stressed:

> a nother lady was there wonnyng
> That hyȝt dame love vnordynate,
> In that place bothe erly and late
> Dame lust, dame wantowne, and dame nyce,
> They ware so there enhabyted, I wate,
> That few token hede to goddys servyse.

The frequent breaking of the vow of obedience is also alluded to:

> another lady there was
> That hyȝt dame dysobedyent
> And sche set nowȝt by her priores.
> Ans than me thowȝt alle was schent.

Of all the faults, Katherine says, this 'was one the most that grevyd me'. The abbey she is shown is, according to Dame Experience, representative, though a few nuns, she admits, do live devout and chaste lives in humility and obedience to the rule:

> I have schewed the nunnes governawnce.
> For as thou seest wythin yonder walle
> Suche bene the nunnes in euery warde,
> As for the most part, I say not alle,
> God forbede, for than hyt were harde,
> For sum bene devowte, holy and towarde,
> And holden the ryȝt way to blysse.

When Katherine's dream ends she awakes and determines not to be a nun until the faults that she has seen are corrected, and there follows a long exhortation to nuns that they should stay within the limits of their convents and seek to live up to the implications of their calling:

> Yowre barbe, your wympplle and your vayle,
> Yowre mantelle and yowre devowte clothyng,
> Maketh men wythowten fayle
> To wene ȝe be holy in levyng.
> And so hyt ys an holy thyng
> To bene in habyte reguler;
> Than, as by owtewarde array in semyng,
> Beth so wythin, my ladyes dere.

The rest of the poem is similarly hortatory. Before the manuscript breaks off there is a catalogue of holy women, some of whom 'weren professed in nunnes habyte', and all of whom led devout lives worthy of imitation.

The hostility here is pointed, but it has none of the viciousness which characterizes that directed against the friars. They differed from monastics in that they did not withdraw from the world but mixed with the laity and preached to them. They were allowed no personal property, nor was their order allowed to possess more land than was required for its buildings. Having no income from estates, friars depended, theoretically, only on the alms of the charitable. The Dominicans arrived in England in 1221, the

Franciscans in 1224, the other orders later. Throughout the thirteenth century friars enjoyed a high reputation as preachers and scholars. But in the latter part of the fourteenth century and throughout the fifteenth, they are subjected to a great deal of criticism, much of it repetitious but no less emphatic for that.

The familiar combination of general and particular criticisms appears in the second fragment of *Mum and the Sothsegger*. The author draws attention to the way in which the Franciscans ('Thees good grey freres', as he sarcastically calls them) had deviated from their rule:

> Thay goon al bare abouue þe foote and by-nethe double
> With smale semyd sockes and of softe wolle,
>
> (*M*, 426–7)

and evaded the injunction that they should touch no money by counting it out with a stick:

> Thay mellen with no monaye more noþer lasse,
> But stiren hit with a sticke and staren on hit ofte
> And doon þaire bisynes þere-with by obedience of þordre;
> But in þe herte ne in þe hande ne may hit not come,
> For þenne þay shuld be shent of þe subpriour.
>
> (*M*, 429–33)

He also criticizes the 'limiters' (those licensed to beg for alms within a specified district) and their methods, whereby they give away trifling presents and hope to receive more valuable ones in return:

> But sum been so courtoys and kinde of þaire deedes
> That with þaire charite þay chaungen a knyfe for a peyre,
> But he wol pille ere he passe a parcelle of whete
> And choise of þe chese þe chief and þe beste.
> He is so cunnyng in þe crafte þat where-so he cometh
> He leueth þe lasse for þe more deele.
>
> (*M*, 442–7)

He contrasts their acquisitiveness with their lack of charity, for even though a friar 'haue a ful coffre/of gold and of good' the needy man 'getys but a lite' of it. Instead of looking after the poor, the poet continues, friars pander to the rich. Through the exploitation of the sacrament of penance they enrich themselves ('mulden vp þe matiere to make þaym fatte') and exert an influence on the powerful men of the kingdom ('gouuernen þe grete' *M*, 465). But despite all this influence, he complains, friars hide the truth. Because of their dependence on the rich they do not reveal how 'symonie shendith al hooly churche' (*M*, 475) or how covetousness has destroyed the aristocracy ('Couetise hath caste þe knyght on þe grene' *M*, 481). Friars themselves care only for money, obtained either through bribes ('spices') or simony ('For Symon-is sermons þay setten al to taske' *M*, 506–7). Other fairly familiar charges appear. There is an allusion to the immorality friars were often accused of: 'Thay been not weddid, wel I wote, þough þay wifes haue' (*M*, 512). And this author also uses the clever acrostic joke which took the initial letters of the four major orders and made up the word CAIM, the normal fifteenth-century spelling of the first murderer's name:

> For who writeth wel þis worde and withoute titil,
> Shal finde of þe figures but euene foure lettres:
> C. for hit is crokid for þees Carmes þou mos take,
> A. for þees Augustines þat amoreux been euer,
> I. for þees Iacobynes þat been of Iudas kynne,
> M. for þees Menours þat monsyd been þaire werkes.
> (*M*, 499–504)

Finally this author makes two charges relating to contemporary incidents. He complains that friars were attempting to obtain permission to preach to the exclusion of parish priests:

> þay stirid a statute in strengthe of bilieue
> That no preste shuld preche saue seely poure freres.
> (*M*, 409–10)

What 'statute', if any, he has in mind is difficult to determine. Normally only a priest with charge of souls was allowed to preach, but between 1400 and 1410, largely as a result of the threat of Lollardy, regulations against unlicensed preaching were tightened. Friars, however, because they were not suspected of heresy, were largely exempted from these regulations, hence perhaps this author's resentment. There is little doubt, however, about the allusion in the line 'At Tibourne for traison y-twyght vp þay were' (*M*, 420.) It refers to the Franciscans who were hanged at Tyburn in 1402 for encouraging the rumour that Richard II was still alive. Of course, friars were not the only ones involved, and it was Franciscans who denounced the conspiracy, but no anti-medicant would choose to ignore such obvious 'traison'. His list of faults is comprehensive, but this author recognizes that not all friars are guilty of them: 'I seye of þaym þat suche been and cesse agaynes oþer' (*M*, 505).

In contrast, the criticism in *Jack Upland* is total: for him friars were 'þe fellist folk þat euer Anticrist foond' (*JU*, 69), and he has no good word to say for any of them. This treatise, which takes the form of a series of questions to the friars, ranges over many topics. There are the familiar sneers that the mendicant orders were the last to be founded ('last brouȝte in to þe chirche' 69–70), that there were too many friars ('so many freris is greet cumbraunce to þe puple' 357–8), and that they had no direct responsibility either to the secular Church or to the Crown ('þei ben not obediente to bisshopis ne lege men to kyngis' 72–3). Predictably, he concentrates on the acquisitiveness of the friars, and contrasts their original vows of poverty with the luxury of contemporary friaries:

> Frere, whi may ȝe for schame lye to þe puple, and seye þat
> ȝe folowe þe apostlis in pouerte more þanne oþere men don;
> & ȝit in curious & costlew housis, & fyne & precious cloþinge,
> delicious & lusti fedynge, in tresorie & iewels & riche ourne-
> mentis, freris passen lordis & oþere riche worldli men; &
> sunnest ȝe bringen aboute ȝoure causis, be þei never so costlew
> or aȝens Goddis lawe? (*JU*, 366–72)

He questions some of their methods of raising money. As often in anti-mendicant satire, there are general accusations that friars sell spiritual things such as prayers and masses 'for alle suche goostli dedis schulden be freeli don as God ȝyueþ freeli, & ellis it were cursid symony' (345–6). More particularly, he mentions the prac-tice of selling a trental of requiem masses 'for a certeyne sum of money—as fyue schylingis or more' (199–200); the way in which friars sought the 'biriynge of oþer mennes parischens' (220–1), particularly the rich, within the precincts of mendicant houses so that their order would benefit financially; the reading of special prayers for benefactors whose names were written down 'in þi tablis' (282); and the granting of 'lettris of fraternyte' to lay benefactors which allowed them the spiritual benefits 'of alle ȝoure massis & oþere good dedis' (336–7) done within the order. He asks, disingenuously, why friars pander to the rich, and why, on the other hand, '. . . coueite ȝe not schrift of pore men, siþ lordis & riche men mai haue prestes more plente þanne pore men?' (222–3). He also accuses the friars of too easily absolving the sins of the rich '. . . as pilinge of her tenauntis & lyuinge in leccherie & glotony & oþere heed synnes' (380–81) which they have no intention of giving up. There is also a miscellany of other accusations. 'Jack Upland' wonders why a friar 'be more punyschid if he breke þe rulis þat his patroun made þan if he breke þe heestis þat God hym silf made' (111–13); why they are secretive about dealings and do 'not suffre ȝoure nouycis to here ȝoure counseile in ȝoure chapitre' (165–6); and why they pay no 'taligis to oure kyng in help of the rewme & supportynge of pore men' (184–5). He accuses them further of beguiling into their orders 'ynnocent children or þei kunne discrescioun' (347–8). The friars' abilities in preaching and scholarship do not impress 'Jack Upland' either: he sneers at the 'fals fablis . . . & feined myraclys' (233) of their sermons, and accuses them of hoarding books 'many mo þanne nediþ ȝou, & putte hem in tresorie, & do prisone hem fro seculer preestis & curatis' (374–5) which hinders the secular clergy in their teaching. The author criticizes friars in their relations with the seculer clergy on several counts: they seek advancement in Church positions 'to be bischopis & prelatis & popis chapleins' (386) and charge 'trewe preestis of erisie & letten þe sowynge of Goddis word' (377–8).

Little can be determined about the author of this piece, though he was certainly influenced by Lollard ideas, for most of the points he makes against the friars are also to be found in the writings of Wycliffe and his followers. He represents himself as a countryman, and his treatise certainly shows no great learning. It is repetitious, not very well organized and sometimes ill-informed: for example, he completely confuses the doctrines of friars on transubstantiation with those of Wycliffe (390–400). But he is confident of the rightness of his criticisms, and at the end of his treatise asks any friar to 'ȝeue Iacke an answere' (409).

This answer was provided in alliterative verse by a friar who calls himself 'Daw Topias'. This seems to be an assumed name and the author is referred to in the colophon to the poem as 'Iohannem Walssingham'. This man has not been satisfactorily identified, and P. L. Heyworth's hypothesis that he was a Dominican from the London Blackfriars is perhaps as near as one can get to him. There is also some doubt about the dating of this *Reply:* both Thomas Wright and W. W. Skeat attributed it to 1402 but Heyworth favours 1419–20.[12] The piece consists of a mixture of anti-Lollard invective and answers (of a sort) to 'Jack Upland's' criticisms of friars. By far the most interesting feature of the *Reply* is 'Friar Daw's debating technique. In part is consists of discrediting 'Jack Upland' because of his lack of education and his humble position in society ('Taking heed of þin estaate þou art but a knave' 757). Similarly, his questions are criticized because 'þei wanten sentence & god thrift boþe' (235). Sometimes 'Friar Daw' exposes the inconsistencies of 'Jack Upland's' arguments, as in the following lines on the accusation of selling the sacraments:

> Alas, Iak, for shame, whi art þou so fals,
> Forto reuerse þi silf in þin owne sawes?
> Þou seidist in þi begynnynge, whan þou seidist of freres,
> Þei sellen seuen sacramentes with Symoundis eyris,
> And now þat we coueite noon but þe sacrament of schrifte,
> For beriynge is no sacrament but an almes dede.
> Þow jawdewyne, þou jangeler, how stande þis to gider?
> (*FDR*, 579–85)

Sometimes he uses a trick of logic, as in his justification of the numbers of friars:

> Þou seist þat God alle þingis haþ maad in mesure, weiȝte
> & noumbre,

> & þat euery frere is sum þing þou maist not denye;
> & þou seist freris ben maad aȝens Goddis wille,
> Þan haþ God maad sum þing þat he wolde not make,
> And so his souereyne goodnesse is contrarious to him silfe.
> Lo! Iakke Iospinel, what folowiþ of þi sawis.
>
> (817–22)

Sometimes he deflects criticism. Thus in one place he seeks to excuse friars from the criticism of selling penances by drawing attention to the rewards that parish priests receive:

> I trowe it be þi paroche preest Iacke þat þou meenest,
> Þat nyl not hosel his parischens til þe peny be paied,
> Ne assoilen hem of her synne wiþouten schrift siluer.
>
> (81–3)

Elsewhere he answers 'Jack Upland's' criticism about 'limiters' and their licences to beg for alms by drawing attention to the similar licences of the Hospitals of St Thomas in Cheapside, St Anthony in Threadneedle Street and St Mary Rouncivall at Charing Cross:

> I trowe þou menys þe pardonysters of Seint Thomas of Acres,
> Of Antoun, or of Runcevale, þat rennen so fast aboute.
>
> (481–2)

Sometimes, as in his refutation of 'Jack Upland's' charge that friaries were more splendid than royal palaces, he argues from the simple facts:

> Iak, where saw þou euer frere houses þourȝout þe rewme,
> Lich in ony realte to þe toure of Londoun,
> To Wyndesore, to Wodestoke, to Wallingforde, to Shene,
> To Herforde, to Eltham, to Westmynster, to Douer?
>
> (469–72)

But usually he argues from the authority of scriptural and patristic texts. In this way he justifies friars' begging for alms. 'Jack Upland' had asked 'on what lawe groundist þou þee þus for to begge' (*JU*, 276–7) and had said (following Wycliffe) that the justification on the grounds that Christ was a beggar was a slander to him 'siþ he had no nede þerto on þat wise' (273–4) because he was lord of all. 'Friar Daw', in his normal condescending tone, first distinguishes between Christ in his divinity and Christ in his human form:

> But for þis mater Iacke, þou most vndirstonde
> Þat Crist in his godhede is lord of alle þingis,
> As testimonie of scripture preueþ in many places.
> As touching his manheed he was nedi & pore.
>
> (*FDR*, 701–4)

He proceeds to support the last statement by various references: to Psalm XL, 17 ('But I am poor and needy, yet the lord thinketh upon me'), to the glosses of Augustine and Jerome on this which see David as a type of Christ, and to Matthew, viii, 20 ('The foxes have holes and the birds of the air have nests; but the son of man hath not where to lay his head'). He also refers to the two blind beggars outside Jericho (Matthew, xx, 30) who were healed by Christ, the lame man outside the temple who asked alms of Peter and John (Acts, iii, 2) '& þer of beggerie vnreproued, of crokidnesse he was heelid' (*FDR*, 734), and the beggar Lazarus (Luke, xvi, 20) who 'criede at his ȝate to cachen his almes' (*FDR*, 736). 'Friar Daw' makes much of the fact that all these beggars received divine favour. He refers to himself as 'lewid as a leke' (45) but he is adept at this kind of argument and quite learned. Elsewhere he admits to having 'lernede Latyn bi roote of clerkes' when he was a 'manciple at Mertoun Halle' (725–6).

'Friar Daw' had ended his *Reply* with the provocative remark to 'Jack Upland' that if his questions were not thought to have been 'sufficientli assoilid' he should say so and it would be 'amendid' (*FDR*, 925–6). Perhaps prompted by this comes a *Rejoinder* written, again in alliterative metre, in the margins of the unique Bodleian MS Digby 41. There is dispute about the date of this poem, as about the dates of the previous two pieces: Thomas Wright suggested 1402, taking the lines

> And þe kyng by his juges trwe execute his lawe
> As he did now late when he hangid ȝou traytoures
>
> (*UR*, 271–2)

to be a reference to the hanging of the friars at Tyburn in that year, but P. L. Heyworth feels that the copy of the poem is the author's holograph and on the basis of the handwriting would date it around 1450. Whatever its date, however, the author's claim to be 'Jack Upland' is clearly a fiction assumed for the purposes of the debate. The author of the *Rejoinder* is clearly much more sophisticated than 'Jack Upland', and he points out to 'Friar Daw' that he is not to be beguiled by the friar's 'gildyn glose' as 'symple hertes' are (*UR*, 71–2). He is a skilful and often witty debater. He can be crudely insulting: 'I meruel þat þou a clerk blaberst þus blyndely' (245), or he can use ingenious devices such as a pun on 'Friar Daw's' name ('Daw' = crow):

> Þow saist þi name is Dawe, it may riȝt wel be so,
> For þou hast condiciones of a tame chowȝe.
> (6–7)

He uses damaging similes: 'Me thynkiþ ȝe ben tapsteres in alle þat ȝe don' (320) or 'ȝe folowen Crist as greyhounde doþe þe hare' (326). Moreover, he is as adroit as 'Friar Daw' in deploying his learning to support his case, as, for example, the way in which he counters 'Friar Daw's' defence of the splendour of friaries by reference to Solomon's temple (1 Kings, vi) with his own references to Jerome and Gratian:

> Daw, þou leggist Salomon for ȝour hie houses,
> Bot olde holy doctoures ben aȝen þee here,
> And specialy Ierom, þat saiþ in þe lawe:
> Who wil allege þe temple for glorie of our chirche,
> Forsake he to be cristen & be he newe a Iewe.
>   12a q 2a Gloria episcopi.
> For siþ þe pore lorde, he saiþ, halowed his pore chirche,
> Take we Cristis crosse, he saiþ, & counte we delices claye.
> (63–70)

There are no important specific charges against the friars that have not already appeared in *Jack Upland*, but a few points are developed: for example, the author of the *Rejoinder* not only accuses friars of immorality 'with wymmen & wifes' but also alludes to 'thair privey sodomye' (*UR*, 58–9). Nor do any new charges appear in the three groups of lines added by a later interpolator in margins of MS Digby 41 left vacant by the writer of the *Rejoinder*.[13] One set of eight lines condemns 'Friar Daw's' tendentious use of texts:

> for summe þou legest kenely to a fals entente
> but of oþer þou blundryst as a blynde buserde.

A sequence of eleven lines deals with the way in which friars prefer their prayers to the Lord's Prayer ('þou legest 3oure selde bedys to þe paternoster þat crist him selue made') and a final twenty-eight lines deal principally with transubstantiation, on which topic the interpolator is scarcely more lucid than 'Jack Upland' or the author of the *Rejoinder*. None the less, he condemns friars roundly: 'þe deuyl & caym with judas ben 3oure fadirs', and 'Friar Daw' in particular whom he regards as 'an asse', a 'jangelyng jay' and 'on of þe falsest þat euer j saw write'.

A few other fifteenth-century verses attack the faults of friars. In the indecent fable *Lyarde*, preserved in the fifteenth-century Lincoln Cathedral MS 91, there are some lines on the sexual immorality of friars:

> Freris hase thame umbythoght, and sworne ilkane to other,
> Salle never a counte betyne mane bycomen ther brother;
> Bot if he may wele swyfe, and bere hym aryghte,
> Twyse or thrise at the leste on a schorte somer nyghte,
> That thane he salle the habete take, and by-come ther brother . . .

but the poem makes no other charges.[14] A more comprehensive list of criticisms occurs in the macaronic verses entitled *Friars, Ministri Malorum* from Trinity College Cambridge MS 1144. The author says that friars cause souls to go to the torments of hell ('ad penas inffernorum' 4) because they perpetuate on earth the sins of those who 'ffelle ffryst ffrom heven' (5). Friars deceive people to obtain money, and if no money is to be had they will beg food: 'fruges petunt isti' (18). He warns those who give lodging to friars of their immorality:

> odur þi wyff or þi doughtour
> hic vult violare;
> or þi sun he weyl prefur . . .
>
> (*HP*, 67, 23–5)

There are the familiar criticisms of the easy penances friars were reputed to allow for money:

> þei weyl assaylle boyth Iacke & gylle,
> licet sunt predones;
> & parte off pennans take hem tylle,
> qui sunt latrones,
>
> (29–32)

and the familiar contrast between the friars' vows of poverty and their splendid buildings

> þer may no lorde of þis cuntre
> sic edifficare
> as may þes ffreers, were þei be,
> qui vadunt mendicare.
>
> (33–6)

He finally accuses them of counterfeiting ('money makers I trow þei be' 37), and of being traitors ('regis proditores' 38). The criticisms are the usual ones. What makes the poem of particular interest, however, is the fact that it was preserved by a priest, for the manuscript in which it appears (a late fifteenth-century miscellany) was evidently copied out by William Womyndham, Canon of Kyrkeby 'super Algam'. This, in itself, is indicative of the bad feeling which existed between the secular clergy and the friars.

Finally, some mention must be made of two short poems written on the front flyleaves of St John's College Cambridge MS 195. It is impossible to assign a precise date to them, but one refers to 'þe gospel in englishe' (*HP*, 69, 10), which almost certainly means they are post-Wycliffe, and both are written down in the same fifteenth-century hand. *The Layman's Complaint* is a three-stanza attack, in simple tail-rhyme, on the acquisitiveness of friars:

Þou þat sellest þe worde of god,
Be þou berfot, be þou schod,
Cum neuere here.
In principio erat verbum
Is þe worde of god, all & sum,
Þat þou sellest, lewed frere.
(*HP*, 68, 1–6)

The author points out that it is 'cursed symonie' to buy or sell spiritual things, and recommends that friars should stay within their houses 'til we þe almis brynge' instead of 'goynge abowte' among lay society 'flatteringe boyþe more & lesse' to acquire money. In two places this writer quotes the Bible (2 Timothy, iii, and Psalm XCI, 6), and this is ostensibly what suggested its companion piece *The Friar's Answer*. This concerns itself largely with the layman's knowledge of the now translated Bible and the implications of this for the mendicants. The friar who supposedly speaks these verses is worried: he thinks that 'þe deuel browȝt it aboute' to have the scriptures in the vernacular, for their availability causes the laity to question his teaching and his role. He gives an example in which the friar's practice of begging for alms is opposed on biblical grounds (Acts, xviii, 3) by some tradesmen:

When I come into a schope
for to say 'in principio',
þei bidine me, 'goo forþ, lewed poppe!'
& worche & win my siluer so!

Yf y sae hit longoþ not
ffor prestis to worche where þei go,
þei leggen for hem holi writ
And sein þat seint polle did soo.
(*HP*, 69, 13–20)

The 'stowt' tradesmen follow this up with other points: that the dress of friars of all orders is richer than their 'werynge cloþes' (24) and that friars ought not simply to receive alms but ought to give away their own wealth to those 'þat nedith þerof' (28). There was considerable support for Lollardy among tradesmen; the positions assumed here are broadly Lollard; and it is therefore likely that the author of these verses was a Lollard sympathizer. He is certainly not the friar he pretends to be, for he uses the word 'desseytis' to describe the friars' techniques of begging for alms. In fact, it seems likely that the final lines—

> Men schul fynde vnneþe a frere
> In englonde wiþin a whille
> (35–6)

—express the author's hopes rather than his fears.

Some of the attacks on the Church considered above, particularly those on friars, were influenced by Lollardy, but it is not easy to assess the importance of this movement in the fifteenth century. One problem was that of definition. Lollard beliefs were not precisely codified, but rather, as J. A. F. Thomson puts it, 'a set of more or less consistent attitudes than . . . a set of carefully worked out doctrines'.[15] The term 'Lollard' (originally an intentional misnomer applied to the sect by its opponents) came to be applied in an indiscriminate way to anything and anybody even vaguely unorthodox. Margery Kempe, the mystic from Lynn, was certainly no heretic, but because her personal behaviour was rather odd, and because she openly discussed scriptural matters, she was on several occasions suspected of heresy, as once at Hessle, Yorkshire '. . . þer men callyd hir loller, & women cam rennyng out of her howsys wyth her rokkys, crying to þe pepil, "Brennyth þis fals heretyk." '[16] After the failure of Oldcastle's rebellion in 1414, the political side of Lollardy was virtually non-existent. But the religious side still appealed enough to alarm the Church authorities, and a few contemporary poets also who tried to use their verses to discredit the sect, its leaders and its doctrines.

The intellectual basis of Lollardy lay in the work of John Wycliffe (1329–85). To his followers he was 'a gret clerke/& in hys tyme knowen wel a vertuouse man' (*UR*, 85–6), but to his opponents he was a gifted philosopher who had misapplied his abilities. For most of his life he was, in fact, an orthodox academic. It was not until his last seven years that he began to attack, with increasing bitterness, various points of the doctrine and the whole of the political structure of the medieval Church:

> Wiþ men in his begynnynge litht lemed he by cunnynge,
> But aftir, with wrong wrytyng, he wrouȝte mykil care,
> And, presumynge perilously, foul fel from þe chirche,
> Missauerynge of þe sacrament, infectyng many oþer.
>
> *(FDR*, 151–4)

The allusion is to his most controversial doctrine, the denial of the real presence of Christ at the Eucharist. But he also denied papal and priestly authority, the necessity for church endowment, the validity of confession, the use of pilgrimages, indulgences and images. In place of what he was attempting to destroy he stressed a reliance on the dictates of the scriptures and on the conscience of the individual. He encouraged translation of the Bible into the vernacular so that it should be available to all. These ideas had first been disseminated in lectures, sermons and treatises in academic Oxford, and most of his early followers were clerics. He also aroused some interest in the higher ranks of lay society: John of Gaunt had protected him for some time, and several knights of Richard II's household, if contemporary chroniclers are to be believed, were Lollards. Of a similar social status was Sir John Oldcastle. But, with his execution in 1417, the earlier recantations of the Lollard knights, and the crushing of Lollardy in academic Oxford, the movement lost both its academic base and its upper-class support.

In the fifteenth century Lollardy became virtually a private religion. It had its ill-informed enthusiasts who mixed a debased form of Wycliffe's ideas with crude superstitions and extravagances of all sorts. It also had its devout adherents who read the translated scriptures or other Lollard books to their families or friends: a neighbour said of Margery Backster, the wife of a carpenter from Martham, that she had secretly desired her, that she and Jean her maid would come secretly, in the night, to her chamber and there she should hear her husband read the law of Christ unto them, which was written in a book that her husband was wont to read to her by night'.[17] Records of trials of fifteenth-century heretics show that Lollardy was almost exclusively a lower-class movement —a fact recognized by contemporary verse writers. One poet stated categorically that 'hit is no gentil mannes game' (*HP*, 64, 76), and refers to supporters of the movement as 'beggars'. Hoccleve refers to Oldcastle's supporters as 'cursied caitifs', but elsewhere speaks more specifically of 'a Baillif or Reeue/or man of craft' (*MP*, II, 143–4) among those influenced by Lollard opinions. 'Friar Daw' refers to

> carpenters ne sowters, cardmakers ne powchers,
> Drapers ne curtellers, girdelers, coferers, ne coruysers
> Ne no maner of artificers . . .
>
> (*FDR*, 865–7)

as being incapable, in his opinion, of discussing the problem of the real presence, the implication being that these were the sorts of people likely to be Lollard supporters. Records of trials for heresy also bear out another charge made in contemporary verses—that there was some support for Lollardy among women. 'Friar Daw' complains that Lollards:

> Wiþ wrenchis and wiles wynnen mennes wyues
> And maken hem scolers of þe newe scole.
>
> (*FDR*, 100–1)

Hoccleve, similarly, regrets that 'Some wommen' although 'hir wit be thynne' will 'argumentes make in holy writ' (*MP*, II, 145–6).

Lollardy was attacked in verse much more than it was supported. And such verses reveal that Lollards were passionately hated, violently feared and little understood. For Hoccleve, Lollards were the servants of the devil: 'The feend is your cheef' (*MP*, II, 468). Similarly, 'Friar Daw' sees them as the soldiers 'In Antichristis vanwarde/And in þe myddil, & in þe rerewarde ful bigly enbatailid' (*FDR*, 217–18). They are often accused of deceit, in particular deceit of their supporters: 'Friar Daw' speaks about their 'cauteles & sleiʒtes/Ech intrikid in oþer to snarre symple soules' (188–9), and Hoccleve of 'the snare of heresie' (*MP*, II, 26) into which they have lured Oldcastle. Their beliefs are, for Hoccleve, like 'mescheuous venyme' (20) and 'Friar Daw' has the same notion:

ȝoure preching is perilouse it poiseneþ sone
As honyed venym it crepith in swot.

(FDR, 127–8)

Elsewhere he compares Lollards to carriers of the plague who 'wiþ ȝour priuy pestilence enpoisoun þe peple' (416). Hoccleve's more persuasive image, that Lollards 'arn of dirknesse þe lanternes' (*MP*, II, 384), implies that they are misguided themselves and that they mislead others. 'Friar Daw' even sees, in the simplicity of the clothes which (he says) Lollards characteristically wear, a kind of deceit:

Whi þat þe lollardis weren moost greye cloþis.
I trowe to shewe þe colour þat signifieþ symplenesse
And wiþinne, seiþ Crist, ȝe ben rauenous wolues.

(383–5)

Hoccleve suggests that their piety is a cover for sexual immorality:

Yee þat pretenden folwers for to be
of Crystes disciples/nat lyue sholde
Aftir þe flesshly lustes/as doon yee
þat rekken nat/whos wyf yee take & holde.

(MP, II, 369–72)

'Friar Daw', using a familiar sermon commonplace, compares Lollards to the army of deadly sins which attack the Church:

Þe deuel is ȝour duke and pride beriþ þe baner,
Wraþþe is ȝoure gunner, envie is ȝour archer,
Ȝour couetise castiþ fer, ȝour leccherie brenniþ,
Glotony gideriþ stickes þerto, & sleuþe myneþ wallis,
Malice is ȝour men of armes & trecherie is ȝour aspie . . .

(219–23)

and elsewhere accuses them of 'arogaunce', 'detraccion', 'woodnesse & foolhardinesse' (170–91). It is a simple matter, of course, for Lollard apologists to point out the inaccuracy of some of these charges. The author of the *Rejoinder*, for example, says, quite correctly, that Lollards wore no specific uniform of grey, but wore anything:

> Þe secte þat þou seggist of, I wot is Iesu Cristis,
> Tellen litil by cloþing, bot now oon now oþer.
>
> (193–4)

But, to their opponents, Lollards obviously represented everything that was evil and practically any accusation, no matter how ill-defined, would suffice.

Somewhat more specific are those accusations which stress the divisiveness of Lollards. According to their opponents they threatened both the security of the state and the unity of the Church. The author of *Defend Us from All Lollardy* stresses the activity of the sect 'Agayns þe kynge & his clergye' (*HP*, 64, 38) and 'Friar Daw' lays the blame for it squarely on Wycliffe:

> siþ þat wickide worme—Wiclyf be his name—
> Began to sowe þe seed of cisme in þe erþe,
> Sorowe & schendship haþ awaked wyde,
> In lordship and prelacie haþ growe þe lasse grace.
>
> (*FDR*, 71–4)

He expands upon the 'erroure & heresie þat rengniþ in þe chirche' (12) because of Lollards, and deploys the full resources of his learning to stress their unorthodoxy. He compares Lollards to various Old Testament figures who rebelled against the chosen religious leaders of Israel:

> Now Achan spoiliþ Ierico & lyueþ of þe þefte
> And so lyuen þis lollardis in her fals fablis.
> Datan & Abiron & Chorees children
> Wiþ newe senceres ensencen þe auters of synne.
> Baal preestes ben bolde sacrifice to make
> And mortel maladi crepiþ in as a canker . . .
>
> (23–8)

He likens the damage that Wycliffe has done to the unity of the Church to that caused by earlier heretics and implies Wycliffe's damnation for it:

> Maximine ne Maniche nevere wrouȝ ten more wrake,
> þerfore from wele he is went, & woo mote him wryng.
>
> (157–8)

He uses the etymology of the word 'heresy' to demonstrate Lollard divisiveness:

> Heresie þat is Grw is diuisioun in Latyn,
> Þe whiche in oure langage meneþ sunderyng & partyng.
> He þanne þat sundriþ him from Crist & his chirche
> And frely forgiþ sentences contrarious to oure feiþ,
> Siche manere of forgers heretikes we callen
>
> (649–53)

—the implication being that Lollard doctrines were 'contrarious to oure feiþ'. He even presses into service the six types of heretic defined by the twelfth-century canonist Henry of Susa to demonstrate to 'Jack Upland' that 'þou & þi secte ben heretikes alle' (672) the implication being that Lollards were guilty of all six types. Here again, however, 'Friar Daw's' anti-heretical zeal leads him into a false position. One of the types of heresy described—that of selling the sacraments ('we clepen hem heretikes þat sacramentis sellyn' 664)—applies in no way specifically to Lollards, and is, in fact, more applicable to friars, as the author of the *Rejoinder* points out:

> þou accusist oþer men þat han bot þe mote
> In þe comparison of alle зour gret synnes.
>
> (323–4)

There are occasions, however, when fifteenth-century poets attempt, with slightly more discrimination, to understand and refute specific Lollard doctrines. One can scarcely dignify these comments by calling them arguments. They bear little relation to the scholarly way in which Wycliffe had sought to establish his position. These poems are little but crude restatements of orthodoxy, mixed with a certain amount of ridicule of Lollard doctrines. Wycliffe had argued for the primacy of the temporal power over the spiritual, but Hoccleve, in his *Address to Sir John Oldcastle*, contradicts this:

> Auctoritee of Preest excedith alle
> Eerthely powers/thogh it seem sour
> To the taast of your detestable errour.
>
> (*MP*, II, 291–3)

His position, such as it is, rests on two analogies: that spiritual power surpasses temporal power in importance 'As moche as dooth the soule the body' (302), and by just as much as the sun does the moon:

> Looke, how moche & how greet dyuersitee
> Betwixt the sonne ther is, & the moone;
> So moche is a popes auctoritee
> Aboue a kynges might. . . .

(313–16)

He defends the Pope by reference to the origin of papal authority: 'The hy power þat is to him committed/As large as petres is' (358–9), and the authority of priests on the grounds that obedience to priests was really obedience to Christ and that priests were mediators between the individual and God:

> To Ihesu Cryst, I seye,
> Principally is þat obedience.
> God hath ordeyned preestes to purveye
> Salue of penance for mannes offense.

(117–20)

He also seeks to get round Lollard strictures on bad priests by saying that the teaching of the priest should be followed not his behaviour:

> I putte cas, a prelat or a preest
> Him viciously gouerne in his lyuynge/
> Thow oghtist reewe on it/whan thow it seest,
> And folowe him nat/but aftir his techynge
> Thow oghtest do. . . .

(129–33)

In the same way he argues that a sinful priest may administer the sacraments because 'Be what he be/the priest is instrument/Of God . . .' (334–5). Against Lollard ideas that priests should live on their tithes, and on what alms their parishioners might give them, but otherwise possess no property, Hoccleve argues in two ways: from biblical precedent—

> While heere on eerthe was our Sauueour,
> Whom Angels diden seruice & honour,
> Purses had he/Why for his chirche sholde
> So haue eek after,
>
> (428–31)

and on the grounds that since the 'entente final' of the Lollards was 'to ryfle' the Church, their motives disqualify their objections (459).

Other Lollard positions also come under attack. Both Hoccleve and the anonymous author of *Defend Us from All Lollardy* speak on behalf of the orthodox use of images and shrines in worship and both find the Lollard position too unsophisticated.

> Ho wor ful lewde þat wolde byleue
> in image mad of stok or ston?
>
> (*HP*, 64, 105–6)

asks the anonymous author, dismayed that anyone should think the image itself was worshipped and not the saint it represented. Hoccleve says that images

> causen men honoure
> The seint/after whom/maad is that figure
> And not worsshippe it/how gay it be wroghte.
>
> (*MP*, II, 412–14)

He develops this, using the unlikely analogy of spectacles, which cause a man 'to see bet than he mighte'. Just as one does not look at the spectacles, but through them to the book, so one does not look upon the image but through it to the saint: 'The sighte vs myngith to the seint to preye' (424). He has no similar justification of pilgrimages, but insists that they are good 'if þat it doon be for deuocioun' (402) and not frivolously for social purposes. He also defends confession, but offers no real arguments in its justification:

> Thow seist 'confessioun auriculeer
> Ther needith noon'/but it is the contrarie;
> Thow lookist mis/thy sighte is nothyng cleer!
> Holy writ ther-in is thyn Aduersarie,

And clerkes alle fro thy conceit varie,
Þat Crystes partie holden & maynteene.

(81–6)

Similarly, he also insists that Lollards err 'in the sacrament/Of the
Auter' but feels he has no need to define 'how in special' because it
'knowen is in many a Regioun' (102). On this Hoccleve was perhaps
wise not to go into too much detail, for the subject of transubstantiation was an intricate one. Wycliffe had maintained that
Christ was present at the Eucharist, but that the bread and the
wine remained in substance after consecration. Th:s was opposed
to the orthodox view that the bread and wine were actually changed
into the body and blood of Christ and that only the 'accidents'
(i.e. the appearances of the bread and wine) remained. 'Friar Daw'
predictably maintains the orthodox view:

we saie wiþ Holy Chirche þat þer is Cristis bodi
& not material breed wiþ Wiclyf ȝour maister

(FDR, 844–5)

and shortly afterwards he enlarges on the position of the friars:

Þei seie breed is turned in to fleish, & wyne in to blood,
Þourȝ þe myȝt of oure God & vertue of his wordis:
Þe fleish is mete, þe blood is drynke, & Crist dwelliþ,
No þing rasyd, no þing diuidid, but oonli broken in signe,
& as moche is in oo partie as is al þe hole.
Þer leeueþ not of þe breed but oonli þe licnesse,
Which þat abidiþ þerinne noon substeyned substans;
It is deþ to yuel, lyf to good, encresing of oure grace.

(855–62)

But this is simply a restatement, made up of phrases from Aquinas,
of orthodox opinion. There is no attempt to refute Wycliffe's
arguments.

Each of the anti-Lollard poets speaks against Lollard notions
that religious truths could be derived from a close study of the
Bible and that the Bible should be available to all. Hoccleve
stresses his preference for former times when the laity accepted the
teaching of the clergy without question:

Oure fadres olde & modres lyued wel,
And taghte hir children/as hem self taght were
Of holy chirche/& axid nat a del
'Why stant this word heere?'/and 'why this word there?'
'Why spake god thus/and seith thus elles where?'
'Why dide he this wyse/and mighte han do thus?'
(153–60)

In this Hoccleve is a natural conservative. For the laity to meddle in religious affairs involves in some sense a disruption of the divinely ordered state of things, a usurpation by the laity of the function of the clergy. But he substantiates this with two other points: that religious truth cannot be arrived at by reason but by faith alone

For if we mighte our feith by reson preeue
We sholde no meryt of our feith haue,
(141–2)

and that clerics alone have the intellectual capacity for understanding religious matters—'To Clerkes grete apparteneth þat aart' (150). The intelligence of the ordinary people, particularly those who support Lollard doctrines, is 'al to feeble to despute of it' (149). 'Friar Daw' puts the same point more harshly by saying that to allow difficult points of doctrine to be discussed by the laity is like casting pearls before swine:

& þe presciouse perlis ȝe strowun to hogges—
þe sutil metis of scripturis to cherlis stomakes
& maken hem als comoun as þe cart weye,
(*FDR*, 880–3)

and he supports his contentions by several biblical references. The essential secrecy of the scriptures, he says, is dissipated by the Lollards: 'þe scripture is scatrid in his priuy pointes' (892). The anonymous author of *Defend Us from All Lollardy* even goes so far as to say that 'þe bibell is al myswent' because Lollards 'construen hit after hir entent' (*HP*, 64, 23).

Such are the direct attacks on Lollardy. Some incidental dis-

I

cussion also appears in the dialogue between the Beggar and Hoccleve in the Prologue to the *Regement of Princes* in which the Beggar gives an account of the burning in March 1410 of John Badby, the Lollard Worcestershire tailor. A few lines are devoted to Badby's heretical opinions on transubstantiation:

> The precious body of oure lorde ihesu
> In forme of brede, he leued not at al,
> (288–9)

and a few to his denial that priests were able to turn the 'brede material' into the body of Christ:

> He seyde, a prestes power was as smal
> As a Rakers, or swiche an oþer wiȝte,
> And to mak it, hadde no gretter myȝt.
> (292–4)

But what is particularly interesting is that the Beggar cites the case of Badby as a warning to Hoccleve against the danger of speculation into the mysteries of religion. His main criticism of Lollards is that they are guilty of intellectual 'Presumpcioun' and 'surquidrie' in believing that reason can solve religious questions. He himself believes that 'mannes reson may not preue oure fey' (331) and asserts his own orthodoxy. He is willing to accept the truth of the Bible without question, for what 'oure lord god seiþ in holy scripture/May not be fals' (337–8) even though some things, such as the immaculate conception, are difficult to understand:

> Was it not eek a moustre as in nature
> Þat god I-bore was of a virgine?
> Ȝit is it soþ, þogh man be coniecture
> Of reson, or what he can ymagine,
> Not sauoure it, ne can it determyne.
> (344–8)

He eschews speculation, and resolves to follow the teaching of the 'worþi prelacie' and the 'suffisant clergye' as 'Oure goode fadres olde han folwyd it' (357). Hoccleve, also, in his own person, stresses that he has 'non inclinacioun' to investigate religious questions:

Of oure feiþ wol I not despute at all;
But, at a word, I in the sacrament
Of þe auter fully bileue, & schal,
With goddes helpe, while life is to me lent;
And, in despyt of the fendes talent,
In al oþer articles of þe feiþ
Byleue, as fer as þat holy writ seiþ.

(379–85)

This is Hoccleve's usual line—a mistrust of reason and a belief attained through faith and through the teachings of the Church. It was back to this mood of humble acquiescence that the orthodox tried to win Lollards and Lollard sympathizers.

Finally, on the subject of Lollardy, something must be said about the interesting *Croxton Play at the Sacrament* which was written and performed in Norfolk at some time around 1461.[18] It is concerned with a story of the desecration of the Host by Jews, a legend known on the continent as early as the fourteenth century but which appears in English nowhere else. The English play tells how Jonathas, a wealthy Jewish merchant, acquires consecrated wafers from a Christian merchant Aristorius. With his four servants the Jew tests the truth of the doctrine of the real presence by putting the Host to various tortures: it is stabbed, thrown into boiling water, and finally cast into a hot oven. The consecrated wafer reveals its miraculous character by bleeding profusely and by speaking to the Jews, who are converted to Christianity. Basically the story is anti-Jewish, but the English version does not stress this aspect. Instead the author seems concerned to emphasize the validity of various po.nts of Christian doctrine. In lines 200–2 Jonathas defines the doctrine of the real presence:

For þe beleue on a cake—methynk yt ys onkynd,
And al they seye how þe prest doth yt bynd,
And be þe myght of hys word make yt flessh and blode

—a doctrine he patently doubts but the validity of which the play demonstrates. The power and authority of the priesthood in administering the sacraments is stressed:

> thys powre he gaue Peter to proclame,
> And how the same shuld be suffycyent to all prechors;
> The bysshoppys and curatys saye the same,
> And soo, as I vnderstond, do all hys progenytors.
>
> (405–8)

Christ himself, in his words to the Jews, had urged upon them the need for confession before they could be forgiven their sins:

> In hys law to make vs stedfast,
> There spake he to vs woordys of grete favore;
> In contrycyon our hartys he cast
> And bad take vs to a confessore.
>
> (944–7)

Both Jonathas and Aristorius resolve at the end of the play to undertake pilgrimages as a part of their penance:

> Now wyll we walke be contre and cost
> Owr wyckyd lyuyng for to restore.
>
> (964–5)

The play makes no mention of Lollardy, but the legend is so interpreted as to serve to confirm many of those doctrines which Lollards challenged, and Cecilia Cutts is perhaps justified in suggesting that it was composed 'by some devout member of the clergy, for presentation in a district (or districts) disturbed by Lollard dissent, in the hope, evidently, of confirming the people in the Catholic faith or of winning them back to it by a vivid illustration of its central doctrine and a strong emotional appeal.'[19]

To demonstrate the validity of the orthodox position by argument or example was one way to combat heresy. But to almost every fifteenth-century poet this way seemed insufficiently forceful. In poem after poem the rulers of England are urged that they have a moral duty to protect the Church and to eradicate heresy by whatever means they have at their disposal. Thus Hoccleve seeks to persuade the newly-crowned Henry V to strengthen the Church

> in chacyng away
> Therrour/which sones of iniquitee

Han sowe ageyn the feith.

(*MP*, IV, 25–7)

Hoccleve was presumably satisfied with Henry's harsh suppressions of heresy, for, in a poem written a little later, he frantically urges him to continue his policies:

Do foorth/do foorth/continue your socour!
Holde vp Crystes Baner/lat it nat falle.

(*MP*, V, 15–16)

In a subsequent stanza he even goes so far as to suggest that Henry should pass a law forbidding discussion of doctrinal questions

Openly among peple/where errour
Spryngith al day/& engendrith rumour.

(28–9)

In another poem Hoccleve stresses the moral obligation of Knights of the Garter to support 'Crystes cause' and to uproot heretical beliefs:

Conqueste of hy prowesse is for to tame
The wylde woodnesse of this mescreance
Right to the roote/rype yee þat same.

(*MP*, VI, 49–51)

Lydgate, in his *Defence of Holy Church* (written in either 1413–14 or 1431–2)[20] urges the 'Most worþi prince' to whom the poem is addressed that he should destroy the enemies of the Church:

And namely hem that of presumpcyoun
Dispraven hir, and hir ornamentes,
And therwithall of indignacioun
Withdrawe wolde hir rich paramenteȝ.

(*Minor Poems* I, 10, 127–30)

Who specifically these enemies are he does not say, but these lines and the later accusation that 'thay hemsilff the riches wolden use' (133) recall Hoccleve's complaint that Lollards intended to 'ryfle' the Church of its property. In some places there is an insistence that the law should be applied with its full rigour to convicted heretics. The Beggar in the Prologue to Hoccleve's *Regement of Princes*, referring to the burning of John Badby, expresses the hope that all heretics should come to a similar end:

> wolde god, to cristes foos echon
> þat as he heelde were I-serued soo,
> ffor I am seur þat þer ben many moo.
>
> (327–9)

Hoccleve does not associate himself with this opinion here, but it was one which he evidently held for in his *Address to Sir John Oldcastle* he expresses the wish that heretics should burn unless they repent:

> but yee do/god, I byseeche a boone,
> þat in the fyr yee feele may the sore!
>
> (*MP*, II, 319–20)

'Friar Daw' is predictably extreme: for him, heretics are 'worþi to noon oþer good but in þe fire to brenne' and therefore, he continues:

> so forto pursue an heretike to fire or to prisoun
> I holde it mor holsum þan to halewe a chirche.
>
> (635–7)

The author of *Defend Us from All Lollardy* tries to frighten heretics by reminding them that it '. . . is a moch folie/for fals beleue to ben brent' (*HP*, 64, 19–20). And everywhere appears the threat, as for example in Hoccleve, that heretics would be condemned to eternal damnation and deprived of the joys of heaven to which the orthodox would come:

> oure soules lift shul be;
> And on þat othir part/yee feendes/yee
> In the dirke halke of Helle schul descende.
>
> (*MP*, II, 476–8)

though, he adds, nobody wishes this upon Lollards, and that the 'desir' of orthodox Christians is 'þat yee yow wolde amende' (480).

It is doubtful, though, whether any of this propaganda had a significant effect. The poems are far from persuasive, for, just as all sorts of repressive action were urged against Lollards, so any argument, however illogical, unlikely or unjustified, would serve in anti-Lollard literature. Most of the verses are more discreditable to their authors than to Lollards. Moreover, the recklessness of the arguments and the frequent metaphors of disease, poison and traps suggest that heretics were feared, whence perhaps the harsh tone of anti-heretical verses. From the number of manuscript copies of them which have survived, it appears they were not very popular. Even the effectiveness of the harsh repressions which they advocate (and which continued throughout the century) was limited. It is obvious from the number of trials for heresy both that the Lollard movement persisted and that the Church authorities remained concerned about it.

NOTES

[1] *The Tale of Beryn* ed. F. J. Furnivall and W. G. Stone, EETS ES 105 1909, lines 147–58.

[2] Quoted by George Holmes, *The Later Middle Ages*, 1962, p. 180.

[3] See Appendix C.

[4] For details of these crusades see Steven Runciman, *A History of the Crusades*, Cambridge 1954, III, 455–63.

[5] Quoted by V. H. H. Green, *The Later Plantagenets*, 1955, p. 52.

[6] *Twenty Six Political and Other Poems*, EETS OS 124 1904, pp. xiv–xvi.

[7] *The Book of Margery Kempe* ed. S. B. Meech and H. E. Allen, EETS OS 212 1940, pp. 36–7.

[8] *Instructions for Parish Priests* ed. E. Peacock, EETS OS 31 1868, line 6.

[9] *Relation of the Island of England* ed. C. A. Sneyd, Camden Society 37, 1847, p. 29.

[10] *Twenty Six Political and Other Poems*, op. cit., p. xxii.

[11] Ed. F. J. Furnivall, *Transactions of the Philological Society*, 1858, Part II, pp. 138–48.

[12] For a summary of the debate on the authorship and date of this and other poems in the 'Jack Upland' sequence, see P. L. Heyworth ed. *Jack Upland, Friar Daw's Reply and Upland's Rejoinder*, Oxford 1968, pp. 6–19.

[13] For these lines see P. L. Heyworth, *ibid.*, pp. 170, 171, 172.

[14] *Reliquiae Antiquae* ed. T. Wright and J. O. Halliwell 1843, II, 280–2.

[15] *The Later Lollards* 1414–1520, Oxford 1965, p. 244.

[16] *The Book of Margery Kempe*, op.cit., p. 129.

[17] Quoted by V. H. H. Green, *op. cit.*, p. 207.

[18] Ed. N. Davis, *Non-Cycle Plays and Fragments*, EETS SS 1 1970, pp. 58–89.

[19] *MLQ* 5, 1944, p. 60.

[20] On the question of the date of this poem see J. Norton-Smith ed. *John Lydgate: Poems*, Oxford 1966, p. 151.

8 : English Society I : The Theoretical Basis

PERHAPS the most important English political thinker of the fifteenth century was Sir John Fortescue, a gifted lawyer from Devon, at various times a justice of the peace, in 1442 chief justice of the King's Bench, and a prominent Lancastrian adviser. Yet even Fortescue's ideas are not particularly original, and, moreover, they tend to be descriptive of English governmental and legal institutions rather than analytical or 'constitutional'. There are in his writings one or two ideas for improving the efficiency of the government, some proposals for increasing royal revenues and for reconstituting the Council, but these ideas are in no way radical. There is also his well-known distinction between 'regal dominion' and 'dominion regal and political'.

> Ther bith ij kyndes off kyngdomes, of the wich that on is a lordship callid in laten *dominium regale* and that other is callid *dominium politicum et regale*. And thai diuersen in that the first kynge mey rule his peple bi suche lawes as he makyth hymself. And therfore he mey sett vppon thaim tayles and other imposicions, such as he wol hym self, withowt thair assent. The secounde kynge may not rule his peple bi other lawes than such as thai assenten unto. And therfore he mey sett vpon thaim non imposicions without thair owne assent.[1]

So begins his *Governance of England* and it is the 'dominion regal and political' which he believes obtains in England. He does not probe the origins of these systems very deeply apart from saying that 'that on kyngdome beganne of and bi the might of the prince, and that oþer beganne bi the desire and institucion of the peple of the same prince.' Nor does he explore the constitutional implications of these systems, though he makes it clear that the English system, in its practical consequences, is a good one. He attributes the impoverished state of France to its system of 'regal dominion' and compares England favourably:

> But blessyd be God this lande is rulid vndir a bettir lawe; and therfore the peple therof be not in such peynurie, nor therby hurt in thair persons, but thai bith welthe, and haue all thinges nescessarie to the sustenance of nature. Wherfore thai ben myghty, and able to resiste the aduersaries of this reaume, and to beete oþer reaumes that do, or wolde do them wronge. Lo this is the fruyt of *Jus polliticum et regale*, vndre wich we live.[2]

In the seventeenth century, particularly, Fortescue's ideas came to be important and influential, but in his own time they do not appear to have been so. When Englishmen of the fifteenth century wrote about their society it was usually in well-tried and conventional terms, as E. F. Jacob puts it: 'English speculation about government and society in the fifteenth century was less political than moral and dogmatic. The study of man and his duties in the community, his moral nature and his rights was, with a few exceptions, left to the homilists or to the regents in the universities, where a handful of teachers in the faculties of arts and theology considered questions about the moral excellence of a citizen mainly as a branch of theology or in relation to the obligations of the classes or grades in society.'[3]

Society was thought to consist of a hierarchy of classes forming an organic whole. Three classes were usually distinguished—the nobility, the clergy and the common people. As Ruth Mohl has shown, this classification was of considerable antiquity and by the fifteenth century was a commonplace.[4] Thus, a sermon writer could state categorically 'There be in þis world þre maner of men: clerkes, kynʒthis and commynalte', without feeling it was necessary to justify his analysis.[5] And these basic categories were found to be useful by writers throughout the period. The author of *Mum and the Sothsegger*, in his first fragment which is to be dated 1399–

1400, speaks of a threefold division, though it differs slightly from the usual one in that there is no mention of the 'clergy' and the 'councillors' are separated off from the 'warriors' not by any social factor but simply by age:

> iche rewme vndir roff/of þe reyne-bowe
> Sholde stable and stonde/be þese þre degres:
> By gouernaunce of grete/and of good age;
> By styffnesse and strengthe/of steeris well y-yokyd,
> Þat beth myȝthffull men/of þe mydill age;
> And be laboreris of lond/þat lyfflode ne fayle.
>
> (III, 248–53)

Writing in 1413, the author of the poems in MS Digby 102 compares the kingdom of England to the stones and flowers around the King's crown and uses the familiar tripartite division of society:

> What doþ a kynges crowne signyfye,
> Whan stones and floures on sercle is bent?
> Lordis, comouns, and clergye
> To ben all at on assent.
>
> (XII, 9–12)

In his translation of *The Mirror of the World* (1481) Caxton affirms that there are '. . . thre maner of peple in the world . . . and that were clerkes, knyghtes, and labourers'.[6] And it is clear that this division of society was useful beyond the fifteenth century. The author of the stanzas, written in a sixteenth-century hand on the flyleaf of BM MS Sloane 4031, refers to the usual classes of society: 'ye that ar comons', 'yov as are en hye degre' and 'ye that are mynystres of god omnypotent'. He also has four stanzas of advice to 'ye ryche' (*HP*, 97, 8–35) but these seem to refer to the rich of any rank and do not disturb the traditional classification.

It is difficult to be sure how far this sort of analysis of society was felt to be satisfactory and how far it was used simply because it had behind it the authority of a long tradition of use. The three estates theory did not usually define the limits of the classes. Nor was it very exhaustive, for distinctions of rank within the three categories were not often made. There are exceptions, however. In one poem from MS Digby 102 the envisaged division seems to be fivefold: a 'Riche comouns', a 'wyse clergy', 'Marchaundes, squyers, chiualry', all ruled over by a 'cheualrous kyng in wittes hy3e' (III, 65–72). Usually, however, the more detailed analyses of society seem to have been prompted by the possibilities of an image, or of a particular type of poem. Thus, in 1442, Bishop Stafford, in his sermon before Parliament, compared the kingdom of England to the throne of Solomon and the six steps leading up to the throne to the estates of society: the nobility was undivided, but within the estate of the clergy he distinguished between the bishops and the ordinary priests, and divided the commons into merchants, cultivators and artificers.[7] In Caxton's version of Jacobus de Cessolis' *Game and Playe of the Chesse* (*c.* 1480) appears not only instructions as to how to play the game, but also advice ('ful of holsom wysedom and requysyte unto every astate and degree') to the various ranks of society, who are represented by the chessmen. In this classification the clergy do not appear. But there are comments on the characteristics and duties of the king and queen, the knights, the king's legates (who are represented by the rooks), the judiciary (who are represented by the alphins or elephants, the forerunners of the modern bishops), and the whole range of the commons (who are represented by the pawns) from merchants to tillers of the soil.[8] The analysis of society here is not meant to be definitive. It took the form it did simply because comparison with the chessmen made such an analysis possible. Similarly, Lydgate, using a Latin version of the 'twelve abuses' poem as a starting point for a poem of advice to the estates, predictably distinguishes twelve divisions in society, including women, the old, the young, rich and poor, as well as some of the categories more usually found (*HP*, 96). In a carol complaining about the lack of 'truth' in contemporary society the author isolates for mention 'grete lordys', ladies, 'men of lawe', monastics and, rather incongruously, 'holy cherche' (*HP*, 59). In another carol, the author seeks to show how money 'rulyst the world ouer all' (*HP*, 51, 2) and organizes his verses loosely by demonstrating how money is coveted by all ranks of society from the highest downwards: he mentions those who live around the 'kynges corte', squires and knights, merchants, women, men of law, 'craftys-men', ploughmen, thieves and beggars. In poems on the inevitability of death a classification of the various orders of society often appears. Lydgate's translated *Dance Macabre*, for example, mentions representatives of various ranks of society from the Pope, Emperor, Cardinal and King down to the Labourer, the Child, the Young Scholar and the Hermit.[9] In his *Prayer to St. Thomas of Canterbury* a more restricted list of the estates of the world appears beginning with the highest:

> Pray for the states of all hooly Cherche,
> For the kynges vertuous gouernaunce,
> For hys Prynces Marcial Puissaunce
> That high discrecioun may ther Brydel leede,
> (*Minor Poems*, I, 31, 91–4)

and continuing with 'Capeleyns', 'Monckes professed, Preestes religious', 'Knyghtes, Squyeres, and yomen for the werre', 'marchauntes that saile fro soo ferre', 'Artificeres that lyue by ther trauaile' and finally 'trew titheres' and 'the poraile'.

Perhaps the most memorable image used to describe society was that of the body politic. It had classical and biblical origins and was frequently used by medieval political theorists. The most exhaustive version of the theory in medieval English verse appears in *The Descryuyng of Mannes Membres* from MS Digby 102. As was commonly the case the author attempts to elaborate. The head is likened to a king 'For he is lord souereyn of al' (XV, 10), and the mouth, nose and eyes to councillors. The neck is likened to a judge 'For, þurgh it, comeþ all wordis of wyt' (20). The priesthood is compared to man's breast 'Most in perile, lest in rest' (27). The author compares the shoulders and backbone to lords, and, appropriately enough, the arms, hands and fingers to those ranks of society whose duties were its defence:

> Þe armes, to knyȝtes to fende fro fon;
> Þe squyers, I likne to þe hondes;
> Þe fyngres to ȝemen þat byfore gon
> Wiþ bent bowes and bryȝt brondes.
> (35–8)

The ribs are compared to men of law, the thighs to merchants (because they travel far) and the legs and feet to craftsmen and ploughmen (because on their efforts all the world depends). The toes are likened to true servants, and here the author makes the point that even the lowliest ranks of society are essential to its well-being: just as a man 'may not stonde þat haþ no toon' (74), so a master cannot exist 'Wiþ-out seruant' (80). The belly is compared to a 'botemeles purs' (82), and the familiar story about how the limbs complained against the belly enforces the usual moral— that moderation should be observed in all things. The author concludes that all ranks of society are interdependent, like all parts of the body:

> I likne a kyngdom in good astate,
> To stalworþe man, myȝty in hele.
> While non of his lymes oþer hate,
> He is myȝty, wiþ anoþer to dele.
>   (121–4)

Lydgate's treatment of this theme in the story of Rehoboam from *The Fall of Princes* is at once more elaborate and less detailed. The prince is compared to the head and the warriors to 'handis & armys off diffence'. The other parts of the body are compared to judges,

> meires, provostes & burgeis in citees,
> Marchauntis also, which seeke in sundri londis,
> With othir crafftis which lyven bi ther hondis,

and the feet and legs are compared to labourers. The estate of the clergy in this version is not part of the body. Lydgate, unlike the MS Digby 102 poet but following a common tradition in medieval political theory, compares the clergy to the soul:

> This bodi must have a soule off liff
> To quyke the membris with gostli mociouns
> Which shal be maad off folk contemplatiff.

Like the MS Digby 102 poet, however, Lydgate uses the image to reinforce the notion that all ranks of society depend upon each other. This image of society was well enough known to be used allusively. Gower, in his *Address to Henry IV*, complains that the papal schism had set an example of division to the princes of Europe in these terms: 'Of that the heved is sick, the limes aken' (*PPS*, II, p. 11). Here, the Pope is conceived as the head, and the princes as the limbs of Christendom.

The most detailed analyses of society, however, come from utilitarian works which sought to instruct would-be servants on the niceties of precedence. One such work is *The Boke of Nurture* written by John Russell 'sum tyme servaunde with Duke Vmfrey of Glowceter, a prynce fulle royalle with whom vschere in chamber was y, and marshalle also in halle'.[10] In his section on the duties of the marshal and usher Russell insists that a detailed knowledge of the various ranks of society is necessary:

> The office of a connynge vschere or marshalle with owt fable
> must know alle estates of the church goodly & greable,
> and þe excellent estate of a kynge with his blode honorable.
>
> (1002–4)

His classification is, as usual, in descending order of rank, but cuts across the normal divisions between clergy and seculars. He begins:

> The pope hath no peere;
> Emperowre is nex hym euery where;
> Kynge corespondent; þus nurture shalle yow lere.
> high Cardynelle, þe dignyte dothe requere;
> Kyngis sone, prynce ye hym Calle;
> Archebischoppe is to hym peregalle.
> Duke of þe blode royalle,
> bishoppe Marques & erle coequalle
>
> (1006–12)

and proceeds in great detail down to

> Worshipfulle merchaundes and riche artyficeris,
> Gentilmen welle nurtured & of good maneris,
> With gentilwommen.
>
> (1037–9)

He says nothing of ranks of society below this, presumably because they did not dine at the sort of gathering where he was accustomed to officiate. He does, however, go on to define which ranks were permitted to eat together, and how many there should be to a table. He also sorts out one or two difficult problems, such as what an usher should do about seating a poor noble and a wealthy commoner, what rank should be assigned to the parents of those people who have risen to important positions, and what should be the status of a 'lady of lowe blode and degre' who is married to a knight. Not so detailed as Russell's analysis, but perhaps based on it, is that which appears in *The Boke of Kervynge*. Like Russell, this author begins with Pope, Emperor, King, Cardinal, Prince and so on, and ends with 'persones & preestes, worshypfull marchauntes & gentylmen'. Briefer still is the list entitled *The Ordre of Goyng or Sittyng* from Balliol College MS 354. This begins in the same way as the books previously quoted and follows substantially the same order, but adds after the rank of 'gentylman' those of 'Artificer' and 'yeman of good name'. An interesting reflection of political change in this manuscript is that a sixteenth-century hand (presumably post-Reformation) has crossed out 'A pope hath no pere' and the rank of 'the popes colectour'.

Medieval writers did not often feel the need to justify the divisions of society they expounded. Sometimes a divine origin for the estates of the world is set out. The author of *Jack Upland*, following Wycliffe, attributes their foundation to God, who made them to correspond to the persons of the Trinity:

> so he sette mannes state: in lordis to represente þe power
> of þe Fadir; preestis to represente þe wisdom of þe Sone;
> and þe comouns to presente þe good lastinge wille of þe Holi
> Goost. (*JU*, 7–10)

Sometimes a biblical origin is suggested. Thus Gower, in his *Vox Clamantis*, finds the origin of the non-noble classes in Adam, who because of his disobedience was expelled from Eden and compelled to labour for his living. Caxton, in his *Game and Playe of the Chesse*, finds in the cursed Cain the origin of churls. *The Boke of St. Albans* uses this idea and makes Seth, Cain's brother who received his father's blessing, the progenitor of gentlemen. Other notions appear here also. After the Flood the descendants of Cain were destroyed, but churls were reborn in Ham who was cursed by Noah, and gentlemen in Shem and Japhet who received his blessing. Nine orders of gentlemen are then distinguished to correspond to the nine orders of angels and the nine colours used in the blazoning of arms.[11] In his *Fall of Princes*, Lydgate, without the use of an analogy, speaks of the divine origin of kings:

> The stat of kynges gan be permyssioun
> Of goddis grace & of his purueyaunce,
> (VIII, 2376–7)

and the MS Digby 102 poet speaks of lords in the same way:

> God made lordis gouernoures
> To gouerne puple in vnyte.
> (III, 129–30)

Such accounts are not simply descriptive. They imply that the particular form of society was divinely justified, and that mankind's duty was to accept it. Thus, after a survey of the various orders of society and their duties, Lydgate writes:

> Remembre you how god hath sette you, lo!
> And doo your parte as ye ar ordeynd to.
> (*HP*, 96, 19–20)

Practical justifications of these social divisions are rare. When they occur the reasoning is of the simplest. The Netmaker, with whom the Pilgrim meets in Lydgate's translation of Deguileville, explains the duties of the various ranks of society and seeks to justify their variety by stressing that if all were of equal status there would be no leadership and

> no maner polycye
> But rather a confusion
> In euery maner Regioun.
> (*Pilgrimage*, 11378–80)

This being the case it followed that one rank of society ought not to assume the duties of another. The Netmaker stresses that the clergy ought not to involve themselves in non-clerical matters: 'Voyde hem ffrom offyce seculer.' Gower said that 'In high astat it is a vice/To go to low . . .', and Lydgate speaks against the presumption of the lower orders:

> What thyng in herte mor froward mai be thouht
> Than is the sodeyn fals presumpcioun
> Off a wrecche that cam vp off nouht,
> To yeue hym lordshepe and dominacioun.
> (*Fall of Princes*, II, 232–5)

Conformity to one's rank was enforced, at least in theory, by the Statutes of Apparel which sought to define what clothes were appropriate for the various ranks of society. Lydgate, in one place, says that these distinctions were divinely ordained:

> God suffreth weel ther be a difference
> Touchyng array, as men been of degre.
> (*Fall of Princes*, VI, 2696–7)

Moral commonplaces, not specifically related to political theory, also inculcated contentment with one's lot and warned against ambition: nobody would have needed reminding that pride was the deadliest of the deadly sins, and everyone would have known that to ride upwards on the ever-moving wheel of Lady Fortune was to risk being cast down. Innumerable tags and almost proverbial verses, such as the quatrain from Cambridge University Library MS Gg iv.12, offered consolation to the lower orders:

> Hiegh Towers by strong wyndes full lowe be cast
> When the lowe Cotages stand sure & fast
> Therfor with surenes yt is better in povertie tabide
> Then hastily to be Riche and sodaynly to slyde.[12]

And, anyway, the poor would have their reward in heaven.

According to these theories, each order of society, by performing its proper function, made an essential contribution to the well-being of the kingdom, and, on occasions, authors defined what they took these duties and responsibilities to be. One sermon writer, for example, writes as follows:

> kny3thes and oþur gentils with hem shuld sett her besines
> abowte þe good gouernaunce in þe temperalltee in þe tyme of
> pees and also abowte diuers poyntes of armes in þe tyme of
> werre . . . prestes shuld principally entermet to lern þe lawe of
> Crist and lawfully to teche itt. And lower men shuld hold hem
> contente with þe questions and þe sotelte of þer own labour.[13]

As this is stated, the duties and responsibilities of each class are of
comparable importance. But, though the part which the common
people and the clergy had to play was often stressed, few doubted
that the policies and behaviour of those who held positions of
power, particularly the King, were crucial. The author of *Advice
to the Several Estates* II from BM MS Sloane 4031, for example,
points out that the character of a ruler is like an example to his
people: he may influence for evil if his own life is evil,

> a vycyovs prynce es as a plage mortall,
> and fovle example to all hes comonte,
> occasyon to folowe hes vyle enormyte,
> > (*HP*, 97, 47–9)

or for good if his own life is good

> lyke-wyse hes lyfe establyd en vertve
> shalbe example to all hes regyon,
> hes lyfe, hes maners, and vertve to ensve.
> > (50–2)

It followed that rulers, particularly young rulers, needed the best
advice they could get, and there were plenty of fifteenth-century
writers eager to give it.

It is not possible, within the compass of this present study, to
give more than a brief account of the major characteristics of some
fifteenth-century 'mirrors for princes', for the *genre* was a popular
one. Hoccleve's *Regement of Princes* is perhaps the earliest and
certainly the most popular poem of this kind in English. As is
clear from the final stanza of the Proem, the advice the poem gives
is meant to help Prince Henry rule well when he attains the throne,
so that God and his people will be satisfied and Henry's own
honour will increase:

Now, gracious prince, agayn that the corone
Honoure you shall with roial dignitee,
Beseche I hym that sitte on hye in trone,
That, when þat charge recueyed han ye,
Swych gouernance men may feele and se
In yow, as may ben vn-to his plesance,
Profet to vs, and your good loos avance.

(2157–63)

Throughout the long, discursive Prologue to his treatise Hoccleve had, as is to be expected, written passages of praise to Prince Henry: for his attempt to save the heretic John Badby's life (lines 295–322), and for his generosity (1842–8); and had also attempted to commend himself to the Prince's patronage by claiming Chaucer as 'dere maistir' and by stressing his need for support by some wealthy patron. But the Prologue amounts to more than this. It consists principally of a discussion between Hoccleve and an old Beggar on a variety of topical problems: each supports an orthodox religious position and condemns Lollardy (281–385); the Beggar laments the extravagance of contemporary fashions (414–553); Hoccleve complains about not being able to get his annuity paid (813–33) and about how heartless noblemen are in not supporting their dependents (862–931); the Beggar exposes some contemporary abuses in the Church (1401–42); Hoccleve complains of the way in which liveried retainers exploit their positions (1492–1554); and finally condemns the greed of the contemporary nobility who seek to consolidate their fortunes through arranged marriages (1623–73). On each of these topics Hoccleve and the Beggar offer sound moral advice, and the Prologue does not differ in essentials from the more formal sections of advice. In fact it could be argued that even the more personalized elements of the Prologue contribute to the advice the poem has to offer. Authority and weight are lent to the Beggar's statements by the fact that he is old:

Age haþ in-sighte how vnsure & vnstable
Þis worldes cours is, by lengthe of his yeeres,
And can deffende hym from his scharpe breres.

(579–81)

He warns against the follies to which young men are disposed, and offers his own career as an example of the way in which a riotous and immoral youth may lead to an impoverished old age:

> where be my gounes of scarlet,
> Sanguyn, murreye, & blewes sadde & lighte,
> Grenes also, and þe fayre violet,
> Hors and harnys, fresche and lusty in syghte?
> My wykked lyf haþ put al þis to flighte.
>
> (694–8)

Hoccleve himself is also preoccupied with growing old. He alludes to his own misspent youth (1219–25) and in one place offers a warning to the young and rich that their prosperity may be temporary:

> Þou þat yclomben art in hy honoures,
> And hast þis worldes welth at thy deuys,
> And bathist now in youthes lusty floures
> Be war, rede I! þou standist on þe ys.
>
> (904–7)

When this was written Prince Henry was about twenty-three years old, and the emphasis on avoiding the follies of youth, which is implicit in the warnings that both the Beggar and Hoccleve give, can scarcely have been accidental.

The main body of advice in the poem is based on three sources— the *Secreta Secretorum*, Egidio Colonna's *De Regimine Principum* and Jacobus de Cessolis' *Liber de Ludo Scacchorum*. Hoccleve claims only that he has made a compilation of these so that Prince Henry will be able to read them more conveniently:

> In short ye may behold and rede
> That in hem thre is skatered ferre in brede.
>
> (2134–5)

But the conventional modesty formula used here obscures his real achievement. For the compilation is not mechanical, but selective, and the moral advice is enlivened and supported by narrative *exempla* and personal reminiscence. Frequently an attempt is made to relate the advice to contemporary social problems. Hoccleve begins his account by considering the duties of kingship 'Consideryng how chargeable a thyng/That ofice is' and urging Prince Henry to behave responsibly:

> Vnto good reule ye yow knytte and bynde;
> Of goddes wreche haue ay drede and awe;
> Do right to grete and smale, and keepe lawe.
> (2168–70)

He continues by warning the Prince that he should weigh his words carefully, and honour his promises, particularly in the matter of repaying merchants:

> Now if it happe, as it haþ happed ofte,
> A kyng in nede borwe of his merchantis,
> Greet wisdom were it trete faire and softe
> (2374–6)

for unless they were treated fairly merchants would not lend money again. The following sections deal with a king's obligation to be just to his people and to keep good laws, and here Hoccleve inserts a long passage on the lawlessness of England (2780–835), five stanzas recommending that the Church be allowed to elect its own bishops (2899–933) and two stanzas against those who seek to gain influential positions through flattery (2934–47). He digresses at length on the prevalence of flattery in England in the course of the next section (3039–101), which is on the need for kings to have pity on those over whom they rule, and to be prepared to forgive transgressions, except murder. The following sections stress the need for mercy, patience and chastity, but though Hoccleve illustrates these virtues by means of exemplary stories no particular parallels with the contemporary situation are drawn. In the next section, however, which is on 'magnanimite' or great-heartedness, he addresses himself directly to Henry and expresses confidence that he will be able with courageous leadership to humble the enemies of England, always provided that he is prudent as well:

> O worthi Prince! I truste in ȝour manhode,
> Medlid wiþ prudence and discrecioun,

That ȝe schulle make many a knyȝtly rode
And the pride of oure foos thristen adoun.
(3963–6)

The following three sections deal with a king's need to be liberal
with his wealth without deviating on the one hand into prodigality
or on the other into covetousness and avarice:

Be infecte wiþ no wrecched chyncherie.
Largesce mesurable vnto yow tye,
And fool largesse voydeth fro yow clene
ffor free largesse is a vertuous mene.
(4743–6)

Hoccleve's personal involvement with the matter of these sections
is considerable. Among the examples of those guilty of prodigality
he instances his own case, much as in the Prologue, as a warning to
Prince Henry:

þogh I neuer were of hy degree,
Ne hadde mochil gode ne gret richesse,
Ȝit hath þe vice of prodigalite
Smerted me sore, & done me hevynesse.
(4362–5)

His poverty, he continues, has been exacerbated by the fact that the
payment of his annuity from the Crown is in arrears, and he asks
Prince Henry to prove himself a liberal ruler by getting it paid:

O liberal prince! ensample of honour!
Vnto your grace lyke it to promoote
Mi poore estat, and to my woo beth boote.
(4387–9)

The following sections advise the Prince to be prudent and to take
the best advice he can from experienced advisers before setting out
his policies, and to put no trust in flatterers (4915–21). The last
section, on peace, begins with moral generalities and arguments in
favour of peace from biblical authorities. But the realities of the
political situation also receive attention. Hoccleve recalls the

trouble caused by the civil wars of the earlier part of Henry IV's reign:

> The ryot þat haþ ben with-in þis lande
> Among our self, many a wyntres space,
> Haþ to þe swerd put many a thousand.
>
> (5216–8)

He reminds the Prince that this sort of war is the 'most harmful/ And perillous' (5230–1), likely to ruin the country's economy and even jeopardise its whole security by making it vulnerable to foreign enemies. For this reason, he continues, he ought to be glad at the civil discord in France, since England is at war with that country; but he feels that any war between Christian countries is bad and urges peace to be made through a marriage between Henry and Katherine:

> Purchaseth pees by wey of mariage,
> And ye þerinne schul fynden auauntage.
>
> (5403–4)

The only just war Hoccleve is prepared to admit is one against the infidel.

The personal involvement and concern for contemporary problems which marked Hoccleve's poem are not present to the same degree in *The Secrees of Old Philisoffres* which Lydgate was engaged on writing for Henry VI when he died in 1449 or 1450. This is a translation of the *Secreta Secretorum*, supposedly written by Aristotle in reply to questions put to him by Alexander. Some fragments of Lydgate's version remain, and he would presumably have given them a coherent order had he lived. More than seven hundred lines are devoted to various prologues before the advice proper begins to be given. The treatment of the topic of the ruler's liberality is long and discursive. It contains what was certainly good advice to Henry VI about his finances, though Lydgate does not make its relevance to the contemporary situation explicit. Lydgate follows the conventional wisdom of his source in recommending the King to be liberal without being prodigal:

> Breffly the vertu of Royal hih largesse,
> Set in A meene of prudent governaunce,
> That ther be nouthir skarsete nor excesse,
> But a ryght Rewle of Attemperaunce.
>
> (*Secrees*, 869–72)

He adds that a King must beware of flatterers and reward only those who are deserving (876–945). In other sections, with unaccustomed brevity, he stresses the need for a king to 'Be voyde of vices' (1053); to keep his people from civil war 'ffor wheer pees Regnyth is al perfeccioun' (1062); to crush heretics 'That been enmyes vnto hooly Cherche' (1074); to conduct himself with the dignity due to his office and insist on his rights (1093–120); and to be merciful and keep his promises. One may detect more personal involvement on Lydgate's part in the stanzas on the value of a university:

> An vniuersite shewith Out his lyght
> In a kyngdom As it shulde be of ryght,
> And by the prynce have dewly favour,
> So clerge beryth a-wey the fflour.
>
> (1173–6)

After this the treatise deals at considerable length with the way in which a king ought to attend to his health (1184–295), and there follows an extended comparison between the four seasons and the stages of a man's life, which is by far the best thing in the poem, but which has no political relevance (1296–491). At this point, according to the rubricator of BM MS Sloane 2464, 'here deyed this translator and nobil poete: and the yonge folowere gan his prologe on this wyse'.

The 'yonge folowere' is Benedict Burgh, at one time rector of Sandon and vicar of Maldon, rector of Sible Hedingham in 1450, archdeacon of Colchester in 1465, prebendary of St Pauls in 1472, and canon of St Stephen's, Westminster, from 1476 until he died in 1483. Many of these positions he must have held through the influence of Henry Bourchier, Earl of Essex, whose children he had tutored, and Bourchier may have been the 'lord' who commissioned him to finish Lydgate's translation. Burgh was the obvious man for the task. He had written in praise of Lydgate as

> the flowre and tresure of poise,
> the garland of Ive, and the laure of victorye,

and had asked to be his 'prentice'.[14] His continuation of *The Secrees of Old Philisoffres* does, in fact, conform to Lydgate's fragments in that it imitates the stanza form, the style, and also the rather impersonal, didactic approach. After a conventionally modest Prologue in which he asks to be excused for his 'Tendirnesse of age and lak of Elloquence' (1492) he continues the translation with a long section on the necessity for a king to enjoy good health and offers much dietary advice (1590–2023). After this the advice is of a more political sort. Burgh stresses the ruler's responsibility to his subjects and the necessity for him to be endowed with 'Rightwysnesse' which is

> Maad to conserve the blood and Richesse
> of his sogettys possessyouns and werkys
> In which his Regalye stant, as sey clerkys.
> (2028–30)

He urges the need for thorough deliberation in the Council:

> Conceyve the Counseyl peyse it in ballaunce
> off eche persone hih or lowe degre,
> (2066–7)

and, once the policy is settled, swift action, because 'to a Reem delayes Cause destruccyoun' (2072). There is much advice on the choosing of councillors:

> He owyth to be lovyd that vices wille eschewe,
> Which lovith trowthe and counseyllith trewly,
> To the thy sogettys stedfast, Iust, and trewe . . .
> (2150–2)

Furthermore, a king should choose only officers who are 'of hool herte and entieer' (2241) and well liked by the king's subjects, a secretary who can

Conceyve in ech thyng
Thyn entent and it redily
To execucioun Can put wittily,
(2329–31)

and messengers who 'Can bere a lettre and repoorte trewly' (2352).
The next section makes the point that bad officers cause rebellion
('Ageyn the thy sogettys shul rebelle' 2394), and stresses the need
for the law to be administered impartially:

have Iuges trewe good and wyse,
not parcial but indifferent men,
Which for lukyr trewthe will not despyse.
(2396–8)

There follows a section on the conduct of war, and the treatise
concludes with a long passage on physiognomy, which, it is stated,
is a relevant subject for a ruler to know about since it enables him
to judge the character of men he has to deal with. No precise date
may be ascribed to Burgh's part of this treatise, nor does he make
any explicit attempt to give it a contemporary relevance. But his
treatment of his source is selective, and it may be that he thought
that much of the advice he had to give—on health, on choosing
councillors, and on the need for justice—was particularly relevant
to Henry VI in the early 1450s.

A precise date may not be assigned to George Ashby's *Active
Policy of a Prince*, but other facts about its composition are conveniently set out in the Latin prefacing the unique version preserved
in Cambridge University Library MS Mm iv 42: it was written for
Prince Edward, son and heir of Henry VI and Margaret, in order
to advise him in policy and wisdom. Ashby begins by compli-
menting Gower, Chaucer and Lydgate for their establishment of
the literary language and ballade forms 'By whome we all may haue
lernyng and lore' (*Poems*, II, 7), and confesses his own inadequacy
for the task he is undertaking by saying that he has 'of makynge
none assurance/Nor of balades haue experience' (40–1), that he is
'fallen/in decrepit age' (64), and most of all that he has not

> seien scripture
> Of many bookes right sentenciall
> In especial of the gloses sure.
>
> (50–2)

He therefore determines to be brief:

> I woll therfor kepe true menyng formal,
> Nor right meche delatyng the rehersall.
>
> (53–4)

It is difficult to know how to take these protestations. Ashby makes
no extensive and direct use of known texts for his treatise, and,
indeed, it is unexpanded by narrative *exempla*. It is, on the other
hand, precisely geared to the contemporary situation: an anxiety
about the civil wars and about the position of the Lancastrian
monarchy is frequently in Ashby's mind. In his dedication, for
for example, when Ashby refers to the Prince as

> youre highnesse Edwarde by name,
> Trewe sone & heire of the high maiestie
> Of oure liege lorde/Kynge Henry & dame
> Margarete, the Quene . . .
>
> (92–5)

it is likely that he intends more than a highly eulogistic compliment.
The heavy emphasis on Edward's lineage was perhaps intended to
scotch the stories of his bastardy circulated at times by the Yorkists.

The treatise is divided into three parts: one dealing with the
lessons to be drawn from past history, one dealing with the contemporary situation, and one with the future. In the first part
Ashby urges Edward to study the past so that he should be 'ful
sure,/Circumspect in his actes, wytt pure' (207–8) through the
example of 'other men. . . . that were polletike' (210). As an
example he refers to the recent civil wars in England, which he sees
as having been caused by the greed of those around Henry VI:

> The high estate of oure king god preserue
> And if deuoided had folke couetous
> From his persoune, his people had not sterue

> With suche grete batellis dispiteous,
> Whiche to here & telle is ful piteous.
>
> (190–4)

But despite the troubled political situation in which he was writing Ashby is confident that Edward will be England's 'grete comfort' (219) and will redress all wrongs and suppress all rebellions. He offers the usual advice for moderation in all things:

> Not to be to hasty in youre wyrkyng,
> Ne to slowe, ne to fcint, for no temptyng,
> Ne to riall, ne in to grete simplesse,
> Ne to liberal for no frendlynesse . . .
>
> (249–52)

and also other recommendations, some of which seem designed to ensure that Edward should not fall into the same errors as his father Henry VI. He is advised, for example, to choose as his servants 'The mooste vertuos folkes and cunnyng' (261) and to 'beware of the couetous' (267). He is urged to live within the income 'of youre Revenues, lyuelode & Rent' (275), to pay 'all that is to youre estate lent' (278), and to act wisely rather than speak wisely (303–5). In the section on the future appears a similar combination of general and particular advice. Of the latter sort Ashby warns the Prince 'to suppresse youre false conspiratours' (381), to 'subdewe al maner rebellyon' (388), and to 'be ye ware of the Reconsiled' (427). He urges Edward to see that the commons 'be welthy/In richesse, goodes and prosperite' (499–500) because then they will be law-abiding:

> And he be of goodes right plentuous,
> He dar not be to lawe contrarious,
>
> (504–5)

and not 'euer wauering in variance' (871) as they were always likely to be. In order that the commons be kept 'in subieccion' Ashby advises Edward to

> Prouide that lawe may be excercised,
> And executed in his formal cours,

Aftur the statutes autorised
By noble Kynges youre progenitours.
(520–3)

More specifically he urges that sumptuary laws be passed so that
the common people should not 'haue precious clothe in theire
Vesture' (535), that the commons 'shude nat bere dagger, ne
Lance' (541), that 'gentilmen' should not give liveries 'But to their
howshold meyne' (549), and that they should 'maynteine no
people' nor 'false quarels take thorugh maintenance' (551–2).
That Ashby had heeded the military lessons of the French wars is
clear from his next piece of advice which is that for the defence of
the realm

By lawe euery man shuld be compellede
To vse the bowe and shetyng for disport.
(569–70)

Furthermore, and doubtless with reference to the mistakes of
Henry VI's reign, he warns Edward against allowing any of his
subjects to be as rich as a king 'If ye wol stande in peas and be set
by' (642), against the resumption of grants because 'Suche variance
hathe be grete rebukyng/To many folk' (727–8), and once more
against being merciful to traitors 'if thoffence touche the sub-
uercion/Of the Realme' (793–4). There is also a great deal of advice,
most of it conventional, on how a king should conduct himself
personally.

The Active Policy of A Prince has no formal envoy and no
explicit. It is followed in the Cambridge University Library MS
Mm iv 42 by the series of translations of Latin maxims which is
usually entitled *Dicta et opiniones diversorum philosophorum*. The
'dicta' are usually treated as a separate item, but they seem to the
present writer to have been conceived as part of the advice Ashby
intended to give. They are written in the same seven-line stanza as
The Active Policy of A Prince and are mentioned in the much-
defaced Latin heading to that poem as if they were part of it:

subditorum securitate & bona custodia sub debita et fidei
obediencia per aduisamenta edicta & opiniones diuersorum

Philosophorum, quorum nomina ... in tractatu breuiter subscribantur.

Furthermore, the method of quoting Latin maxims and then following them by loose translations in English verse, which Ashby follows all through the 'dicta', is frequently in evidence in *The Active Policy of A Prince*: before line 296, for example, appears

Docet Regem satisfacere/de stipendiis stipendiariis suis
Alioquin societas despiciet eum et dominium suum; hec Plato,

and similar maxims appear before lines 331, 352, 653, 695, 793, 821, 828 and 842. Moreover, the nature of the advice appearing in the 'dicta'—sententious moral and political platitudes—is the same as that of the previous poem, and similarly addressed to a king. The second stanza of the 'dicta' is typical:

> Truste nat oonly in menis multitude,
> Ne in thair myght, ne in Comon clamour,
> But in god & in goode consuetude
> Of trewe iustice, without any rigour,
> Otherwise than god wolde, owre Saueour:
> A Kynge, Reulyng al thynges rightfully
> With lawe reigneth with al folk plesantly.
> *(Poems, III, 8–14)*

The advice here, however, is conventional and generalized, with no specific relevance to Prince Edward. More than twelve hundred and sixty lines of the 'dicta' survive, and Ashby's capacity for producing more seems infinite, but the manuscript breaks off at this point in the middle of a stanza and the end is lost.

In one stanza of the 'dicta' Ashby speaks of the way in which a king may be persuaded from his faults if 'a wise man'

> showe to hym demonstracion
> Of stories exemplificacion
> Playnly, that he may vnderstand the blame,
> To eschewe of mysgouernance the name.
> (1075–8)

Lydgate frequently uses this method. *The Troy Book* (1412–20), for example, appears to have been intended to function as, amongst other things, a 'mirror for princes'. In his Prologue Lydgate says that Prince Henry, who commissioned the work

> hath desire, sothly for to seyn,
> Of verray kny3thod to remembre ageyn
> The worthynes, 3if I schal nat lye,
> And the prowesse of olde chiualrie,
> By-cause he hath Ioye and gret deynte
> To rede in bokys of antiquite,
> To fyn only, vertu for to swe
> Be example of hem. . . .
>
> (75–82)

Lydgate uses some of the events of the story to provide advice on the right behaviour of a prince. Telemon's unknightly treatment of Hesione, daughter of King Lamedon, provoked 'ful hy3e vengeaunce' (I, 4374), all of which goes to show, Lydgate recalls later, that terrible wars may often spring from trifling causes:

> Strife and debate, here vnder þe sonne
> Wer meved first of smal occasioun,
> That caused after gret confusioun.
>
> (II, 126–8)

Princes are further advised to take heed of King Lamedon ('Make 3ow a merour of þis Lamedon') who died because he showed 'violence/vnto straungers' (II, 85–6). Lydgate cites Priam as an example of an overhasty king:

> late Priam alwey 3our merour ben
> Hasty errour be tymes to correcte.
>
> (II, 1898–9)

Above all he warns against discord within a country, particularly among its leaders:

> For whan hertis in loue ben nat oon,
> Farewel Fortune, her grace is clene a-goon:

> For where Discord holdeth residence
> It is wel wers þan swerd or pestilence.
>
> (IV, 4513–16)

Advice such as this—decent, sensible and commonplace—can have had little topical relevance. D. A. Pearsall has pointed out that some of it is, in fact, inappropriate. He refers, for example, to Lydgate's lines on the murder of Agamemnon:

> O myȝti God, þat in þin inward loke
> Sest euery þing þoruȝ þin eternal myȝt,
> Whi wiltow nat of equite and riȝt
> Punishe and chastise so horrible a þing,
> And specialy þe mordre of a kyng?
>
> (V, 1046–50)

and concludes rightly that a poem written so shortly after the usurpation and murder of Richard II would have to be 'innocent of contemporary reference' to allow its inclusion.[15]

In the medieval mind the story of Troy was associated with that of Thebes, and versions of the two are sometimes found together in French and in English translations. So it was natural that Lydgate's attention should switch easily from the one to the other, and immediately he finished the *Troy Book* he seems to have set to work on *The Siege of Thebes* which he completed in 1422. His source was some French version of the Thebes story similar to the *Roman de Edipus*, and some of Lydgate's characteristic expansions and additions show the kinds of concern with advising rulers which appeared in his earlier poem on Troy.[16] Early in the first part of the poem, for example, the traditional story of the way in which the walls of Thebes were raised by King Amphion's music provides the opportunity for an excursus on kingship. Lydgate, following Boccaccio, interprets the story as being about the power of eloquence, for the music

> was no thyng but the crafty speche
> Of this kyng ycalled Amphioun
>
> (226–7)

through which he persuaded the neighbouring peoples to build Thebes for him. This prompts reflections on the advantages of a pleasant demeanour in a king:

> Her may ȝe see how myche may avaylle
> The goodlihed and lownesse of a kyng,
> And specealy in cher and in spekyng,
> To his lyeges and to bern hym fayre
> In his apport and shewe hym debonayre . . .
> (244–8)

and there follow warnings against being 'to straunge ne soleyn/In contenaunce' (249–50) to the common people who 'bereþ hym vp' and are his 'Pyler' in his 'moste nede' (265–7). Elsewhere he warns rulers that they should be truthful:

> ȝe kyngges and lordes beth wel war
> ȝour bihestes Iustly forto holde.
> (1774–5)

They should not squander the nation's wealth for their own pleasures while their people suffer:

> And in a prince it is ful gret offence
> As clerkes seyn, and a gret repreef,
> Suffre his puple lyven at myscheef.
> It is ful hevy and greuous in her thoght
> ȝif he habound and they han right noght.
> (2688–92)

Liberality is what wins the hearts of a king's subjects:

> in his courte lat hym first devise
> To exile scarshed and couetise;
> Than is he likly with fredam ȝif he gynne,
> loue of his puple euermore to wynne.
> (2709–12)

Most of all, however, the poem explores the problems of peace and war. Lydgate is capable of seeing the justness of Polynices' cause for going to war—that he was the 'Rightful kyng' of Thebes (3773).

K

He also sets out the brave resolve of the Greek soldiery that it is better

> Manly to deye with worship and honour,
> Than lik a coward with the lyf endure.
> (4124–5)

But he concludes the poem with a long passage on the disadvantages of war which spares 'hegh estat nor lowh condicioun' (4646) and in which both sides are bound to 'felyn gret damage' (4656). To enjoin a ruler to strive for peace was usual, but here Lydgate's words coincide opportunely with the signing of the Treaty of Troyes, some phrases of which he seems to echo in the conclusion to his poem.

The habit of offering advice to princes was obviously well established in Lydgate before he came to write his greatest work *The Fall of Princes* (1431–8). This is a translation of Laurent de Premierfait's French version of Boccaccio's *De Casibus illustrium Virorum,* much expanded. It demonstrates, by a succession of exemplary stories from Adam and Eve to King John of France who was captured at Poitiers in 1356, 'the chaung off worldi variaunce' (I, 434) wrought by Fortune on even the most powerful among princes. In a lengthy Prologue Lydgate reveals how he was commissioned to undertake the work by Humphrey, Duke of Gloucester, to whom it appealed as a 'mirror for princes':

> Off gret noblesse and reputacioun,
> And onto pryncis gretli necessarie
> To yive exaumple how this world doth varie.
> (I, 425–7)

Thus, in accordance with his patron's wishes (and no doubt his own too) Lydgate intersperses moral advice to princes throughout the nine books of his work, particularly in the Envoy to each tragedy. The story of the fall of Adam and Eve prompts reflections on pride and disobedience:

> Wherfore, ye Pryncis, auisili doth see,
> As this tragedie in maner berth witnesse,
> Whereas wantith in any comounte

Subieccioun, for lakkyng off meeknesse
And with pouert pride hath an interesse,
Ther folwith afftir thoruh froward insolence
Among the peeple fals inobedience.

(I, 988–94)

The quarrel of Polynices and Eteocles and the fall of Thebes pro-
vokes the reflection that 'Kyngdamys deuyded mey no while
endure' (I, 3822). The story of Theseus, which concentrates on his
desertion of Ariadne and also alludes to his expulsion from Athens
by rebellious subjects, is made to enforce a moral against inconstancy, the inconstancy of a prince being the worst of all:

off alle chaungis, that chaung is most to dreede,
And most feerful is that variaunce
Whan that pryncis, which may the peeple leede,
Be founde vnstable in ther gouernaunce,

(I, 4565–8)

because it sets a bad example to his people. A little further on he
warns against 'hasti credence, withoute auisement' (I, 4823)
especially of the counsel of flatterers. The Envoy to the story of
Samson urges that princes should 'Keep your conceitis vnder
couerture' (I, 6508) especially from women, and the story of
Canace's death on the instigation of her father Eolus is made to
convince princes to be

prudent and attempre,
Differrith vengaunce, of hih discrecioun;
Til your ire sumwhat asuagid be,
Doth neuer off doom non execucioun.

(I, 7064–7)

Book I is characteristic of Lydgate's procedure and concerns.
Essentially he responds to each story or sequence of stories with
the appropriate moral. There is little evidence of a coherent
attempt at 'the beginnings of a formal theory of politics' which
W. F. Schirmer finds especially in Book II, or at least, if Lydgate
did have a consciously worked out theory, it seems to have been
extremely conventional.[17] His lengthiest description of society uses

the commonplace image of the 'body politic' and concludes in the normal way by stressing that a country which is rich and well governed is like a healthy body:

> And as a bodi which that stant in helthe
> Feelith no greef off no froward humours,
> So eueri comoun contynueth in gret welthe,
> Which is demened with prudent gouernours. . . .
> (II, 869–72)

Similarly, the most comprehensive passage of advice to princes amounts only to a series of platitudes. Kings should avoid 'tirannye', 'Fals extorsion', and 'sensualite'. The king's throne should be 'supportid with iustise and clemence' and the king should 'egal iuge stonde/Tween riche & poore'. Just as a parent looks after his children

> Riht so a kyng in his estat roiall
> Sholde of his offis dilligentli entende
> His trewe leeges to cherisshe hem & diffende.
> (VIII, 2364–6)

His kingdom should 'Resemble the kyngdam which that is dyuyne', and the king himself 'sholde be the merour and the liht' of his subjects and surpass them 'be vertuous excellence'. The king should be 'stable as eny ston' in joy or in adversity, and have as his councillors those who 'Tueen good and euel . . . knowe the difference'. He should exclude from his court 'Rowners, flaterers and such folk as kan lie', those 'Coueitous peeple that poore folk oppresse', those 'that doon a thyng for meede' and those' Riotous peeple that loue to wachche al niht'. If this is the sort of advice Humphrey of Gloucester wished to hear he could have obtained it elsewhere. None of Lydgate's ideas on society and kingship are original.

The authors of the poems so far discussed all wrote under the patronage of the establishment. But before this chapter ends something should be said about two writers who—from outside the patronage system and in the non-Chaucerian tradition of alliterative verse—sought to give advice to kings. It is clear from his Prologue that the author of *Mum and the Sothsegger* sees himself as a 'truthteller' fitted to advise, and that he considered his poem as one of advice to a king:

> euery Cristen kyng/þat ony croune bereth,
> So he were lerned on þe langage/my lyff durst I wedde,
> ʒif he waite well þe wordis/ and so werche þer-after,
> Ther nys no gouernour on þe grounde/ne sholde gye him þe better,
> For all is tresour of þe trinite/þat turneth men to gode.
>
> (42–6)

But it is equally clear that the first fragment of the poem offers a discursive but fairly specific critique of Richard II's rule, and that the second is a similar critique of English politics and society in the early years of Henry IV's reign. On occasions, however, general principles are elicited. Once the three estates theory is expounded briefly (III, 248–53), but the most notable passage on the relation of a king to society is that part of the author's dream in which the old man he meets explains to him (probably following Bartholomaeus Anglicus' *De Proprietatibus Rerum*) the social organization of bees, which 'of alle best/beste is y-gouuerned'.

> Thay haue a king by kinde þat þe coroune bereth,
> Whom þay doo sue and serue as souurayne to þaym alle,
> And obeyen to his biddyng,
>
> (999–1001)

he says, and next in authority under the king are princes, who owe allegiance to him:

> alle þe principallz to þe prince fal prest þay been at nede,
> To rere þaire retenue to righte alle þe fautes.
>
> (1014–15)

The different bees have different duties: some go to the fields to 'sovke oute þe swettenes of þe somer floures' (1020); some 'abiden at home to bigge vp þe loigges' (1021); and others 'waiten þe wedre, þe wynde and þe skyes' (1024). The king rules through the consent of the others:

> by reason/and by right-ful domes,
> Thorough contente of þe cumpaignie/þat closeth alle in oone
> (1036–7)

and is 'The moste merciful among þaym and meukest of his deedes' (1031). In return for the king's merciful rule the bees support him when necessary:

> yf he fleuble or feynte/or funder dovneward,
> The bees wollen bere hym til he be better amended.
> (1042–3)

At the end of the old man's exposition the poet feels that what has been said 'hath muche menyng' but professes not to understand its significance: 'hit is to mistike for me' (1089). It is, however, obviously a simple description of the ideal society, and in particular of the ideal relationship between the king and his subjects. The only cause of trouble in this society are the 'drones'—the useless, unproductive, parasitical elements of society—who 'trauaillen not no tyme of þe day' but who, nevertheless, 'growen grete and fatte/And fillen þaire bagges brede-ful/of þat þe bees wyrchen' (1046–8). These are tolerated in prosperous times, but are killed off when their uselessness threatens the other bees:

> But as sone as þay see/þaire swynke is y-stole,
> Thenne flocken þay to fighte/þair fautes to amende,
> And quellen þe dranes quicly and quiten alle þaire wrongz.
> (1084–6)

Since the poem is meant to be exemplary, the ideal social situation described in this parable is clearly one to which the author felt rulers should aspire, and the treatment of 'drones' here is similar to what the author advises the king to do about grasping courtiers in an earlier passage:

> 'He shulde haue hadde hongynge/on hie on þe forckis,
> Þouȝ ȝoure brother y-born/had be þe same.
> Than wolde oþer boynardis/haue ben abasshyd
> To haue meved ȝou to ony maters/þat myssheff had ben ynne.'
> (I, 108–11)

In places other pieces of advice for kings appear. A king should not seek to maintain his rule over the people by force 'For legiance without loue/litill þinge availlith' (I, 24). By means of a proverb he warns a king against allowing his servants too much power:

> Þer gromes and þe goodmen/beth all eliche grette,
> Woll wo beth þe wones/and all þat woneth þer-in.
>
> (I, 66–7)

Kings should not allow the young and inexperienced to have high positions in the Council:

> For it fallith as well to fodis/of xxiiij ʒeris,
> Or yonge men of yistirday/to ʒeue good redis,
> As becometh a kow/to hoppe in a cage.
>
> (III, 260–2)

This is followed by some advice about personal behaviour. Kings, says the author, ought not to devote themselves to 'likynge/and lust of þe world' (III, 266) or waste their time and money on pleasures:

> And spende of the spicerie/more þan it nedid,
> Bothe wexe and wyn/in wast all abouʒte,
> With deyntes y-doublid/and daunsinge to pipis,
> In myrthe with moppis/myrrours of synne.
>
> (III, 273–6)

Instead they should devote themselves to government and fulfil their obligations to the people: 'laboure on þe lawe/as lewde men on plowes' (III, 267). But though advice of this sort is frequent in the poem it does not add up to a cogent and articulated theory of kingly behaviour. Each comment appears to be prompted by what the author takes to be contemporary failings.

The final poem to be considered here, *The Crowned King* from Bodleian MS Douce 95, was written just before Henry V's invasion of France in 1415. It relates a dream the author had 'on corpus cristi even/Six other vij myle oute of Suthampton' (*HP*, 95, 19–20) in which a 'clerk' addressed some words of wisdom to the 'crowned kyng' (51). The advice is fairly conventional though the author does not follow any known source and there are references to the specific political situation, for example, to the 'subsidie' (36) which Henry V had asked of the Commons in November 1414. The 'clerk' begins by speaking about the responsibility a king has ('Thi-self hast lyfe, lyme, and lawes for to keep' 52) and enjoins him to be perfect in his own life: 'rule the be reson, and vpright sitte' (54). The king should be strong ('dred for thy domes and dowted for thy myght' 56), but should remember that his prosperity and power are built upon the labours of the people:

> Moche worship they wynne the in this worlde riche,
> Of thy gliteryng gold and of thy gay wedes,
> Thy proude pelure, and palle with preciouse stones,
> Grete castels and stronge, and styff walled townes.
>
> (67–70)

In return for his wealth he should 'gouerne hem euen' (73). He urges that the king should work along with his parliament ('Thi peres in parlement pull hem to-geders' 77), but should be suspicious of flatterers: 'kepe the fro glosyng of gylers mowthes' (86). Those he should favour, says the 'clerk', are 'thi clergi' and

> thy champyons and chief men of armes;
> And suche as presoners mowe pike with poyntes of werre,
> Lete hem wilde that they wynne, & worþyly hem þonke;
> And suche as castels mowe cacche, or eny clos tounes,
> Geve hem as gladly—than shalt þou gete hertes.
>
> (94–8)

(The question about prisoners belonging to their captors was one discussed in 1414 when the subsidy was settled.) He further advises the king as to the benefits which learning gives ('lere lettrewre in þy youthe, as a lord befalleth' 113) and finally urges him to be generous: 'be not gredy gyftes to grype' (125). After this advice the poet draws his poem to an end: 'of this mater y meve you no more' (135). He also shifts the focus of the poem by drawing the attention of the worldly 'crowned kyng' to the example of 'that crowned kyng that on cros dyed' (141) implying, what is usually in these 'mirrors for princes' explicitly stated, that is that the ruler was expected to conform morally and spiritually to Christian doctrine, and that his behaviour on earth would be judged, by the same standards as anyone else's behaviour, by God in Heaven.

It should be clear from what has been said above that fifteenth-century ideas on society and kingship, as they are expressed in verse, are hardly ever original, often not very cogently worked out, and only infrequently related specifically to the contemporary situation. But though the ideas current were conventional and generalized the relevance they were thought to have is indicated by the fact that they appear in this century for the first time in English, and by the fact that they were frequently re-used. When intelligent fifteenth-century Englishmen thought about the structure of society it was usually in terms of a hierarchy of classes, and when the performance of their rulers was measured it was against the standards laid down in such 'mirrors for princes' as have been described.

NOTES

[1] *The Governance of England* ed. C. Plummer, Oxford 1885, p. 109.

[2] *Ibid.*, p. 115.

[3] *The Fifteenth Century*, Oxford 1961, p. 305.

[4] *The Three Estates in Medieval and Renaissance Literature*, Columbia 1933. My whole account of ideas about society is much indebted to this work.

[5] *Middle English Sermons*, ed. W. O. Ross, EETS OS 209, 1938, p. 237.

[6] Ed. O. H. Prior, EETS ES 110, 1913, p. 29.

[7] *Rotuli Parliamentorum* V, 35.

[8] Ed. W. E. A. Axon, 1883.

[9] Ed. F. Warren and B. White, EETS OS 181, 1931.

[10] This text, and the two others mentioned in this paragraph are edited by F. J. Furnivall, EETS OS 32, 1868.

[11] See the edition of W. Blades, 1881; and for further comments on the social ideas it expresses Sylvia Thrupp, *The Merchant Class of Medieval London*, Michigan 1962, pp. 295-7.

[12] Ed. H. Person, *Cambridge Middle English Lyrics*, Seattle 1962, No. 60 lines 1–4.

[13] *Middle English Sermons*, op. cit. p. 224.

[14] Ed. R. Steele, *Secrees of Old Philisoffres*, EETS ES 66, 1894, pp. xxxi–xxxii.

[15] *John Lydgate*, 1970, p. 139.

[16] See particularly R. W. Ayers, 'History, Moral Purpose and the Structure of Lydgate's *Siege of Thebes*', *PMLA* 72, 1958, 463–74; and A. Renoir, *The Poetry of John Lydgate*, 1967, pp. 110–135.

[17] *John Lydgate*, translated by Ann E. Keep 1961, p. 213.

9 : English Society II : Some Aspects of Social Change

As the previous chapter indicated, the theoretical basis of medieval society was frequently expounded by fifteenth-century authors. Within its own terms the system appeared to be perfect, provided that kings ruled in accordance with all the advice given to them, that the various ranks of society behaved in an appropriate fashion, that there was no gross exploitation of one rank by another, and that there was no undue aspiration on the part of a person of one rank to the condition of another. Predictably, this was not the case. The author of a fifteenth-century sermon from BM MS Royal 18 B xxiii describes the contemporary situation in terms which show a reversal of the usual social ideal:

> Loke qwethir þe comon peple sey not oponly þat þe extorcion and þe misgouernaunce of þe lordes is cause of all þis werre and þis myschef þat is fallen in þis reme. On þe oþur side þe lordes and þe grette men seyn þat þe pride and þe nyse aray þat reyneþ among commeners is cause of þis myschef. Also þe lay men seþ þat þe couetise of men of holychurche is cause of þis. And þei sey þat þe wrathe and enuy þat reyneþ a-monge þe comon pepull vil be cause of þe confucion and destruccion of þe world. So þat lordes accuseþ þe commeners, and þei accusen holy churche, and þus ichon accuseþ oþur.[1]

For this writer England was a confused country, demoralized and seriously divided against itself. The various ranks of society— lords, clergy and commons—did not sustain each other as the theory said they should, but were naturally suspicious and blamed each other for the 'myschef' that troubled them. It goes without saying that this is a partial view and that denunciation seemed always to come more readily from the pulpit than praise. But, even so, the sheer bulk of complaint of this sort compels attention. Many another disillusioned sermon writer voices the same or similar complaints. Nor are these sentiments only to be found in sermons. A considerable amount of verse, dealing with a variety of social grievances is extant from the fifteenth century. Some of these poems are generalized indictments of the whole of society, and others deal with more precise contemporary problems.

The generalized complaints dealing with society as a whole may be treated as a body in that they have a great deal in common. They concentrate usually on large abstract issues rather than particular events. The sentiments these poems reveal are also surprisingly repetitive. This is partly due to the fact that the abuses they speak of were common, and general enough to apply to almost any time or place. But this is not the only reason. In political verse, as in other types, medieval writers did not invent where they could copy and reapply. Like prophecies, verse complaints were often re-used slightly altered in different political contexts. The generality of the sentiments in most of these verses makes them especially amenable to this treatment, but they share also a way of looking at political and social problems in moral and religious terms. R. H. Robbins has made the very necessary observation that 'many of the Middle English religious poems lamenting the sins of the age, although they use the terminology of doctrine, are really political.'[2] In fact, it is often impossible to separate moral and religious complaints from political ones, principally because their authors did not distinguish them. If they complained on one ground they usually complained on all.

This treatment of the political in religious and moral terms also derives in part from the nature of the material on which many of these complaints were based. The ultimate origin of some is to be found in the widely known tract of the 'twelve abuses' variously ascribed in manuscripts of the ninth, tenth and eleventh centuries to Cyprian, Augustine and Origen. The Preface conveniently summarizes its contents:

Duodecim abusiva sunt sæculi, hoc est: sapiens sine operibus, senex sine religione, adulescens sine obedientia, dives sine eleemosyna, femina sine pudicitia, dominus sine virtute, christianus contentiosus, pauper superbus, rex iniquus, episcopus neglegens, plebs sine disciplina, populus sine lege, sic soffocatur iustitia. . . .[3]

In this form the 'abuses' had a wide popularity in England and after the tenth century vernacular versions appear frequently. But some of the popularity of these complaints is to be attributed to their use in the 'sexta tabula' of the well-known *Speculum Christiani* or in the *Gesta Romanorum* in the form of the 'sayings of the four philosophers'. Here the story tells how a king, whose land had been beset by various misfortunes, called together the four wisest men in the kingdom for an explanation. In enigmatic speeches each gives three reasons, which differ somewhat in the various versions of the story, but which have in common the fact that they attribute the country's misfortunes to moral degeneracy and sin. Most of the many English complaints which draw on this version of the 'abuses' usually omit the story framework and often quote a selection of the original twelve. At first the 'abuses' had no explicit political dimension, but it is not difficult to see how this was acquired. Late medieval writers readily saw an analogy between the unsatisfactory state of England and the country alluded to in the 'sayings of the four philosophers' story. And they were just as ready to cast themselves in the role of wise men and attribute English national disasters to moral degeneracy and sin. Here, in a ready-made and authoritative form, was a brief but pointed expression of the generalized discontent which many evidently felt.

Poems based on this material are early found in Middle English. Like the original 'abuses' many are overtly moral and religious rather than political. 'Abuse' poems appear as early as the thirteenth century and more frequently in the fourteenth, but their real vogue was in the fifteenth century. Most are short, vigorous pieces. Like their originals the majority rely on a series of parallel statements which describe a situation in which normal moral values, accepted modes of behaviour and usual social roles are reversed. Perhaps

the poem which most closely preserves the original 'abuses' is
that from St John's College Cambridge MS 37 which translates
into short couplets the Latin prefixed to it:

> ʒeft is domesman,
> & gyle is chapman;
> Lords ben owtyn lawe,
> & chylderen ben withowtyn awe;
> Wyth is trechery
> & loue is lechery. . . .
>
> (*HP*, 55, 9–11)

Another ten lines of English verse follow, then more Latin with its
English translation, all equally generalized and offering no clue as
to a specific political context.

In this body of verse the complaints are usually predictable and
there is little variation of mood and tone. More ingenuity was,
however, devoted to the form of the complaints. The traditional
material sometimes appears in the guise of a prophecy, such as the
verses from MS Trinity College Dublin 516:

> When lordes wille is londes law,
> Prestes wylle trechery, and gyle hold soth saw,
> lechery callyd pryve solas,
> And robbery is hold no trespace—
> Then schal the lond of Albyon
> torne in-to confusioun.
>
> (*HP*, 47, 1–6)

Almost certainly this is not meant to refer to future events, and the
manuscript attribution to Merlin and the prophecy form are used
only to give its rather trite observations some sort of authority and
interest. Most likely it was meant to indicate that the first four lines
were currently true, and that the prospect hinted at in the last line
would become a reality unless things improved. It is simply an
expression of discontent. The date 1461 appears in an odd couplet
following this poem in the manuscript, but whether it is significant
is doubtful. The confused conditions at around the time of the
Battle of Towton (1461) could have given rise to these verses, but

they could equally well refer to any situation or date. So too could the following lines:

> Nowe the lawe is led by clere conciens;
> full sylde/couetise hath damnacion;
> In euery place/ryȝt hath residencs;
> nethir in towne ne fylde/simulacion;
> ther is trewly in euery case/consolacion;
> the pore pepull no tyme hath/but ryȝt;
> men may fynd day ne nyȝt/adulacion;
> now rayneth trewly In euery mannys syȝt. . . .[4]

This is the opening of one of the several 'punctuation' poems which deal with political topics, and it exploits the possibilities of ambiguity inherent in the form. If the verse is set out as here and also end stopped, it proclaims a perfect state of things. Punctuated another way (shown here by means of the / sign) its meaning is reversed. It becomes a complaint of the familiar kind, here, incidentally, with its own rhyme scheme. Something of the same ironic reversal in what at first sight appears to be glowing praise of contemporary society is involved in *The World Upside Down* of which a typical stanza is as follows:

> Amongge the comyns pride is now exilid;
> Louers vsyn no fayned countenaunce;
> In knyghthod largesse nwli ys reuyued.
> Ho can in court fynd eny variaunce?
> Prestus in litille han there suffisaunce;
> Conschiaunce with Marchaundice is cheffe lord & syre;
> And stablenesse founden and spesialli in a-tire.
>
> (*HP*, 63, 8–14)

Because the last line, which is also the refrain, is so clearly improbable within the conventions of medieval literature (fashions were traditionally always changing) and because this patently untrue statement parallels the previous statements, the truth of the previous statements is thereby called in question. This topic of the 'world upside down' would have been familiar enough to a medieval audience. It was frequently used from classical times as the framework for denunciations. But here in the final stanza the ironic intention of the poem is made explicit:

> Aill these lightli shold tornyn up so dovne,
> Ne were of wommen þe perfight stablenesse.
>
> (43–4)

'these' refers to the statements of the preceding stanzas and the invitation to reverse their meanings is plain (since women were traditionally fickle). Read in these terms the poem appears as a conventional complaint against the moral and political decadence of the times.

This type of poem seems to have appealed to Lydgate as a way of varying the conventional 'abuses' material. The poem entitled *So as the Crabbe Goth Forward* is a loose and expanded translation of a French *ballade*, according to Trinity College Cambridge MS R. 3. 20 written by 'le plus grande poetycal Clerk du Parys'. It presents an ideal world in which all the moral virtues prevail:

> Þis worlde is ful of stabulnesse,
> Þer is þer inne no varyaunce;
> But trouthe, feyth, and gentylesse,
> Secrenesse, and assuraunce,
> Plente, ioye, and al playsaunce . . .
>) (*Minor Poems*, II, 19, 1–5)

and in which all classes of society behave as they ought,

> Prynces soustene Rightwysnesse,
> Knyghthood inTrouthe haþe whett his launce,
> Lawe haþe putte Meede in gret distresse
> And avoyded hir acqueyntaunce . . .
>
> (17–20)

but this picture is turned upside down by the refrain: 'so as þe crabbe goþe forward'. Lydgate evidently felt he needed to explain the joke, for he includes some lines (not in the French original) which inform the reader 'þat þe crabbe gooþe bakward', and that 'þe reuers' of the statements in the poem represents the true state of affairs. In *A Resoun of the Rammes Horne* a similar set of statements about the moral nature of contemporary society, such as

> Marchauntes of lucre take noon hede,
> And vsure lith fetred yn distresse;
> And for to speke or write of womanhede,
> Thei banished han from hem Nowfangelnesse;
> And laborers done ay ther besynesse
> That of the daie they wille none owre be lorne . . .
> *(Minor Poems*, II, 18, 17–22)

are reversed by the ironic refrain which compares their truth with the straightness of a ram's horn: 'right as a rammes horne'. In this poem, however, Lydgate does not explain the reversal at greater length.

Other fifteenth-century verses of general complaint depend somewhat less on this traditional material. Consequently, they are often more individual in manner, more selective in their choice of contemporary evils, and occasionally a tentative date can be suggested. A carol from MS Eng. poet e 1 complains that the natural moral order of things is reversed:

> Vycyce be wyld and vertues lame,
> And now be vicyce turned to game,
> Therfore correccion is to blame. . . .
> *(EEC* No. 386, 1–3)

This state of affairs is attributed to social grievances such as the pretensions of the young, the corruption of the court and the lack of political goodwill among nations:

> envy causyth gret distaunce
> Both in Englond and in Fraunce.
> (18–19)

These lines are vague in their reference, but if the dissension ('distaunce') alluded to here refers to the differences between the two countries (rather than to differences within the two countries) the poem is probably to be dated sometime before 1453 when the wars virtually ended. Perhaps dating from shortly after this and possibly prompted by the widespread disillusionment at the losses in France comes a lament in seven quatrains from CUL MS Hh ii 6 which opens:

> Nowe is Englond perisshed in fight,
> With moche people & consciens light,
> Many knyghtes & lytyll myght
> Many lawys & lityll right. . . .[5]
>
> (*HP*, 62, 1–4)

The following stanzas elaborate on this with similar pointed antitheses and the same resigned tone. Here, as often in this type of poem, political disasters are attributed to the moral shortcomings of the nation.

A somewhat longer complaint, entitled, after its refrain, *The Bisson Leads the Blind*, may be more precisely dated. This is not due to any precision on the author's part, however, but to the astuteness of modern scholarship. In the list of examples of contemporary corruption and decadence appear the lines:

> He ys louyd þat wele can lye,
> And theuys tru men honge.
>
> (*HP*, 49, 41–2)

At first sight this just looks like another example of the way in which true values are reversed. But, as R. H. Robbins showed, it refers without doubt to a notorious law case of 1456.[6] A convicted thief, Thomas Whytehorn, informed on and falsely gave evidence against his former acquaintances, most of whom were as a result found guilty of treason and hanged. For this Whytehorn was not only pardoned but also rewarded by the King, who himself profited from the confiscation of the traitors' property. Robbins' supposition is borne out by a note in the same hand as copied this poem in the single BM MS Harley 5396 in which it occurs, containing the date 'Monday aftyr seynt barthylmewys day the xxxiiij ȝere of Kyng Harry the vj'. Once this is established the precise implications of other passages emerge. Lines 69–77, in particular, refer to the outbreak of the civil wars. But what is especially interesting is the fact that this author sees the political aftermath of the first Battle of

St Albans of 1455 and the Thomas Whytehorn incident in general terms, as part of a pattern of contemporary decadence. The generalizing tendency of medieval complaint poems is most marked here. Though it would appear that this poet's discontent was provoked by particular events which he found deplorable, he expressed his dissatisfaction as a generalized list of complaints, relying heavily in form and expression on the well-known 'abuse' poems. This is apparent in the opening stanza:

> ffulfyllyd ys þe profesy for ay
> Þat merlyn sayd & many on mo,
> Wysdam ys wel ny away,
> No man may knowe hys frend fro foo,
> Now gyllorys don gode men gye;
> Ryȝt gos redles all behynde;
> Truthe ys turnyd to trechery;
> ffor now þe bysom ledys þe blynde.
>
> (1–8)

The refrain is proverbial; the reference in the first two lines must be to a prophecy somewhat similar to that quoted above from MS Trinity College Dublin 516; the notions in all the other lines may easily be paralleled in other 'abuse' poems; and even the precise wording of 'Truthe ys turnyd to trechery' is to be found elsewhere.

Despite the completeness of their attacks and despite the very real feelings of frustration and dissatisfaction evident in them, these poems were not revolutionary. They contain no proposals for overthrowing and renewing the decadent society they deplore. In spirit they are conservative. Though they criticize contemporary society, they unfailingly endorse, either overtly or by implication, those assumptions and values upon which it was based. And this way of thinking is plain from the formal organization of some of the poems: descriptions of the ideal society are implied in one of the possible readings of the punctuation poem quoted, and also in the 'world upside down' verses before their ironic refrains. Contemporary evils are defined here as a reversal of an accepted set of social and moral values, and the poet's certainty of the rightness of these values sharpens his sense of how far contemporary society had deviated from them. The implicit assumptions are always that a perfect society existed somewhere in the past and that the natural sinfulness of man and the propensity for change for the worse inherent in all human activities have disrupted it. A basic conservatism of this sort also produced the more precisely directed discontent at the fairly basic and far-reaching changes in the pattern of English society which took place in the fifteenth century.

In terms of their social consequences the changes in the patterns of agricultural organization were perhaps most far-reaching, for medieval society was based on land and land tenure. This period witnessed the final and irrevocable break-up of the older patterns of arable demesne farming based on the three- or four-field system and maintained largely on the labour services of an unfree peasantry. The causes which contributed to this break-up are complex, but an agricultural slump in the earlier part of the fourteenth century seems to have first provoked some landowners (secular lords more readily than monastics) into seeking financial security in leasing parts of their demesne lands for rents. Labour services tended increasingly to be commuted for money and landowners came to rely more on wage labourers. The plague of 1348 and the later outbreaks, particularly that of 1361, also furthered these changes in that the considerable decrease in the population created a labour shortage and consequent demands for higher wages. The Ordinances and Statutes of Labourers of 1349 and 1351 sought, with little success, to fix maximum wages. As the scarcity of labour grew more pronounced, landowners were increasingly forced to pay wages higher than those sanctioned by the regulations, and as their costs increased and their profits declined they were forced to lease more and more arable land, or turn it over to pasture, which demanded less outlay on labour. By the end of the fourteenth century even pasture farming on a large scale was found by some landowners to be unprofitable and pasture lands as well as arable lands were leased. In the fifteenth century these processes of agricultural change continued, and though some magnates came to possess vast estates (often through shrewd investment, through commerce, or through astutely arranged marriages), increasingly the richer peasants were renting and sometimes buying agricultural land.

With the break-up of this feudal pattern of demesne farming went a weakening of tenurial ties. In place of the old feudal relationship between a lord and his vassals emerged new forms of relationship, organized on the principle of personal contracts freely negotiated. The powerful magnate might promise to be 'good lord' to lesser men, which is to say that he would seek to promote their interests (if for example they were smaller landowners). He might alternatively undertake to pay them wages and allow them to live under his protection, which was usually indicated by the fact that they would wear his badge or livery. The lesser man might promise to help the greater if and when his help were needed, or he might undertake to serve in the lord's personal retinue, or perform other services. Late medieval legislation distinguished three categories of retainer: resident household retainers, estate managers and legal advisers formed one group; those who undertook by written indenture to serve their lord in peace and war formed the second; and those who had no formal contract but who accepted the lord's fees and wore his livery in return for certain services, formed the third. Retinues or 'affinities' of this sort were not new. They are to be found as early as the thirteenth century. But the extent to which lords built up their retinues in the late fourteenth and fifteenth centuries was new. Whether this 'bastard feudalism' was or was not conducive to political and social stability is a matter of dispute.[7] But certainly it helped to destroy traditional loyalties, and since the contract depended on self-interest it frequently collapsed in adversity. A retainer would change his allegiance if he thought it was advantageous to do so: Edmund Paston said of a steward '. . . I fele by him he wold forsake his master and get hym a newh, yf he wyste he schuld rewle; and so wene I meche of all the contre is so disposyd' (*Paston Letters*, No. 69). That the keeping of retinues (which were in some cases virtually like private armies) might lead to abuse was not immediately apparent. But from the late fourteenth century onwards there is frequent legislation to restrict them. Richard II, in a Statute of 1390, limited to peers the right to take retainers, and forbade the taking of service to all below the rank of esquire. Furthermore, those not employed as household retainers, estate managers or legal advisers, had to be indentured to serve the lord for life. Later legislation sought, with varying success, to impose further restraints.

As they adjusted to these changes in society the social roles and behaviour patterns of the upper classes also changed. Whether for the better or the worse is disputable. But contemporary writers tended to identify a supposed falling away from the ideal behaviour of former years with these social changes. Hoccleve's regret at the passing of the old feudal world and its values is representative:

> For that I wolde that the hye degree
> of Chiualrie vniuersally
> Bare vp his hede, & bente not awry.
> (*Regement*, 2453–5)

To find perfect noblemen he looked to the past: to Henry, first Duke of Lancaster, in whom was found '. . . al þat longith to knyȝthode' (*ibid.*, 2652), to Edward III and to John of Gaunt. A misgiving frequently expressed was that knights of the fifteenth century had the appearance of nobility without the necessary substance to go with it:

> Many galantes & penylese,
> Great courtears & small wages,
> Many gentilmen & fewe pages.
> (*HP*, 62, 5–8)

The late fourteenth-century author of the sermon in MS Additional 41321 makes the point with reference to the past: '. . . thei that ben in the estaat of knyȝthode, thoru this foule synne of pride stieth faste and passeth hili hir estaat in al maner aparaile that longeth unto hem above hire auncetres that weren bifore hem, whiche hadden myche more lifelode than thei have now'.[8] Hoccleve is slightly more precise in his analysis:

> In dayes olde, whan smal apparaille
> Suffisid vn-to hy estat or mene,
> Was gret houshold wel stuffid of victaille;

But now housholdes ben ful sclender & lene,
ffor al þe good þat men may repe or glene,
Wasted is in outrageous array,
So that housholdes men nat holde may.

(Regement, 491–7)

And some nobles, it is true, were notoriously extravagant and could be said to have 'wasted' their wealth. There seems to have been a competitiveness among them, in the opinion of the author of a sermon from British Museum MS Royal 18B xxiii: 'everi lord bi-holdeth othur, how he is arayed, how he is horsid, how he is manned, and so envyeth other' and he adds pointedly '. . . for to parforme this, her owne lyflodes wolen not suffice'.[9] It was widely felt that the upper classes sought to flaunt their wealth to the extent that they lived beyond their means. Apart from the 'outrageous' clothes Hoccleve refers to, they indulged in rich foods, instituted costly building projects and maintained large retinues. The author of *Mum and the Sothsegger* had marvelled at this extravagance:

Þat þe hie houusinge/herborowe ne myghte
Halfdell þe houshould/but hales hem helped,

(III, 217–18)

and had reflected that it frequently led to extortion from the poor and to debts. At about the same time a sermon writer had come to the same conclusions: 'I am siker . . . that other thei must be stronge thefes to robbe here neiboris in the cuntre, or wrongful extorcioneris, to meyntene with hire proude estaat, or falle in to dette, for borwynge to that proude araie. . . .'[10] Even the greatest nobles were sometimes forced to borrow money. And those who sought to remedy or consolidate their fortunes by responding to the changed social conditions are also criticized. It was evidently felt that the upper classes demeaned themselves by living off anything but the proceeds of their manors. One anonymous author regrets that 'Lordes be led all out of kynde' (*HP*, 49, 30) because they had taken up professions ('Lordys þe lawe þey lere' 49) or commercial activity ('Knyȝtus be made custemerys' 27). Another means of enriching themselves and their families, widely used by the fifteenth-century nobility, was the seeking of advantageous marriages for their children, although sometimes such matches were absurdly inappropriate. Hoccleve observes:

> Among þe ryche also is an vsage,
> Eche of hem his childe vnto oþres wedde,
> Þogh þei be al to yong & tendre of age,
> No wher ny rype ynow to go to bedde,
>
> (*Regement*, 1639–42)

and goes on to characterize accurately 'al þe gilt/of þis' as due to 'couetyse'. Of course, the arranged marriage was a generally accepted social phenomenon (and had been for centuries) particularly among the upper classes. But others, besides Hoccleve, felt that it was inappropriately exploited in the fifteenth century: for example, the marriage between Catherine, dowager Duchess of Norfolk (who was over eighty), to Sir John Woodville (who was twenty) was widely condemned. At the bottom of most of the criticism of the upper classes was the feeling that they no longer conducted themselves, in social or in moral matters, in the manner expected from men in their positions.

But not only was there dissatisfaction about the conduct of the upper classes. The retainers they employed are also frequently the subjects of criticism. Feed retainers were becoming increasingly important as a social group. Lords were entrusting more and more of their activities to councillors, advisers and servants. Bishop Reginald Pecock remarks that many lords were incapable of the simple arithmetic involved in their accounts and for this reason had to appoint 'officers under them for to attend sufficiently to all the worldly needs of their lands'.[11] This left some lords virtually at the mercy of their advisers, and that these advisers were not always thought to be honest is clear from the way in which Edward IV is reported to have rebuked Sir William Brandon, one of the Duke of Norfolk's men: 'Brandon, thow thou can begyll the Dwk of Norffolk and bryng hym abow the thombe as thow lyst, I let the wet thow shalt not do me so; for I undyrstand thy fals delyng well inow.' (*Paston Letters*, No. 716). Because a lord was so dependent upon his retainers it was felt to be imperative that he should choose true and loyal men of ability, not deceitful flatterers whose only object was to retain the lord's favour. Hoccleve makes the point in his poem of advice to Prince Henry:

> Þe moste lak þat han þe lordes grete,
> Is of hem that hir soothes shuld hem telle;
> Al in þe glose folk labour and swete;
> Thei stryuen who best rynge shal þe belle
> of fals plesance, in þat hir hertes swelle
> If þat oon can bet than other deceyue;
> And swich deceyt, lordes blyndly receyue,
> *(Regement, 1926–32)*

with the obvious implication that contemporary lords had surrounded themselves with the wrong kind of adviser. There are frequent complaints against flattering advisers. One anonymous author says that the abuse was general: 'Gabberys glosen euery whare' (*HP*, 49, 61) but was especially pernicious in the households of the great because 'flattererys be made knyȝtus perys' (29) and 'Iaperys syt lordys ful nere' (51). The author of the verses in MS Digby 102 puts into the mouth of a complaisant retainer a cynical admission of his flattering behaviour.

> I plese my lord at bed and bord,
> Þouȝ y do but strype a stre,
> And florische fayre my lordis word,
> And fede hem forth with nay and ȝee.
> *(II, 25–8)*

Some authors are more precise in their criticisms. Hoccleve says that retainers often fail to correct a lord's errors because they fear that their criticism will lose for them the lord's favour:

> A gloser also kepith his silence
> Often, where he his lord seeth hym mystake.
> *(Regement, 3088–9)*

He points out elsewhere that retainers often misinterpret to their lord the way in which his policies were regarded:

Many a seruant/vnto his lord seith,
'Þat al the world spekith of him honour',
Whan the contrarie of þat/is sooth in feith.
(*MP*, III, 217–19)

The MS Digby 102 poet says that a lord's secrets are frequently
disclosed by his retainers:

What a glosere here or see,
Þou3 it shulde to shame falle,
He knoweþ in chambre preuytee,
Telleþ his felow in þe halle.
(IV, 201–4)

He elsewhere makes the point that while in a lord's service retainers
worked principally for their own financial gain:

3if a lord 3eue fee or rent
For to do a gret office,
To serve hym wel is þyn atent,
For thy profyt, but not for his,
For he fyndeþ þe þy vaunsement;
Þy loue vppon þe profyt lys,
(XVII, 17–22)

and he goes on to add the caution that persons who thus prosper
in the world are 'gostly blent'. In the view of the author of *Mum and
the Sothsegger* the men who acquired influential positions in a
lord's retinue were often not of real ability:

For I say for my-self/and schewe, as me thynchith,
That ho is riall of his ray/that light reede him folwith;
For al his witte in his wede/ys wrappid for sothe,
More þan in mater to amende/þe peple þat ben mys-led.
3it swich fresshe foodis/beth feet in-to chambris,
And for hir wedis so wyde/wyse beth y-holde,
(III, 122–7)

but rather fashionable nonentities. The power and influence retainers came to have aroused a lot of resentment against them.

What frequently seems to have offended fifteenth-century critics of the new system of relations which grew up between lord and retainer was the self-interest it seemed to demand from everyone. Hoccleve complains that lords may no longer be relied upon for their customary charity:

> welaway! as harde as is a post—
> A post? nay; as a stoon—ben hertes now!
> Lordes, for shame! what þing eyleth yow?
> (*Regement*, 4695–7)

and again a few lines later:

> Allas! þogh þat a man disceuere & pleyne
> To many a lord his mescheuous myserie,
> The lord naght deyneth vnderstonde his peyne;
> He settith noght þerby a blakberie.
> (4712–15)

In passages such as this it may be suspected that Hoccleve's own disappointed hopes of advancement were never far from his mind. But, in one place, he draws attention to a notable instance of the more general harshness of contemporary society, in which disabled soldiers who had fought in France were neglected by the lords for whom they had fought:

> How many a gentilman may men nowe se,
> Þat whilom in þe werres olde of fraunce
> Honoured were, & holde in grete cheerte
> ffor hire prowesse in armes, & plente
> Of frendes hadde in youþe, & now, for schame,
> Allas! hir frendeschipe is croked & lame.
> (870–5)

This was written in 1412, and it is interesting to note, in a poem which J. Kail dates from 1400, that a retainer justifies his own self-interested behaviour by an allusion to the misfortune that may befall the soldier who fights unselfishly on his lord's behalf:

> My flateryng, glosyng, not me harmes.
> I gete loue, and moche richesse,

> When wel-faryng men of armes
> In fight, in presoun, and distresse.
> When thou art old and feble, y gesse,
> Who wole the fynde fode or wede?
> (MS Digby 102, II, 49–54)

Though the author disapproves of this speaker's position, there was clearly a case to be made in favour of a retainer consulting his own interests. Hoccleve recognizes but deplores the fact that financial self-interest was often the only reason why retainers were anxious to enter a lord's service:

> Whil þat þe swetnesse of riches endurith,
> Vnto þe riche is manny man plesaunt;
> Only þe richesse þerto hem lurith;
> What he comaundiþ, þei ben obysaunt
> To do, whil þat he of goode is habundaunt;
> But whan þe pray, þe richesse, is agoo,
> The man forsaken þei for euermo.
> (*Regement*, 3067–73)

But it was well known that influential positions were hard to come by and that tenure of them was often short. Thus it was necessary for the fortunate retainer to make the most of his chances while he could. The author of a fifteenth-century carol recognized that 'lordis loue schaungit oft' and advised those who 'serue a lord of prys':

> In thin welthe werk sekyrly,
> For seruyse is non erytage.
> (*EEC* No. 381, 11–12)

The second line of this quotation is proverbial and it is evident that many acted upon its implications. The Commons often complained about the dishonesty of royal and other officials, and taxes and customs dues were frequently misappropriated. Often the official enriched himself at the expense of his employer: Ralph, Lord Cromwell, admitted at his death that he had misappropriated £3,481 1s. 6d.; Stephen Preston, a squire in Edward IV's household, sold, for his own gain, much of the standing timber in the King's forest of North Pederton.[12] But usually retainers used their authority and the influence of a lord's protection to extort money from the common people. The author of a sermon in BM MS Harley 2398 compares them to 'day theves' who wait in the woods, and their 'seculer lordes beth trees of this wode, under whos power they lurketh and spoyleth the peple'.[13] There is an account of how men 'maintained' by a lord might exploit their positions in Hoccleve. It is told from the point of view of a Privy Seal clerk, and so presumably reflects his own experience. Lord's men, he says, take the fees which properly belong to the clerks:

> if a wyght haue any cause to sue
> To vs, som lordes man schal vndertake
> To sue it out; & þat þat is vs due
> ffor oure labour, hym denyeþ vs nat take.
> (*Regement*, 1499–1502)

The clerks are promised by the retainer that his 'lord schal þanken vs an oþer day'. But though they know that this is the beginning of the process whereby they will be deprived of their rewards, they can do nothing about it:

> we dar non argument
> make a-geyn him, but fayre & wel him trete,
> Leste he roporte amys, & make vs schent.
> (1513–15)

The reason for this is that the retainer enjoys the protection of a lord and 'Hard is, be holden suspect with þe grete'. Hoccleve remarks a few stanzas later that all retainers are not like this ('I seye nat, al lordes men þus do/þat sue vnto oure courte' 1541–2) but he adds that many 'Han þus don ofte' and one may assume that abuses such as the one he describes were not uncommon.

The most serious abuse, however, was that the law tended to be corrupted by these networks of influence which developed. Those 'maintained' by the great could twist the law to their own ends and were virtually immune from punishment for wrongdoings: on one occasion, William Paston advised a client to drop a lawsuit on the grounds that his opponent was a friend of the Duke of Norfolk. The author of a sermon in BM MS Royal 18 B xxiii roundly denounces the 'affinities' of great men who extort money from the ordinary people either through manipulating the law or disregarding it: '. . . officers of gret men that wereth her lyverethes . . . by colour of lawe and aȝens lawe, robbeth and dispoyleth the poure people, now betynge, now sleyinge, now puttynge hem from hous and landes.'[14] Hoccleve points out to Prince Henry that 'Lawe is nye flemed out of þis cuntre' and lays the blame for it squarely on the rich and those they maintain. It is, he continues, a dangerous tendency:

> and this forth growe,
> This londe shal it repent and sore abye;
> And al such mayntenance, as men wel knowe,
> Sustened is naght by persones lowe,
> But Cobbes grete þis ryot sustene;
> Correct it, gode is, whil þat it is grene.
>
> (*Regement*, 2802–7)

He speaks here as if the abuses of maintenance are a new social phenomenon, but some years earlier the author of *Mum and the Sothsegger* had made much the same point:

> Thus is þe lawe louyd/þoru myȝhty lordis willys,
> Þat meynteyne myssdoers/more þan oþer peple.
> For mayntenance many day/well more is þe reuþe.
>
> (III, 310–12)

In another place (again for the reason that it is likely to cause corruption of the law) he condemns the giving of liveries:

> Now for to telle trouþe/þus þan me thynketh,
> That no manere meyntenour/þe lawe ne apeire,
> Neiþer bragger ne boster/for no breme wordis.
>
> (II, 77–9)

All these instances are from the early years of the century but the problem still persisted as late as about 1470 when George Ashby, on the topic the ruler's duty to keep the law, advised Prince Edward:

gentilmen shuld nat yeve clothyng
But to their howshold meyne, for surance
That no man be their power excedyng,
Ne maynteine no people, by youre puissance,
Ner false quarels take thorough maintenance
(Poems, II, 548–52)

—a recommendation for a restrictive policy very similar to that in Edward IV's legislation of 1468.

Though these writers were oversimplifying the situation by attributing the lawless condition of England solely to the growth of liveried retinues, the problem of lawlessness was, nevertheless, a serious one. Because the law was not strongly administered people tended not to rely upon it, and frequently tried to solve their own problems privately through force or cunning. The lawlessness of the nobility is most completely documented. Typical of many private feuds was that between the Earl of Devon and William, Lord Bonville, which caused it to be recorded in parliament in 1441 that 'there ben grete & grevous riotes down in the Weste Countrey, betwene Th'erle of Devonshire and the Lord Bonevile, by the whiche som Men have be murdred, some robbed, & Children & Wymen taken'.[15] The disputed ownership of three Gloucestershire manors—Wotton, Symondshall and Cowley—led first to legal action between the Talbot family and the lords of Berkeley, and then to violence. In 1470 Thomas Talbot, despairing of a solution by legal means, challenged William, Lord Berkeley, either to single combat or to a pitched battle between their private armies to settle the matter:

William, called Lord Berkeley. I merveill ye come not forth with all your carts of gunnes, bowes, with oder ordinance, that yet set forward to come to my manor of Wotton to bete it down upon my hand. I let you wit ye shall not nede to come soe nye. For I trust to God to mete you nere home with Englishmen of my own nation and neighbours, whereas ye by suttle craft have blown it about in diverse places of England that I should intend to bring in Welshmen for to destroy and hurt my own nation and country. I lete thee wit, I was never soe disposed, nere never will be. And to the proof hereof, I require thee of knighthood and of manhood to appoynt a day to meet me half way, there to try between God and our two hands all our quarrell and title of right, for to eschew the shedding of Christian menns blood. Or els at the same day bringe the uttermost of thy power, and I shall mete thee. An answere of this by writinge, as ye will abide by, according to the honour and order of Knighthood. Thomas Talbot the Viscount Lisle.[16]

The result of this was the Battle of Nibley Green at which about one hundred and fifty men, including Thomas Talbot, lost their lives. Most disputes, such as this one, were concerned with the possession of property. The ownership of many of the properties bequeathed to the Paston family by Sir John Fastolf was frequently questioned, and not only in the lawcourts: in 1450 Lord Moleyns' men attacked and wrecked Margaret Paston's house at Gresham; in 1465 the Duke of Suffolk forcibly seized the Pastons' property at Hellesdon; and in 1469 the Duke of Norfolk besieged and eventually took Caister Castle. But throughout English society, not only among the nobility and the gentry, there was a high level of crime. An Italian visitor to England at the end of the century remarked that 'There is no country in the world where there are so many thieves and robbers as in England.' Travelling on the roads was dangerous and round the coasts piracy was frequent. There was often open contempt for the law: one woman, for example, who had been served with a writ 'reysed vpp her neghebors with wepyns drawen forto slee and mordre ye said bryngers of ye writte . . . and compellyd hem forto devour the same Writte . . . bothe Wex and parchement.' It is little wonder that in 1459 one chronicler should write that 'In this same tyme, the reame of Englonde was oute of alle good governaunce, as it had be many dayes before.[17]

Quarrels and disputes and the crimes which resulted from them prompted a great increase in litigation, with the consequence that law courts and lawyers became increasingly important. To try to avoid litigation disputes were sometimes put to arbitration, and on occasions those involved would be reconciled in this way. But it was often difficult to get impartial arbitrators, and frequently impossible to implement decisions reached. Therefore the law was usually invoked: Sir John Fastolf and John Paston were continually involved in lawsuits; it was said that at one time Sir William Plumpton was suing every true man in the Forest of Knaresborough for one reason or another; and the *Household Book* of Sir John Howard shows him to have been a frequent litigant.[18] But it was not only the aristocracy and the gentry who went to law. Burgesses were frequently involved in cases, as were some churches also. Lawyers prospered and their numbers increased. In London extra accommodation had to be provided for law students: in 1454 Barnard's Inn was handed over to them and by 1463 Staple Inn, which was originally a customs house, had become an Inn of Chancery. But the law was notoriously corrupt and open to all sorts of exploitation. Judgements were sometimes blatantly partial, as, for example, that of Justice Prisot on the complaints of the city of Norwich, the town of Swaffham and Sir John Fastolf against the activities of Sir Thomas Tuddenham and John Heydon. The 'open partialitie' of Prisot's handling of the case was so marked that even his colleague Justice Yelverton remarked upon it (*Paston Letters*, No. 192). Bribery was frequently the means towards a favourable decision: on one occasion Sir John Fastolf urges his agent to 'entreat the Sheriff as well ye can by resonable rewards' (*Paston Letters*, No. 188) and the whole Paston correspondence reveals similar attitudes. Juries could also be rigged: Fastolf, for example, orders his representative to 'Labour to the Sheriff for the return of such panels as will speak for me'; Sir Thomas Tuddenham once frightened a jury into a false verdict by 'horrible menaces'; and on one occasion the King ordered such juries to be formed as would acquit Lord Moleyns of an indictment whether he was guilty or not (*Paston Letters*, No. 193). Practices such as these to manipulate the law were so frequent as to be expected, even if they were not acceptable: a certain Thomas Playter even entered money paid out in bribes in his official accounts.[19]

Of course, these practices cannot have been general, but examples of corruption must have occurred often enough to account for the frequent anxious recommendations that the law should be administered fairly. The author of the verses in MS Digby 102 points out that the corrupt administration of the law endangers a country because it encourages crime:

> Lete not lawe be fauoured ne sold.
> Suche maken fals men be bold,
> And false men myghte stroye a thede.
> (I, 156–8)

Hoccleve warns judges against personal bias:

> Naght ought a iuge, for hatrede or loue
> Othir wey deme þen trouth requirith
> (*Regement*, 2689–90)

and against accepting bribes:

> A iuges purs, with golde noght shulde swelle;
> If one iustice he shape his dome to bilde,
> His iugementes he ʒifteles must ʒilde.
> (2714–16)

But most authors roundly condemn the administration of the law in all its aspects. The author of the sermons in MS Royal 18 B xxiii writes that '. . . bothe Cristen courte and seculere courte . . . goon for golde and eftes, and trewthe is forsokon',[20] and in the opinion of the chronicler John Hardyng:

> The lawe is lyke vnto a Walshmannes hose
> To eche mannes legge that shapen is and mete. . . .[21]

In other fifteenth-century poems a variety of charges appear. One author says that the law has very little to do with truth:

> With men of lawe he haʒt non spas—
> Þey louyn trewþe in non plas.
> (*HP*, 59, 9–10)

Another draws attention, at one and the same time, to the great number of laws on the statute book and to their ineffectiveness:

L

> Many lawys, and lytylle ryght;
> Many actes of parlament,
> And few kept wyth tru entent.
>
> (*PPS*, II, p. 252)

Hoccleve points out that the rich and poor are not treated equally before the law:

> The riche and myghty man, thogh he trespace,
> No man seith ones þat blak is his eye;
> But to þe pore, is denyed al grace;
> He snybbyd is, and put to tormentrie.
>
> (*Regement*, 2822–5)

But the most frequent complaint is that the law could be corrupted through money. The MS Digby 102 poet complains of this:

> In alle kyngdomes, here lawe is wryten;
> For mede ne drede, þey chaunge it nouȝt.
> In Engeland, as all men wyten,
> Law, as best, is solde and bouȝt.
>
> (XIII, 25–8)

No matter what crime a man has committed, says one author, even murder, if he has sufficient money to offer a bribe he will be able to escape punishment:

> Þow I haue a man I-slawe
> & forfetyd þe kynges lawe,
> I xal fyndyn a man of lawe
> Wyl takyn my peny & let me goo.
>
> (*SL XIV and XV* No. 57, 5–8)

On the other hand, says another author, the man who has no money is powerless in legal matters:

> Whate-so-euer he be, and yf that he
> whante money to plede the lawe,
> do whate he cane In ys mater than
> shale proue not worthe a strawe.
>
> (*HP*, 51, 45–8)

The complaint is most pointed in the first half of the anonymous *London Lickpenny*, which tells of a Kentishman, one of 'the pore that wold proceede' (*HP*, 50, 6), who goes to London for legal redress because, as he says, 'my goodes were defravded me by falshood' (26). He goes to the various courts, but is confused by the bustle of activity, as at the King's Bench, where

> sat clarkes a gret Rout,
> which fast dyd wryte by one assent;
> There stoode vp one and cryed about,
> 'Rychard, Robert, and Iohn of Kent!'
> I wyst not well what this man ment,
> (15–19)

and can get nobody to act for him because he is too poor, even though his case is a good one:

> I gave them my playnt vppon my knee,
> they lyked it well, when they had it reade;
> but, lackyng mony, I could not be sped.
> (33–5)

He returns home dissatisfied and disappointed, vowing 'of the law wold I meddle no more' (107).

Particularly interesting in its attitudes to the law is the *Instructions to his Son* written around 1445–50 by Peter Idley, for a long time bailiff of Wallingford, later gentleman falconer and under keeper of the royal mews and falcons, and after 1456 Controller of the King's Works throughout the kingdom. Idley had a good deal of practical legal experience, and his preoccupation with the law emerges in his treatise. He deplores the prevalence of theft in contemporary society and regrets that punishments are not more severe:

> The lawes were vsed in the dayes before
> A theif to be hanged for xiiij en pens;
> But now they stele many a score
> And it is thought but a litell offence.
> (II A, 2610–13)

He also draws attention to those lords who promote servants skilled in using the law unjustly for the lord's advantage:

> Ffor somme lordis be of that condicioun,
> If they haue a seruaunt can toille and tangle
> And can gete hem goodis by subtell extorcioun
> And with the lawe also can wrastill and wrangle,
> Spare for non othes, fast chide and Iangle—
> He shall be cheif of counceill and speciall secretarie,
>
> (II B, 1051–6)

and makes the point that both the lords and the servant will suffer 'egall paynes' in hell because 'of the synne they beith bothe party-ners'. In a long passage in his second book he exposes the way in which those appointed as executors sometimes fail to carry out the dead man's wishes. They do not distribute his property as alms, or use it to pay for masses for his soul, but think only of keeping it for themselves:

> And when he is thus to churche ybrought,
> fful symple almes for hym ther is deeled;
> The sely soule shall haue litell or nought
> When the cors with clay is clooselie heelid;
> Ther mynde is on the baggis that streitly be sealled.
>
> (II B, 1632–6)

He follows this with a highly circumstantial account of three such false executors, and the arguments they use to justify their actions. His most frequent complaints, however, are on the extent of perjury in fifteenth-century lawcourts:

> Somme swere also at Sessions and at assise,
> Somme for mannes lyff and somme for londe,
> And beere fals wittenes in diuers wyse;
> To sey the trouthe they holde vp her honde,
> But for money they woll not wonde
> To be as fals as falshode hymsilf,
>
> (II A, 2708–13)

and, as a warning, he relates the story of a perjurer who was struck dead in court. But though Peter Idley recognizes the extent to which the law was corrupted, he, none the less, insists that his son Thomas should study the law:

> I conceyve thy witte bothe goode and able,
> To the lawe, therfore, now haue I ment
> To set the.
>
> (I, 127–9)

Nor is he above using coercion to get his son to follow this profession:

> And if þou do the contrarie, trust me well,
> I woll put fro the without nay
> Londe and goodis eueri deell
> And all þat euer I goodly may.
>
> (I, 134–7)

The reason for this insistence appears in the next stanza:

> To grete worshippe hath the lawe
> Brought forth many a pouere man
> That wolde flee vices and to vertu drawe,
> Many a thousande sith þe world beganne.
>
> (141–4)

For the middle-class boy of some intelligence, the law, with all its faults, was, as Peter Idley recognized, a means towards prosperity.

Another way in which the energetic and ambitious might rise in the social hierarchy and achieve financial security was through taking advantage of developments in industry and commerce. Though England in the fifteenth century was still basically a rural society a certain amount of industry had developed. Round the coasts there was an increase in off-shore fishing, particularly for herring, from the east coast ports, and some ships went to the waters around Iceland for cod. In some places minerals were being mined: there was a little silver, lead from Cumberland, Derbyshire and Somerset, coal from most northern and western counties from Somerset to Northumberland, and iron principally from the north, but also from Gloucestershire, Kent and Sussex. It must have been an iron-master's factory which kept awake one fifteenth-century poet and prompted his indignant verses:

> Swarte smekyd smeþes, smateryd wyth smoke,
> Dryue me to deth wyth den of her dyntes.
> Swech noys on nyghtes ne herd men neuer.
> What knauene cry, & clateryng of knockes!
> Þe kammede kongons cryen after 'Col, Col!'
> & blowen here bellewys þat al here brayn brestes.
> *(SL XIV and XV* No. 118, 1–6)

But the most important commodity was wool which was so plentiful and of such fine quality in England.

> 'Of Brutis Albion his wolle is cheeff richesse
> In prys surmountyng euery othir thyng
> Sauff greyn & corn'
> *(Minor Poems*, II, 23, 351–3)

writes Lydgate in one place. But increasingly throughout the fifteenth century the English were not simply producing the raw material for export, but were manufacturing fine woollen cloth of various sorts—the broadcloth from the Cotswolds, kerseys from the south-west, East Anglia and the West Riding of Yorkshire, worsted from Norfolk, the green Kendal cloth and the famous 'blue' cloth from Coventry. Manpower, often that released by agricultural changes, was switched to cloth-making, and a considerable number of lower-class workers came to depend upon this industry. In the early 1460s, for example, one author recommends that the export of wool should be restricted so that there would be full employment in England:

> And in especyall restrayne strayttly þe wool
> That þe comyns of thys land may wyrke at the full.
> *(HP*, 70, 55–6)

Writing a little later, George Ashby gives very similar advice to Prince Edward:

> Yif ye wol bryng vp ayen clothe makyng
> And kepe youre Comyns oute of ydelnesse,

Ye shull therfore haue many a blessyng
And put the pore people in busynesse.
(*Poems*, II, 527–30)

As these lines imply, the cloth-making industry was liable to the odd recession, but mainly it prospered, and those areas which produced wool and cloth were among the richest in England.

But as significant as these developments in industry were those in commerce, for England was becoming increasingly a trading nation. The main imports of wine came from Gascony, and salt from Bourgneuf. From northern Europe came corn (in years of scarcity), timber from Prussia, tar, pitch, wax and furs. From the Low Countries came certain dyes essential for the cloth-making industry. From Spain, mainly through Bristol, came a variety of goods: wine and oil; foreign fruits such as raisins, dates and figs; honey, almonds, licorice, saffron; some raw materials such as iron, wax, tallow, rosin, and some dyes; leather work, skins and soap. From Portugal, which had long-standing treaties of peace, friendship and alliance with England and whose people were 'oure frendes wyth there commoditez' came, according to the author of *The Libelle of Englyshe Polycye*, very similar merchandise:

oyle, wyne, osey, wex and greyne,
Fygues, reysyns, hony and cordeweyne,
Dates and salt hydes and suche marchaundy.
(132–4)

The Italian merchants from Genoa, Venice and Florence brought, mainly to London, Southampton and Sandwich, the luxury goods the rich desired:

clothes of golde; silke and pepir blake
They bringe wyth hem, and of woade grete plente
Woll-oyle, wood aschen by vessell in the see,
Coton, roche-alum and gode golde of Jene,
(333–6)

medicinal drugs and sugar, together with a range of trivial merchandise, which, according to this author, was not of very much use,

All spicerye and other grocers ware,
Wyth swete wynes, all manere of chaffare,
Apes and japes and marmusettes taylede,
Nifles, trifles that litell have availed.

(346–9)

The west coast ports, particularly Bristol and Chester, conducted a lucrative trade with Ireland, from whose 'sure, wyde and depe' harbours, particularly Waterford, the English shipped principally raw materials and foodstuffs:

Hydes and fish, samon, hake and herynge;
Irish wollen and lynyn cloth, faldynge,
And marterns gode bene in here marchaundye;
Hertys hydes, and other hydes of venerye,
Skynnes of oter, squerel and Irysh hare,
Of shepe, lambe and fox is here chaffare,
Felles of kydde and conyes grete plente.

(658–64)

Merchants were also venturing to Iceland, particularly from Bristol, Hull, Lynn and Newcastle, for stockfish, and by 1436 the trade had reached, according to the author of the *Libelle of Englyshe Polycye*, such an extent that the demand for fish had outstripped the supply:

And now so fele shippes thys yere there were
That moche losse for unfraught they bare.

(806–7)

English exports varied from country to country. Iceland was so poor in resources except for fish that grain and wood were shipped there, minerals, metalware such as pots, pans and knives, and all kinds of manufactured goods. Similarly, though Gascony was rich in wines it was short of such commodities as corn, fish and coal, and these were supplied by English merchants. But always the main exports were wool and, increasingly, cloth. Part of this overseas trade was in the hands of the German merchants of the Hanse, and part was conducted by the Italians who had licences

to buy English wool and ship it. This aroused the commercial
jealousy of the English merchants, who felt themselves to be dis-
criminated against in their own country.

> In Cotteswolde also they ryde aboute
> And al Englande and bien wythouten doute
> What them liste wythe fredome and fraunchise,
> More then we Englisshe may getyn in any wyse
> (456–9)

wrote the author of the *Libelle of Englyshe Polycye* of the Italians.
But increasingly the trade was becoming dominated by English
merchants, who, by the end of the fifteenth century, shipped almost
all the wool, mainly through the Staple at Calais, and the majority
of the cloth. This had the effect of enriching the principal trading
ports—London, Bristol and Southampton—and producing merchants of enormous wealth, such as William Canynges (died 1474)
of Bristol.

Attitudes towards these developments in commerce varied.
Political theorists recognized well enough that trade and merchants
were important. George Ashby stresses that Prince Edward should
cherish 'Marchaudes' (II, 612) along with pilgrims, scholars and
poets. In his analysis of the 'body politic' the author of the MS
Digby 102 poems emphasizes the worth of merchants who put
themselves at risk ('in perile ride and gon') in order to gain wealth
for themselves and the community:

> Bryngen wynnyng, gold, and fee,
> Make hiȝe houses of lym and ston,
> Mayntene burgh, toun and cyte.
> (XV, 52–4)

The patriotic author of *The Libelle of Englyshe Polycye* goes
further than this and makes a simple equation between the wealth
of merchants and the economic well-being of the country:

> For yef marchaundes were cherysshede to here spede,
> We were not lykely to fayle in ony nede;

> Yff they bee riche, thane in prosperite
> Schalbe oure lande, lordes and comonte.
>
> (482–5)

He then proceeds to eulogise Richard Whittington, the London merchant who died in 1423. His contribution to the wealth and prosperity of England is especially emphasized:

> in worship nowe think I on the sonne
> Of marchaundy Richarde of Whitingdone,
> That loodes sterre and chefe chosen floure.
> Whate hathe by hym oure England of honoure,
> And whate profite hathe bene of his richesse,
> And yet lasteth dayly in worthinesse,
> That penne and papere may not me suffice
> Him to describe, so high he was of prise.
>
> (486–93)

Those towns and cities whose prosperity depended on trade also naturally show themselves acutely aware of its importance. On one of Henry VII's early progresses he was greeted at Bristol by a pageant in which one character first spoke verses about the former prosperity of the city:

> This Towne lefte I in great Prosperitie,
> Havyng Riches and Welthe many folde,
> The Merchaunt, the Artyficier, ev'ryche in his Degre
> Had great Plente both of Silver and Golde
> And lifed in Joye as they desire wolde. . . .

He continued then by pointing out that 'Bristow is fallen into Decaye' and that this would be 'Irrecuparable' unless the King showed his favour to the city and its people:

> that a due Remedy
> By you, ther herts Hope and Comfort in this Distresse,
> Proveded be, at your Leyser convenyently,
> To your Navy and Cloth-making, whereby I gesse
> The wele of this Towne, standeth in Sikernesse,
> May be maynteigned, as they have bee
> In days hertofor in Prosperitie.[22]

Trade, of course, was a chancy business. Both community and individual alike were hit by economic recessions and changes in political alliances. Valuable ships and their cargoes were sometimes lost in storms or pirated. The rich squire in *The Childe of Bristowe* advised his son against becoming a merchant because trading 'is but caswelte'. But, in the fifteenth century, there were increasingly men who, like the 'Childe', ignored the risk and bound themselves apprentice for 'vii yer' the 'science for to lere':

> Hit hath ever be myn avise
> to lede my lyf by marchandise
> to lerne to bye and selle;
> That good getyn by marchantye,
> it is truthe, as thynketh me,
> there with will I melle.[23]

For the fortunate and the skilful the rewards of trade were great, as those engaged in it realized very well. A knowing, and accurate, rhymed proverb quoted in a fifteenth-century commercial handbook for the instruction of merchants referred to the profits made by Bristol men from their trade with Ireland:

> Heryng of Slegothe
> and salmon of Bame
> heis made in Brystowe
> many a ryche man.

A proverbial couplet alludes to the prosperity of a Dartmouth shipowning family:

> Blow the wind high blow the wind low
> It bloweth good to Hauleys hoe.

In a window of his house the Nottinghamshire merchant John Barton, who had grown wealthy on the wool trade, had set a rhymed posy which gave thanks to God and recognized the source of his prosperity:

> I thank God and ever shall
> It is the sheep hath payed for all.

Nor did his piety consist only in words. On his death in 1491 Barton was buried in his local church of St Giles at Holme beside Newark, which had been substantially rebuilt in a lavish perpendicular style with his money. Even in the church, however, the connection with the wool trade is obvious, for one of the frieze of shields over the two-storeyed south porch bears the arms of the Staple of Calais.[24]

Even such obvious piety as this, however, did not save merchants from the opprobrium of the moralists. Nor did that line of reasoning which said that the commercial activity of merchants was necessary for the public good, nor that the profit merchants made was justified because it paid for the labour they had expended in transporting goods, nor that their profits compensated for the risks they took, though these views were frequently expounded.[25] Merchants were economic individualists in a society whose values did not fully allow for their activities, a society which held that it was the duty of all men to work for the common good. The feeling was inescapable that merchants exploited other men: they bought cheap and sold dear. They helped themselves grossly, when the theory said that they should have laboured only for enough to sustain themselves and keep up their social positions. Merchants are frequently denounced by sermon writers. According to the author of a sermon preserved in BM Harley MS 2398 the merchant's lust for gain on earth was likely to destroy him:

> ne suffreth him nouȝt to have slepe, ne reste, by niȝte ne by day; bot maketh him travayle in water and in londe, in chele and in hete, in feyntyse and in werynesse. Ryȝt as a spythur destroyeth here-self in makynge a webbe for to take a flye, ryȝt so the coveytous man destroyeth his owene body for to gete thys worldes goed. . . .[26]

And elsewhere writer after writer, as G. R. Owst has shown, exposes the 'wilis and falsede' practised by merchants in order to make a profit from the gullible public. In contemporary verses the same disapproval is also to be found. A stanza from a carol on *Money, Money,* from Royal MS 17B xlvii emphasizes the enormity of their avarice:

money to Incresse, marchandys neuer to cease
wyth many a sotell wyle;
Men say the wolde for syluer and golde
Ther owne faders begyle.
(*HP*, 51, 33–6)

This author does not enlarge upon the 'many a sotell wyle' likely
to be used, but no doubt the sort of thing he had in mind appears
in some lines of the metrical *Sermon on the Feast of Corpus Christi*
which denounce those wholesalers who exploit the poor by corner-
ing the market in order to create a shortage and force up prices:

He buggeþ Corn aȝeyn þe ȝere
And kepeþ hit til hit beo dere.
'Þer-of he doþ wysliche,
ȝif he departe hit skilfulliche.'
Nay forsoþe þenkeþ he nouht
To pore men parten ouht;
Bouȝte he neuere so good chepe,
He reweþ nout þe pore wepe;
He ne rouhte how al þe worlde ȝode,
So þat his owne biȝete were goode.
(51–60)

To those poor men who ask for corn his answer is 'Goþ or wey,
Corn is dere', but, says the sermon writer, the unscrupulous trader
will regret this, for when he comes to enter heaven God will say:
'Goþ to helle, for heuene is dere' (92).[27] Elsewhere appear complaints about the use of false weights and measures, and a few jibes
against particular traders, such as Lydgate's three stanzas *Against
Millers and Bakers*. They should form a guild and build a chapel
under the pillory:

Let mellerys and bakerys gadre hem a gilde,
And alle of assent make a fraternite;
Vndir the pillory a litil chapell bylde,
(*Minor Poems*, II, 15, 17–19)

an appropriate place, he says, since they ought to spend most of
their time there as a result of their false dealing.

These criticisms of merchants and traders were part of a more general feeling of unease at the acquisitiveness and materialism of contemporary society. The author of the *Italian Relation* felt that the Englishman's concern with money was worth commenting upon, and disapproving poems on the power of money and the lengths men would go to in order to acquire it were frequent. Of course, poems on money were not new, but certain factors (also touched upon in contemporary verses) made this type of poem particularly relevant in the fifteenth century.²⁸ The expansion in trade made it necessary for the financial system to be flexible, and the use of money became general. Former methods of payment in goods were on the decline and attempts to revert to them met with resistance. In the early 1460s, for example, the author of *A Trade Policy* complained on behalf of the workers in the cloth industry that they were being forced to take half of their goods in merchandise:

> Lytyll þei take for theyre labur, yet halff ys merchaundyse.
> Alas! for rewth, yt ys gret pyte,
>
> (*HP*, 70, 87–8)

and he follows this up with a demand that they should be 'payd in good mone'. The severe treatment of those who debased the coinage of the realm is further evidence of the importance of money. In 1410 the MS Digby 102 poet had spoken against those who clipped coins:

> That clippen money, þey haue þe curs
> ffoure tymes in þe ȝere,
>
> (IX, 49–50)

and in 1415 the clipping, filing or washing of coins was made a treasonable offence.

The increase in the demand for money meant that great care had to be taken to maintain supplies of bullion. England was not rich in precious metals and most had to be imported. The author of *The Libelle of Englyshe Polycye* recognized that the 'plate of sylvere, of wegges gode and sure' that the Germans brought from Bohemia and Hungary was 'encrese ful grete unto thys londe' One of his

arguments in favour of consolidating English positions in Ireland
was that Ireland (he thought) was rich in precious metals, and could
be used as a source of bullion to remedy England's shortage:

> For of sylvere and golde there is the oore
> Amonge the wylde Yrishe, though they be pore,
> For they ar rude and can thereone no skylle;
> So that, if we had there pese and gode wylle
> To myne and fyne and metall for to pure,
> In wylde Yrishe myght we fynde the cure.
>
> (686–91)

He went on to speak of the fine quality of Irish gold. In a rather
tortuous passage the author of *A Trade Policy* argued that a mint
should be built close to silver mines in England, so that the silver
could be coined there and some of it used to pay the workers
('Wherby þat the wyrkfolk myght trewly be payd' 119). This, he
said, would result in more men wishing to work in the silver mines
and an increase in the output of silver:

> ayenst oon man then schuld ye haue x,
> for the good payment of the wyrkmen;
> And the moe peopyll þat wyrk in þe mynys,
> The more syluer schuld be had vp at all tymys.

> And thus þe kyng schold be enrychyd for his parte
> More than he is now, I dare playnly Ioparte,
> After the rate of theyre gret wynnyng
> The wich schold be to hym a profytable thyng.
>
> (*HP*, 70, 121–8)

But bullion remained scarce, and the weight of both gold and
silver coins was reduced during the century. Various acts of
parliament also forbade the export of money, but it still went on.
The author of *The Libelle of Englyshe Polycye* blames the Italian
merchants for taking English gold abroad:

> Also they bere the golde oute of thys londe
> And souke the thryfte awey oute of oure honde.
>
> (396–7)

It was even necessary for an act of parliament to forbid goldsmiths from melting down coins for use in gilding objects. The currency crisis was at times so acute that one writer could say that coin was the best merchandise of all:

> In marchandys who can deuyse
> so good a ware, I say?
> at al tymys the best ware ys
> Euer redy money.
>
> (*HP*, 51, 29–32)

This shortage of money had the effect of emphasizing the acquisitiveness of fifteenth-century society. Money represented wealth; it made possible the good things of life; with it one could acquire status. There was, it is true, a body of opinion which warned against the dangers of acquisitiveness, particularly of money. A brief gnomic verse, for example, from Caius College Cambridge MS 261 provides a warning, in traditional terms, that those who hoard money are guilty of avarice, and that they burden themselves with the cares of wealth:

> Spende, and god schal sende,
> Spare, and ermor care;
> non peni, non ware;
> non catel, non care.
>   go, peni, go.
>
> (*SL XIV and XV*, 60, 1–5)

There were also arguments which reconciled men to poverty, such as that which said that the poor man was at least secure against the uncertainty of Fortune, since he could be cast down no lower. Hoccleve, in 1412, in a passage lamenting his own lack of money, rehearses this argument in order to console himself:

> I thought eek, if I in-to povert creepe
> Than am I entred in-to sykirnesse.
>
> (*Regement*, 43–4)

But in the next stanza but one he impatiently rejects it on the grounds that the only 'certainty' ('sykirnesse') provided by poverty is the certainty that one is miserable:

'Allas!' þoghte I, 'what sykirnesse ys þat
To lyue ay seur of greef and of nuisaunce.'

(57–8)

And increasingly, in the fifteenth century, the practical and the
ambitious found no virtue in poverty. Peter Idley, for example,
devotes several stanzas to warning his son that 'nede causeth
sorow to multeplye'. Poverty, he says, is spiritually dangerous,
because it can make a man take to crime: 'She dryueth a man to
thefte and murdre alsoo'; it degrades a man so that he has 'to
begge and borowe with shame'; and makes him unhappy 'And
wrastell with the worlde in care and woo'. It is true that he also
warns his son that the misuse of wealth could cause him to have
'Helle perpetually to thyn enhabitacion', but he is emphatic that
wealth in itself is no bad thing:

> sith the world first beganne
> The goodis temporall in euery lande
> If they be in the possession of a good man
> Then be they good.
>
> (I, 701–4)

He insists that he 'who hath goodis temporall hath a noble frende'
(684) and that the man 'without goodis temporall may not longe
endure' (672). Above all he extols the virtues of money:

> Who that hath money shal haue men at nede
> And frendis not a fewe to defende hym of his foo;
> Richesse in euery reawme spareth not to spede:
> He is Godde vndre God, goo wher he goo,
>
> (687–90)

with which, he says, one may 'purchase blisse and voyde payn'.

Though Idley was not blind to the possible misuses of wealth he
passes over such considerations quickly. There were others, however, who deplored, in greater detail, what they took to be the
contemporary obsession with money and the disproportionate
power that money came to have. The author of the carol *Gramersy*

Myn Owyn Purs from BM MS Sloane 2593 regrets that money wins a man friends, who are lost when he is poor:

> Quan I have in myn purs inow,
> I may have bothe hors and plow,
> And also fryndis inow,
> Thorow the vertu of myn purs.

> Quan my purs gynnyght to slak,
> And ther is nowt in my pak,
> They wil scyn, 'Go farwil, Jak;
> Thou xalt non more drynke with us.
>
> (*EEC* No. 390, 1–8)

The *Narracio de Domino Denario* from MS Cotton Galba E ix treats money, in the conventional way, as the all-powerful knight 'Sir Peny':

> Sir peny ouerall gettes þe gre,
> both in burgh and in cete,
> in castell and in towre;
> with-owten owþer spere or schelde
> es he þe best in frith or felde,
> and stalworthest in stowre.
>
> (*SL XIV and XV*, 58, 94–9)

He expands on this by showing how 'both ȝong & alde' of all ranks of society are in the power of 'Sir Peny' and corrupted by him. He is master 'In kinges court'; he controls spiritual matters to the extent that 'He may by both heuyn and hell'; women may be seduced through money 'be þai neuer so strange of will'; money corrupts the law because 'þe domes-men he mase so blind', and 'he makes mani be forsworne'. Another author, writing of *The Power of the Purse* from MS Eng. poet. e I makes the familiar points that money is necessary if one is to 'haue out to do with þe law to plete', if 'þou be a marchant to by or to sell', or if 'þou be a lettryd man' with ambitions 'to bere estat in scole'. But particularly he warns that money is necessary for social advancement:

> If þou be a ȝeman, a gentyllman wold be,
> Into sum lordes cort þan put þou þe;

> Lok þou haue spendyng larg & plente,
> & alwey þe peny redy to tak to,
> (*SL XIV and XV*, 59, 5–8)

—and he gives the same advice to the gentleman who wishes to be a squire, and the squire who aspires to knighthood. The author of *Money, Money* from BM MS Royal 17 B xlvii stresses the way in which all ranks of society are obsessed by money, and deplores the fact that some will even take to robbery in order to obtain it:

> sume for money lye by the wey
> another mannes purse to gett;
> but they that long vse yt amonge
> ben hangyd by the neke.
> (*HP*, 51, 61–4)

But he regrets most of all that the value set on a man is not determined by his abilities, but by the amount of money he has:

> Yt ys all-wayes sene now-a-dayes
> That money makythe the man.
> (79–80)

Many other poems of this sort are extant which make these or similar points. In some, the author is capable of an ironic self-awareness which tends to undercut his criticisms. The author of this last poem quoted, for example, laments his own lack of money while at the same time deploring the obsession of contemporary society with it:

> money, money, thow gost away
> & wylt not byde wyth me.
> (refrain)

But despite all this, and despite the fact that many of the criticisms made are traditional, the conclusion is inescapable that the acquisitiveness and materialism of an increasingly money-oriented society greatly offended many contemporaries, who, in the predictable way, lament the passing of the old values.

But the materialism of the fifteenth-century Englishman did not show itself only in the acquisition of money. Though coin itself was scarce most classes of society, except for the landowning aristocracy, were better off than they had been previously. This prosperity they used to provide themselves with houses of greater comfort, food of a more luxurious sort, and clothes of increased richness and extravagance. Fashionable apparel, in fact, was the object of much criticism. Fashions changed throughout the century, of course (and this was one of the things for which they were ridiculed), but the nature of the criticism remained fairly constant. It was widely felt that the fashions were unnatural, ridiculous and immoral, and that they were examples of the deadly sin of pride. Hoccleve, in 1412, has the Beggar in the Prologue to the *Regement of Princes* complain about the extravagance of contemporary male attire with its wide gowns and long, full sleeves:

> But þis me þinkiþ an abusioun,
> To se on walke in gownes of scarlet,
> xij ȝerdes wyd, wit pendant sleues downe
> On þe grounde, & þe furrour þer-in set
> Amountyng vnto twenty pound or bet.
> (421–5)

He also has harsh words for the tippets that were worn:

> Also ther is another newe get,
> A foul wast of cloth and an excessyf;
> Ther goth no lesse in a mannes tipet
> Than of brood cloth a yerde, by my lyf.
> (449–52)

He points out the impracticality of these fashions, particularly for the servants of lords. If a lord is attacked by his enemies servants wearing fashionable dress would literally not be able to lift a hand in his defence because of the weight of their garments:

> His armys two han ryght ynow to done,
> And sumwhat more, his sleeues vp to holde.
> (470–1)

The only use for these garments, he says, is to sweep the streets:

> Now hath þis lord but litil neede of broomes
> To swepe a-wey þe filthe out of the street,
> Syn syde sleues of penylees gromes
> Wile it vp likke, be it drye or weet.
>
> (533–6)

But though such fashions are impractical and absurd, such is the contemporary vogue for them that people will impoverish themselves, says the Beggar, and deprive themselves of food so that they can be well dressed:

> ffor al þe good þat men may repe or glene,
> Wasted is in outrageous aray.
>
> (495–6)

Yet, he laments, these lavishly dressed men are esteemed:

> Who now moost may bere on his bak at ones
> Of cloth and furrour, hath a fressch renoun.
> He is 'a lusty man' clept for þe nones.
>
> (484–6)

Towards the middle of the century fashions had changed. Peter Idley, writing between 1445 and 1450, comments upon the vogue for long hair: 'the here is not shorn/But hangeth downe to the browe beforne' (II B, 25–6), and on the ridiculously short and inelegant doublets:

> They be cutted on the buttok even aboue the rompe.
> Euery good man truly such shappe lothes;
> It makyth hym a body short as a stompe,
> And if they shull croke, knele othir crompe,
> To the middes of the backe the gowne woll not reche.
>
> (44–8)

From about this time too come various comments on the extravagance of women's fashions. Lydgate, in a poem on the horned head-dresses women wore, points out, with a wealth of learned reference, that classical heroines such as Helen, Penelope, Polyxena and Lucrece did not wear horned head-dresses yet were accounted beautiful. He characterizes them as 'A thyng contrarie to ffemynyte' and attributes the wearing of them to pride:

> They haue despit, and ageyn concyence,
> Lyst nat of pryde, ther hornes cast away.
> (*Minor Poems*, II, 38, 39–40)

Less learned, but no less pointed, are some lines from MS Ashmole 59 which call upon Christ to destroy the extravagance of contemporary fashions, particularly womens' head-dresses:

> Fell dovne þe pryde of wommens hornes,
> And suffre hem longer with longe tayles
> Ne none oþer vicyous entayles,
> Of noþer of males ne femayles,
> Ne hodes, ne tyres lyche carrake sayle.
> (*HP*, 53, 2–6)

The criticism is made all the more effective here by the fact that the author recalls that Christ's head-dress was 'þe crowne of thornes' (1).

From this period too come some of the earliest poems against 'gallants'—a *genre* which was to continue to be popular into the sixteenth century. The treatment of one of these overdressed braggarts in *Huff, A Galaunt* from MS Rawlinson poet. 34 is typical. The poet begins by describing the gallant's extravagant clothes: his 'stomager . . . byforne', his 'pykyd schone', his 'gownys be sett with pleytys fele', his long hair 'ffowre enchys by-neth hys ere', and his 'hosyn of red'. But it emerges that the gallant is not such a splendid creature as he appears: he has a purse as part of his apparel, but no money in it:

> Galaunt, by thy gyrdyl hangyth a purss;
> Ther-in ys neyther peny nor crosse.
> (*HP*, 52, 33–4)

Furthermore, though the gallant looks fine from the front, his 'schyrtte by-hynd ys all to-torne', and though he wears a dagger the poet considers his bravery 'worse than nought'. He is fit only for playing with the 'iij dysse' he has in his purse, and for petty theft:

'Thow art ful abyl to stele a horse' (39). Much the same position is assumed by the author of the verses *On the Corruption of Public Manners* from BM MS Harley 372. He comments on the long hair, extravagant hats, short doublets and 'piked' shoes of fashionable contemporaries but sets this against his opinion that they are 'hertlesse', 'witlesse' and 'thriftlesse':

> Ye prowd galonttes hertlesse,
> With your hyghe cappis witlesse,
> And youre schort gownys thriftlesse,
> Have brought this londe in gret hevynesse.
>
> With youre longe peked schone,
> Therfor your thrifte is almost don,
> And with youre long here into your eyen,
> Han brought this lond to gret pyne.
>
> (*PPS*, II, p. 251)

Much more elaborate and much more ambitious, but still basically in the same tradition, is the *Treatyse of A Gallant*, which also seems to date from somewhat later.[29] As usual there is much comment on the fashions themselves: on the 'warrocked hoode' and 'parrocked pouche' of the gallant, on the perverseness of 'men arayed as women/and woman as man', on the 'many poyntes' on contemporary dress, the 'taters' of contemporary cloaks, the 'purfled garmentes', the 'small gyrdynge in the waste', the

> rolled hodes/stuffed with flockes
> The newe broched doublettes/open at the brestes
> Stuffed with pectoll/of theyr loues smockes
> Theyr gownes and they cotes schredde all in lystes,
>
> (183–6)

the 'typettes be wrythen/lyke to a chayne', and 'All these newe bulwarkes' worn around the hose. The author blames the extravagance of these fashions for the sinfulness of contemporary society:

> As in this name Galaunt/ye may expresse
> Seuen letters for some cause in especyall
> That fygureth the vii deedly synnes & theyr wretchednes

and he follows this up with an acrostic on GALAWNT. More precisely, he complains that the fashions are unnatural ('dysfygurynge nature'), conducive to lechery

> Our women in theyr parte/laboure as they may
> In theyr aray with chere and countenaunce.
> Our men on theyr syde make them fresshe and gay
> And laboure to purchace womens plesaunce,
>
> (155–8)

and ruinous to the country's economy: 'we have exyled our welthe'.

The criticisms of contemporary fashions cited up to now have principally had a moral basis. But there was a very real sense, shared by many, that these fashions were politically dangerous. George Ashby advises Prince Edward of the need for legislation:

> Lete not the pouer Comyns be dysguised
> Ne haue precious clothe in theire vesture,
> But in thair excesse be ther supprised
> And obserue a resonable mesure.
>
> (*Poems*, II, 534–7)

Statutes of Apparel did, in fact, exist, but they were ineffective, as a piece of legislation dated 1463 recognized. This refers to the 'dyvers Ordenauncez and Statutez' enacted earlier to the effect that the Commons should 'use nor were noon inordynat Aray', and continues '. . . which Statutez and Ordenauncez notwithstondyng, for lak of punysshment and puttyng them in due execution, the Commyns of this youre seid Reame, as well men as women, have used, and daily usen, excessive and inordynat Arayes . . .'. Before setting out precisely what dress it was permissible for the various ranks of society to wear the Statute defines the reasons behind the prohibition of extravagant dress: '. . . the grete displeasure of God, enpoverysshing of this youre seid Reame, and enriching of straunge Reames and Cuntrees, and fynall distroiyng of the Husbondrie of this youre seid Reame.'[30] Contemporary poets frequently argue in the same way and stress that extravagant fashions render the country decadent and impoverished. The author of the

Treatyse of a Gallant contrasts what he took to be the former state of England—rich, moral, respected

> Ryght late stode our londe in suche prosperyte
> Of chyvalry, manhode, and ryche marchaundyse,
> Thrughe all crysten realmes sprange our felycyte . . .

—with what by implication is its present state of sin and poverty. Frequently he regrets that 'our Englysshe nacyon', that 'sumtyme was so wyse', should have allowed itself to 'be so blynde' as to indulge in the extravagant fashions which, he claims, came from France:

> O Fraunce/why dyde not these galauntes abyde there?
> England may wayle that euer it came here.
>
> (55–6)

The Beggar in the Prologue to Hoccleve's *Regement of Princes* believes that contemporary fashions should be resisted because they are dangerous to the country:

> O engelond, stande vp-ryght on thy feet!
> So foul a wast in so symple degree
> Banysshe! or sore it schal repente the.
>
> (537–9)

The anonymous author of a single stanza squib from MS Corpus Christi College Oxford 274 cites

> Furres of ferly bestes,
> Costefulle crouperes with crestes,
>
> (*PPS*, II, p. 252)

and 'Robes made of schredes' as among the things which have 'schent Englond'.

It was also widely felt that contemporary fashions were a mark of unwarranted social aspiration when they were worn by the lower classes, and ultimately destructive of those niceties of social distinction which social theories defined. Legislation, in fact, was careful to say that people should wear only that dress appropriate to their ranks ('oonly accordyng to their degreez'). The author of a sermon from BM MS Additional 41321 forcefully makes the point about social aspiration and furthermore blames the extravagance of their dress to the fact that the lower classes were demanding higher wages:

Nouȝ also the comyn peple is hie stied into the synne of pride. For now a wrecchid cnave, that goth to the plouȝ and to carte, that hath no more good but serveth fro ȝer to ȝer for his liflode, there-as sumtyme a white curtel and a russet gowne wolde have served suchon ful wel, now he muste have a fresch doublet of fyve schillynges or more the price; and above, a costli gowne with bagges hangynge to his kne, and iridelid undir his girdil as a newe ryven roket, and an hood on his heved, with a thousande ragges on his tipet; and gaili hosid an schood as thouȝ it were a squyer of cuntre; a dagger harneisid with selver bi his gurdel, or ellis it were not worth a pese. This pride schulle ther maistirs a-buye, whanne that thei schul paie hir wages. For, there-as thei weren wont to serve for x or xii schillingis in a ȝer, now thei musten have xx oor thritti and his lyverei also therto; not for he wol do more werk, but for to meynten with that pride.[31]

The Beggar in the Prologue to the *Regement of Princes* is also worried by the blurring of social distinctions, and, characteristically, looks to the past for a damaging comparison:

> Som tyme, after men myghten lordes knowe
> Be there array, from oþer folke; but now
> A man schal stody and musen a long throwe
> whiche is whiche.
>
> (442–5)

He is aware that this situation is somehow a threat to the upper classes, for he advises 'lordes'

> If twixt yow and youre men no difference
> Be in array, lesse is youre reuerence.
>
> (447–8)

Peter Idley is even more explicit. Not only does he complain about the blurring of rank—

A man shall not now kenne a knave from a knyght,
ffor al be like in clothyng and array

(II B, 50–1)

—but he also relates this observation to his comments on the proper ordering of the social structure. He argues the necessity for 'Eche man to kenne hymsilf and his better', and for dress to vary according to rank:

And as they be in ordre set of degree,
Right so shall her clothyng and arraie bee.

(69–70)

In heaven, he says, 'an ordre is Kepte', and unless on earth there are 'Somme to obeie and somme to gouerne above' all 'welthe, worship and love' will be destroyed.

The theoretical assumption (which underlies Idley's comments here) that society was, in its perfect state, a hierarchy of classes which depended upon each other was never seriously challenged by a theory of comparable weight in the fifteenth century. But various developments in agriculture, industry, commerce, finance and fashion brought the traditional theory into conflict with contemporary realities for which it did not allow. As feudalism declined the relevance of the social theory it produced also diminished. Whereas feudal society was hierarchic, fairly static and reasonably protective, the society which was beginning to emerge in fifteenth-century England put more stress on individuality and self-reliance. A man's possibilities were not as limited by the conditions of his birth as they had been. A certain amount of social mobility was possible—at least, as far up the scale as the lesser gentry. William Paston, for example, the son of Clement Paston who was 'a good plain husbandman', became a rich landowner, a Justice of the Common Pleas in 1429, married Agnes the daughter and heiress of a knight, Sir Edmund Berry, and in 1463 his grandson was knighted. In the towns and villages journeymen could become merchants; artisans sometimes became skilled craftsmen or traders. In rural society bondmen could become tenant farmers, or could leave their own districts and become wage labourers. Some, particularly professional retainers, lawyers and merchants, cheerfully accepted the new possibilities that society offered and exploited them to amass wealth, to achieve influence, to buy land, to build houses and to wear fine clothes. Those imbued with the more traditional notions of social theory, on the other hand, saw everywhere in contemporary society only extravagance, ambition, greed and self-interest, which they felt were destroying the set of values which they accepted and disrupting the stability of the social order they knew.

NOTES

[1] *Middle English Sermons* ed. W. O. Ross, EETS OS 209, 1940, p. 311.

[2] 'Middle English Verses of Protest', *Anglia* 78, 1960, p. 193.

[3] See Robbins *HP*, p. 324, for a text.

[4] Ed. J. R. Kreuzer, *RES* 14, 1938, pp. 321–3, and for another text R. H. Robbins, *SL XIV and XV*, No. 111.

[5] But compare the version of this in MS Corpus Christi College Oxford 237 f. 237 v, printed by Thomas Wright *PPS* II, p. 252, which reads in line 1 'Now ys Yngland alle in fyght.' Is this a reference to the civil wars?

[6] *MLN* 70, 1955, 473–6.

[7] See the important article of K. B. McFarlane, 'Parliament and Bastard Feudalism', *TRHS*, 25, 1944, pp. 53–79, to which my account is indebted.

[8] Quoted by G. R. Owst, *Literature and Pulpit in Medieval England*, Cambridge 1933, p. 337.

[9] Quoted by G. R. Owst, *op. cit.*, p. 311.

[10] Quoted by G. R. Owst, *op. cit.*, p. 337.

[11] *Repressor* ed. C. Babington, Rolls Series 19, 1860, II, 306 (quoted by McFarlane, *op. cit.*).

[12] See J. R. Lander, *Stability and Conflict in Fifteenth Century England*, 1969, p. 167.

[13] Quoted by G. R. Owst *op. cit.*, p. 324.

[14] Quoted by G. R. Owst, *op. cit.*, p. 324.

[15] *Rotuli Parliamentorum* V, 285.

[16] Quoted by Jonathan Blow, 'Nibley Green 1470: the Last Private Battle Fought in England', *History Today* II, 1962, pp. 598–610.

[17] For the incidents referred to in this paragraph see A. Abram, *Social Life in England in the Fifteenth Century*, 1909, pp. 80–8 where full references are given.

[18] *Ibid.*, pp. 89–90 for references.

[19] *8th Report of the Historical MSS Commission*, p. 268 (quoted by H. S. Bennett, *The Pastons and their England*, Cambridge 1922, p. 168).

[20] Quoted by G. R. Owst, *op. cit.*, p. 341.

[21] C. L. Kingsford, 'Extracts from the First Version of Hardyng's Chronicle' *EHR* 27, 1912, p. 749.

[22] See Sydney Anglo, *Spectacle Pageantry and Early Tudor Poetry*, Oxford 1969, pp. 33–4.

[23] Ed. C. Hopper in *The Camden Miscellany* No. 4, 1859. See further E. M. Carus Wilson, *Medieval Merchant Venturers* 1957, p. 81.

[24] For the verse on Ireland see *The Noumbre of Weyghtes* (BM MS Cotton Vespasian E ix) f. 100d quoted by E. M. Carus Wilson, *op. cit.*, p. 21. For the verse on Dartmouth see A. S. Green, *Town Life in the Fifteenth Century*, 1894, II, 73; and for John Barton's posy see *Testamenta Eboracensia* IV, 61 (quoted by E. E. Power in *Studies in English Trade in the Fifteenth Century* ed. E. E. Power and M. M. Postan, 1933, p. 41). For details of St Giles Holme beside Newark see Nikolaus Pevsner, *The Buildings of England: Nottinghamshire*, 1951, pp. 83–4.

[25] On this whole question see R. H. Tawney, *Religion and the Rise of Capitalism*, 1926, Chapter 1.

[26] Quoted by G. R. Owst, *op. cit.*, p. 352.

[27] Ed. C. Horstmann, *Minor Poems of the Vernon MS*, EETS OS 98, 1892, I, 168–97.

[28] On the tradition of medieval venality satire see J. A. Yunck, *The Lineage of Lady Meed*, University of Notre Dame 1963.

[29] Ed. F. J. Furnivall, *Ballads from MSS*, 1868–72, I, 445–53.

[30] *Rotuli Parliamentorum* V, 504.

[31] Quoted by Owst, *op. cit.*, p. 369.

10 : English Society III : Verses of Protest and Revolt

In 1276–7 the tenants of the village of Stoughton in Leicestershire complained before the royal court that the Abbot of Leicester, William Schepished, had imposed upon them illegal labour services. R. H. Hilton points out that their attempt to get legal redress from the King's court is significant in that it indicates 'that the villeins had considerable confidence that they would succeed'. But their complaint failed and the court, amongst other things, confirmed the fact that they were unfree. An eighty-three line Latin poem, perhaps written by a canon of the abbey, triumphantly derides their presumption, and points out that they will stay villeins, with no hope of social advancement:

> Quid faciet servus nisi serviet, et puer eius?
> Purus servus erit et libertate carebit.
> Judicium legis probat hoc et curia legis.[1]

Most peasants of the time must reluctantly have accepted this view. Yet over the next two centuries, with the decline of feudalism, the conditions of the peasantry began to improve considerably. With the break-up of the large demesnes peasants were able to rent and even buy land. Labour services owed by a bondman to his lord were increasingly commuted for money. Personal bondage declined, though it did not entirely disappear, for some lords still valued the profits from such institutions as *chevage* (the sum paid by a bond-man for permission to live outside the manor), *heriot* (payable from the possessions of a dead bondman), or *merchet* (the sum paid by a bondman for permission to give his children in marriage). Moreover, food prices remained over the fifteenth century fairly stable, and because of the shortage of labour after the Black Death, and despite legislation to peg them, the wages of labourers tended to rise.

But though conditions had improved they were not, by any stretch of the imagination, good, and because they were poor and exploited the lower classes complain, sometimes in verses. These verses are unfortunately few in number. The means by which verse was usually preserved did not favour the survival of that reflecting lower-class sympathies, for those people who collected verses in manuscripts tended to be from the aristocracy and the middle classes. In addition the lower classes were the least well educated, and the least literate, and verses intended for them must frequently have had only an oral existence. Some of the poems to be considered in this chapter, for example, though now preserved in written form, were originally oral in their delivery. None the less, a few poems have survived, often in unlikely places—chronicles, city records, legal records, sermons and so on. But whether these are sufficient to give an overall picture of lower-class protest must remain doubtful. Moreover, it is very often difficult to be certain of the intention of these poems, or to attribute them to a specific context or date, and almost all are anonymous.

Bearing these difficulties in mind, it is nevertheless possible to discern a development in this type of verse, and therefore it is necessary first of all to say something about verses prior to the fifteenth century. The tone of the earliest verses representing lower-class opinions is one of resignation, as for example in *The Song of the Husbandman* from BM MS Harley 2253. It is impossible to ascribe this poem to any precise context, but from the language it appears to have been written around 1300 by a south-western author. In technique the poem is highly accomplished—the rhyme scheme is demanding, the alliteration heavy and the poet uses the device of stanza-linking fairly consistently. Yet the point of view represented is that of poor tenant farmers. They are oppressed chiefly by manorial officials:

> þe hayward heteþ vs harm to habben of his;
> þe bailif bockneþ vs bale & weneþ wel do;

> þe wodeward waiteþ vs wo, þat lokeþ vnder rys;
> ne mai vs ryse no rest, rycheis ne ro.
> þus me pileþ þe pore þat is of lute pris.
>
> (*HP*, 2, 15–19)

But the weight of exchequer taxation, presumably to pay for Edward I's wars, also causes them hardship:

> ʒet comeþ budeles, wiþ ful muche bost;
> 'greyþe me seluer to þe grene wax;
> þou art writen y my writ, þat þou wel wost!'
>
> (37–9)

In order to meet these demands each farmer has to sell his equipment, his livestock and even his seed corn, thus rendering himself practically destitute. It is impossible to doubt the reality of the grievances this poet isolates for comment, or his passionate concern about the plight of those who suffer under them. But for all this he accepts the situation in that he feels he can do nothing about it. There is no revolt, scarcely the indignation one might expect, only the despair of the last line: 'as god in swynden anon as so forte swynke' (72).

The only alternative to this resignation seems to have been a whimsical escapism. So the author of *The Man in the Moon*, again from BM MS Harley 2253, conceives the well-known folk story in his own contemporary terms.[2] According to the story the 'Man in the moon' was supposed to have been a peasant who had been caught cutting sticks from the lord's hedges. He had forfeited a pledge to the bailiff as a token of his guilt, but rather than face his punishment it seems he has fled the manor. The poet plans to help the fugitive peasant by recovering his pledge from the bailiff, whom he plans to invite home and get drunk:

> We shule preye þe haywart hom to vr hous
> Ant maken hym at heyse for þe maystry,
> Drynke to hym deorly of fol god bous,
> Ant oure Dame Douse shal sitten hym by.
> When þat he is dronke ase a dreynt mous,
> Þanne we shule borewe þe wed ate bayly.
>
> (27–32)

This is clearly not in any way a conventional political poem, though the situation it describes—a peasant has been forced to flee the manor for an offence against the vert—was not an unusual one. But the humorous and indirect treatment prevents the poet from seeing the situation in simple social terms. He has some awareness of the problem in these terms, and his sympathy with the cold and fearful peasant, though humorously expressed, is convincing enough. But he evades the social issue through a whimsical solution to the problem. Perhaps no solution other than the exploitation of the human weaknesses of the representatives of manorial authority was conceivable to him.

Somewhat more than this—a 'beginning of hope' among the lower classes for better conditions is apparent in *The Land of Cockaygne*, if A. L. Morton's reading of it is accepted.[3] It is difficult to judge the intention of this poem: it is certainly in part a clever anti-clerical satire, but the utopia it describes seems intended by the poet to be available only to the lower classes:

> whose wl com þat lond to,
> ful grete penance he mot do;
> Seue ȝere in swineis dritte
> he mote wade, wol ȝe iwitte,
> al anon vp to þe chynne,
> so he schal þe lond winne. . . .
> (*HP*, 48, 177–82)

The essentially lower-class sympathies of the writer are further indicated by the fact that these lines seem to be his own, for the French poem on which this is in part based would admit only those of somewhat higher rank: 'Esquiers, vadletz, e serjauntz' and forbid entry to 'ribaldz e a pesauntz'.[4] But that the poem is basically wishful and not reformist is shown by the terms in which the paradise is described: there is no work, plenty of food, the rivers are of 'oile, milk, honi and wine' and the buildings of crystal, green jasper and red coral. The unrealistic and impractical dimension of these aspirations shows that any alleviation to the meanness and hardship of lower-class life was barely conceivable, for as Morton says: 'If the hope had been stronger or better grounded it

M

would not have taken shape as a fantasy, a grotesque dream of a society wished for but not seen as an actual possibility.'

The earliest verses to be written in the context of a revolt date from 1381 when the peasants of Kent and Essex left their manors and marched on London. The immediate cause of the revolt was the imposition of Poll Taxes in 1377, 1379 and 1380, but the manifestoes presented by the rebels at Blackheath and Smithfield mention other things. They demand the abolition of villeinage, that labour services should be based on free contract and that there should be no more lordship except the lordship of the King, that all men should be equal, and that the estates of the Church should be confiscated. This is a somewhat incoherent programme, but it is radical. Similarly, when John Ball preached at Blackheath on the text:

> When Adam dolve and Eve span
> Who was then a gentleman?

he argued the basic equality of all men and the overthrow of the social structure. In the verses associated with the rising, however, radicalism is notably absent. It is possibly a little invidious to seek for political ideas in these verses. Those that survive are intended to buttress the intentions of people already committed to the cause rather than to convince and convert by political argument. None the less, it is surprising that the form and language of these verses is so extremely conventional. R. H. Robbins has shown that John Ball's *Letter I* is only a slightly altered version of a well-known 'abuses of the age' type of poem. He asks that contemporary society be reformed:

> God doe boote for nowe is time,
> (*HP*, 17, 7)

but his criticisms here are not political. Instead he draws attention to contemporary moral failings: 'pride', 'covetise', 'lechery', 'gluttonie', 'envye' and 'sloath'. Verses written by other rebels show these same characteristics: 'Iak trewman' complains about the spread of 'gile' and 'synne', and draws attention to the prevalence of bribery:

trewþe hat bene set under a lokke
and falsness regneth in everylk flokke
No man may come trewþe to
but he syng si dedero,[5]

in lines which may be paralleled elsewhere. Even John Ball's
warnings to the commons of Essex, about trusting only those who
were loyal to the cause, are set out in almost proverbial terms:

be war or þe be wo.
knoweþ ȝour freend fro ȝour foo.
haueþ y-now & seith hoo.
(*HP*, 18, 3–5)

It may be that John Ball and his followers were attempting to play
safe in these verses by using unobjectionable moral commonplaces. It may be, as John Stow suspected, that they are 'full of
riddles and dark sentences', and mean more than they say.[6] But it
is most likely that the rebels had no more appropriate way of
speaking in verse.

The revolt of 1381 failed. The authorities reasserted themselves
and the leaders of the rising were caught and executed. The
demands set out in the manifestoes came to nothing and the
conditions of the lower classes did not immediately improve. The
rising, however, did have a significant effect on opinion. One poet
writing in 1381, who is hostile to the rebels, none the less recognizes
that the revolt had brought the grievances and aspirations of the
lower classes to the notice of all:

Iak strawe made yt stowte
Cum profusa comitiua,
And seyd al schuld hem lowte
Anglorum corpora viua.
(*HP*, 19, 25–8)

Another poet, writing in 1382, says that the rising came as a shock
to the complacency of the aristocracy:

Whon þe Comuynes bigan to ryse
Was non so gret lord, as I gesse,

> Þat þei in herte bigon to gryse
> And leide heore Iolyte in presse,
>
> (*HP*, 20, 17–20)

and his refrain stresses that it 'was a warnyng to beware'. After 1381 awareness of lower-class rights and interests increased, and along with this went a new confidence on the part of the lower classes. It shows immediately in verses of protest, as, for example, in those written by John Berwald of Cottingham near Hull in 1392. In tail-rhyme verses of colloquial vigour and directness, he expresses the solidarity of the lower classes:

> yet will ilke-an hel up other
> and meyntene him als his brother,
> Both in wrong & right,
>
> (*HP*, 21, 7–9)

and insists on their human dignity

> hething will we suffer non—
> Neither of Hobb nor of Ion,
> With what man he be.
>
> (16–18)

To allow themselves to be treated in a less than respectful manner, he adds, would be unnatural ('vnkind' 19).

In the fifteenth century these trends continued. Almost all writers on political affairs stress that the lower classes are important to the well-being of the kingdom, and that they should be treated by their rulers with justice and respect. These are not strikingly new views, but the degree to which they are insisted upon is new. The author of the verses from MS Digby 102, which were written between 1401 and 1421, constantly returns to the topic of the proper treatment of the common people. There are frequent exhortations to those 'that over puple hast gouernaunce' to 'Brynge not a comone in greuaunce' (I, 12); to those who 'leden law' to 'holde no pore men in awe' (IX, 59); and to the rich that they should not revel in their wealth 'and leue þe pore in hunger and pyn' (X, 203). They are to be cursed, he says, who 'Wiþ wrong take pore mennys thrift' (XXI, 58). This author is no radical. He believes that the common people would be 'shent' without 'kyng or gouernour', but since the labours of the common people provide the kingdom's wealth he insists that

> comouns is þe fayrest flour
> þat euere god sette on erþely crown.
>
> (XII, 143–4)

In some verses dated 1401, however, another aspect of his reasoning emerges—a fear that the lower classes will revolt if they are not well treated:

> ffor fawte of lawe ȝif comouns rise,
> þan is a kyngdom most in drede.
> ffor whanne vengeaunce a comouns lede,
> þei do gret harm er þey asses.
>
> (III, 27–30)

Though he does not say as much, he doubtless writes with the disturbances of the previous century and the lesser troubles of his own time in mind. A similar warning comes from Hoccleve in 1412:

> ffor þei þat nought ne haue, with knyfe I-drawe,
> wol on hem þat of good be myghty, renne,
> And hurt hem, and hir houses fire & brenne,
> And robbe and slee, and do al swich folye,
> Whan þer no lawe is, hem to iustifie.
>
> (*Regement*, 2782–6)

Writing some time later George Ashby advised the ill-fated Prince Edward that a king should make certain that the common people were prosperous:

> Kepe youre Comyns bi helpe of your lordeship,
> That they may growe in richesse and worship,
>
> (*Poems*, II, 516–17)

the implication being that he could expect trouble from them if they were impoverished. Clearly, in the fifteenth century there were felt to be both moral and practical reasons for treating the lower classes well.

These attitudes towards the lower classes differ significantly from those expressed by the anonymous canon of Leicester in 1276–7, and the verses of protest also reflect this changed situation. Fifteenth-century writers, it is true, nowhere envisage a society structured in a radically different way from the one in which they lived. But their verses of protest touch on a wider set of grievances than the earlier verses and tend to be more outspoken and violent in their sentiments. The least violent are those fairly general expressions of class antagonism of no precisely determinable intention, such as the verses which are quoted in a sermon in Bodleian MS Lat. theol. d 1, which R. H. Robbins dates 1434:

> Þin ffadere was a bond man,
> Þin moder curtesye non can.
> Euery beste þat leuyth now
> Is of more fredam þan þow.
> (*HP*, 22, 5–8)

This is clearly meant to be an expression of discontent at the bond-man's condition of villeinage, and H. G. Pfander has suggested that it was originally a fragment of a worker's song.[7] But how resentful the bondman is is difficult to decide. Since he feels 'Euery beste' to be freer than he is he has cause for resentment. But he appears to accept his condition and only consoles himself in the last stanza, playing on words, with the realization that the poor man is at least 'free' from the cares of wealth:

> ȝif þou art pore, þan art þou fre.
> ȝif þou be riche, þan woo is þe.
> for but þou spendyte wel ere þou goo,
> þin song for euer is 'well-ay-woo',
> (9–12)

and from the danger of suffering in hell (the implication of the everlasting 'well-ay-woo' of the last line). In another poem, according to R. L. Greene[8] a New Year carol and dated by R. H. Robbins as 1445, the democratic feeling is more definite:

> Anoþer ȝere hit may befall
> Þe lest þat is withyn this hall

To be more mastur þan we all;
Cryste may send now sych a ȝere.

(*HP*, 23, 5–8)

On the face of it this stanza could be simply a commonplace expression of the vagaries of fortune: in a year it may come about that everyone's condition will be altered. For this particular author, though, its implication seems to be that some sort of social mobility is possible, and that therefore it is pointless to be overawed by one's social superiors. This emerges more clearly from the sentiments of the last stanza:

> This lordis that ben wonder grete,
> They threton powre men for to bete;
> Hyt lendith lytull in hur threte;
> Cryste may send sich a yere.
>
> (9–12)

The author's contempt for his social superiors here seems genuine enough. But the uncertainty of his freedom from 'hur threte' is plain from the thrice repeated 'may send' and the poem is basically wishful.

Among the most interesting of these generalized poems is *The Prophecy of the Dice*, which was evidently quite popular since it has survived in five manuscripts. R. H. Robbins suggests that 'one might speculate whether this has any reference to the 1381 revolt', but all the manuscripts of it date from the fifteenth century and the poem's generalized sentiments belong as well to this period as to the previous century:

> Euermore schalle the ⚅ be the best cast on the dyce;
> Whan that ⚀ beryth vp the ⚅ ynglond schal be an paradice.
> And ⚁ and ⚃ set al on oone syde,
> Then schal the name of the ⚅ spring vonder wyde.
> ⚃ set A-side and ⚋ clene schent,
> ye schal have a new king At a new parlement.
> ⚅ schal vp and ⚀ schal vnder . . . .
>
> (*HP*, 46, 1–7)

As it stands this is enigmatic, but it differs from other dice poems in that it clearly has a political significance. In the Trinity College MS 516 version the various numbers are glossed in Latin: one represents *rex*, the King; two *bilingue*, perhaps those who speak French and English, but more likely flatterers; three *proditores*, traitors; four *domini*, the lords; five *religiosi*, the clergy; and six *vulgus*, the people. Read with this gloss, the poem becomes a protest of distinctively lower-class sympathies with emphasis on removing flatterers and traitors and disregarding the lords and the clergy. The attitude to the King is interesting. Usually, in verse of this sort, the King is seen as a friend to the lower classes, their protector against corrupt officials, avaricious judges, overbearing lords and so on. But here, from line 6, it appears that the removal of the King is argued, and from line 7 it seems that the desired state of things is one in which the King is subjected to the will of the people. On the other hand, 'beryth vp' in line 2 may mean 'support', in which case the envisaged situation would be the usual one in which the King and the lower orders stood together. This interpretation is supported by the last line of the poem: 'Yet schal the ▦ ber the pryce, and the ▯ schal helpe ther-to' (10). Popular resentment was usually directed at those most immediately in authority over the people.

The conditions and the grievances of the agrarian lower classes are touched upon in two remarkable mystery plays written around 1425 by the same author and preserved in the Towneley cycle. In the *First Shepherds' Play*, Gyb enters and complains that he has been ruined because his sheep have all died of the rot: 'Now beg I and borow' (*Towneley Plays* XII, 27). He is meant to be a tenant farmer because he next complains that rents are due to be paid:

> ffermes thyk ar comyng/my purs is bot wake,
> I haue nerehand nothyng/to pay nor to take,
> (30–31)

and he may have to give up farming and 'the countre forsake' unless matters improve. The second shepherd, John Horne, agrees that 'pore men ar in the dyke' (94) and complains about the 'bosters and bragers' who terrorize and exploit the poor:

If he hask me oght/that he wold to his pay,
ffull dere bese it boght/if I say nay.

(73–4)

He is not precise about who these men are, but they must presumably be the 'maintained' servants of the local lord. Coll, in the *Second Shepherds' Play*, is more explicit, and forthrightly blames the oppressive exactions of the rich for his poverty:

We ar so hamyd,
ffor-taxed and ramyd,
We ar mayde hand tamyd,
With thyse gentlery men.

(XIII, 15–18)

He also complains about the lord's servants who 'refe vs oure rest' and 'hold . . . vs hunder', and who arrogantly commandeer his equipment: 'he must borow my wane/my ploghe also' (38). But though he lives thus 'in payne/Anger and wo' he is powerless to alter the situation because his oppressors are supported 'thrugh mantenance' of 'men that are gretter'. A similar aggrieved complaint comes from Daw, who does not seem to be a tenant, as Coll is, but a servant. What angers him most is the realization that he has to perform unpleasant manual tasks while his master sleeps:

Sich seruaundys as I/that swettys and swynkys,
Etys oure bred full dry/and that me forthynkys;
We ar oft weytt and wery/when master-men wynkys,
yit commys full lately/both dyners and drynkys . . .

(154–7)

and even after this, he says, his wages are likely to be reduced or paid to him late ('Thay can nyp at oure hyre/And pay vs full lately' 161–2). He resolves to work only as hard as his reward warrants, and for the rest of the time plans to enjoy himself:

Bot here my trouth, master,/for the fayr that ye make,
I shall do therafter/wyrk as I take;
I shall do a lytyll, sir,/and emang euer lake. . . .

(163–5)

Of course, the scene has a comic dimension: the 'master' Daw addresses so impudently is far away. The whole tone of these complaints is difficult to judge. Their social grievances are not the only things the shepherds complain about. They also talk about the weather and their wives in much the same grumbling way. Perhaps they were simply meant to be comic. But the plays in question were performed in Wakefield, a town which was becoming wealthy and important as a result of the woollen industry, so the grievances of these shepherds were in all probability not without local significance. It is interesting to note, however, that if these grievances were allowed to be expressed in the public performances of the plays, they were probably not regarded as being particularly dangerous.

A much more violent set of attitudes is to be found in the medieval ballads of Robin Hood. There has been much speculation about his origins and identification, and dates from as far back as 'about the time of Richard I' have been suggested for him.[9] But no early reference to him antedates 1377 and many come from fifteenth-century writers. The earliest ballads, including the important *Gest of Robyn Hode*, are all preserved in fifteenth-century copies, and their concerns appear to have been contemporary. Maurice Keen has shown that the emphasis on proficiency in archery, on questions of livery and maintenance, and on offences against the 'venison' make it possible to 'identify the world of the ballads with the England of the later fourteenth and fifteenth centuries'.[10] Some scholars have denied any 'sort of political character' to Robin Hood,[11] and on the basis of ballads dating from the sixteenth century and later this is true enough. But the medieval ballads are best taken, in the words of G. H. Gerould, as 'a trustworthy index to the restiveness of the common people under political, economic and social abuses'.[12] As early as about 1450 the historian Walter Bower had located the popularity of these stories among the 'solid rustics'.[13] The poems themselves are addressed to 'gentilmen/That be of frebore blode' (*GRH*, stanza 1) and 'god yemen/Comley, corteys, and god' (*RHP*, stanza 2), and their hero is conceived in just these terms. He is a lower-class hero, but not a villein, rather 'a gode yeman' (*GRH*, stanza 1) who 'was boyt corteys and ffre' (*RHP*, stanza 3). His natural allies tend to be from among the 'yeomanry'—a class of society made up of independent, free, but fairly humble persons:

> What man that helpeth a good yeman
> His frende than wyll I be.
>
> (*GRH*, stanza 269)

However his sympathy extends to all who are oppressed or the victims of injustice, from the destitute knight Sir Richard at the Lee to the poorest man he may chance to meet:

> whether he be a messengere
> Or a man that myrthes can,
> Of my good he shall haue some
> Yf he be a pore man.
>
> (*GRH*, stanza 210)

Robin Hood is no indiscriminate robber. In what amounts almost to a policy statement he instructs his men to harm no farmer 'That tilleth with his ploughe', no 'gode yeman' and 'no knyght ne no sqvyer' who 'wol be a gode felawe.' He is equally clear in his definition of who the natural enemies of the outlaws were:

> The bisshoppes and these archebisshoppes,
> Ye shall them bete and bynde;
> The hye sherif of Notingham,
> Hym holde ye in your mynde.
>
> (*GRH*, stanza 15)

Such explicit statements as this are rare in these ballads, but the stories tend to show the results of these attitudes in action.

As usual in Middle English political verse, the protest is not in any way ideologically based. The hatred is not directed at the political system which gave rise to exploitation and injustice. Still less is there any dislike of the King, who is always 'our comly Kynge' and of whom Robin Hood once says:

> I loue no man in all the worlde
> So well as I do my kynge.
>
> (*GRH*, stanza 386)

Nor is there any feeling against the aristocracy, but rather a positive deference to rank: Robin Hood asks Little John to be the servant of the destitute Sir Richard at the Lee because it is wrong, he feels, for a knight to travel unattended:

> 'It were greate shame', sayde Robyn,
> 'A knight alone to ryde.'
> (*GRH*, stanza 80)

The right of anyone to this social status is never questioned. Most of the hatred generated in these poems is rather towards those whose behaviour more directly antagonized the lower classes: the representatives of the law (particularly the sheriff and those who administered the forest laws) and grasping and unscrupulous landowners (particularly Church landowners). The attitude towards 'These bisshoppes and these archbishoppes' must not be taken to indicate a general anti-religious or anti-clerical position for Robin Hood. His devotion to the Blessed Virgin 'that he loved allther moste' (*GRH*, stanza 9) is emphasized throughout the ballads, and one of the few things about the outlaw life which upsets him is:

> Þat I may not no solem day
> To mas or matyns goo.
> (*RHM*, stanza 6)

Nor does any hatred of the lower clergy appear in these ballads; as early as 1475 Friar Tuck, in a dramatic fragment, appears associated with the outlaws. On the other hand, highly ranked monastics are always represented as tenaciously avaricious and utterly lacking in Christian charity, as in the incident in the *Gest of Robyn Hode* where the Abbot of St Mary's York seeks to get possession of the lands of Sir Richard at the Lee for non-payment of a debt:

> 'Do gladly, syr abbot', sayd the knyght,
> 'I am come to holde my day:'
> The fyrst word the abbot spake
> 'Hast thou brought my pay'.
> (stanza 103)

When the knight asks for more time to pay so that he shall not lose his hereditary lands:

> The abbot sware a full grete othe,
> 'By God that dyed on a tree,
> Get the londe where thou may,
> For thou getest none of me.'
>
> (stanza 110)

In this incident the corruption of the law is also demonstrated, for when the unfortunate knight appeals to the 'hye iustyce of Englonde' for a more lenient interpretation of the law he reveals that he is 'maintained' by the Abbot, whose fees he accepts and whose livery he wears:

> 'I am holde with the abbot', sayd the iustyce
> 'Both with cloth and fee.'
>
> (stanza 107)

And when Sir Richard asks the sheriff to speak on his behalf he meets the same brusque refusal: ' "Nay, for God", sayd he.' The 'hye sherif of Notyingham' and his hirelings are the most hated individuals in the ballads. They are invariably shown as treacherous, cruel and corrupt, probably, as R. H. Hilton suggests, because the duties of sheriffs, 'delivery of writs, attachment of accused persons, distraint on property, enpanelling of juries . . .', and their use of force 'to compel tenants to pay rent, to perform services, or to dispel and arrest rioters' were such as to bring them into frequent conflict with the lower classes.[14]

The attitudes embodied in these ballads to the sheriff and his men are violent. In the *Gest of Robyn Hode* the outlaw hero hits the sheriff with an arrow and then:

> or he myght vp aryse
> on his fete to stonde,
> He smote of the sherifs hede
> With his brighte bronde.
>
> (stanza 348)

In *Robin Hood and Guy of Gisborne* the head of the sheriff's hireling is struck off, fixed on the end of a bow, and mutilated:

Robin pulled forth an Irish kniffe
And nicked Sir Guy in the fface,
That he was neuer on a woman borne
Cold tell who Sir Guye was.

(*RHGG*, stanza 42)

In another ballad two outlaws capture a monk, who has betrayed
Robin Hood, and his page:

John smote of þe munkis hed,
No longer wold he dwell;
So did Much þe litull page,
Ffor ferd lest he wolde tell.

(*RHM*, stanza 52)

But though there is no place for pathos and sentimentality in these
ballads, there is apparent an element of wishfulness. Here the forces
of oppression and injustice are always defeated. Here too the outlaw life is presented as enviable. There is a great plenty of sumptuous foods available to the outlaws:

Brede and wyne they had right ynoughe
And noumbles of the dere,

(*GRH*, stanza 32)

followed by 'Swannes and fessauntes . . . full gode', 'fowles of the
ryvere', and every other type of bird that was 'bred on bryre',
yet this is described as 'simple chere'. Robin Hood also makes
extravagant gestures to those he helps: a generous £400 in gold
coin, liberal amounts of cloth, the 'best coresed hors' that was ever
seen and so on. Little John's proposition to the sheriff's cook that
as an outlaw he would get two suits of livery and 20 marks a year
is also meant to be an attractive one. The livery is important.
Because he gives liveries of Lincoln green, Robin Hood comes to be
something like a great lord, to whom is paid the highest compliment possible when, after one adventure, the King consents to
wear 'a grene garment' in his honour (*GRH*, stanza 421). But all
this, of course, is pure fantasy. What emerges from these ballads is
clearly in no sense an accurate picture of outlaw life, and it is only
rarely that the ballads afford any insight into its less attractive

side. On one occasion it is stated that the outlaws 'lyve by our kynges dere' because they have no 'other shyft' (*GRH*, stanza 377). On another the captured sheriff of Nottingham complains of the harshness of the outlaws' life after he has been committed to spending a night in the forest as the outlaws habitually did:

> 'This is harder order', sayde the sherief,
> 'Than any ankir or frere;
> For all the golde in mery Englonde
> I wolde nat longe dwell her.'
>
> (*GRH*, stanza 198)

But even incidental expressions of the shortcomings of the outlaw life, such as these, are rare. In general Robin Hood is made to fulfil all the latent aspirations of his yeoman audience: he is rich and free, not tied to service or toil, not dominated by authority, in no way a starved and hunted criminal but an agent for moral good who rectifies the abuses of contemporary society. The poems convey a very different impression of the outlaw life from that given in the early fourteenth-century verses on the 'trailbastons' where, despite the pleasant setting in which he finds himself, the outlaw's greatest wish is to be back in normal society:

> Je pri tote bone gent qe pur moi vueillent prier
> Qe je pus a mon pais aler y chyvaucher.[15]

So far this chapter has been concerned with fifteenth-century verses of protest of a fairly general nature with no reference to specific contexts. But a few verses have survived which may be fairly precisely dated and related to specific problems and events. The earliest of these date from 1418 and concern the jurisdiction of the city of Cambridge. They were posted up on the mayor's door, and the mayor is the versifier's principal target:

> Looke out here Maire with thie pilled pate,
> And see wich a scrowe is set on thie gate;
> Warning thee of hard happes,
> For and it lukke thou shalt have swappes:
> Therefore I rede keepe the at home;

For thou shalt abey for that is done;
Or els kest on a coate of mayle;
Truste well thereto withouten faile.

(*Lost Lit.*, p. 200)

As if to mark him off from the rest, the couplets end here and the verses continue in a simple tail-rhyme form but with the same mixture of threats and insults, now against the mayor's supporters: the 'great Golias Joh. Essex' shall 'have a clowte with my karille axe', 'the hosteler Bambour with his goats beard' shall be 'made afeard', 'that harlot Hierman with his calves snowte' shall be buffeted 'For his werkes sake', 'Hankyn Attilbrigge' shall have 'swappes', and the 'catchepoles' and 'other knaves' shall 'take knockes full good chepe'. These verses are preserved in a complaint made to the King's Council by the mayor about the riotous behaviour of certain students from the university and others, and students were blamed for the verses though this was strongly denied by the university authorities. There is certainly nothing in the verses which makes it intrinsically likely that a student was the author. These are not 'learned' verses. Practically anyone who hated the city authorities and had a modicum of literary ability in the vernacular would have been capable of writing them. But it may be that students were responsible since the threats the verses contained were shortly proved to be seriously meant.[16] Later in this same year the mayor and burgesses complained in a petition to the Duke of Bedford that 'certain clerks armed in a warlike manner, by night broke the windows and rails of Richard Barix, goldsmith, and of John Bilney, the Mayor, and beat William Weggewood, and Robert Norres, and wounded and ill-treated one John Burte who came out of his house to quell the riot'. On another occasion 'they exclaimed "come out of your houses, you villains, whoremongers and scoundrels, or you shall be burnt in them" ', and there are charges of ill-using Robert Attilbrigge, John Knapton, John Metham and others. The violence of these riots is matched by the violence of the verse, which is direct and colloquial. The author, student or not, has achieved a mode of expressing his discontent which is in no way derivative.

The next verses date from 1450 when the Kentishmen rose under Jack Cade and marched on London. The court was at Leicester, but an army was gathered and Henry VI came to the capital to negotiate with Cade. This was perhaps a ploy to gain time, for the King soon broke off negotiations. Counter-measures by the royal forces were rather ineffectual, however, and the rebels had some success. They managed to defeat a royal army at Sevenoaks on 18 June, and occupied the city of London for a time. They also caught and executed the hated treasurer Lord Say and Sele and his son-in-law William Crowmer, sheriff of Kent. But the revolt lost its momentum. The rebels disbanded under the promise of a general pardon and Cade was killed on 12 July in Sussex. The rising was not exclusively confined to the lower classes, though the majority of rebels were from these ranks of society. One knight, eighteen esquires, seventy-four gentlemen and many priests were involved, together with commercial men, for the Kentish ports, particularly Sandwich, had been badly hit by the French wars: exports were badly down owing to the embargo on wool imposed by Holland, Brabant and Flanders, and so too were the imports of wine. The rebel grievances were mixed. Some related to local affairs: Lord Say and Crowmer were thought to have threatened to turn Kent into a deer forest as a punishment for the murder by Kentishmen of William de la Pole, Duke of Suffolk, earlier in the year; there are hints of rigged elections in Kent; and Kentish law was apparently badly administered. But other grievances related to national affairs: the court party, according to the rebels, was misleading the King; and too many royal lands had been granted away so that the King was impoverished. But though the discontent was both local and national only the national grievances find expression in the verse, and these are set out with nothing like the precision they have in the rebel manifestoes:

> God be oure gyde,
> and then schull we spede.
> Who soeuur say nay,
> ffalse for their money reuleth!
> Trewth for his tales spolleth!

God seend vs a ffayre day!
awey traytours, awey.
(*HP*, 24, 1-7)

There is no defined social programme here: the writer criticizes, in general terms, those who rule because of their money, those who advise badly and traitors. These are commonplaces of the same sort as those in John Ball's verses of 1381. If there is a significant difference it is one of tone: the 1450 verses appear to embody a greater conviction that the rebels will be successful.

Dating from the early 1460s come some verses which are the earliest extant to bring into opposition capital and labour in an urban context in anything like modern terms. The poem, which R. H. Robbins entitles *A Trade Policy*, is interesting for various reasons. It is partly derivative in that some of its author's political attitudes and also whole lines of verse are copied from *The Libelle of Englyshe Polycye* (1436), but it has, none the less, its own distinct character. Whereas its 'source' was addressed to the lords of the King's Council, this appears to have been written by a cloth worker and is perhaps intended for the ears of his fellow workers and the cloth manufacturers. As in his 'source', this author stresses the political usefulness of trade as an instrument of foreign policy, but concerns himself with other topics too: a plan for increasing the output of silver in England, and, most importantly in this context, proposals for the proper treatment of workers in the cloth industry. His concern is always with the working conditions of the 'pore pepyll' and the 'poore porayle' of the cloth industry, the 'spynners, carders, wevers . . . toukers, dyers . . .' and so on. Not only does he suggest that exports of raw wool should be restricted so that there may be full employment in the English cloth industry ('That þe comyns of thys land may wyrke at the full' 56), but he also exposes the dishonest means by which the manufacturers exploited the workers. Some were paying their workers half in money and half in merchandise, a bad enough practice in itself, says the poet, but made yet worse by the fact that some manufacturers were calculating the value of the merchandise by its inflated market price, not its wholesale price:

wyche makyth the poreyll to morne & wepe.
Lytyll þei take to theyre labur, yet halff ys merchaundyse.
Alas! for rewth, yt ys gret pyte!

Þat they take for vjd, yt ys dere ynow of iij;
And thus þei be defrawdyd in euery contre;
The pore haue þe labur, the ryche the wynnyng.
This acordythe now3te, it is a heuy partyng.

(HP, 70, 86–92)

The 'merchaundes & cloth-makers' were also further reducing the workers' real wages by exploiting the difference between spun and unspun wool:

ffor ix li, I wene, they schall take xij.
This is very trewth, as y know my selff;
Theyre wages be batyd theyre weyte ys encresyd;
þus the spynners & carders auaylys be all seasyd.

(101–4)

As a remedy for all this he suggests that

syche wyrkfolk be payd in good mone,
ffrom þis tyme forth by suffycyent ordynaunce
þat þe poreyll no more be putte to such greuaunce.

(93–6)

The 'ordynaunce' the author hoped for was passed by parliament in 1463 and 1464, forbidding manufacturers from making their workers 'to take grete part of their wages in Pynnes, Girdels and other unprofitable Merchandise', insisting that wools should be weighed 'accordyng to the true pounde', and that workers should be paid in 'lawfull money for all their lefull wages'.[17] These clumsy and repetitious verses were probably used as propaganda in the years preceding the ordinances and it is tempting to feel that they had some influence.

Finally there are the three sets of verses written in Coventry in 1495–6 by supporters of Laurence Saunders, a dyer who was a constant opponent of the mayor and the ruling oligarchy over a number of years. The city oligarchy was made up of a body of twenty-four *potentiores* who chose the mayor and officers for the coming year. The mayor and the *potentiores* then chose another twenty-four persons to make up the council, but the mayor was not obliged to consult them and usually ruled with the help of a few advisers. The *potentiores* who elected the mayor virtually made up the Leet (a legislative and judicial body in whose records these poems are preserved) and, as P. M. Kendall has said, 'The town government was beautifully self perpetuating'.[18] There had been considerable discontent among the common people under this rule for many years before the protests of Laurence Saunders. The surprising thing is that Saunders was a member of one of the ruling families (his father had been mayor in 1469), and it was his position as one of the two elected chamberlains of the city in 1481 which first gave him an opportunity for action. Part of his duties involved the supervision of the common land which bordered the city and it came to his notice that parcels of it had been illegally enclosed by the richer landowners (with the connivance of the city oligarchy), and also that members of the oligarchy were grazing more sheep on it than they were legally allowed to. As he was entitled to, Saunders impounded animals that were being illegally allowed to graze the commons, but the city authorities refused to fine their owners. For the over-zealous prosecution of his duties Saunders was imprisoned. When he was released, he appealed to Prince Edward's Council at Ludlow, knowing that he would get no satisfaction in Coventry. Saunders' charges were incontestable, and the royal Council ordered an investigation, but they also found that Saunders had been guilty of defying the city authorities and allowed them to correct and punish him according to his desert. He was again gaoled and only allowed out on a large surety. There followed riots among the common people who threw down the fences of illegally enclosed lands and disrupted civic ceremonies. In 1482 Saunders again opposed the city council on the question of enclosures and was again imprisoned. When he was released, it was with a grim warning from the Prince's Council: 'þat this was the secunde tyme þat he had ben in warde for his disobeysaunce, & for such commocions as he had made amonges the pepull; therefore they bad hym be ware; for yf he came the iij de tyme in warde for such matieres, hit schulde cost hym his hedde. . . .'[19] Perhaps because of this threat nothing is heard of Saunders for twelve years. But the events of 1481–2 reveal his preoccupations and form an indispensable background to the troubles of 1494–6.

For it was probably the vexed question of illegal enclosures which caused Saunders suddenly, in 1494, to confiscate Will Boteler's oats (which had presumably been grown on illegally enclosed land) and to incite the people to 'take þis Corn who so wyll as youre owne'.[20] He had also stirred the people '. . . to comocion & insurrecion' by telling a crowd of forty: 'Sirs, here me! We shall never have oure ryght till we have striken of the hedes of iij or iiij of thes Churles hedes that rulen vs.' This incident took place appropriately enough on 1 August (Lammas Day, when traditionally the common lands were thrown open to all) but it was not until 17 September that Saunders was put in prison where he remained until he had found further sureties. At Easter 1495 he was discharged from the mayor's council, the common council '& all oþer Counceils hereafter' and also forbidden from riding with the chamberlains in the Lammas Day procession.[21] This public disgrace of their champion provoked a good deal of discontent among the common people. So did certain impositions by the city authorities. The right of poor cloth-makers to sell in the porch of St Michael's Church had been lately taken away and they were obliged to sell in the Drapery (controlled by the rich Holy Trinity Guild) and to pay for the rent of a stall. In a similar way wool could only be sold at the Wool Hall. Compulsory registration of apprentices for 13d was also enforced. Some verses nailed up on the door of St Michael's Church 'be some evell disposed person vnknowen' touch on these grievances and also express support for Saunders in the last couplet:

> Be it knowen & vnderstand
> This Cite shuld be free & nowe is bonde.
> Dame goode Eve made it free
> & nowe þe custome for woll & þe draperie.
> Also hit is made þat no prentes shalbe
> but xiij penyes pay shuld he.
> Þat act did Robert Grene,

þerfore he had many a Curse, I wene.
And nowe anoþer rule ye do make
þat non shall ryde at Lammas but they þat ȝe take.
When our ale is Tunned
ȝe shall haue drynk to your Cake.
Ye haue put on man like a Scot to raunsome.
Þat wolbe remembred when ȝe haue all Forgoten.
Caviat.

(Lost Lit., p. 198)

Whether the threats at the end impressed the city authorites or not is impossible to say. But the mood of the verses probably well enough represents that of the majority of the common people, and the authorities decided to act leniently with Saunders. They halved the £40 fine imposed upon him for his latest offences.

Saunders was not satisfied. He appealed to Henry VII against his fine and drew attention to the still unresolved business of the illegal enclosures. A privy seal ordered the Coventry authorities to forgo the fine and also to look into the charges about enclosures. Saunders at once presented his accusations in detail to the city council and taunted the mayor, John Dove, there and at his house. He was once again imprisoned and was allowed to procure his freedom only on a large surety for good behaviour. He refused to accede to this because he knew it was merely a device to silence him, and while he was in prison two more sets of verses in his favour were posted up. The first is written in a simple tail-rhyme form, and unlike the verses of the previous year is not very specific. It is addressed to the city authorities ('Ye þat be of myght') and urges them to behave justly ('Se that ye do right') to Saunders, whom they have 'in a snare'. If he does not receive justice, the poet says, the city authorities had better guard themselves against unforseen disasters ('after-clappys'). He warns them that the common people are like bees and wasps—not individually big or powerful, but capable of wounding:

> Where as they light
> The been will byte
> And also styng.

Loke þat ye do right.
Both day & nyght
Beware of wappys.[22]

The other verses, which follow without a break in the manuscript
but which form a distinct entity, are in couplets. They begin by
complaining that Coventry is wrongfully subjected ('bond') to the
wills of the city oligarchy, and that the common people are treated
unjustly: 'right is holden fro þe Cominalte!' Then, in more particular terms, the author defines his grievances: common lands have
been 'closed in & hegged full fast' (4) instead of thrown open, and
Laurence Saunders, a member of the Holy Trinity and Corpus
Christi Guilds who 'speketh for our right', has been imprisoned.
This author, however, shows a more comprehensive awareness of
the situation than is usually shown in these verses, in that he treats
these precise grievances as part of a larger pattern. He continues,
in a more general way, about how the city authorities consistently
deceive and impoverish the common people, stresses the importance of the people and memorably expresses their resentment:

We haue no more to lose, þe soth for to say,
ffor eny fauour or frenship þe comiens with yowe fynde,
But pyke awey our thryfte & make vs all blynde.
And euer ye haue nede to þe Cominalte—
Such favour as ye shewe vs, such shall ye see:
We may speke feir & bid you good morowe,
But luff with our hertes shull ye have non.
Cherish þe Cominalte & se they haue their right,
ffor drede of a worse chaunce be day or be nyght!
Þe best of you all, litell worth shuld be,
And ye had not helpe of the Cominalte.
                                        (*HP*, 25, 10–20)

He ends with some veiled threats to the council about what will
come about ('what shal be þe ende' 24) if matters are not put right.
The protracted affair was finally brought to some sort of conclusion,
but not one that this poet would have liked, for after an examination
of the case before the King's Council, the mayor had Saunders

'commyt vnto þe Flete, there to abide vnto þe tyme the kynges pleasure were knowen what ferther punysshement he shuld haue'.[23] Popular risings rarely had any tangible or immediate effect in improving lower-class conditions. Nor, with the possible exception of the *Trade Policy*, did poems written in connection with them. If the verses had an influence at all it was probably indirect. They doubtless served to inform and to encourage. But perhaps their greatest effect derived from the fact that they existed at all. A few men, writing in unfavourable circumstances, managed to express, however inadequately, the grievances and aspirations of a class of medieval society which normally suffered in silence.

NOTES

[1] Ed. R. H. Hilton, 'A Thirteenth Century poem on disputed Villein Services', *EHR* 56, 1941, pp. 90–7. *Translation:* 'what should a villein do but serve, and his son after him? You will be a villein unconditionally and without liberty. The verdict of the law proves that, and the law court.'

[2] Ed. Carleton Brown, *English Lyrics of the Thirteenth Century*, Oxford 1932, No. 89.

[3] *The English Utopia*, London 1952, pp. 1–35.

[4] 'The Order of Fair Ease' ed. Thomas Wright, *Political Songs of England*, London 1839, pp. 137–48.

[5] *Chronicon Henrici Knighton* ed. J. R. Lumby, Rolls Series 92, 1889–95, II, 139.

[6] *Annales*, London 1615, p. 294.

[7] *Popular Sermon*, New York 1937, p. 49.

[8] *A Selection of English Carols*, Oxford 1962, No. 27. But in his notes Greene suggests the carol may relate to the discontent at Hailes Abbey, Gloucestershire over its impoverishment rather than be 'a general proletarian protest' (p. 206).

[9] For references, and criticisms of these views, see R. H. Hilton, 'The Origin of Robin Hood', *Past and Present*, 14, 1958, pp. 30–44, and Maurice Keen, *The Outlaws of Medieval Legend*, London 1961, pp. 174–90. My whole account of Robin Hood is much indebted to these studies.

[10] *Op. cit.*, p. 142.

[11] F. J. Child, *English and Scottish Popular Ballads*, 5 vols., 1882–95, III, 43, whence also the texts of these ballads.

[12] *The Ballad of Tradition*, Oxford 1932, p. 134.

[13] Quoted by Keen, *op. cit.*, p. 177.

[14] *Op. cit.*, p. 41.

[15] See Isabel S. T. Aspin, *Anglo Norman Political Songs*, ANTS 9 1953, pp. 67–78. *Translation:* 'I beg all good people that they pray for me so that I may ride to my own country.'

[16] For details and references for what follows see G. G. Coulton, *Social Life in Britain*, Cambridge 1918, pp. 66ff.

[17] For details see *Statutes of the Realm* II, 403–7 and R. H. Robbins, *MLN* 71, 1956, pp. 245–8.

[18] *The Yorkist Age*, London 1962, p. 121. What follows is much indebted to this account of Laurence Saunders.

[19] *The Coventry Leet Book*, ed. M. D. Harris, EETS OS, 134–5, 1907–8, pp. 511–12.

[20] *Ibid.*, p. 557.

[21] *Ibid.*, p. 564.

[22] *Ibid.*, p. 577.

[23] *Ibid.*, p. 580.

Abbreviations

ANTS	Anglo Norman Text Society
Ashby *Poems*	*George Ashby's Poems* ed. Mary Bateson, EETS ES 76 1899.
BM	British Museum
Digby 102 Poems	*Twenty Six Political and Other Poems* ed. J. Kail, EETS OS 124 1904.
EEC	*The Early English Carols* ed. R. L. Greene, Oxford 1935.
EETS OS/ES/SS	Early English Text Society Original Series/Extra Series/Supplementary Series.
EHR	*English Historical Review*
Fall of Princes	John Lydgate's *Fall of Princes* ed. H. Bergen, EETS ES 121–4, 1918–19.
GRH, RHGG, RHM, RHP	'Gest of Robyn Hode', 'Robin Hood and Guy of Gisborne', 'Robin Hood and the Monk', 'Robin Hood and the Potter' in F. J. Child, *English and Scottish Popular Ballads*, 5 vols., 1882–95.
HP	*Historical Poems of the Fourteenth and Fifteenth Centuries* ed. R. H. Robbins, New York 1959.
Idley Instructions	*Peter Idley's Instructions to his Son* ed. Charlotte d'Evelyn, Boston 1935.
Index	C. F. Brown and R. H. Robbins, *An Index of Middle English Verse*, New York 1943, and *Supplement* by Robbins and J. Cutler, 1965.

JU, FDR, UR	*Jack Upland, Friar Daw's Reply, and Upland's Rejoinder* ed. P. L. Heyworth, Oxford 1968.
JWCI	*Journal of the Warburg and Courtauld Institutes*
Libelle	*The Libelle of Englyshe Polycye* ed. Sir George Warner, Oxford 1926.
Lost Lit.	R. M. Wilson, *The Lost Literature of Medieval England*, 1952.
Minor Poems	*The Minor Poems of John Lydgate* ed. H. N. MacCracken, EETS ES 107, 192, 1911, 1934.
MLN	*Modern Language Notes*
MLQ	*Modern Language Quarterly*
MLR	*Modern Language Review*
Mod. Phil.	*Modern Philology*
MP	*Thomas Hoccleve's Minor Poems*, ed. F. J. Furnivall, EETS ES 61, 73, 1892, 1925.
Mum and the Sothsegger	*Mum and the Sothsegger*, ed. Mabel Day and R. Steele, EETS OS 199, 1936.
Nicolas	N. H. Nicolas ed. 'Henry V's Invasion of France' in *The Battle of Agincourt*, 1832, pp. 301–29.
Paston Letters	*The Paston Letters*, ed. J. Gairdner, 6 vols., 1904.
Pilgrimage	John Lydgate's *Pilgrimage of the Life of Man*, ed. F. J. Furnivall and Katherine B. Locock, EETS ES 77, 83, 92, 1899–1904.
PMLA	*Publications of the Modern Language Association of America*
PPS	*Political Poems and Songs*, ed. Thomas Wright, 2 vols., Rolls Series 14, 1859–61.

Regement	Thomas Hoccleve's *Regement of Princes*, ed. F. J. Furnivall, EETS ES 72, 1897.
RES	*Review of English Studies*
RL XV	*Religious Lyrics of the Fifteenth Century*, ed. C. F. Brown, Oxford 1939.
Secrees	John Lydgate and Benedict Burgh's *Secrees of Old Philisoffres*, ed. R. Steele, EETS ES 66, 1894.
SL XIV and XV	*Secular Lyrics of the Fourteenth and Fifteenth Centuries*, ed. R. H. Robbins, Oxford 1952.
Towneley Plays	*The Towneley Plays*, ed. G. England and A. W. Pollard, EETS ES 75, 1897.
TRHS	*Transactions of the Royal Historical Society*
Troy Book	John Lydgate's *Troy Book*, ed. H. Bergen, EETS ES 97, 103, 106, 126, 1906–20.

Appendix A

From British Museum MS Lansdowne 762 ff. 52r–53r.

Index 3945

52r   When a m cccc togyther be knett
and xxiiij w*ith* them be mett
as merlyon sayith in his story of bryttayne
of kynge henry of englond certayne
And thempoure & the kynge of ffraunce & flaunders also   5
and other lord*is* many moo
by trew p*ro*phecy that sholde befall
of m*er*velous amonge them all

52v   Thuse sayeth merlyon in his p*ro*phecye
That in no wise kepyth to lye   10
ffirst the lylie that faire flowre
that many yeres shall kepe his color
After that he shall sprede into lyons land*is*
And grow amonge the thornis ʒonder stond*is*
After that a mans son shall mete w*ith* the mone   15
bryngyng in his armes best*is* many oon
Thus mannys son all nacions hym shall drede
Above all the worlde in eu*er*y stede
w*ith* many a creature the lyon shall mete
and enter in to his londe that socorles shalbe lefte   20
w*ith* them they shall bere both flessh and fell
w*ith* wylde beste of the region full cruell
The same yere shall com an Egill oute from the east
Spredyng his wing*is* abowte the son in hast
Many of his chikyns w*ith* hym will he bryng   25

to helpe the manys sone wi*th* grete joyng
ffirst many a castell they shall ou*er*throw
wi*th* pillers and towres that shalbe full low
Also in one p*ar*te of the lyons londe
shalbe a grete battaile I vnderstonde   30
for many kynge shall fight there foo
That of red blode a grete flode shall goo
There shall the lylie lose his crowne so gay
wi*th* the which the mans son shalbe crowned p*ar* fay
So grete a battayle shall then there be   35
that fewe on lyve men shall see
The moste p*ar*te of the worlde deth shall tast
wel be he þ*at* shall scape in haste
53r   Then after this grete battayle
The hed of the worlde his myght shall faile   40
To the erthe wi*th* hed makyng inclinacion
Prayng to god for manns salvasion
After this the egill and the mans son
shall reigne togither wi*th*outen mone
In all the worlde then shalbe pease   45
wi*th* cris*t*en and hethen dowtles
Also of frute grete plentie
Ioy may they that thus Ioy may see
Then shall manns son for cryst*is* sake
a m*er*velous thing vpon hym take   50
And take his way to the lond of p*ro*mission
And thus gode hath p*ro*uyded for kynge henrys salvacion.

MS Lansdowne 762 is a quarto volume written partly on vellum and partly on paper. From the items in it which may be dated, and from the handwriting, it appears to have been compiled in the earlier part of the sixteenth century. Its 106 folios contain a miscellaneous collection of items (fully described in the *Catalogue of the Manuscripts of the Lansdowne Collection*, 1819, No. 762) mainly of historical interest, including a great many prophecies in verse and prose. This text is prefaced on f. 52r by a 'key' to its interpretation.

The lylie that faire flowre
is the kyng of ffraunce that sewr
The lyon that fferefull is
is the londe of fflaunders
The lyons son I saye certayne   5
is the duke of f[l]aunders p. burgeyn
The man son *with* the wilde best*is*
is the kynge of inglonde by conquest*is*
The londe of the mone I vnderstonde
is englonde walis and Irelond   10
The Egill w*ith* the birde in bower
is the nobyll emp*er*our
The son that so high is
is the londe of fflaunders ywis
The hed of the worlde also   15
is the pope w*ith*outen woo
the m*er*velous Signe is pa fay
The holy crosse god died on good fryday.

The existence of this 'key' makes the prophecy it refers to more amenable to interpretation than is usually the case.

line 1: *when a m ccccc togyther be knett* MS. Were this reading to be accepted the date would be 1524, which the interpretation in the 'key' shows to be impossible: 'the duke of f[l]aundres p. burgeyn' must refer to Philip the Good who was Duke of Burgundy from 1419–67. So the date is probably a mistake for 1424.

line 28: MS reads *townes* for 'towres', but this would not give very good sense.

line 36: MS reads *that fewe of on lyve* . . ., but the *of* is crossed through. This is obviously a mistake caused by attraction with the 'of' of the following line.

N

Appendix B

From British Museum MS Lansdowne 762 ff. 63v–65r.

Index 3510

63v The yere of our lorde m cccc lxxx iij
betuext the departyng of Aprell and not far from may
The bull shall dep*ar*te & passe away
The same yere shalbe moche adoo
Walles shall bere armys and to Albion goo   5
Which shall cause men to sofer moch woo
Wood*is* & waters downe shalbe cast
And sey that eu*er* they were borne alasse
The other shalbe wrongid at the last
The . . . shall dye in the same stowre   10
The yere of our lorde m cccc lxxx iiij
A dragon with a Rede rose þ*at* grete is his fame
A bastarde vnder wedelok shall he bee
The crowne to opteyne he will chalenge by name
But yf the thirde aryse þe bore shall have degree   15
Of the reason take good hede
This councellyth yow seint Bede
ffor betwext iiij & fyve þ*at* is to vnderstonde
moche sorowe shalbe do be see and be londe
A blake cowe shal aryse ageyne of a trew lyne   20
Ne the blode of Cadwalidus a grete gentilman is he
A banysshed man ys he far beyonde the see
ffraunce and flaunders shall aryse
Spayne shall supporte them w*it*h all þ*er* myght
The danes shall take enterpryse   25

And to all englonde geve a lyght
Now holy Chirch thow þer take good hede
for then shalt thow nowght be set by
preest*is* monk*is* chanons fryers nor religeous
This may not be forde wi*th*oute gre prayours   30
A knyghte name shalbe called C
The best borne man in the worlde is he
This knyght shalbe faire yonge & of the blod of Iesse
And kyn to mary quene of me*r*cy
The Egill shall aryse & wi*th* hym com   35
64r The bore shall mete hym in the wey
The facon and the grey gryffon
That the forsaid . . . shall syng well awey
Then men shall aryse one ageyne another
And fare as men that were all wood   40
The son shall slee the father the broder the broder
That the stretes of London shall ron all on blod
Then shall this noble prynce C
To troye ontrewe styfly com
The Egyll the Gryffon grene & the bore wi*th* hym shalbe   45
But the gentyll ffacon shall aske a peticyon
That the cytie of London be not put to confucyon
Ne dowte of Aldermen XX and three
Shall leese their hede in that cytie
Then P shall ryse and com oute of the T   50
And iij battaylls shalbe and that full stronge
So that no man shall knowe who shall have þe victory
The terme of iij yere þ*at* shall laste so longe
Now yf I tell you of a marvell take yt for no wonder
Withoute the grace of god helpe soden deth shalbe and
    hongry   55
The six shall arise the sinke shall vnder
Ryse shall ageyne beryed in fight yf that he were
Which to all the worlde shalbe grete wonder
A grete rebuke shall haue the bretheles bere
A grete acorde shalbe made betwixt ij knight*is*   60
And in the ryght shalbe set the ryght heire

Then in the londe shalbe grete warre
and eu*er*y man ageyne other shall ryse
downe shalbe cast the woode and water
a bastarde shall com and take enterpryse   65
A rede rose this bastard in wedelok borne
w*ith* hym a dredefull dragon a man of grete fame
the gilden bolle his lyvelode to put from
the ix of cadwaladrus blode by name
64v he thynkyth to put E to grete shame   70
and all his hospryng for ever more
a wycked woman shalbe cause of blame
the which sholde longe lye in the hande of a bore
a blake cowe shall come thorow Brettayne to albion
w*ith* hym a yong knyght whos name shalbe P   75
borne of the lyne of a kynge crowned w*ith* thorne
and shalbe callid cosyn to Iesse
A childe w*ith* a chaplet shall come ou*er* the see
w*ith* an Egill ryall hauyng no pere
Except Ih*es*u that dyed on Caluere   80
Which sofered his body to be persed w*ith* a spere
The rede rose and the white dragon so ferse shalbe
on the dowghtye bull w*ith* their myght and mayne
that he shalbe fayne for to flee
vnto a castell that was made of stone   85
w*ith* the ffete of his moyle his flessh shalbe torne
which that he sholde trust most vpon
alas for shame in his most nede all his shall torne hym fro
The ffete of the . . . flessh shalbe tore
And the welth of his ospryng shalbe t*or*ned to woo   90
The cok of the north shalbe fayne to flee
his ffethers shalbe pluked on eu*er*y syde
and corse the tyme that eu*er* lorde was he
downe shall he be put from all his pride
The blew bore and mollette thorow inglonde shall ryde   95
Troy ontrew shall trembill and quake
for fere of a childe w*ith* chaplet þ*at* will in clide
þe molett in troy xiij dayes Iustis shall make

Than shall a bere þat longe hath he tyed at a stake

65r Causer of debate chefe as yt shalbe see   100

a many his cheine shall be shake

and be chefe maker of pease and vnytie

A dede man shall aryse that beryed was in fight

and make acorde betwene ij men enuious

and put the heire in his very ryght   105

Then shall they pase forth vnto pontus

Then shall the deman say evyn thus

their matter hath stonde longe in mykyll woo

Theirfore ryse trew R & take þi son K & crowne E eius filius

but before all this there shalbe mykill adoo   110

The bull and the rede Rose shall stonde at grete stryff

They shall cause englonde to suffer mykell woo

and many a man shall lese their lyff

so fiersly the battaylle betwext them shall goo

Betwyxt Glocetor and Wales the first shalbe   115

the seconde at the vij downe on a grete playne

There shall many a mothers son dye

The chife lord perteynyng and the bull shalbe slayne

Than shall a . . . felysch with myght and mayne

com to busbery and mete at the crose of stone   120

the Raven and the mylfote their shall sofer her last payne

and many a kny[ght] with her men that neuer shall goo home

The red rose and the dragon their presoune downe shall cast

At honnysley heyth another shalbe

to charen crose that battaile shall last   125

and so go downe from Seton to the see

above all places he and merlin make mone

take tente to his talkyng where he tellyth

how a lyon shalbe banysshed and to berwyk gon

the rose and the Raged tree folowith be ffrethes & be fellis 130

A stowte knyght in a storme a bewgle shall blowe

to reve vp his Ratches & ron with open mouth

and sle hym that neuer was borne for the blake crow

because of the vengaunce that shall fale in the sowth.

Though it is clear from the dates in lines 1 'm cccc lxxxiij' and line 11 'm cccc lxxx iiij' that this prophecy refers to the reign of Richard III to interpret each individual reference here would be very difficult. Part of the difficulty is this author's propensity for mixing two styles of prophecy, the Sibylline (which refers to persons by the initial letter of their names) and the Galfridian (which refers to persons as animals). This author also seems to have worked into his prophecy parts of others: line 56, for example, appears to have been taken from a dice prophecy (compare *HP* 46); and lines 23–6 may be paralleled elsewhere, as, for example, on f. 53v of this manuscript, where they appear to be meant to stand as a prophecy in their own right:

> ffrance and flaunders than shall ryse
> Spane shall supporte them w*ith* all thei3 myght
> The Danes will com to take enterpryse
> nowght shall they do but all abowght lyght.
> *(Index* 864.5)

lines 10, 38, 89, 119: the scribe has left a gap in each of these lines, omitting in each case a name. This was presumably either a name he wished to omit, or one he could not read in his exemplar.

line 72: MS has þ*er* written above 'of'.

line 82: MS has *white* written above 'rede'.

line 122: MS has *kny*.

line 133: MS has *brone*.

Appendix C

From National Library of Wales MS Peniarth 50 ff. 126r–126v.

f. 126r In þe seson of somer surly who lykes
þe fare of þe ferlyes þat schal fal in hast
In Iule ys ioyned þe ioynt of þe tyme
þat þis ferly befel not in ferre landys
When a m [cccc] xxx & iij yer ar ended   5
Som cccc haly holden togedre
þen was told me þe tale þat Y tel schal
Y was meuyd in my mynd at mydaystyme
& wandred in a way by a wode syde
By þe greues so grene as þe gate lay   10
Whilys þat Y came to a scarre by a clonch syde
And þer for slomer Y syled & settilled down þere
& not slomred ne slept but sothly Y waked
Y sygh a pepyl prest come prikand by þe way
Lyke as a lord had lad hem a bowne   15
But þei ledde a lady þat leue Y for sothe
þat was borne to abyde not but a while
ffor she raythly rad fro þis renkes a awey
& bowede to a banke þat Y abade vndyre
& bade me ryse raythly & rest me no lengre   20
ffor þer was woos waland in the web about
þat Y was stoned in þat stond and studydd a whil
& al for ferde Y fel flat down to þe grownd
But Y refinnyd my reson & ros vp ageyn
f. 126v & frayned at þe fre what ferly hit was   25
Scho sayd Y shal say þe soþ surly & none oþer

þe pope schal be poysned & put out of Rome
& þe were shal be veroncle & wainer deprived
Then shal clerly þe clergy comyn togedre
In þe bourgh of basyl & byde many a day   30
But basyl þe burgh shal be broght to grond
ffor þe falsnes of þe freckes þat ar fond þerin
þen schal Borgoyn yn bale byde many yerys
& al þe feyrnes of France frusshed at budres
þus þe werre schal be wakned in þis wyde landes   35
ffro Rom into Reynes renk shal dey
ffor þeir pride pestolences shal put hem at bud
& warres shal wakyn þe wyes with wondres
þen shul þei passe ouer þe path pepyl enarmyd
& hongr schal enhance þeym trow þu none oþer   40
Sauoy shal haue sorow of many fere landes
& melan shal be marked for many long yeres
Al þe feyrnes of Fraunce & þe fresshe pepyl
Shal be snaped for here & surly at vnder
Then schal a breton hym bound ouer þe brad streme   45
& care to paleys & þer a court hold
He schal ferr fflaunders and al þe ferre landes
& ryde into Rom with renkes ynow

MS Peniarth 50 is a small book of vellum and paper of 165 folios measuring about $5\frac{1}{2} \times 4\frac{1}{2}$ inches. It is often attributed to Gwilym Tew, on the basis of a note on f. 1v, but this attribution is to be doubted. In any case, it appears from the handwriting that at least three people were responsible for its contents. Several dates appear: on f. 34v, 1425; on f. 41r, 1445; on f. 110v, 1451; and on f. 150v, 1456. The manuscript is in bad condition. Six folios are missing and from f. 128 to the end there is evidence of considerable disarrangement. In places the manuscript is deeply stained so that some parts cannot be read at all, and others only with difficulty. The two folios containing the poem printed here are badly stained at top and bottom and the text is difficult to establish accurately. The manuscript contains a miscellany of items in Welsh, Latin and English, but many are prophecies.

line 5: MS reads *When a m xxx & iij*, that is 1033, which cannot be right, if the poem refers to the Council of Basle which took place in 1433. Perhaps the scribe omitted 'cccc' because he was distracted by the appearance of that number in the following line.

line 15: in the MS 'lyke as a' is inserted above 'lord had lad . . .'

Bibliography

1. *Bibliographies*

Bateson, F. N. W., *The Cambridge Bibliography of English Literature*, 5 vols., Cambridge 1940–57, I, 163–8, 200–1, 270.

Brown, C. F. and Robbins, R. H., *An Index of Middle English Verse*, New York 1943, and *Supplement* by Robbins and J. Cutler, 1965.

Renwick, W. L. and Orton, H., *The Beginnings of English Literature to Skelton 1509*, 1939, pp. 317–18.

Wells, J. E., *A Manual of the Writings in Middle English*, New Haven 1910, Chapter 4; and Supplements.

2. *Primary Texts*

(i) *Texts of Political Verses*

Aspin, Isabel S. T., *Anglo Norman Political Songs*, ANTS 9, 1953.

Bateson, Mary, *George Ashby's Poems*, EETS ES 76, 1899.

Bergen, H., *John Lydgate's Troy Book*, EETS ES 97, 103, 106, 126, 1906–20.

——, *John Lydgate's Fall of Princes*, EETS ES 121–4, 1918–19.

Brotanek, R., *Mittelenglische Dichtungen*, Halle 1940.

Brown, C. F., 'Lydgates Verses on Queen Margaret's Entry into London', *MLR* 7, 1912, 225–34.

——, *English Lyrics of the Thirteenth Century*, Oxford 1932.

——, *Religious Lyrics of the Fifteenth Century*, Oxford 1939.

Child, F. J., *English and Scottish Popular Ballads*, 5 vols., 1882–95.

Davis, N., *Non Cycle Plays and Fragments*, EETS SS 1, 1970.

Day, Mabel and Steele, R., *Mum and the Sothsegger*, EETS OS 199, 1936.

d'Evelyn, Charlotte, *Peter Idley's Instructions to his Son*, Boston 1935.

England, G. and Pollard, A. W., *The Towneley Plays*, EETS ES 75, 1897.

Furnivall, F. J., 'Why I Can't Be a Nun', *Translations of the Philological Society*, 1858, Part II, pp. 138–48.

——, *Political Religious and Love Poems*, EETS OS 15, 1866.

——, *Ballads From Manuscripts*, 2 vols., 1868–72.

——, *Meals and Manners in Olden Time*, EETS OS 32, 1868.

——, *Thomas Hoccleve's Minor Poems*, EETS ES 61, 73, 1892, 1925.

——, *Thomas Hoccleve's Regement of Princes*, EETS ES 72, 1899.

——, and Lacock, Katherine B., *John Lydgate's Pilgrimage of the Life of Man*, EETS ES 77, 83, 92, 1899–1904.

—— and Stone, W. G., *The Tale of Beryn*, EETS ES 105, 1909.

Gairdner, J., *Collections of a London Citizen*, Camden Society 1876.

Greene, R. L., *The Early English Carols*, Oxford 1935.

——, *A Selection of English Carols*, Oxford 1962.

Hall, J., *Poems of Laurence Minot*, Oxford 1897.

Heyworth, P. L., *Jack Upland, Friar Daw's Reply and Upland's Rejoinder*, Oxford 1968.

Hopper, C., 'The Childe of Bristowe' in *Camden Miscellany No. 4*, 1859.

Horstmann, C., *Minor Poems of the Vernon MS*, EETS OS 98, 1892.

Kail, J., *Twenty Six Political and Other Poems*, EETS OS 124, 1904.

Kreuzer, J. R., 'Some Earlier Examples of the Rhetorical Device in Ralph Roister Doister III, iv, 33', *RES* 14, 1938, 321–3.

Macaulay, G. C., *The Works of John Gower*, 4 vols., Oxford 1899–1902.

MacCracken, H. N., *John Lydgate's Serpent of Division*, 1910.

——, 'An English Friend of Charles of Orleans', *PMLA* 26, 1911, 142–80.

——, *The Minor Poems of John Lydgate*, EETS ES 107, 192, 1911, 1914.

Nicolas, N. H., *The Battle of Agincourt*, 1832.

Norton-Smith, J., *John Lydgate: Poems*, Oxford 1966.

Pantin, W. A., 'A Medieval Collection of Latin and English

Proverbs and Riddles from Rylands Latin MS 394', *Bulletin of the John Rylands Library* 14, 1930, 81–114.

Peacock, E., *John Mirk's Instructions for Parish Priests*, EETS OS 31, 1868.

Person, H., *Cambridge Middle English Lyrics*, Seattle 1962.

Robinson, F. N., *The Complete Works of Geoffrey Chaucer* 2nd edition, Oxford 1957.

Robbins, R. H., *Secular Lyrics of the Fourteenth and Fifteenth Centuries*, Oxford 1952.

——, *Historical Poems of the Fourteenth and Fifteenth Centuries*, New York 1959.

Steele, R., John Lydgate and Benedict Burgh, *Secrees of the Old Philisoffres*, EETS ES 66, 1894.

Warren, F. and White, Beatrice, *Dance Macabre*, EETS OS 181, 1937.

Warner, Sir G., *The Libelle of Englyshe Polycye*, Oxford 1926.

Withington, R., 'Queen Margaret's Entry into London, 1445' *Mod. Phil.* 13, 1916, 53–7.

Wright, T., *Political Songs of England*, Camden Society 1839.

——, *Political Poems and Songs*, 2 vols., Rolls Series 14, 1859–61.

—— and Halliwell, J. O., *Reliquae Antiquae*, 2 vols., 1843.

(ii) *Other Texts*

Axon, W. E. A., *William Caxton's Game and Play of the Chesse*, 1883.

Babington, C., *Reginald Pecock's Repressor*, Rolls Series 19, 1860, 2 vols.

Blades, W., *The Book of St. Albans*, 1881.

Brie, W. F. D., *The Brut*, EETS OS 131, 136, 1906–8.

Davies, J. S., *English Chronicle, 1377–1461*, Camden Society 1858.

Ellis, H., *Robert Fabyan's New Chronicles of England and France*, 1811.

——, *Hardyng's Chronicle*, 1812.

——, *Three Books of Polydore Vergil's English History*, Camden Society 1844.

Gairdner, J., *Memorials of Henry VII*, 1858.

——, *The Paston Letters*, 6 vols., 1904.

Harris, M. D., *The Coventry Leet Book*, EETS OS 134, 135, 1907–8.

Hearne, T., *Vita Ricardi II*, 1727.

Hingeston, F. C., *John Capgrave's Chronicle of England*, Rolls Series 1, 1858.

Holinshed, R., *Chronicles*, 1808 edition, 6 vols.

Kingsford, C. L., *Chronicles of London*, Oxford 1905.

——, 'Extracts from the First Version of John Hardyng's *Chronicle*', *EHR* 27, 1912, 462–82 and 740–53.

Le Prevost, A., *Ordericus Vitalis Historiae Ecclesiasticae*, Paris 1838–55, 5 vols.

Madden, Sir F., *Matthew Paris Historia Anglorum*, Rolls Series 44, 1866, 3 vols.

Meech, S. B. and Allen, Hope Emily, *The Book of Margery Kempe*, EETS OS 212, 1940.

Plummer, C., *Sir John Fortescue's Governance of England*, Oxford 1885.

Prior, H. O., *William Caxton's Mirror of the World*, EETS ES 110, 1913.

Raine, A., *York Civic Records*, Yorkshire Archaeological Society 1939.

Riley, H. T., *Annales a Johanne Amundesham*, Rolls Series 28, 1870–1, 2 vols.

——, *Registrum Abbatiae Johannis Whetamstede*, Rolls Series 28, 1872–3, 2 vols.

Ross, W. O., *Middle English Sermons*, EETS OS 209, 1938.

Rymer, T., *Foedera*, 20 vols., 1704–35.

Sneyd, C. A., *Relation of the Island of England*, Camden Society 1847.

Stow, J., *Annales*, 1615.

Stubbs, W., *Roger of Hoveden's Chronica*, Rolls Series 51, 4 vols.

Thompson, E. M., *Chronicon Angliae*, Rolls Series 64, 1874.

Vinaver, E., *The Works of Malory*, Oxford 1947, 3 vols.

3. Secondary Material

Abram, A., *Social Life in England in the Fifteenth Century*, 1909.

Adamson, J. W., 'The Extent of Literacy in England in the Fifteenth and Sixteenth Centuries', *The Library* 10, 1929–30, 163–93.

Anglo, S., *Spectacle, Pageant and Early Tudor Policy*, Oxford 1969.

Aston, Margaret, *The Fifteenth Century: the Prospect of Europe*, 1968.

Ayers, R. W., 'History, Moral Purpose and the Structure of Lydgate's *Siege of Thebes*', *PMLA*, 72, 1958, 463–74.

Bagley, J. J., *Historical Interpretation*, 1965.

Baugh, A. C., *A History of the English Language*, 2nd edition, 1957.

Bennett, H. S., *The Pastons and their England*, Cambridge 1922.

Blow, J., 'Nibley Green 1470: the last private battle fought in England', *History Today* 1962, II, 598–610.

Carus Wilson, E. M., *Medieval Merchant Venturers*, 1957.

Chambers, E. K., *The Medieval Stage*, Oxford 1903, 2 vols.

——, *English Literature at the Close of the Middle Ages*, Oxford 1945.

Chrimes, S. B., *Lancastrians, Yorkists and Henry VII*, 2nd edition, 1966.

Coulton, G. G., *Social Life in Britain*, Cambridge 1918.

Courthope, W. J., *History of English Poetry*, 1895–1910, 6 vols.

Cutts, Cecilia, 'The Croxton Play: an anti-Lollard piece', *MLQ* 5, 1944, 45–60.

Daiches, D., *A Critical History of English Literature*, 1961, 2 vols.

Fisher, J. H., *John Gower: Moral Philosopher and Friend of Chaucer*, 1965.

Gerould, G. H., *The Ballad of Tradition*, Oxford 1932.

Green, A. S., *Town Life in the Fifteenth Century*, 1894, 2 vols.

Green, V. H. H., *The Later Plantagenets*, 1955.

Hilton, R. H., 'A thirteenth century poem on disputed villein services', *EHR* 56, 1941, 90–7.

——, 'The Origin of Robin Hood', *Past and Present*, 14, 1958, 30–44.

Holmes, G., 'The Libelle of Englyshe Polycye,' *EHR* 76, 1961, 193–216.

Jacob, E. F., *Henry V and the Invasion of France*, 1947.

——, *The Fifteenth Century*, Oxford 1961.

Keen, M., *The Outlaws of Medieval Legend*, 1961.

Kendall, P. M., *The Yorkist Age*, 1962.

Kingsford, C. L., *English Historical Literature in the Fifteenth Century*, 1913.

——, *English History in Contemporary Poetry: Lancaster and York*, 1913.

Lander, J. R., *Stability and Conflict in Fifteenth Century England*, 1969.

MacFarlane, K. B., 'Bastard Feudalism', *TRHS* 25, 1944, 53–79.

——, *John Wycliffe and the Beginnings of English Nonconformity*, 1952.

McKenna, J. W., 'Henry VI of England and the Dual Monarchy', *JWCI* 28, 1965, 145–62.

McLeod, Enid, *Charles of Orleans*, 1969.

Mohl, Ruth, *The Three Estates in Medieval and Renaissance Literature*, Columbia 1933.

Moore, S., 'Patrons of Letters in Norfolk and Suffolk c. 1450', *PMLA* 27, 1912, 188–207 and *ibid*. 28, 1913, 79–105.

Morton, A. L., *The English Utopia*, 1952.

Myers, A. R., *England in the Late Middle Ages*, 1952.

Owst, G. R., *Literature and Pulpit in Medieval England*, Cambridge 1933.

Pearsall, D. A., *John Lydgate*, 1970.

Perroy, E., *The Hundred Years War*, English translation 1965.

Pevsner, N., *The Buildings of England: Nottinghamshire*, 1951.

Pfander, H. G., *Popular Sermon*, New York 1937.

Power, E. E., *Medieval English Nunneries*, 1922.

—— and Postan, M. M., eds. *Studies in English Trade in the Fifteenth Century*, 1933.

Renoir, A., *The Poetry of John Lydgate*, 1967.

Robbins, R. H., 'A Political Action Poem', *MLN* 70, 1955, 245–9.

——, 'On Dating a Middle English Moral Poem', *MLN* 71, 1956, 473–6.

——, 'Middle English Verses of Protest', *Anglia* 78, 1960, 193–203.

——, 'John Crophill's Ale Pots', *RES* 20, 1969, 182–9.

Rowe, B. J. H., 'King Henry VI's claim to France in picture and poem', *The Library* 13, 1933, 77–88.

Runciman, S., *A History of the Crusades*, Cambridge 1954, 3 vols.

Savage, E. A., *Old English Libraries*, 1911.

Scattergood, V. J. [On BM MS 1735] *RES* 21, 1970, 337–8.

Schirmer, W. F., *John Lydgate*, translated by Ann E. Keep 1961.

Tawney, R. H., *Religion and the Rise of Capitalism*, 1926.

Taylor, R., *The Political Prophecy in England*, New York 1911.

Ten Brink, B., *History of English Literature*, translated by H. M. Kennedy 1887.

Thomson, J. A. F., *The Later Lollards 1414–1520*, Oxford 1965.

Thrupp, Sylvia L., *The Merchant Class of Medieval London*, Michigan 1962.

Weiss, R., *Humanism in England during the Fifteenth Century*, 3rd edition, 1967.

Wilson, R. M., *The Lost Literature of Medieval England*, 1952.

Yunck, J. A., *The Lineage of Lady Meed*, University of Notre Dame 1963.

Index